Picturing Theology

REVISED EDITION

Picturing Theology

A Topical Collection of
The Urban Ministry Institute's
Key Diagrams, Charts, Graphics, and Articles

Rev. Dr. Don L. Davis *with contributions by*
Rev. Terry Cornett, Rev. Don Allsman, *and* Rev. Ryan Carter

World Impact Press
3701 East 13th St. North, Suite 100
Wichita, Kansas 67208

Picturing Theology: A Topical Collection of The Urban Ministry Institute's Key Diagrams, Charts, Graphics, and Articles (Revised Edition)

Published by World Impact Press
3701 East 13th St North, Suite 100
Wichita, Kansas 67208

© 2019 by The Urban Ministry Institute
Revised Edition © 2025 by World Impact Inc.

All rights reserved.

ISBN: 978-1-62932-452-4

All Scripture quotations, unless otherwise noted, are from The Holy Bible, English Standard Version, copyright © 2001 by Crossway Bible, a division of Good News Publishers. Used by permission. All Rights Reserved.

Table of Contents

Introduction 13

General Topics

Once Upon a Time:
The Cosmic Drama through a Biblical Narration of the World 17

From Before to Beyond Time: The Plan of God and Human History . . 19

The Nicene Creed. 21

The Nicene Creed with Biblical Support. 22

The Apostles' Creed 24

The Story of God: Our Sacred Roots 25

Jesus of Nazareth: The Presence of the Future. 26

The Theology of Christus Victor: A Christ-Centered Biblical Motif
for Integrating and Renewing the Urban Church 27

Christus Victor: An Integrated Vision for the Christian Life 28

There Is a River: Identifying the Streams of a
Revitalized Authentic Christian Community in the City 29

Living in the Already and the Not Yet Kingdom 30

The Story God Is Telling 31

Jesus Christ, the Subject and Theme of the Bible 32

Summary Outline of the Scriptures 33

Traditions: (*Paradosis*) 37

Documenting Your Work:
A Guide to Help You Give Credit Where Credit Is Due 44

General Biblical Studies

Understanding the Bible in Parts and Whole 51

General Facts Concerning the New Testament 52

Chronological Table of the New Testament. 54

Translation Methodology 55

Conversion and Calling

Theories of Inspiration 59
Getting a Firm Grasp of Scripture 60
Picking Up on Different Wavelengths:
Integrated vs. Fragmented Mindsets and Lifestyles 61

Bible Interpretation

Keys to Bible Interpretation:
Some Keys to Interpreting the Scriptures Accurately 67
Chart of Biblical Studies 74
Figures of Speech 75
Bible Study Tools Worksheet 82
Use of Reference Tools for Interpreting the Bible 84
How to Interpret a Narrative (Story) 86
The Compass of Narrative Elements:
Charting a Course toward a Story's Meaning 88

The Old Testament Witness to Christ and His Kingdom

Old Testament Witness to Christ and His Kingdom 91
Summary of Messianic Interpretations in the Old Testament . . . 92
Messiah Yeshua in Every Book of the Bible 96
Old Testament Names, Titles, and Epithets for the Messiah . . . 98
Promise vs. Prediction:
The Apostolic Hermeneutic of the Old Testament 100
Messiah Jesus: Fulfillment of the Old Testament Types 101
Principles Behind Prophecy 103
Analytical vs. Christocentric Approach to Old Testament Study . .104
The Prophetic Vision as Source of Biblical Faith Commitment . . .105
The Tabernacle of Moses 106
Arrangement of the Twelve Tribes around the Tabernacle 107
Degrees of Authority Given to Fruit of
Christocentric Use of the Old Testament 108

The New Testament Witness to Christ and His Kingdom

Communicating Messiah: The Relationship of the Gospels. 111

Messianic Prophecies Cited in the New Testament 112

Preaching and Teaching Jesus of Nazareth as
Messiah and Lord Is the Heart of All Biblical Ministry 118

A Harmony of the Ministry of Jesus 119

Appearances of the Resurrected Messiah 120

Biblical Justification for the Resurrection of Messiah Jesus. . . .121

General Theology and Ethics

The Shadow and the Substance:
Understanding the Old Testament as God's Witness to Jesus Christ . .125

In Christ. 126

The Picture and the Drama:
Image and Story in the Recovery of Biblical Myth 127

Apostolicity:
The Unique Place of the Apostles in Christian Faith and Practice . . .128

Giving Glory to God 129

God's Three-In-Oneness: The Trinity 138

The Kingdom of God

Ethics of the New Testament:
Living in the Upside-Down Kingdom of God 149

A Theology of the Church in Kingdom Perspective 150

Representin': Jesus as God's Chosen Representative. 151

Faithfully Re-Presenting Jesus of Nazareth. 152

Models of the Kingdom. 153

God the Father

The Names of Almighty God 157

Theological Visions and Approaches. 160

The Father, Son, and Holy Ghost Share the Same
Divine Attributes and Works: Supporting Scriptures. 164

God the Son

The Self-Consciousness of Jesus Christ	.167
The Principle of Substitution	.168
Portrayals of Jesus in the New Testament Books	.169
The Miracles of Jesus	.170
The Parables of Jesus	.171
The Life of Christ according to Seasons and Years	.172

God the Holy Spirit

Spiritual Gifts Specifically Mentioned in the New Testament	.177
St. Basil, the Nicene Creed, and the Doctrine of the Holy Spirit	.179
Examples of Denominational Statements on "Baptism in the Holy Spirit" Which Illustrate the Differing Views	.181
Areas of Disagreement among Christians Concerning Spiritual Gifts	.185
The Role of the Holy Spirit in Spiritual Guidance	.190
Denominational Statements on "Sanctification"	.196
Some of the Ways in Which Christians Disagree about Sanctification	.200

General Christian Ministry

The Hump	.207
Fit to Represent: Multiplying Disciples of the Kingdom of God	.208
Our Declaration of Dependence: Freedom in Christ	.209
Thirty-Three Blessings in Christ	.211
Substitute Centers to a Christ-Centered Vision: Goods and Effects Which Our Culture Substitutes as the Ultimate Concern	.215

Theology of the Church

The Lord's Supper: Four Views	.219
Perception and Truth	.220
Paul's Partnership Theology: Our Union with Christ and Partnership in Kingdom Ministry	.221
Six Kinds of New Testament Ministry for Community	.222
The Role of Women in Ministry	.223
A Theology of the Church	.227

Foundations of Christian Leadership

Discerning the Call: The Profile of a Godly Christian Leader 247

Investment, Empowerment, and Assessment:
How Leadership as Representation Provides Freedom to Innovate . .248

Understanding Leadership as Representation:
The Six Stages of Formal Proxy 249

Re-Presenting Messiah 250

Paul's Team Members 251

Nurturing Authentic Christian Leadership 253

Lording Over vs. Serving Among:
Differing Styles and Models of Leadership 254

Dealing with Old Ways 255

Delegation and Authority in Christian Leadership 256

"You Can Pay Me Now, Or You Can Pay Me Later" 257

Hindrances to Christlike Servanthood 258

Practicing Christian Leadership

A Guide to Determining Your Worship Profile 261

Capturing God's Vision for His People:
The "Enduring Solidarity" of Our Search for the Land of Promise . .263

Dynamics of Credible Spiritual Vision 264

The Church Leadership Paradigm:
The Case for Biblical Leadership 265

Roles of Representational Leadership 266

A Sociology of Urban Leadership Development:
A Tool for Assessment and Training 267

The Equipping Ministry

The Three-Step Model 271

The Obedient Christian in Action 272

Spiritual Growth Diagrams 273

Living the Disciplines 275

Steps to Equipping Others 276

Discipleship Diagram 278

Circle of Jewish Calendar 279

Following the Life of Christ throughout Each Year 280

The Plot Line of the Church Year 281
The Church Year (Western Church) 282
Spiritual Service Checklist 284

General Urban Mission

How to Start Reading the Bible 287
A Schematic for a Theology of the Kingdom and the Church . . .288
From Deep Ignorance to Credible Witness 290
Suffering: The Cost of Discipleship and Servant-Leadership . . .291
The Way of Wisdom 292

Foundations for Christian Mission

Story: The Crux of Revelation 295
Developing Ears That Hear:
Responding to the Spirit and the Word 296
Toward a Hermeneutic of Critical Engagement 297
Let God Arise!
The Seven "A's" of Seeking the Lord and Entreating His Favor . . .298
The Oikos Factor: Spheres of Relationship and Influence 299
Kingdom of God Timeline 300
That We May Be One: Elements of an Integrated
Church Planting Movement among the Urban Poor 301
Selecting Credible Criteria for Independence:
Navigating Toward a Healthy Transition 310
Salvation as Joining the People of God 313

Evangelism and Spiritual Warfare

Translating the Story of God 321
Culture, Not Color: Interaction of Class, Culture, and Race . . .322
Targeting Unreached Groups in Churched Neighborhoods . . .323
Receptivity Scale 324
Relationship of Cost and Effectiveness
in Disciple-Making Endeavors 325

Focus on Reproduction

Equipping the Church Plant Team Member:
Developing Workable Training Strategies 329

The Communal Context of Authentic Christian Leadership 330

Church Planting Models 331

Overview of Church Plant Planning Phases 333

Creating Coherent Urban Church Planting Movements:
Discerning the Elements of Authentic Urban Christian Community . . .334

Apostolic Band: Cultivating Outreach for Dynamic Harvest 335

The Church Plant Team: Forming an Apostolic Band 336

Three Levels of Ministry Investment 337

Doing Justice and Loving Mercy: Compassion Ministries

Five Views of the Relationship between Christ and Culture 341

Advancing the Kingdom in the City:
Multiplying Congregations with a Common Identity 342

Authentic Freedom in Jesus Christ 344

Empowering People for Freedom, Wholeness, and Justice 345

Jesus and the Poor 371

Introduction

It is hard to argue against the value of graphics, symbols, diagrams, and charts to simplify the presentation of difficult theological themes. Who doesn't like pictures and graphics when given to explain thorny ethical and theological issues? In many ways, we are image-making creatures, addicted to both symbol and metaphor as we communicate with others in the course of our everyday lives. The old adage, "A picture is worth a thousand words," proves true in daily conversation as well as in poetry, science, or any other intellectual work.

More often than not, I find it difficult to fully comprehend the significance of an idea until I have illustrated, graphed, or symbolized the concept in some fashion or other. Good graphs and metaphors are ready tools to represent and summarize the key concepts and categories of any serious subject or field of study. The use of diagrams and picture graphs can greatly aid us as we seek to comprehend the deeper meanings of complex or hard-to-understand theological notions or spiritual concepts.

Of course, all such effort in schematizing ideas and concepts via graphs and charts is more than a little oversimplifying the truth, to say the least. Still, depicting complex ideas visually in graphs and diagrams is an essential and helpful aid to helping us look into and understand something that is extremely complex and difficult to understand. Although a graphic may sometimes be offered as a poor substitute for clear reasoning about an idea or concept, good metaphors, diagrams, or symbols can often be just the tool to help us grasp some mystery with better comprehension.

The prophets and apostles often used visual pictures and metaphors to help God's people understand God's analysis of a situation, or lean into the meaning of some mystery or concept God was communicating with them. For example, the apostles used pictures of ordinary and familiar things to help us better comprehend the mysteries of God. Think of the metaphors related to the Church: it is the family of God, the body of Christ, and temple of the Holy Spirit. In order to know truly what the church is, you must delve into the meaning what a family is, how a body functions, and what a temple's purpose consists of. Actually, without those pictures, you will never come to understand or fully appreciate what the Church really is, and what she should be doing in the world.

I offer to you, the reader, these graphs, tables, and diagrams with humility and with some reserve. They were drawn to help my students wrestle with the meaning of the Bible's deep truths and mysteries. From the positive feedback from my students, I can say that they did prove helpful to many. I pray that with the independent release of these pictures and graphs that they will also prove beneficial in your study and reflections. I am convinced that with some meditation the graphics in this collection will boost your confidence and willingness to engage the truth of the Scriptures for the sake of maximum impact in your life. Truly, if a picture is worth a thousand words, this collection has much to say about the wonder and depth of the truths of God's Word.

Rev. Dr. Don L. Davis
Wichita, Kansas

General Topics

Once Upon a Time: The Cosmic Drama through a Biblical Narration of the World

Rev. Dr. Don L. Davis

From everlasting to everlasting, our Lord is God

From everlasting, in that matchless mystery of existence before time began, our Triune God dwelt in perfect splendor in eternal community as Father, Son, and Holy Spirit, the I AM, displaying his perfect attributes in eternal relationship, needing nothing, in boundless holiness, joy, and beauty. According to his sovereign will, our God purposed out of love to create a universe where his splendor would be revealed, and a world where his glory would be displayed and where a people made in his own image would dwell, sharing in fellowship with him and enjoying union with himself in relationship, all for his glory.

Who, as the Sovereign God, created a world that would ultimately rebel against his rule

Inflamed by lust, greed, and pride, the first human pair rebelled against his will, deceived by the great prince, Satan, whose diabolical plot to supplant God as ruler of all resulted in countless angelic beings resisting God's divine will in the heavenlies. Through Adam and Eve's disobedience, they exposed themselves and their heirs to misery and death, and through their rebellion ushered creation into chaos, suffering, and evil. Through sin and rebellion, the union between God and creation was lost, and now all things are subject to the effects of this great fall–alienation, separation, and condemnation become the underlying reality for all things. No angel, human being, or creature can solve this dilemma, and without God's direct intervention, all the universe, the world, and all its creatures would be lost.

Yet, in mercy and loving-kindness, the Lord God promised to send a Savior to redeem his creation

In sovereign covenantal love, God determined to remedy the effects of the universe's rebellion by sending a Champion, his only Son, who would take on the form of the fallen pair, embrace and overthrow their separation from God, and suffer in the place of all humankind for its sin and disobedience. So, through his covenant faithfulness, God became directly involved in human history for the sake of their salvation. The Lord God stoops to engage his creation for the sake of restoring it, to put down evil once and for all, and to establish a people out of which his Champion would come to establish his reign in this world once more.

So, he raised up a people from which the Governor would come

And so, through Noah, he saves the world from its own evil, through Abraham, he selects the clan through which the seed would come.

Through Isaac, he continues the promise to Abraham, and through Jacob (Israel) he establishes his nation, identifying the tribe out of which he will come (Judah). Through Moses, he delivers his own from oppression and gives them his covenantal law, and through Joshua, he brings his people into the land of promise. Through judges and leaders he superintends his people, and through David, he covenants to bring a King from his clan who will reign forever. Despite his promise, though, his people fall short of his covenant time after time. Their stubborn and persistent rejection of the Lord finally leads to the nation's judgment, invasion, overthrow, and captivity. Mercifully, he remembers his covenant and allows a remnant to return – for the promise and the story were not done.

Who, as Champion, came down from heaven, in the fullness of time, and won through the Cross

Some four hundred years of silence occurred. Yet, in the fullness of time, God fulfilled his covenant promise by entering into this realm of evil, suffering, and alienation through the incarnation. In the person of Jesus of Nazareth, God came down from heaven and lived among us, displaying the Father's glory, fulfilling the requirements of God's moral law, and demonstrating the power of the Kingdom of God in his words, works, and exorcisms. On the Cross he took on our rebellion, destroyed death, overcame the devil, and rose on the third day to restore creation from the Fall, to make an end of sin, disease, and war, and to grant never-ending life to all people who embrace his salvation.

And, soon and very soon, he will return to this world and make all things new

Ascended to the Father's right hand, the Lord Jesus Christ has sent the Holy Spirit into the world, forming a new people made up of both Jew and Gentile, the Church. Commissioned under his headship, they testify in word and deed the gospel of reconciliation to the whole creation, and when they have completed their task, he will return in glory and complete his work for creation and all creatures. Soon, he will put down sin, evil, death, and the effects of the Curse forever, and restore all creation under its true rule, refreshing all things in a new heavens and new earth, where all beings and all creation will enjoy the shalom of the triune God forever, to his glory and honor alone.

And the redeemed shall live happily ever after . . .

The End

From Before to Beyond Time: The Plan of God and Human History

Adapted from Suzanne de Dietrich. *God's Unfolding Purpose*. Philadelphia: Westminster Press, 1976.

I. Before Time (Eternity Past) 1 Corinthians 2:7

    A. The Eternal Triune God
    B. God's Eternal Purpose
    C. The Mystery of Iniquity
    D. The Principalities and Powers

II. Beginning of Time (Creation and Fall) Genesis 1:1

    A. Creative Word
    B. Humanity
    C. Fall
    D. Reign of Death and First Signs of Grace

III. Unfolding of Time (God's Plan Revealed Through Israel) Galatians 3:8

    A. Promise (Patriarchs)
    B. Exodus and Covenant at Sinai
    C. Promised Land
    D. The City, the Temple, and the Throne (Prophet, Priest, and King)
    E. Exile
    F. Remnant

IV. Fullness of Time (Incarnation of the Messiah) Galatians 4:4-5

    A. The King Comes to His Kingdom
    B. The Present Reality of His Reign
    C. The Secret of the Kingdom: the Already and the Not Yet
    D. The Crucified King
    E. The Risen Lord

V. The Last Times (The Descent of the Holy Spirit) Acts 2:16-18

    A. Between the Times: the Church as Foretaste of the Kingdom
    B. The Church as Agent of the Kingdom
    C. The Conflict Between the Kingdoms of Darkness and Light

VI. The Fulfillment of Time (The Second Coming) Matthew 13:40-43

    A. The Return of Christ
    B. Judgment
    C. The Consummation of His Kingdom

VII. Beyond Time (Eternity Future) 1 Corinthians 15:24-28

    A. Kingdom Handed Over to God the Father
    B. God as All in All

From Before to Beyond Time: Scriptures for Major Outlines Points

I. Before Time (Eternity Past)

1 Corinthians 2:7 (ESV) – But we impart a secret and hidden wisdom of God, which God decreed before the ages for our glory (cf. Titus 1:2).

II. Beginning of Time (Creation and Fall)

Genesis 1.1 (ESV) – In the beginning, God created the heavens and the earth.

III. Unfolding of Time (God's Plan Revealed Through Israel)

Galatians 3:8 (ESV) – And the Scripture, foreseeing that God would justify the Gentiles by faith, preached the Gospel beforehand to Abraham, saying, "In you shall all the nations be blessed" (cf. Romans 9:4-5).

IV. Fullness of Time (The Incarnation of the Messiah)

Galatians 4:4-5 (ESV) – But when the fullness of time had come, God sent forth his Son, born of woman, born under the law, to redeem those who were under the law, so that we might receive adoption as sons.

V. The Last Times (The Descent of the Holy Spirit)

Acts 2:16-18 (ESV) – But this is what was uttered through the prophet Joel: "'And in the last days it shall be,' God declares, 'that I will pour out my Spirit on all flesh, and your sons and your daughters shall prophesy, and your young men shall see visions, and your old men shall dream dreams; even on my male servants and female servants in those days I will pour out my Spirit, and they shall prophesy.'"

VI. The Fulfillment of Time (The Second Coming)

Matthew 13:40-43 (ESV) – Just as the weeds are gathered and burned with fire, so will it be at the close of the age. The Son of Man will send his angels, and they will gather out of his Kingdom all causes of sin and all lawbreakers, and throw them into the fiery furnace. In that place there will be weeping and gnashing of teeth. Then the righteous will shine like the sun in the Kingdom of their Father. He who has ears, let him hear.

VII. Beyond Time (Eternity Future)

1 Corinthians 15:24-28 (ESV) – Then comes the end, when he delivers the Kingdom to God the Father after destroying every rule and every authority and power. For he must reign until he has put all his enemies under his feet. The last enemy to be destroyed is death. For "God has put all things in subjection under his feet." But when it says, "all things are put in subjection," it is plain that he is excepted who put all things in subjection under him. When all things are subjected to him, then the Son himself will also be subjected to him who put all things in subjection under him, that God may be all in all.

The Nicene Creed

We believe in one God, the Father Almighty, maker of heaven and earth and of all things visible and invisible.

We believe in one Lord Jesus Christ, the only begotten Son of God, begotten of the Father before all ages, God from God, Light from Light, True God from True God, begotten not created, of the same essence as the Father, through whom all things were made.

Who for us men and for our salvation came down from heaven and was incarnate by the Holy Spirit and the virgin Mary and became human. Who for us too, was crucified under Pontius Pilate, suffered and was buried. The third day he rose again according to the Scriptures, ascended into heaven and is seated at the right hand of the Father. He will come again in glory to judge the living and the dead, and his Kingdom will have no end.

We believe in the Holy Spirit, the Lord and life-giver, who proceeds from the Father and the Son. Who together with the Father and Son is worshiped and glorified. Who spoke by the prophets.

We believe in one holy, catholic, and apostolic church.

We acknowledge one baptism for the forgiveness of sin, and we look for the resurrection of the dead and the life of the age to come. Amen.

The Nicene Creed with Biblical Support

Deut. 6:4-5; Mark 12:29; 1 Cor. 8:6	We believe in one God,
Gen. 17:1; Dan. 4:35; Matt. 6:9; Eph. 4:6; Rev. 1:8	the Father Almighty,
Gen. 1:1; Isa. 40:28; Rev. 10:6	Maker of heaven and earth
Ps. 148; Rom. 11:36; Rev. 4:11	and of all things visible and invisible.
John 1:1-2; 3:18; 8:58; 14:9-10; 20:28; Col. 1:15, 17; Heb. 1:3-6	We believe in one Lord Jesus Christ, the only Begotten Son of God, begotten of the Father before all ages, God from God, Light from Light, True God from True God, begotten not created, of the same essence as the Father,
John 1:3; Col. 1:16	through whom all things were made.
Matt. 1:20-23; John 1:14; 6:38; Luke 19:10	Who for us men and for our salvation came down from heaven and was incarnate by the Holy Spirit and the virgin Mary and became human.
Matt. 27:1-2; Mark 15:24-39, 43-47; Acts 13:29; Rom. 5:8; Heb. 2:10; 13:12	Who for us too, was crucified under Pontius Pilate, suffered, and was buried.
Mark 16:5-7; Luke 24:6-8; Acts 1:3; Rom. 6:9; 10:9; 2 Tim. 2:8	The third day he rose again according to the Scriptures,
Mark 16:19; Eph. 1:19-20	ascended into heaven, and is seated at the right hand of the Father.
Isa. 9:7; Matt. 24:30; John 5:22; Acts 1:11; 17:31; Rom. 14:9; 2 Cor. 5:10; 2 Tim. 4:1	He will come again in glory to judge the living and the dead, and his Kingdom will have no end.
Gen. 1:1-2; Job 33:4; Ps. 104:30; 139:7-8; Luke 4:18-19; John 3:5-6; Acts 1:1-2; 1 Cor. 2:11; Rev. 3:22	We believe in the Holy Spirit, the Lord and life-giver,
John 14:16-18, 26; 15:26; 20:22	who proceeds from the Father and the Son,
Isa. 6:3; Matt. 28:19; 2 Cor. 13:14; Rev. 4:8	who together with the Father and Son is worshiped and glorified,
Num. 11:29; Mic. 3:8; Acts 2:17-18; 2 Pet. 1:21	who spoke by the prophets.
Matt. 16:18; Eph. 5:25-28; 1 Cor. 1:2; 10:17; 1 Tim. 3:15; Rev. 7:9	We believe in one holy, catholic, and apostolic Church.
Acts 22:16; 1 Pet. 3:21; Eph. 4:4-5	We acknowledge one baptism for the forgiveness of sin,
Isa. 11:6-10; Mic. 4:1-7; Luke 18:29-30; Rev. 21:1-5; 21:22-22:5	And we look for the resurrection of the dead and the life of the age to come. Amen.

Memory Verses for the Nicene Creed

The Father	Revelation 4:11 (ESV) – Worthy are you, our Lord and God, to receive glory and honor and power, for you created all things, and by your will they existed and were created.
The Son	John 1:1 (ESV) – In the beginning was the Word, and the Word was with God, and the Word was God.
The Son's Mission	1 Corinthians 15:3-5 (ESV) – For what I received I passed on to you as of first importance: that Christ died for our sins according to the Scriptures, that he was buried, that he was raised on the third day according to the Scriptures, and that he appeared to Peter, and then to the Twelve.
The Holy Spirit	Romans 8:11 (ESV) – If the Spirit of him who raised Jesus from the dead dwells in you, he who raised Christ Jesus from the dead will also give life to your mortal bodies through his Spirit who dwells in you.
The Church	1 Peter 2:9 (ESV) – But you are a chosen race, a royal priesthood, a holy nation, a people for his own possession, that you may proclaim the excellencies of him who called you out of darkness into his marvelous light.
Our Hope	1 Thessalonians 4:16-17 (ESV) – For the Lord himself will descend from heaven with a cry of command, with the voice of an archangel, and with the sound of the trumpet of God. And the dead in Christ will rise first. Then we who are alive, who are left, will be caught up together with them in the clouds to meet the Lord in the air, and so we will always be with the Lord.

The Apostles' Creed

I believe in God, the Father Almighty, Maker of heaven and earth; and in Jesus Christ his only Son, our Lord; who was conceived by the Holy Spirit, born of the Virgin Mary, suffered under Pontius Pilate, was crucified, dead, and buried; he descended into hell; the third day he arose again from the dead; he ascended into heaven and sits on the right hand of God the Father Almighty; from thence he shall come to judge the quick and the dead.

I believe in the Holy Spirit, the holy catholic church, the communion of saints, the forgiveness of sins, the resurrection of the body, and the life everlasting. Amen.

The Story of God: Our Sacred Roots

Rev. Dr. Don L. Davis

The Alpha and the Omega	Christus Victor	Come, Holy Spirit	Your Word Is Truth	The Great Confession	His Life in Us	Living in the Way	Reborn to Serve
The LORD God is the source, sustainer, and end of all things in the heavens and earth. All things were formed and exist by his will and for his eternal glory: the triune God, Father, Son, and Holy Spirit, Romans 11:36.							
THE TRIUNE GOD'S UNFOLDING DRAMA — God's Self-Revelation in Creation, Israel, and Christ				**THE CHURCH'S PARTICIPATION IN GOD'S UNFOLDING DRAMA** — Fidelity to the Apostolic Witness to Christ and His Kingdom			
The Objective Foundation: The Sovereign Love of God — God's Narration of His Saving Work in Christ				**The Subjective Practice: Salvation by Grace through Faith** — The Redeemed's Joyous Response to God's Saving Work in Christ			
The Author of the Story	*The Champion of the Story*	*The Interpreter of the Story*	*The Testimony of the Story*	*The People of the Story*	*Re-enactment of the Story*	*Embodiment of the Story*	*Continuation of the Story*
The Father as Director	Jesus as Lead Actor	The Spirit as Narrator	Scripture as Script	As Saints, Confessors	As Worshipers, Ministers	As Followers, Sojourners	As Servants, Ambassadors
Christian Worldview	Communal Identity	Spiritual Experience	Biblical Authority	Orthodox Theology	Priestly Worship	Congregational Discipleship	Kingdom Witness
Theistic and Trinitarian Vision	Christ-centered Foundation	Spirit-Indwelt and -Filled Community	Canonical and Apostolic Witness	Ancient Creedal Affirmation of Faith	Weekly Gathering in Christian Assembly	Corporate, Ongoing Spiritual Formation	Active Agents of the Reign of God
Sovereign Willing	Messianic Representing	Divine Comforting	Inspired Testifying	Truthful Retelling	Joyful Excelling	Faithful Indwelling	Hopeful Compelling
Creator True Maker of the Cosmos	Recapitulation Typos and Fulfillment of the Covenant	Life-Giver Regeneration and Adoption	Divine Inspiration God-breathed Word	The Confession of Faith Union with Christ	Song and Celebration Historical Recitation	Pastoral Oversight Shepherding the Flock	Explicit Unity Love for the Saints
Owner Sovereign Disposer of Creation	Revealer Incarnation of the Word	Teacher Illuminator of the Truth	Sacred History Historical Record	Baptism into Christ Communion of Saints	Homilies and Teachings Prophetic Proclamation	Shared Spirituality Common Journey through the Spiritual Disciplines	Radical Hospitality Evidence of God's Kingdom Reign
Ruler Blessed Controller of All Things	Redeemer Reconciler of All Things	Helper Endowment and the Power	Biblical Theology Divine Commentary	The Rule of Faith Apostles' Creed and Nicene Creed	The Lord's Supper Dramatic Re-enactment	Embodiment Anamnesis and Prolepsis through the Church Year	Extravagant Generosity Good Works
Covenant Keeper Faithful Promiser	Restorer Christ, the Victor over the powers of evil	Guide Divine Presence and Shekinah	Spiritual Food Sustenance for the Journey	The Vincentian Canon Ubiquity, antiquity, universality	Eschatological Foreshadowing The Already/Not Yet	Effective Discipling Spiritual Formation in the Believing Assembly	Evangelical Witness Making Disciples of All People Groups

Picturing Theology, Revised Edition | 25

Jesus of Nazareth: The Presence of the Future
Rev. Dr. Don L. Davis

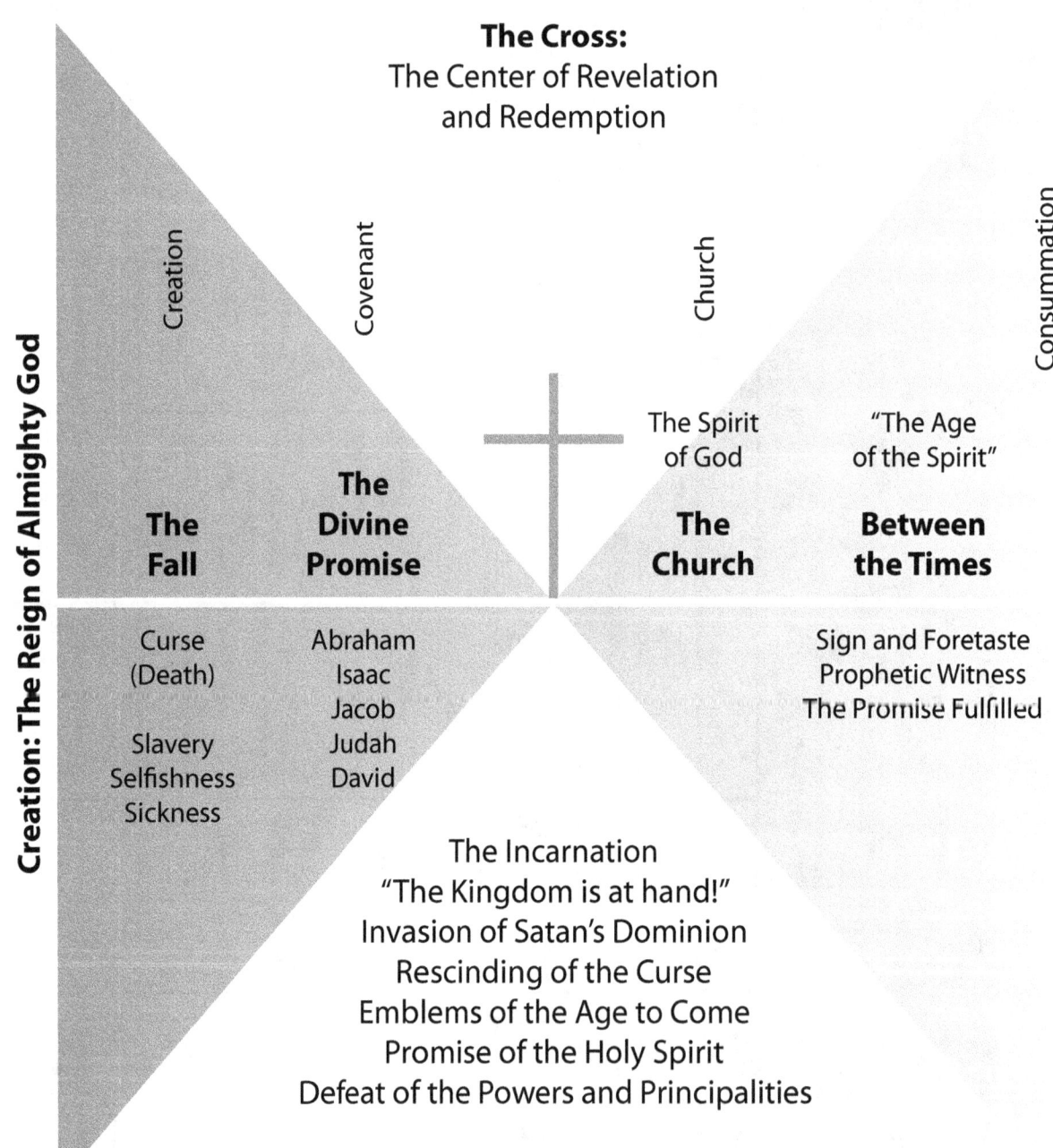

The Theology of Christus Victor:
A Christ-Centered Biblical Motif for Integrating and Renewing the Urban Church

Rev. Dr. Don L. Davis

	The Promised Messiah	The Word Made Flesh	The Son of Man	The Suffering Servant	The Lamb of God	The Victorious Conqueror	The Reigning Lord in Heaven	The Bridegroom and Coming King
Biblical Framework	Israel's hope of Yahweh's anointed who would redeem his people	In the person of Jesus of Nazareth, the Lord has come to the world	As the promised king and divine Son of Man, Jesus reveals the Father's glory and salvation to the world	As Inaugurator of the Kingdom of God, Jesus demonstrates God's reign present through his words, wonders, and works	As both High Priest and Paschal Lamb, Jesus offers himself to God on our behalf as a sacrifice for sin	In his resurrection from the dead and ascension to God's right hand, Jesus is proclaimed as Victor over the power of sin and death	Now Reigning at God's right hand till his enemies are made his footstool, Jesus pours out his benefits on his body	Soon the risen and ascended Lord will return to gather his Bride, the Church, and consummate his work
Scripture References	Isaiah 9:6-7 Jeremiah 23:5-6 Isaiah 11:1-10	John 1:14-18 Matthew 1:20-23 Philippians 2:6-8	Matthew 2:1-11 Numbers 24:17 Luke 1:78-79	Mark 1:14-15 Matthew 12:25-30 Luke 17:20-21	2 Corinthians 5:18-21 Isaiah 52-53 John 1:29	Ephesians 1:16-23 Philippians 2:5-11 Colossians 1:15-20	1 Corinthians 15:25 Ephesians 4:15-16 Acts 2:32-36	Romans 14:7-9 Revelation 5:9-13 1 Thessalonians 4:13-18
Jesus's History	The pre-incarnate, only begotten Son of God in glory	His conception by the Spirit, and birth to Mary	His manifestation to the Magi and to the world	His teaching, exorcisms, miracles, and mighty works among the people	His suffering, crucifixion, death, and burial	His resurrection, with appearances to his witnesses, and his ascension to the Father	The sending of the Holy Spirit and his gifts, and Christ's session in heaven at the Father's right hand	His soon return from heaven to earth as Lord and Christ: the Second Coming
Description	The biblical promise for the seed of Abraham, the prophet like Moses, the son of David	In the Incarnation, God has come to us; Jesus reveals to humankind the Father's glory in fullness	In Jesus, God has shown his salvation to the entire world, including the Gentiles	In Jesus, the promised Kingdom of God has come visibly to earth, demonstrating his binding of Satan and rescinding the Curse	As God's perfect Lamb, Jesus offers himself up to God as a sin offering on behalf of the entire world	In his resurrection and ascension, Jesus destroyed death, disarmed Satan, and rescinded the Curse	Jesus is installed at the Father's right hand as Head of the Church, Firstborn from the dead, and supreme Lord in heaven	As we labor in his harvest field in the world, so we await Christ's return, the fulfillment of his promise
Church Year	Advent	Christmas	Season after Epiphany Baptism and Transfiguration	Lent	Holy Week Passion	Eastertide Easter, Ascension Day, Pentecost	Season after Pentecost Trinity Sunday	Season after Pentecost All Saints Day, Reign of Christ the King
	The Coming of Christ	The Birth of Christ	The Manifestation of Christ	The Ministry of Christ	The Suffering and Death of Christ	The Resurrection and Ascension of Christ	The Heavenly Session of Christ	Reign of Christ
Spiritual Formation	As we await his Coming, let us proclaim and affirm the hope of Christ	O Word made flesh, let us every heart prepare him room to dwell	Divine Son of Man, show the nations your salvation and glory	In the person of Christ, the power of the reign of God has come to earth and to the Church	May those who share the Lord's death be resurrected with him	Let us participate by faith in the victory of Christ over the power of sin, Satan, and death	Come, indwell us, Holy Spirit, and empower us to advance Christ's Kingdom in the world	We live and work in expectation of this soon return, seeking to please him in all things

Christus Victor:
An Integrated Vision for the Christian Life
Rev. Dr. Don L. Davis

Christus Victor
*Destroyer of Evil and Death
Restorer of Creation
Victor o'er Hades and Sin
Crusher of Satan*

For the Church
- The Church is the primary extension of Jesus in the world
- Ransomed treasure of the victorious, risen Christ
- Laos: The people of God
- God's new creation: presence of the future
- Locus and agent of the Already/Not Yet Kingdom

For Theology and Doctrine
- The authoritative Word of Christ's victory: the Apostolic Tradition: the Holy Scriptures
- Theology as commentary on the grand narrative of God
- Christus Victor as the core theological framework for meaning in the world
- The Nicene Creed: the Story of God's triumphant grace

For Spirituality
- The Holy Spirit's presence and power in the midst of God's people
- Sharing in the disciplines of the Spirit
- Gatherings, lectionary, liturgy, and our observances in the Church Year
- Living the life of the risen Christ in the rhythm of our ordinary lives

For Gifts
- God's gracious endowments and benefits from Christus Victor
- Pastoral offices to the Church
- The Holy Spirit's sovereign dispensing of the gifts
- Stewardship: divine, diverse gifts for the common good

For Worship
- People of the Resurrection: unending celebration of the people of God
- Remembering, participating in the Christ event in our worship
- Listen and respond to the Word
- Transformed at the Table, the Lord's Supper
- The presence of the Father through the Son in the Spirit

For Evangelism and Mission
- Evangelism as unashamed declaration and demonstration of Christus Victor to the world
- The Gospel as Good News of kingdom pledge
- We proclaim God's Kingdom come in the person of Jesus of Nazareth
- The Great Commission: go to all people groups making disciples of Christ and his Kingdom
- Proclaiming Christ as Lord and Messiah

For Justice and Compassion
- The gracious and generous expressions of Jesus through the Church
- The Church displays the very life of the Kingdom
- The Church demonstrates the very life of the Kingdom of heaven right here and now
- Having freely received, we freely give (no sense of merit or pride)
- Justice as tangible evidence of the Kingdom come

There Is a River: Identifying the Streams of a Revitalized Authentic Christian Community in the City[1]

Rev. Dr. Don L. Davis • Psalm 46:4 (ESV) – There is a river whose streams make glad the city of God, the holy habitation of the Most High.

Tributaries of Authentic Historic Biblical Faith			
Recognized Biblical Identity	*Revived Urban Spirituality*	*Reaffirmed Historical Connectivity*	*Refocused Kingdom Authority*
The Church Is One	The Church Is Holy	The Church Is Catholic	The Church Is Apostolic
A Call to Biblical Fidelity *Recognizing the Scriptures as the anchor and foundation of the Christian faith and practice*	A Call to the Freedom, Power, and Fullness of the Holy Spirit *Walking in the holiness, power, gifting, and liberty of the Holy Spirit in the body of Christ*	A Call to Historic Roots and Continuity *Confessing the common historical identity and continuity of authentic Christian faith*	A Call to the Apostolic Faith *Affirming the apostolic tradition as the authoritative ground of the Christian hope*
A Call to Messianic Kingdom Identity *Rediscovering the story of the promised Messiah and his Kingdom in Jesus of Nazareth*	A Call to Live as Sojourners and Aliens as the People of God *Defining authentic Christian discipleship as faithful membership among God's people*	A Call to Affirm and Express the Global Communion of Saints *Expressing cooperation and collaboration with all other believers, both local and global*	A Call to Representative Authority *Submitting joyfully to God's gifted servants in the Church as undershepherds of true faith*
A Call to Creedal Affinity *Embracing the Nicene Creed as the shared rule of faith of historic orthodoxy*	A Call to Liturgical, Sacramental, and Catechetical Vitality *Experiencing God's presence in the context of the Word, sacrament, and instruction*	A Call to Radical Hospitality and Good Works *Expressing kingdom love to all, and especially to those of the household of faith*	A Call to Prophetic and Holistic Witness *Proclaiming Christ and his Kingdom in word and deed to our neighbors and all peoples*

---

1   This schema is an adaptation and is based on the insights of the Chicago Call statement of May 1977, where various leading evangelical scholars and practitioners met to discuss the relationship of modern evangelicalism to the historic Christian faith.

Living in the Already and the Not Yet Kingdom

Rev. Dr. Don L. Davis

The Spirit: The pledge of the inheritance (*arrabon*)
The Church: The foretaste (*aparche*) of the Kingdom
"In Christ": The rich life (*en Christos*) we share as citizens of the Kingdom

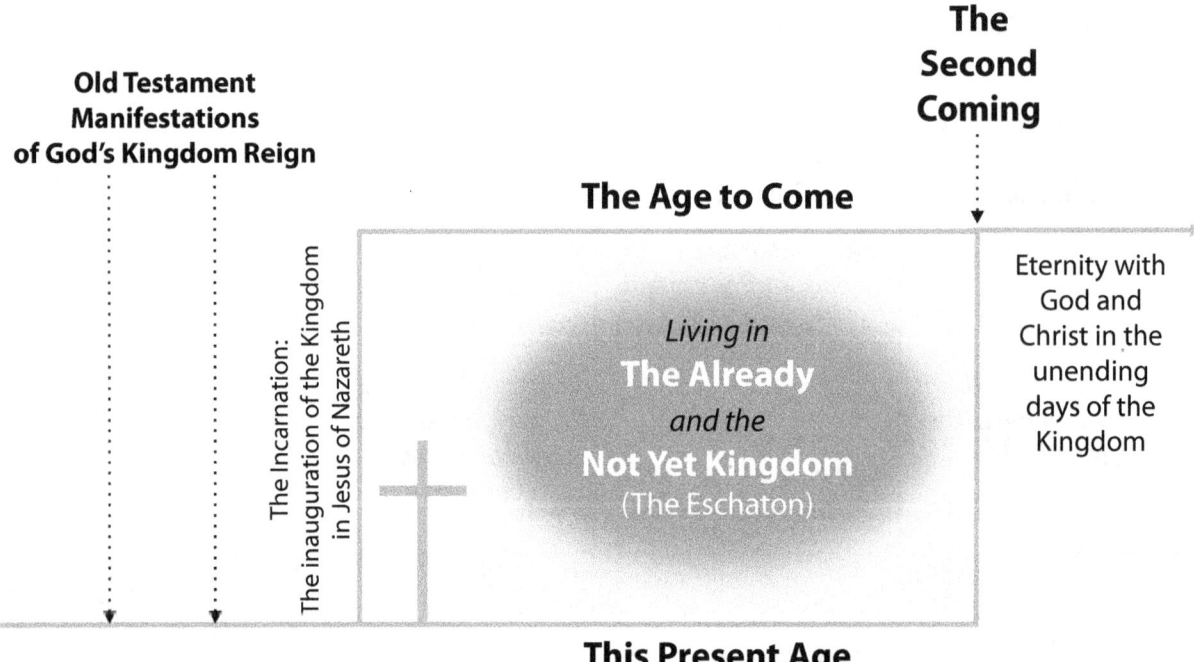

Internal enemy: The flesh (*sarx*) and the sin nature
External enemy: The world (*kosmos*) the systems of greed, lust, and pride
Infernal enemy: The devil (*kakos*) the animating spirit of falsehood and fear

Jewish View of Time

This Present Age • The Age to Come

The Coming of Messiah

The restoration of Israel
The end of Gentile oppression
The return of the earth to Edenic glory
Universal knowledge of the Lord

The Story God Is Telling

Rev. Don Allsman

Chapter Title	Chapter Summary	Theme Verse
An Attempted Coup (Before Time) Genesis 1:1a	God exists in Perfect Fellowship before creation. The devil and his followers rebel and bring evil into existence.	In the beginning was the Word, and the Word was with God and the Word was God. He was in the beginning with God. All things were made through him, and without him was not any thing made that was made (John 1:1-3).
Insurrection (Creation and the Fall) Genesis 1:1b – 3:13	God creates man in his image, who joins Satan in rebellion	Therefore, just as sin came into the world through one man, and death through sin, and so death spread to all men because all sinned (Romans 5:12).
Preparing for Invasion (The Patriarchs, Kings, and Prophets) Genesis 3:14 – Malachi	God contends to set apart a people for his own, out of which will come a King to deliver mankind, including Gentiles. Clues to his battle plans are hinted at along the way.	They are Israelites, and to them belong the adoption, the glory, the covenants, the giving of the law, the worship, and the promises. To them belong the patriarchs and from their race, according to the flesh, is the Christ who is God over all, blessed forever. Amen (Romans 9:4-5).
Victory and Rescue (Incarnation, Temptation, Miracles, Resurrection) Matthew – Acts 1:11	The Savior comes to deal a disarming blow to his enemy.	The reason the Son of God appeared was to destroy the works of the devil (1 John 3:8b).
The Army Advances (The Church) Acts 1:12 – Revelation 3	The Savior reveals his plan of a people assigned to take progressive ownership from the enemy as they enjoy a foretaste of the Kingdom to come.	So that through the church the manifold wisdom of God might now be made known to the rulers and authorities in the heavenly places. This was according to the eternal purpose that he has realized in Christ Jesus our Lord (Ephesians 3:10-11).
The Final Conflict (The Second Coming) Revelation 4 – 22	The Savior returns to destroy his enemy, marry his bride, and resume his rightful place on the throne.	Then comes the end, when he delivers the Kingdom to God the Father after destroying every rule and authority and power. For he must reign until he has put all his enemies under his feet. The last enemy to be destroyed is death (1 Corinthians 15:24-26).
The War between the Kingdoms	The common thread of the Bible narrative is warfare.	The kingdom of the world has become the kingdom of our Lord and of his Christ. And he shall reign forever and ever (Revelation 11:15b).

"It is a world where terrible things happen and wonderful things too. It is a world where goodness is pitted against evil, love against hate, order against chaos, in a great struggle where often it is hard to be sure who belongs to which side because appearances can be deceptive. Yet for all its confusion and wildness, it is a world where the battle goes ultimately to the good, who live happily ever after, and where in the long run everybody, good and evil alike, becomes known by his true name."

– Frederick Buechner. *Telling the Truth.*

Jesus Christ, the Subject and Theme of the Bible

Rev. Dr. Don L. Davis
Adapted from Norman Geisler, *A Popular Survey of the Old Testament*. Grand Rapids, MI: Baker Books, 1977, pp. 11ff.

Jesus Christ, the Subject and Theme of the Bible Luke 24:27, 44; Hebrews 10:7; Matthew 5:17; John 5:39	**Two-fold Structure of the Bible**	**Four-fold Structure of the Bible**	**Eight-fold Structure of the Bible**
	Old Testament: *Anticipation* Concealed Contained The precept In shadow In ritual In picture As foretold In prophecy In pre-incarnations	**The Law** *Foundation for Christ*	***The Law:*** Foundation for Christ (Genesis-Deuteronomy)
			History: Preparation for Christ (Joshua-Esther)
		The Prophets *Expectation of Christ*	***Poetry:*** Aspiration for Christ (Job-Song of Solomon)
			Prophets: Expectation of Christ (Isaiah- Malachi)
	New Testament: *Realization* Revealed Explained Its perfection In substance In reality In person As fulfilled In history In the Incarnation	**The Gospels** *Manifestation of Christ*	***Gospels:*** Manifestation of Christ (Matthew-John)
			Acts: Propagation of Christ (The Acts of the Apostles)
		The Epistles *Interpretation of Christ*	***Epistles:*** Interpretation of Christ (Romans-Jude)
			Revelation: Consummation in Christ (The Revelation of John)

Summary Outline of the Scriptures

Rev. Dr. Don L. Davis

Old Testament

1. GENESIS – Beginnings
   a. Adam
   b. Noah
   c. Abraham
   d. Isaac
   e. Jacob
   f. Joseph
	11. 1 KINGS – Solomon's Glory, Kingdom's Decline
	   a. Solomon's glory
	   b. Kingdom's decline
	   c. Elijah the prophet

2. EXODUS – Redemption, (out of)
   a. Slavery
   b. Deliverance
   c. Law
   d. Tabernacle
	12. 2 KINGS- Divided Kingdom
	   a. Elisha
	   b. Israel (N. Kingdom falls)
	   c. Judah (S. Kingdom falls)

3. LEVITICUS – Worship and Fellowship
   a. Offerings, sacrifices
   b. Priests
   c. Feasts, festivals
	13. 1 CHRONICLES – David's Temple Arrangements
	   a. Genealogies
	   b. End of Saul's reign
	   c. Reign of David
	   d. Temple preparations

4. NUMBERS – Service and Walk
   a. Organized
   b. Wanderings
	14. 2 CHRONICLES – Temple and Worship Abandoned
	   a. Solomon
	   b. Kings of Judah

5. DEUTERONOMY – Obedience
   a. Moses reviews history and law
   b. Civil and social laws
   c. Palestinian Covenant
   d. Moses's blessing and death
	15. EZRA – The Minority (Remnant)
	   a. First return from exile – Zerubbabel
	   b. Second return from exile – Ezra (priest)

6. JOSHUA – Redemption (into)
   a. Conquer the land
   b. Divide up the land
   c. Joshua's farewell
	16. NEHEMIAH – Rebuilding by Faith
	   a. Rebuild walls
	   b. Revival
	   c. Religious reform

7. JUDGES – God's Deliverance
   a. Disobedience and judgment
   b. Israel's twelve judges
   c. Lawless conditions
	17. ESTHER – Female Savior
	   a. Esther
	   b. Haman
	   c. Mordecai
	   d. Deliverance: Feast of Purim

8. RUTH – Love
   a. Ruth chooses
   b. Ruth works
   c. Ruth waits
   d. Ruth rewarded
	18. JOB – Why the Righteous Suffer
	   a. Godly Job
	   b. Satan's attack
	   c. Four philosophical friends
	   d. God lives

9. 1 SAMUEL – Kings, Priestly Perspective
   a. Eli
   b. Samuel
   c. Saul
   d. David
	19. PSALMS – Prayer and Praise
	   a. Prayers of David
	   b. Godly suffer; deliverance
	   c. God deals with Israel
	   d. Suffering of God's people – end with the Lord's reign
	   e. The Word of God (Messiah's suffering and glorious return)

10. 2 SAMUEL – David
   a. King of Judah (9 years – Hebron)
   b. King of all Israel (33 years – Jerusalem)	

Old Testament, continued

20. PROVERBS – Wisdom
   a. Wisdom versus folly
   b. Solomon
   c. Solomon – Hezekiah
   d. Agur
   e. Lemuel
	30. AMOS – God Judges Sin
	   a. Neighbors judged
	   b. Israel judged
	   c. Visions of future judgment
	   d. Israel's past judgment blessings

21. ECCLESIASTES – Vanity
   a. Experimentation
   b. Observation
   c. Consideration
	31. OBADIAH – Edom's Destruction
	   a. Destruction prophesied
	   b. Reasons for destruction
	   c. Israel's future blessing

22. SONG OF SOLOMON – Love Story	32. JONAH – Gentile Salvation
	   a. Jonah disobeys
	   b. Others suffer
	   c. Jonah punished
	   d. Jonah obeys; thousands saved
	   e. Jonah displeased, no love for souls

23. ISAIAH – The Justice (Judgment) and Grace (Comfort) of God
   a. Prophecies of punishment
   b. History
   c. Prophecies of blessing	

	33. MICAH – Israel's Sins, Judgment, and Restoration
	   a. Sin and judgment
	   b. Grace and future restoration
	   c. Appeal and petition

24. JEREMIAH – Judah's Sin Leads to Babylonian Captivity
   a. Jeremiah's call; empowered
   b. Judah condemned; predicted Babylonian captivity
   c. Restoration promised
   d. Prophesied judgment inflicted
   e. Prophesies against Gentiles
   f. Summary of Judah's captivity
	34. NAHUM – Nineveh Condemned
	   a. God hates sin
	   b. Nineveh's doom prophesied
	   c. Reasons for doom

	35. HABAKKUK – The Just Shall Live by Faith
	   a. Complaint of Judah's unjudged sin
	   b. Chaldeans will punish
	   c. Complaint of Chaldeans' wickedness
	   d. Punishment promised
	   e. Prayer for revival; faith in God

25. LAMENTATIONS – Lament over Jerusalem
   a. Affliction of Jerusalem
   b. Destroyed because of sin
   c. The prophet's suffering
   d. Present desolation versus past splendor
   e. Appeal to God for mercy	

	36. ZEPHANIAH – Babylonian Invasion Prefigures the Day of the Lord
	   a. Judgment on Judah foreshadows the Great Day of the Lord
	   b. Judgment on Jerusalem and neighbors foreshadows final judgment of all nations

26. EZEKIEL – Israel's Captivity and Restoration
   a. Judgment on Judah and Jerusalem
   b. Judgment on Gentile nations
   c. Israel restored; Jerusalem's future glory	

	37. HAGGAI – Rebuild the Temple
	   a. Negligence
	   b. Courage
	   c. Separation
	   d. Judgment

27. DANIEL – The Time of the Gentiles
   a. History; Nebuchadnezzar, Belshazzar, Daniel
   b. Prophecy	

28. HOSEA – Unfaithfulness
   a. Unfaithfulness
   b. Punishment
   c. Restoration
	38. ZECHARIAH – Two Comings of Christ
	   a. Zechariah's vision
	   b. Bethel's question; Jehovah's answer
	   c. Nation's downfall and salvation

29. JOEL – The Day of the Lord
   a. Locust plague
   b. Events of the future day of the Lord
   c. Order of the future day of the Lord
	39. MALACHI – Neglect
	   a. The priest's sins
	   b. The people's sins
	   c. The faithful few

New Testament

1. MATTHEW – Jesus the King
    a. The Person of the King
    b. The Preparation of the King
    c. The Propaganda of the King
    d. The Program of the King
    e. The Passion of the King
    f. The Power of the King
	7. 1 CORINTHIANS – The Lordship of Christ
	    a. Salutation and thanksgiving
	    b. Conditions in the Corinthian body
	    c. Concerning the Gospel
	    d. Concerning collections

2. MARK – Jesus the Servant
    a. John introduces the Servant
    b. God the Father identifies the Servant
    c. The temptation initiates the Servant
    d. Work and word of the Servant
    e. Death, burial, resurrection
	8. 2 CORINTHIANS – The Ministry in the Church
	    a. The comfort of God
	    b. Collection for the poor
	    c. Calling of the Apostle Paul

3. LUKE – Jesus Christ the Perfect Man
    a. Birth and family of the Perfect Man
    b. Testing of the Perfect Man; hometown
    c. Ministry of the Perfect Man
    d. Betrayal, trial, and death of the Perfect Man
    e. Resurrection of the Perfect Man
	9. GALATIANS – Justification by Faith
	    a. Introduction
	    b. Personal – Authority of the Apostle and glory of the Gospel
	    c. Doctrinal – Justification by faith
	    d. Practical – Sanctification by the Holy Spirit
	    e. Autographed conclusion and exhortation

4. JOHN – Jesus Christ is God
    a. Prologue – the Incarnation
    b. Introduction
    c. Witness of Jesus to his Apostles
    d. Passion – witness to the world
    e. Epilogue
	10. EPHESIANS – The Church of Jesus Christ
	    a. Doctrinal – the heavenly calling of the Church
	        - A Body
	        - A Temple
	        - A Mystery
	    b. Practical – The earthly conduct of the Church
	        - A New Man
	        - A Bride
	        - An Army

5. ACTS – The Holy Spirit Working in the Church
    a. The Lord Jesus at work by the Holy Spirit through the Apostles at Jerusalem
    b. In Judea and Samaria
    c. To the uttermost parts of the Earth
	11. PHILIPPIANS – Joy in the Christian Life
	    a. Philosophy for Christian living
	    b. Pattern for Christian living
	    c. Prize for Christian living
	    d. Power for Christian living

6. ROMANS – The Righteousness of God
    a. Salutation
    b. Sin and salvation
    c. Sanctification
    d. Struggle
    e. Spirit-filled living
    f. Security of salvation
    g. Segregation
    h. Sacrifice and service
    i. Separation and salutation
	12. COLOSSIANS – Christ the Fullness of God
	    a. Doctrinal – In Christ believers are made full
	    b. Practical – Christ's life poured out in believers, and through them

	13. 1 THESSALONIANS – The Second Coming of Christ:
	    a. Is an inspiring hope
	    b. Is a working hope
	    c. Is a purifying hope
	    d. Is a comforting hope
	    e. Is a rousing, stimulating hope

New Testament, continued

14. 2 THESSALONIANS – The Second Coming of Christ
    a. Persecution of believers now; judgment of unbelievers hereafter (at coming of Christ)
    b. Program of the world in connection with the coming of Christ
    c. Practical issues associated with the coming of Christ
	21. 1 PETER – Christian Hope in the Time of Persecution and Trial
	    a. Suffering and security of believers
	    b. Suffering and the Scriptures
	    c. Suffering and the sufferings of Christ
	    d. Suffering and the Second Coming of Christ

15. 1 TIMOTHY – Government and Order in the Local Church
    a. The faith of the Church
    b. Public prayer and women's place in the Church
    c. Officers in the Church
    d. Apostasy in the Church
    e. Duties of the officer of the Church
	22. 2 PETER – Warning Against False Teachers
	    a. Addition of Christian graces gives assurance
	    b. Authority of the Scriptures
	    c. Apostasy brought in by false testimony
	    d. Attitude toward Return of Christ: test for apostasy
	    e. Agenda of God in the world
	    f. Admonition to believers

16. 2 TIMOTHY – Loyalty in the Days of Apostasy
    a. Afflictions of the Gospel
    b. Active in service
    c. Apostasy coming; authority of the Scriptures
    d. Allegiance to the Lord
	23. 1 JOHN – The Family of God
	    a. God is Light
	    b. God is Love
	    c. God is Life

17. TITUS – The Ideal New Testament Church
    a. The Church is an organization
    b. The Church is to teach and preach the Word of God
    c. The Church is to perform good works
	24. 2 JOHN – Warning against Receiving Deceivers
	    a. Walk in truth
	    b. Love one another
	    c. Receive not deceivers
	    d. Find joy in fellowship

18. PHILEMON – Reveal Christ's Love and Teach Brotherly Love
    a. Genial greeting to Philemon and family
    b. Good reputation of Philemon
    c. Gracious plea for Onesimus
    d. Guiltless illustration of Imputation
    e. General and personal requests
	25. 3 JOHN – Admonition to Receive True Believers
	    a. Gaius, brother in the Church
	    b. Diotrephes
	    c. Demetrius

19. HEBREWS – The Superiority of Christ
    a. Doctrinal – Christ is better than the Old Testament economy
    b. Practical – Christ brings better benefits and duties
	26. JUDE – Contending for the Faith
	    a. Occasion of the epistle
	    b. Occurrences of apostasy
	    c. Occupation of believers in the days of apostasy

20. JAMES – Ethics of Christianity
    a. Faith tested
    b. Difficulty of controlling the tongue
    c. Warning against worldliness
    d. Admonitions in view of the Lord's coming
	27. REVELATION – The Unveiling of Christ Glorified
	    a. The person of Christ in glory
	    b. The possession of Jesus Christ – the Church in the World
	    c. The program of Jesus Christ – the scene in Heaven
	    d. The seven seals
	    e. The seven trumpets
	    f. Important persons in the last days
	    g. The seven vials
	    h. The fall of Babylon
	    i. The eternal state

Traditions:
(*Paradosis*)
Rev. Dr. Don L. Davis and Rev. Terry G. Cornett

Strong's Definition

Paradosis. Transmission, i.e. (concretely) a precept; specifically, the Jewish traditionary law

Vine's Explanation

denotes "a tradition," and hence, by metonymy, (a) "the teachings of the rabbis," . . . (b) "apostolic teaching," . . . of instructions concerning the gatherings of believers, of Christian doctrine in general . . . of instructions concerning everyday conduct.

1. **The concept of tradition in Scripture is essentially positive.**

   Jeremiah 6:16 (ESV) – Thus says the Lord: "Stand by the roads, and look, and ask for the ancient paths, where the good way is; and walk in it, and find rest for your souls. But they said, 'We will not walk in it'" (cf. Exodus 3:15; Judges 2:17; 1 Kings 8:57-58; Psalm 78:1-6).

   2 Chronicles 35:25 (ESV) – Jeremiah also uttered a lament for Josiah; and all the singing men and singing women have spoken of Josiah in their laments to this day. They made these a rule in Israel; behold, they are written in the Laments (cf. Genesis 32:32; Judges 11:38-40).

   Jeremiah 35:14-19 (ESV) – The command that Jonadab the son of Rechab gave to his sons, to drink no wine, has been kept, and they drink none to this day, for they have obeyed their father's command. I have spoken to you persistently, but you have not listened to me. I have sent to you all my servants the prophets, sending them persistently, saying, 'Turn now every one of you from his evil way, and amend your deeds, and do not go after other gods to serve them, and then you shall dwell in the land that I gave to you and your fathers.' But you did not incline your ear or listen to me. The sons of Jonadab the son of Rechab have kept the command that their father gave them, but this people has not obeyed me. Therefore, thus says the Lord, the God of hosts, the God of Israel: Behold, I am bringing upon Judah and all the inhabitants of Jerusalem all the disaster that I have pronounced against them, because I have spoken to them and they have not listened, I have called to them and they have not answered." But to the house of the Rechabites Jeremiah said, "Thus says the Lord of hosts, the God of Israel: Because you have obeyed the command of Jonadab your father and kept all his precepts and done all that he commanded you, therefore thus says the Lord of hosts, the God of Israel: Jonadab the son of Rechab shall never lack a man to stand before me."

2. **Godly tradition is a wonderful thing, but not all tradition is godly.**

   Any individual tradition must be judged by its faithfulness to the Word of God and its usefulness in helping people maintain obedience to Christ's example and teaching.[1] In the Gospels, Jesus frequently rebukes the Pharisees for establishing traditions that nullify rather than uphold God's commands.

   Mark 7:8 (ESV) – You leave the commandment of God and hold to the tradition of men" (cf. Matthew 15:2-6; Mark 7:13).

   Colossians 2:8 (ESV) – See to it that no one takes you captive by philosophy and empty deceit, according to human tradition, according to the elemental spirits of the world, and not according to Christ.

3. **Without the fullness of the Holy Spirit, and the constant edification provided to us by the Word of God, tradition will inevitably lead to dead formalism.**

   Those who are spiritual are filled with the Holy Spirit, whose power and leading alone provides individuals and congregations a sense of freedom and vitality in all they practice and believe. However, when the practices and teachings of any given tradition are no longer infused by the power of the Holy Spirit and the Word of God, tradition loses its effectiveness, and may actually become counterproductive to our discipleship in Jesus Christ.

   Ephesians 5:18 (ESV) – And do not get drunk with wine, for that is debauchery, but be filled with the Spirit.

   Galatians 5:22-25 (ESV) – But the fruit of the Spirit is love, joy, peace, patience, kindness, goodness, faithfulness, gentleness, self-control; against such things there is no law. And those who belong to Christ Jesus have crucified the flesh with its passions and desires. If we live by the Spirit, let us also walk by the Spirit.

   2 Corinthians 3:5-6 (ESV) – Not that we are sufficient in ourselves to claim anything as coming from us, but our sufficiency is from God, who has made

---

[1] "All Protestants insist that these traditions must ever be tested against Scripture and can never possess an independent apostolic authority over or alongside of Scripture." (J. Van Engen, "Tradition," *Evangelical Dictionary of Theology*, Walter Elwell, Gen. ed.) We would add that Scripture is itself the "authoritative tradition" by which all other traditions are judged. See "Appendix A, The Founders of Tradition: Three Levels of Christian Authority," following.

us competent to be ministers of a new covenant, not of the letter but of the Spirit. For the letter kills, but the Spirit gives life.

4. **Fidelity to the Apostolic Tradition (teaching and modeling) is the essence of Christian maturity.**

   2 Timothy 2:2 (ESV) – and what you have heard from me in the presence of many witnesses entrust to faithful men who will be able to teach others also.

   1 Corinthians 11:1-2 (ESV) – Be imitators of me, as I am of Christ. Now I commend you because you remember me in everything and maintain the traditions even as I delivered them to you (cf. 1 Corinthians 4:16-17; 2 Timothy 1:13-14; 2 Thessalonians 3:7-9; Philippians 4:9).

   1 Corinthians 15:3-8 (ESV) – For I delivered to you as of first importance what I also received: that Christ died for our sins in accordance with the Scriptures, that he was buried, that he was raised on the third day in accordance with the Scriptures, and that he appeared to Cephas, then to the twelve. Then he appeared to more than five hundred brothers at one time, most of whom are still alive, though some have fallen asleep. Then he appeared to James, then to all the apostles. Last of all, as to one untimely born, he appeared also to me.

5. **The Apostle Paul often includes an appeal to the tradition for support in doctrinal practices.**

   1 Corinthians 11:16 (ESV) – If anyone is inclined to be contentious, we have no such practice, nor do the churches of God (cf. 1 Corinthians 1:2; 7:17, 15:3).

   1 Corinthians 14:33-34 (ESV) – For God is not a God of confusion but of peace. As in all the churches of the saints, the women should keep silent in the churches. For they are not permitted to speak, but should be in submission, as the Law also says.

6. **When a congregation uses received tradition to remain faithful to the "Word of God," they are commended by the apostles.**

   1 Corinthians 11:2 (ESV) – Now I commend you because you remember me in everything and maintain the traditions even as I delivered them to you.

   2 Thessalonians 2:15 (ESV) – So then, brothers, stand firm and hold to the traditions that you were taught by us, either by our spoken word or by our letter.

   2 Thessalonians 3:6 (ESV) – Now we command you, brothers, in the name of our Lord Jesus Christ, that you keep away from any brother who is

walking in idleness and not in accord with the tradition that you received from us.

Appendix A

The Founders of Tradition: Three Levels of Christian Authority

Exodus 3:15 (ESV) – God also said to Moses, "Say this to the people of Israel, 'The Lord, the God of your fathers, the God of Abraham, the God of Isaac, and the God of Jacob, has sent me to you.' This is my name forever, and thus I am to be remembered throughout all generations."

1. The Authoritative Tradition: the Apostles and the Prophets (The Holy Scriptures)

Ephesians 2:19-21 (ESV) – So then you are no longer strangers and aliens, but you are fellow citizens with the saints and members of the household of God, built on the foundation of the apostles and prophets, Christ Jesus himself being the cornerstone, in whom the whole structure, being joined together, grows into a holy temple in the Lord.

– The Apostle Paul

Those who gave eyewitness testimony to the revelation and saving acts of Yahweh, first in Israel, and ultimately in Jesus Christ the Messiah. This testimony is binding for all people, at all times, and in all places. It is the authoritative tradition by which all subsequent tradition is judged.

2. The Great Tradition: the Ecumenical Councils and their Creeds[2]

What has been believed everywhere, always, and by all.

– Vincent of Lerins

The Great Tradition is the core dogma (doctrine) of the Church. It represents the teaching of the Church as it has understood the Authoritative Tradition (the Holy Scriptures), and summarizes those essential truths that Christians of all ages have confessed and believed. To these doctrinal statements the whole Church, (Catholic, Orthodox, and Protestant)[3] gives its assent. The worship and theology

---

2 See Appendix B, "Defining the Great Tradition."

3 Even the more radical wing of the Protestant reformation (Anabaptists) who were the most reluctant to embrace the creeds as dogmatic instruments of faith, did not disagree with the essential

of the Church reflects this core dogma, which finds its summation and fulfillment in the person and work of Jesus Christ. From earliest times, Christians have expressed their devotion to God in its Church calendar, a yearly pattern of worship which summarizes and reenacts the events of Christ's life.

3. Specific Church Traditions: The Founders of Denominations and Orders

The Presbyterian Church (U.S.A.) has approximately 2.5 million members, 11,200 congregations and 21,000 ordained ministers. Presbyterians trace their history to the 16th century and the Protestant Reformation. Our heritage, and much of what we believe, began with the French lawyer John Calvin (1509-1564), whose writings crystallized much of the Reformed thinking that came before him.

– The Presbyterian Church, U.S.A.

Christians have expressed their faith in Jesus Christ in various ways through specific movements and traditions which embrace and express the Authoritative Tradition and the Great Tradition in unique ways. For instance, Catholic movements have arisen around people like Benedict, Francis, or Dominic, and among Protestants people like Martin Luther, John Calvin, Ulrich Zwingli, and John Wesley. Women have founded vital movements of Christian faith (e.g., Aimee Semple McPherson of the Foursquare Church), as well as minorities (e.g., Richard Allen of the African Methodist Episcopal Church or Charles H. Mason of the Church of God in Christ, who also helped to spawn the Assemblies of God), all of which attempted to express the Authoritative Tradition and the Great Tradition in a specific way consistent with their time and expression.

The emergence of vital, dynamic movements of the faith at different times and among different peoples reveals the fresh working of the Holy Spirit throughout history. Thus, inside Catholicism, new communities have arisen such as the Benedictines, Franciscans, and Dominicans; and outside Catholicism, new denominations have emerged (Lutherans, Presbyterians, Methodists, Church of God in Christ, etc.). Each of these specific traditions have "founders," key leaders whose energy and vision helped to establish a unique expression of Christian faith and practice. Of course, to be legitimate, these movements must adhere to and faithfully express both the Authoritative Tradition and the Great Tradition. Members of these specific

---

content found in them. "They assumed the Apostolic Creed–they called it 'The Faith,' Der Glaube, as did most people." See John Howard Yoder, Preface to *Theology: Christology and Theological Method*. Grand Rapids: Brazos Press, 2002. pp. 222-223.

traditions embrace their own unique practices and patterns of spirituality, but these unique features are not necessarily binding on the Church at large. They represent the unique expressions of that community's understanding of and faithfulness to the Authoritative and Great Traditions.

Specific traditions seek to express and live out this faithfulness to the Authoritative and Great Traditions through their worship, teaching, and service. They seek to make the Gospel clear within new cultures or subcultures, speaking and modeling the hope of Christ into new situations shaped by their own set of questions posed in light of their own unique circumstances. These movements, therefore, seek to contextualize the Authoritative tradition in a way that faithfully and effectively leads new groups of people to faith in Jesus Christ, and incorporates those who believe into the community of faith that obeys his teachings and gives witness of him to others.

Appendix B
Defining the "Great Tradition"

The Great Tradition (sometimes called the "classical Christian tradition") is defined by Robert E. Webber as follows:

> [It is] the broad outline of Christian belief and practice developed from the Scriptures between the time of Christ and the middle of the fifth century.
>
> – Webber. *The Majestic Tapestry*.
> Nashville: Thomas Nelson Publishers, 1986. p. 10.

This tradition is widely affirmed by Protestant theologians both ancient and modern.

> Thus those ancient Councils of Nicea, Constantinople, the first of Ephesus, Chalcedon, and the like, which were held for refuting errors, we willingly embrace, and reverence as sacred, in so far as relates to doctrines of faith, for they contain nothing but the pure and genuine interpretation of Scripture, which the holy Fathers with spiritual prudence adopted to crush the enemies of religion who had then arisen.
>
> – John Calvin. *Institutes*. IV, ix. 8.

> . . . most of what is enduringly valuable in contemporary biblical exegesis was discovered by the fifth century.
>
> – Thomas C. Oden. *The Word of Life*.
> San Francisco: HarperSanFrancisco, 1989. p. xi

> The first four Councils are by far the most important, as they settled the orthodox faith on the Trinity and the Incarnation.
>
> – Philip Schaff. *The Creeds of Christendom*. Vol. 1. Grand Rapids: Baker Book House, 1996. p. 44.

Our reference to the Ecumenical Councils and Creeds is, therefore, focused on those Councils which retain a widespread agreement in the Church among Catholics, Orthodox, and Protestants. While Catholic and Orthodox share common agreement on the first seven councils, Protestants tend to affirm and use primarily the first four. Therefore, those councils which continue to be shared by the whole Church are completed with the Council of Chalcedon in 451.

It is worth noting that each of these four Ecumenical Councils took place in a pre-European cultural context and that none of them were held in Europe. They were councils of the whole Church and they reflected a time in which Christianity was primarily an eastern religion in it's geographic core. By modern reckoning, their participants were African, Asian, and European. The councils reflected a church that "... has roots in cultures far distant from Europe and preceded the development of modern European identity, and [of which] some of its greatest minds have been African" (Oden, *The Living God*, San Francisco: HarperSanFrancisco, 1987, p. 9).

Perhaps the most important achievement of the Councils was the creation of what is now commonly called the Nicene Creed. It serves as a summary statement of the Christian faith that can be agreed on by Catholic, Orthodox, and Protestant Christians.

The first four Ecumenical Councils are summarized in the following chart:

Name/Date/Location	Purpose	
First Ecumenical Council 325 A.D. Nicea, Asia Minor	Defending against:	Arianism
	Question answered:	Was Jesus God?
	Action:	Developed the initial from of the Nicene Creed to serve as a summary of the Christian faith
Second Ecumenical Council 381 A.D. Constantinople, Asia Minor	Defending against:	Macedonianism
	Question answered:	Is the Holy Spirit a personal and equal part of the Godhead?
	Action:	Completed the Nicene Creed by expanding the article dealing with the Holy Spirit
Third Ecumenical Council 431 A.D. Ephesus, Asia Minor	Defending against:	Nestorianism
	Question answered:	Is Jesus Christ both God and man in one person?
	Action:	Defined Christ as the Incarnate Word of God and affirmed his mother Mary as *theotokos* (God-bearer)
Fourth Ecumenical Council 451 A.D. Chalcedon, Asia Minor	Defending against:	Monophysitism
	Question answered:	How can Jesus be both God and man?
	Action:	Explained the relationship between Jesus's two natures (human and divine)

Documenting Your Work: A Guide to Help You Give Credit Where Credit Is Due

The Urban Ministry Institute

Avoiding Plagiarism

Plagiarism is using another person's ideas as if they belonged to you without giving them proper credit. In academic work it is just as wrong to steal a person's ideas as it is to steal a person's property. These ideas may come from the author of a book, an article you have read, or from a fellow student. The way to avoid plagiarism is to carefully use "notes" (textnotes, footnotes, endnotes, etc.) and a "Works Cited" section to help people who read your work know when an idea is one you thought of, and when you are borrowing an idea from another person.

Using Citation References

A citation reference is required in a paper whenever you use ideas or information that came from another person's work.

All citation references involve two parts:

- Notes in the body of your paper placed next to each quotation which came from an outside source.

- A "Works Cited" page at the end of your paper or project which gives information about the sources you have used

Using Notes in Your Paper

There are three basic kinds of notes: parenthetical notes, footnotes, and endnotes. At The Urban Ministry Institute, we recommend that students use parenthetical notes. These notes give the author's last name(s), the date the book was published, and the page number(s) on which you found the information. Example:

> In trying to understand the meaning of Genesis 14:1-24, it is important to recognize that in biblical stories "the place where dialogue is first introduced will be an important moment in revealing the character of the speaker . . ." (Kaiser and Silva 1994, 73). This is certainly true of the character of Melchizedek who speaks words of blessing. This identification of Melchizedek as a positive spiritual influence is reinforced by the fact that he is the King of Salem, since Salem means "safe, at peace" (Wiseman 1996, 1045).

Creating a Works Cited Page

A "Works Cited" page should be placed at the end of your paper. This page:

- lists every source you quoted in your paper
- is in alphabetical order by author's last name
- includes the date of publication and information about the publisher

The following formatting rules should be followed:

1. **Title**

   The title "Works Cited" should be used and centered on the first line of the page following the top margin.

2. **Content**

   Each reference should list:

   - the author's full name (last name first)
   - the date of publication
   - the title and any special information (Revised edition, 2nd edition, reprint) taken from the cover or title page should be noted
   - the city where the publisher is headquartered followed by a colon and the name of the publisher

3. **Basic form**
   - Each piece of information should be separated by a period.
   - The second line of a reference (and all following lines) should be indented.
   - Book titles should be underlined (or italicized).
   - Article titles should be placed in quotes.

   Example:

   Fee, Gordon D. 1991. *Gospel and Spirit: Issues in New Testament Hermeneutics*. Peabody, MA: Hendrickson Publishers.

4. **Special forms**

   A book with multiple authors:

   > Kaiser, Walter C., and Moisés Silva. 1994. *An Introduction to Biblical Hermeneutics: The Search for Meaning.* Grand Rapids: Zondervan Publishing House.

   An edited book:

   > Greenway, Roger S., ed. 1992. *Discipling the City: A Comprehensive Approach to Urban Mission.* 2nd ed. Grand Rapids: Baker Book House.

   A book that is part of a series:

   > Morris, Leon. 1971. *The Gospel According to John.* Grand Rapids: Wm. B. Eerdmans Publishing Co. *The New International Commentary on the New Testament.* Gen. ed. F. F. Bruce.

   An article in a reference book:

   > Wiseman, D. J. "Salem." 1982. In *New Bible Dictionary.* Leicester, England – Downers Grove, IL: InterVarsity Press. Eds. I.H. Marshall and others.

   (An example of a "Works Cited" page is located on the next page.)

For Further Research

Standard guides to documenting academic work in the areas of philosophy, religion, theology, and ethics include:

> Atchert, Walter S., and Joseph Gibaldi. 1985. *The MLA Style Manual.* New York: Modern Language Association.

> *The Chicago Manual of Style.* 1993. 14th ed. Chicago: The University of Chicago Press.

> Turabian, Kate L. 1987. *A Manual for Writers of Term Papers, Theses, and Dissertations.* 5th edition. Bonnie Bertwistle Honigsblum, ed. Chicago: The University of Chicago Press.

Works Cited

Fee, Gordon D. 1991. *Gospel and Spirit: Issues in New Testament Hermeneutics.* Peabody, MA: Hendrickson Publishers.

Greenway, Roger S., ed. 1992. *Discipling the City: A Comprehensive Approach to Urban Mission.* 2nd ed. Grand Rapids: Baker Book House.

Kaiser, Walter C., and Moisés Silva. 1994. *An Introduction to Biblical Hermeneutics: The Search for Meaning.* Grand Rapids: Zondervan Publishing House.

Morris, Leon. 1971. *The Gospel According to John.* Grand Rapids: Wm. B. Eerdmans Publishing Co. *The New International Commentary on the New Testament.* Gen. ed. F. F. Bruce.

Wiseman, D. J. "Salem." 1982. In *New Bible Dictionary.* Leicester, England-Downers Grove, IL: InterVarsity Press. Eds. I. H. Marshall and others.

General Biblical Studies

Understanding the Bible in Parts and Whole

Rev. Don Allsman

The Bible is the authoritative account of God's plan to exalt Jesus as Lord of all, redeem all creation, and put down God's enemies forever. The subject of the Bible is Jesus Christ (John 5:39-40):

- The Old Testament is the anticipation and promise of Christ
- The New Testament is the climax and fulfillment in Christ

"In the Old Testament the New Testament lies hidden; in the New Testament the Old Testament stands revealed."

Elements of plot development: beginning, rising action, climax, falling action, resolution

1. Beginning: Creation and fall of man (the problem and need for resolution), Genesis 1:1 – 3:15
2. Rising Action: God's plan revealed through Israel (Genesis 3:15 – Malachi)
3. Climax: Jesus inaugurates his Kingdom (Matthew – Acts 1:11)
4. Falling Action: The Church continues Jesus's kingdom work (Acts 1:12 – Revelation 3)
5. Resolution: Jesus returns to consummate the Kingdom (Revelation 4 – 22)
6. Commentary: The people of God describe their experiences to provide wisdom (The Wisdom literature: Job, Psalms, Proverbs, Ecclesiastes, Song of Solomon)

The Bible in Book Order

Genesis, Exodus, Leviticus, Numbers, Deuteronomy, Joshua, Judges, Ruth, 1-2 Samuel	History from Creation to the reign of King David
1-2 Kings	Israel's history from David to Exile
1-2 Chronicles	Various historical accounts from Creation to Exile
Ezra, Nehemiah, Esther	Accounts of Israel in Exile and return
Job (contemporary of Abraham) Psalms (primarily of David), Proverbs, Ecclesiastes, song of Solomon (Solomon's time)	Wisdom Literature
Isaiah, Jeremiah, Lamentations, Ezekiel, Daniel, Hosea, Joel, Amos, Obadiah, Jonah, Micah, Nahum, Habakkuk, Zephaniah, Haggai, Zechariah, Malachi	Writings of Israel's prophets from the time of the Kings through the return from Exile
Matthew, Mark, Luke, John	The account of Jesus of Nazareth (Gospels)
Acts, Romans, 1-2 Corinthians, Galatians, Ephesians, Philippians, Colossians, 1-2 Thessalonians, 1-2 Timothy, Titus, Philemon, Hebrews, James, 1-2 Peter, 1-3 John, Jude, Revelation	The account of the Church after Jesus's ascension, including letters of apostolic instruction to the Church (Epistles)
Revelation	The future and the end of the age (Jesus's return)

General Facts Concerning the New Testament

A Comparative Chart of the Four Gospels

Robert H. Gundry. *A Survey of the New Testament*. Grand Rapids: Zondervan, 1981.

	Probable Date of Writing	Probable Place of Writing	First Intended Audience	Theme and Focus
Mark	50s	Rome	Gentiles in Rome	Jesus's redemptive activity
Matthew	50s or 60s	Antioch in Syria	Jews in Palestine	Jesus the Jewish Messiah, and the disciples as the new people of God
Luke	60s	Rome	Interested Gentile seekers	The historical certainty of the Gospel account
John	80s or 90s	Ephesus	General Population in Asia Minor	Believing in Jesus as the Messiah for eternal life

Old Testament Apocrypha

Walter A. Elwell and Robert W. Yarbrough. *Encountering the New Testament*. Grand Rapids: Baker Books, 1998.

Roman Catholics and some Eastern Orthodox churches recognize the writings listed below as Scripture. Protestants acknowledge their literary value and historical significance but do not view them as possessing spiritual authority		
Additions to Esther	Judith	Prayer of Manasseh
Baruch	Letter of Jeremiah	Psalm 151
Bel and the Dragon	1 Maccabees	Song of the Three Jews
Ecclesiasticus (Wisdom of Jesus Son of Sirach)	2 Maccabees	Susanna
	3 Maccabees	Tobit
1 Esdras	4 Maccabees	Wisdom of Solomon
2 Esdras	Prayer of Azariah	

General Facts about the New Testament

1. The New Testament is the testament of God's saving work in more recent times and announces the Savior that the Old Testament awaits.

2. The New Testament contains 27 books, four dealing with Jesus's life and ministry called *Gospels*, one dealing with history of the Church, Acts, and 21 *Epistles* or letters, and one book of prophecy.

3. The collection of books in the New Testament comprise the canon, an authorized collection that came together over 3 centuries.

4. New Testament manuscripts were first written on papyrus (a paper made from reeds, and then on leather). Nearly 300 others are written on *uncials*, in capital letters, usually on leather. *Minuscules* represent the largest group and display a kind of cursive writing that developed in *Byzantium* around the ninth century. *Lectionaries*, books used in Church worship, include portions of Scripture as well.

5. The New Testament is reliable because of 1) the extensive evidence supporting it; 2) the authors wrote them within the first generation or two of Christian history, and 3) ancient versions were widely distributed.

6. The personal tone of the New Testament is seen in the fact that of the 27 books, 24 are personal letters, and 3 are personalized accounts of the life and work of Christ.

7. The Apocrypha includes 14 non-canonical books written between 200 B.C. and A.D. 100.

8. Jesus was seen as a threat by the Jews because he made controversial claims about himself and took liberties with Jewish customs.

9. Jesus appeared at a time when the traditions of Judaism dictated much of Jewish life and practice. A knowledge of these customs can greatly aid our understanding of the New Testament.

Chronological Table of the New Testament

Rev. Dr. Don L. Davis, adapted from Robert Yarbrough

Date	Christian History	New Testament	Roman History
c. 28-30	Public ministry of Jesus	Gospels	14-37, Tiberius, emperor
c. 33	Conversion of Paul	Acts 9:1-13	—
c. 35	Paul's first post-conversion Jerusalem visit	Galatians 1:18	—
c. 35-46	Paul in Cilicia and Syria	Galatians 1:21	—
—	—	—	c. 37-41, Gaius, emperor c. 41-54, Claudius, emperor
c. 46	Paul's second Jerusalem visit	Galatians 2:1; Acts 11:27-50	—
c. 47-48	Paul and Barnabas in Cyprus and Galatia (1st Journey)	Acts 13-14	—
c. 48?	Letter to the Galatians	—	—
c. 49	Council of Jerusalem	Acts 15	—
c. 49-50	Paul and Silas from Syrian Antioch through Asia Minor to Macedonia and Achaia (2nd Journey)	Acts 15:36-18:21	—
c. 50	Letters to the Thessalonians	—	—
c. 50-52	Paul in Corinth	—	c. 51-52, Gallio, proconsul of Achaia
Summer 52	Paul's third Jerusalem visit	—	c. 52-59, Felix, procurator of Judea
c. 52-55	Paul in Ephesus	—	c. 54-68, Nero, emperor
c. 55-56	Letters to the Corinthians	—	—
c. 55-57	Paul in Macedonia, Illyricum, and Achaia (3rd Journey)	Acts 18:22-21:15	—
Early 57	Letter to the Romans	—	—
May 57	Paul's fourth (and last) Jerusalem visit	Acts 21:17	—
c. 57-59	Paul's imprisonment in Caesarea	Acts 23:23	c. 59, Festus succeeds Felix as procurator of Judea
Sept. 59	Paul's voyage to Rome begins	Acts 27-28	—
Feb. 60	Paul's arrival in Rome	—	—
c. 60-62	Paul's house arrest in Rome	—	—
c. 60-62?	Captivity Letters (Ephesians, Philippians, Colossians, Philemon)	—	c. 62, death of Festus; Albinus procurator of Judea
c. 65?	Paul visits Spain (4th Journey?)	—	c. 64, Fire of Rome
c. ??	Pastoral Letters (1 and 2 Timothy, Titus)	—	—
c. 65?	Death of Paul	—	—

Translation Methodology

Rev. Terry G. Cornett

	Grade Level	Formal Equivalence	Dynamic Equivalence	Paraphrase
Hard to Read	12th 11th 10th 9th	King James Version (KJV) New American Standard Bible (NASB)		
Average Adult Level	8th 7th 6th	New International Version (NIV)	New Living Translation (NLT)	The Living Bible (TLB) The Message
Children's Bibles	5th 4th 3rd	New International Reader's Version (NIrV)	Contemporary English Version (CEV) International Children's Bible (ICB)	

Conversion and Calling

Theories of Inspiration

Rev. Terry G. Cornett

Theory of Inspiration	Explanation	Possible Objection(s)
Mechanical or Dictation	The human author is a passive instrument in God's hands. The author simply writes down each word as God speaks it. This direct dictation is what protects the text from human error.	The Books of Scripture show diverse writing styles, vocabularies, and manners of expression which vary with each human author. This theory doesn't seem to explain why God would use human authors rather than giving us a direct written word from himself.
Intuition or Natural	Gifted people with exceptional spiritual insight were chosen by God to write the Bible	The Bible indicates that Scripture came from God, through human authors (2 Peter 1:20-21).
Illumination	The Holy Spirit heightened the normal capacities of human authors so that they had special insight into spiritual truth.	The Scriptures indicate that the human authors expressed the very words of God ("Thus saith the Lord" passages; Romans 3:2).
Degrees of Inspiration	Certain parts of the Bible are more inspired than others. Sometimes this position is used to argue that portions dealing with key doctrines or ethical truths are inspired while portions dealing with history, economics, culture, etc. are less inspired or not inspired.	The biblical authors never indicate that some of Scripture is more inspired or treat only one kind of biblical material as inspired in their use of it. Jesus speaks about the entire scriptural revelation up to his day as an unchanging word from God (Matthew 5:17-18; John 3:34-35).
Verbal-Plenary	Both divine and human elements are present in the production of Scripture. The entire text of Scripture, including the words, are a product of the mind of God expressed in human terms and conditions, through human authors that he foreknew (Jeremiah 1:5) and chose for the task.	It seems unlikely that the human elements which are finite and culture-bound could be described as the unchanging words of God.

Getting a Firm Grasp of Scripture

From Leroy Eims, *The Lost Art of Disciple Making*, p. 81.

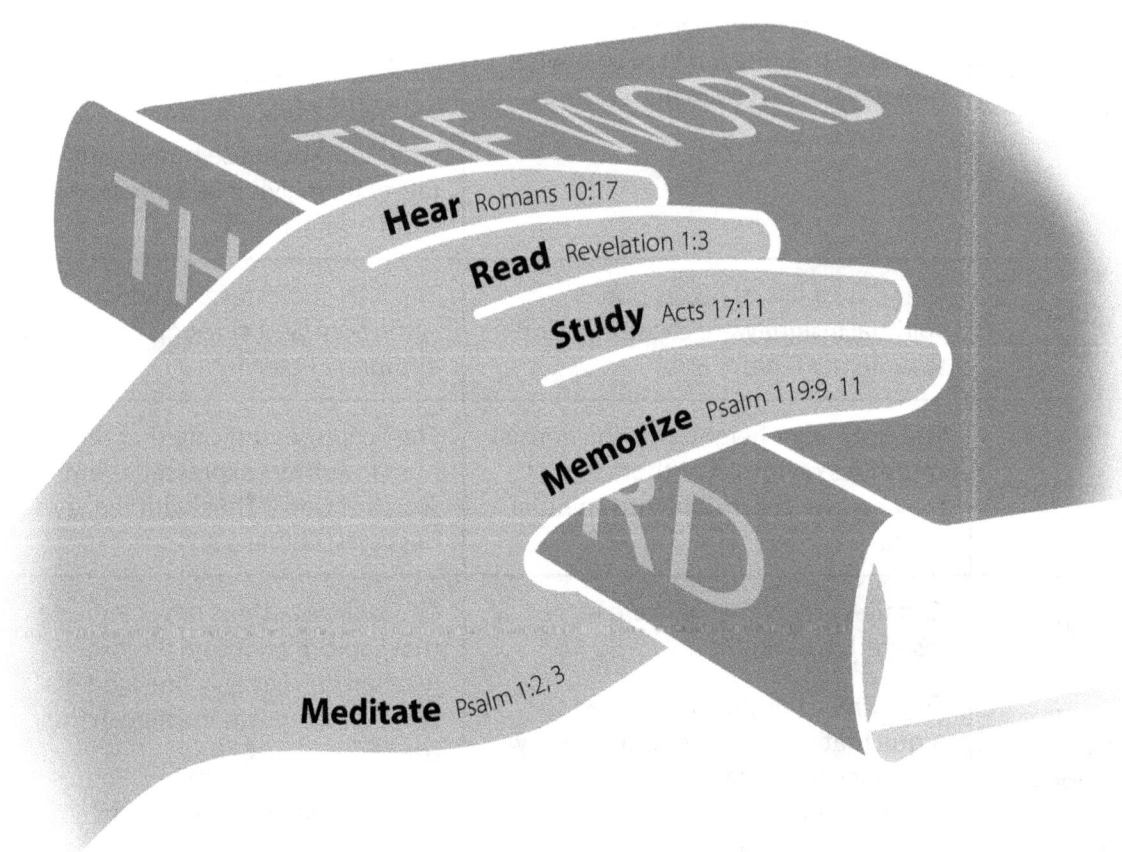

Picking Up on Different Wavelengths:
Integrated vs. Fragmented Mindsets and Lifestyles

Rev. Dr. Don L. Davis

A Fragmented Mindset and Lifestyle	An Integrated Lifestyle and Mindset
Sees things primarily in relation to one's own needs	Sees all things as one and whole
Sees something other than God as a substitute point of reference and coordination for meaning and truth	Sees God in Christ as the ultimate point of reference and coordination for all meaning and truth
Seeks God's blessing upon one's own personal enhancement	Aligns personal goals with God's ultimate plan and purposes
Understands the purpose of life to experience the greatest level of personal fulfillment and enhancement possible	Understands the purpose of life to make the maximum contribution possible to God's purpose in the world
Only relates to others in connection to their effect upon and place within one's individual personal space	Deeply identifies with all people and things as an integral part of God's great plan for his own glory
Defines theology as seeking to express someone's perspective on some religious idea or concept	Defines theology as seeking to comprehend God's ultimate designs and plans for himself in Jesus Christ
Applications are rooted in seeking right responses to particular issues and situations	Applications are byproducts of understanding what God is doing for himself in the world
Focuses on the style of analysis (to discern the processes and make-up of things)	Focuses on the style of synthesis (to discern the connection and unity of all things)
Seeks to understand biblical revelation primarily from the standpoint of one's private life ("God's plan for my life")	Seeks to understand biblical revelation primarily from the standpoint of God's plan for whole ("God's plan for the ages")
Governed by pressing concerns to ensure one's own security and significance in one's chosen endeavors ("My personal life plan")	Decision making is governed by commitment to participate as co-workers with God in the overall vision ("God's working in the world")
Coordinates itself around personal need as a working paradigm and project	Connects and correlates itself around God's vision and plan as a working paradigm
Sees mission and ministry as the expression of one's personal giftedness and burden, bringing personal satisfaction and security	Sees mission and ministry as the present, practical expression of one's identity vis-a-vis the panoramic vision of God
Relates knowledge, opportunity, and activity to the goals of personal enhancement and fulfillment	Relates knowledge, opportunity, and activity to a single, integrated vision and purpose
All of life is perceived to revolve around the personal identity and needs of the individual	All of life is perceived to revolve around a single theme: the revelation of God is Jesus of Nazareth

Scriptures on the Validity of Seeing All Things as Unified and Whole

Psalm 27:4 (ESV) – One thing have I asked of the Lord, that will I seek after: that I may dwell in the house of the Lord all the days of my life, to gaze upon the beauty of the Lord and to inquire in his temple.

Luke 10:39-42 (ESV) – And she had a sister called Mary, who sat at the Lord's feet and listened to his teaching. [40] But Martha was distracted with much serving. And she went up to him and said, "Lord, do you not care that my sister has left me to serve alone? Tell her then to help me." [41] But the Lord answered her, "Martha, Martha, you are anxious and troubled about many things, [42] but one thing is necessary. Mary has chosen the good portion, which will not be taken away from her."

Philippians 3:13-14 (ESV) – Brothers, I do not consider that I have made it my own. But one thing I do: forgetting what lies behind and straining forward to what lies ahead [14] I press on toward the goal for the prize of the upward call of God in Christ Jesus.

Psalm 73:25 (ESV) – Whom have I in heaven but you? And there is nothing on earth that I desire besides you.

Mark 8:36 (ESV) – For what does it profit a man to gain the whole world and forfeit his life?

Luke 18:22 (ESV) – When Jesus heard this, he said to him, "One thing you still lack. Sell all that you have and distribute to the poor, and you will have treasure in heaven; and come, follow me."

John 17:3 (ESV) – And this is eternal life, that they know you the only true God, and Jesus Christ whom you have sent.

1 Corinthians 13:3 (ESV) – If I give away all I have, and if I deliver up my body to be burned, but have not love, I gain nothing.

Galatians 5:6 (ESV) – For in Christ Jesus neither circumcision nor uncircumcision counts for anything, but only faith working through love.

Colossians 2:8-10 (ESV) – See to it that no one takes you captive by philosophy and empty deceit, according to human tradition, according to the elemental spirits of the world, and not according to Christ. [9] For in him the whole fullness of deity dwells bodily, [10] and you have been filled in him, who is the head of all rule and authority.

1 John 5:11-12 (ESV) – And this is the testimony, that God gave us eternal life, and this life is in his Son. [12] Whoever has the Son has life; whoever does not have the Son of God does not have life.

Psalm 16:5 (ESV) – The Lord is my chosen portion and my cup; you hold my lot.

Psalm 16:11 (ESV) – You make known to me the path of life; in your presence there is fullness of joy; at your right hand are pleasures forevermore.

Psalm 17:15 (ESV) – As for me, I shall behold your face in righteousness; when I awake, I shall be satisfied with your likeness.

Ephesians 1:9-10 (ESV) – making known to us the mystery of his will, according to his purpose, which he set forth in Christ [10] as a plan for the fullness of time, to unite all things in him, things in heaven and things on earth.

John 15:5 (ESV) – I am the vine; you are the branches. Whoever abides in me and I in him, he it is that bears much fruit, for apart from me you can do nothing.

Psalm 42:1 (ESV) – As a deer pants for flowing streams, so pants my soul for you, O God.

Habakkuk 3:17-18 (ESV) – Though the fig tree should not blossom, nor fruit be on the vines, the produce of the olive fail and the fields yield no food, the flock be cut off from the fold and there be no herd in the stalls, [18] yet I will rejoice in the Lord; I will take joy in the God of my salvation.

Matthew 10:37 (ESV) – Whoever loves father or mother more than me is not worthy of me, and whoever loves son or daughter more than me is not worthy of me.

Psalm 37:4 (ESV) – Delight yourself in the Lord, and he will give you the desires of your heart.

Psalm 63:3 (ESV) – Because your steadfast love is better than life, my lips will praise you.

Psalm 89:6 (ESV) – For who in the skies can be compared to the Lord? Who among the heavenly beings is like the Lord?

Philippians 3:8 (ESV) – Indeed, I count everything as loss because of the surpassing worth of knowing Christ Jesus my Lord. For his sake I have suffered the loss of all things and count them as rubbish, in order that I may gain Christ.

1 John 3:2 (ESV) – Beloved, we are God's children now, and what we will be has not yet appeared; but we know that when he appears we shall be like him, because we shall see him as he is.

Revelation 21:3 (ESV) – And I heard a loud voice from the throne saying, "Behold, the dwelling place of God is with man. He will dwell with them, and they will be his people, and God himself will be with them as their God.

Revelation 21:22-23 (ESV) – And I saw no temple in the city, for its temple is the Lord God the Almighty and the Lamb. [23] And the city has no need of sun or moon to shine on it, for the glory of God gives it light, and its lamp is the Lamb.

Psalm 115:3 (ESV) – Our God is in the heavens; he does all that he pleases.

Jeremiah 32:17 (ESV) – Ah, Lord God! It is you who has made the heavens and the earth by your great power and by your outstretched arm! Nothing is too hard for you.

Daniel 4:35 (ESV) – all the inhabitants of the earth are accounted as nothing, and he does according to his will among the host of heaven and among the inhabitants of the earth; and none can stay his hand or say to him, "What have you done?"

Ephesians 3:20-21 (ESV) – Now to him who is able to do far more abundantly than all that we ask or think, according to the power at work within us, [21] to him be glory in the Church and in Christ Jesus throughout all generations, forever and ever. Amen.

Bible Interpretation

Keys to Bible Interpretation: Some Keys to Interpreting the Scriptures Accurately

Rev. Terry G. Cornett and Rev. Dr. Don L. Davis. Revised ed.

Key Principles

To gain an accurate understanding of a book or passage from the Bible, the interpreter must:

Presuppositions

1. Believe that the Scriptures are inspired, infallible and the authoritative rule for life and doctrine.

2. Realize that it is not possible to fully understand and apply the Scriptures without:

    - having been "born from above" by faith in Christ
    - being filled with God's Holy Spirit
    - being diligent to pursue its meaning through regular study
    - being willing to obey its message, once revealed

3. Allow the process of interpretation to engage the "whole person." The study of Scripture should captivate your emotions and your will as well as your mind. "We aim to be objective but not disinterested readers."

4. Understand that all Scripture is in some way a testimony to Christ. Christ is the Bible's subject; all of its doctrine, teaching and ethics point to him.

5. Take into account both the divine and the human side of Scripture.

6. Seek to "extract" or take out the meaning that is in the text (exegesis), not read into the text his or her own beliefs or ideas (eisegesis).

7. Seek to explain:

    - the "unclear" passages by the clearer statements
    - the symbolic portions by the stated teachings of Scripture
    - the Old Testament by the New Testament

8. Take into account the whole context of the book and the passage where any particular text is found.

Understanding the Original Situation

9. Identify the human author and the intended audience. Start by attempting to discover what the author was trying to say to the original audience. "A passage cannot mean what it never meant."

10. Use information about the manuscripts, languages, grammar, literary forms, history, and culture to help discover the author's intended meaning.

11. Take seriously the genre and types of language used by the author, then interpret the Scriptures literally, meaning that we take the plain sense of the language as it is normally used in that genre.

Finding General Principles

12. Look for the ideas, values, and truths that a story, command, or prophecy is trying to communicate. Seek to state those principles in a way that is true and useful for all people, at all times, and in all situations.

13. Use Scripture to interpret Scripture. In order to understand any individual part of Scripture, compare that portion to the message of the whole Bible.

    Once this understanding has been reached, one must also reinterpret his/her understanding of the whole of Scripture (theology and doctrine) in light of the new information gained from the passage (The Hermeneutical Circle).

14. Understand that reason, tradition, and experience are significant factors in the process of interpreting Scripture. Principles must be clear, logical and defensible; they must be compatible with the way Christians have interpreted the Scriptures throughout history; and they must help to make sense out of human experience.

Applying General Principles Today

15. Carefully move from what Scripture "meant" to its original audience to what it "means" for the current reader.

16. Apply the general truths to specific situations faced by people today.

    - Remember that the Holy Spirit is the primary guide in the application of truth. Ask him for guidance about the meaning for today and then prayerfully meditate on the meaning of the passage.

    - Seek the Spirit's guidance by seeing how he has led other Christians (both inside and outside your own denominational tradition) to interpret the meaning and application of the passage for today.

17. Put the principles and the applications in language that makes sense to modern readers.

18. Keep the proper "end goals" in view. The intent of all Bible study is to mature the reader in the life and love of Jesus Christ, to the glory of God. Not knowledge alone, but life transformation is the goal of Bible interpretation.

Key Perspective

Discovering the Word and Works of God in the Lives of the People of Scripture

Note: In this diagram, Kuhatschek's categories refer to the three steps of Biblical interpretation outlined by Jack Kuhatschek in *Applying the Bible* Downer's Grove: IVP, 1990.

Their Ancient World: Physical Environment, Religions, Worldviews, Cultures, Beliefs, Peoples, Languages, History, Politics

What it meant to them then

What it means to us now

The Eternal Truth of the Living God

Our Contemporary Situation: World, Job, Family, Character, Neighborhood, Relationships, Church

Kuhatschek's Categories
- Understanding the Original Situation
- Finding General Principles
- Applying General Principles today

Applying Principles of God's Word to Our Lives in the Church and in the World

Key Steps to Interpretation

Step One: Understanding the Original Situation

The focus of this step is on understanding the *world of the Bible, the author, and God's message to a particular group of people at a particular time and place.*

A. Ask God to open your eyes to truth through the ministry of the Holy Spirit as you read his Word.

Tell God that you want to be changed as well as informed by your reading of the Scriptures. Ask him to reveal specific actions and attitudes in your own life which need to be changed or disciplined. Ask God to use the Word to reveal Jesus and to make you more like his Son. Thank God for the gifts of his Spirit, his Son, and the Scriptures. Many believers began their study of God's Word by simply praying the words of Psalm 119:18.

Heavenly Father, open my eyes to see wonderful things in your word. Amen.

B. Identify the author of the book, the approximate date it was written, why it was written, and to whom it was written.

Key Tools: Bible Dictionary, Bible Handbook, or Bible Commentary

C. Read the context around the passage.

Key Tool: A standard translation (not a paraphrase) of the Bible

- Look to see where natural "breaks" are in and around the passage and make sure that you are looking at the entire passage during the process of interpretation.

- Read the material around the passage. It is a good rule of thumb to read at least one chapter before and one chapter following the passage you are studying.

- The shorter the passage selected for interpretation, the greater the danger becomes in ignoring context. The old proverb is correct: "A text without a *context* is a *pretext*."

D. Observe the passage carefully.

- Identify who is speaking and who is being spoken to.
- Observe the main ideas and the details.
    » Make a simple outline of the passage.
    » Identify the main ideas.
    » Look for repeated words or images.
    » Find "cause-and-effect" relationships.
    » Look for comparisons, contrasts, and connections.

E. Read the passage in another translation of Scripture.

Key Tool: A translation or paraphrase of the Scriptures that uses a different translation philosophy than the version of Scripture you regularly use

- Write down any questions that this new translation raises in your mind and stay alert for answers as you do further study.

F. Read any parallel accounts or passages from other parts of Scripture.

Key Tool: A concordance and/or a Bible which includes cross-references

- Note what details are added to the passage you are studying from the other accounts in Scripture.

- Why did the author choose to omit some details and emphasize others? What significance does this have for understanding the author's intent.

G. Study the words and the grammatical structures.

Key Tools: Hebrew and Greek Lexicons and Expository Dictionaries help deepen our understanding of word meanings and usage. Exegetical Commentaries help explain grammatical constructions and how they affect the meaning of the text.

- Make a note of words that are being used in a unique way by the writer and of special grammatical forms like imperatives, verbs that show continuous action, etc.

H. Identify the genre (type of literature) and consider any special rules that apply to it.

Key Tool: Bible Dictionary and Bible Commentaries

- Each type of literature has to be taken seriously for what it is. We must not interpret poetry in the same way we interpret prophecy, or narratives in the way we interpret commands.

I. Look for literary structures that might influence the way the text is understood.

Key Tool: Exegetical Commentaries

- Literary structures include figures of speech, metaphors, typologies, symbols, poetic structures, chiasmic structures, etc.

J. Identify the historical events and the cultural issues which might effect the people or influence the ideas described in the passage.

Key Tools: Bible Dictionaries and Bible Commentaries

- Constantly ask, "What was happening in history and society that would affect the way the audience heard the message in this text?"

K. Summarize what you believe the author was trying to say and why it was important for the original audience.

- Your goal in this step is to write the key truths of the passage in such a way that the original author and the original listeners would agree with them if they heard them.

Step Two: Finding General Principles

The focus of this step is identifying *the central message, commands, and principles in a portion of Scripture* which teach God's purposes for all people.

A. List in sentence form what you believe are the general principles in the passage which apply to all people, at all times, in all cultures.

B. Check these statements against other parts of Scripture for clarity and accuracy.

Key Tools: Concordance, Topical Bible

Ask yourself:

- Are the principles I listed supported by other passages in the Bible?
- Which of these principles might be difficult or impossible to explain when compared with other passages of Scripture?
- Must any of these principles be ruled out in light of other passages of Scripture?
- What new information about God and his will does this passage add to my overall knowledge of Scripture and doctrine?

C. Adjust or modify your statements of God's principles in light of the discoveries you made above.

- Rewrite your key principles to reflect the insight gained from other portions of Scripture.

D. Read commentaries to discover some of the key principles and doctrines that others in the Church have drawn from this passage.

- Compare and contrast the information from the commentaries with your own reading. Be willing to abandon, change, or defend your views as necessary as you come across new information.

E. Again adjust or modify your statements of God's principles in light of the discoveries you made above.

Step Three: Applying General Principles Today

The focus of this step is on moving *from what Scripture "meant" to what it "means."* What does obedience to God's commands and purposes look like today in our culture, with our families and friends, and with the problems and opportunities that we face in our lives?

A. **Ask God to speak to you and reveal the meaning of this passage for your life.**
   - Meditate on the passage and the things you have learned from your study so far while asking the Holy Spirit to point out the specific applications of the truths discovered for yourself and those around you.

B. **How is this passage "Good News" to me and others?**
   - How does it reveal more about Jesus and his coming Kingdom?
   - How does it relate to God's overall plan of salvation?

C. **How should knowing the truth from this passage:**
   - Affect my relationship with God?
     » Try to determine how the principles and examples from these Scriptures might help you to love and obey God more perfectly.
   - Affect my relationships with others?
     » This includes my church family, my physical family, my co-workers, my friends, my neighbors, my enemies, strangers, and the poor or oppressed.
   - Challenge beliefs, attitudes, and actions that my culture views as normal?
     » How must my thinking and acting be different from those in the world around me?

D. **Attempt to answer the questions "What am I to believe?" and "What am I to do?" now that I have studied this passage.**
   - Do I need to repent from old ways of thinking and acting?
   - How can I act on this truth so that I become a wise person?

E. **How can I share what I have learned with others in a way that draws attention to Christ and builds them up?**

Chart of Biblical Studies

Rev. Dr. Don L. Davis

Type of Criticism	The Task in Bible Study	What Is Studied	View of the Bible	Proof Level	Strengths	Weaknesses	Level of Criticism
Form Criticism	Trace the oral traditions and earliest stories associated with the texts	Oral traditions of the people of God, along with the early Church	Product of human tradition	Low	Evolving sense of the Bible's origin	Too speculative	Higher
Source Criticism	Discover the written sources used in the creation of the books	Comparing texts in various books to see similarities and contrasts	Product of human ingenuity	Low	Ability to identify key sources	No way to prove its claims	Higher
Linguistic Criticism	Study the ancient languages, words, and grammar	Comparing texts in various books to see similarities and contrasts	Product of human culture	Mid	In-depth meaning of ancient language	Too far removed from the language	Lower
Textual Criticism	Compare the variant manuscripts to find the best reading	Focus on different manuscripts and their families of texts	Product of textual research	High	Multitude of reliable manuscripts available	Far too extensive number	Lower
Literary Criticism	Determine the author, style, recipient, and genre	Different types of literature, background study on the books	Product of literary genius	High	Discovering what types of literature mean	We tend to read too much into it	Higher
Canonical Criticism	Analyze the Church's acceptance, view and use of the text	History of the Bible in ancient Israel and the early Church (councils, conventions)	Product of religious community	High	Taking the community's view of the Bible Seriously	Tends to make the Bible merely a group book	Higher
Redaction Criticism	Focus on the theology of the person who wrote it	Intense study of individual books to understand the meaning of the author's theme and views	Product of creative personality	Mid	Deep analysis of an author's entire collection of writings	Does not correlate the Bible with other books	Higher
Historical Criticism	Investigate the historical setting, culture, and background	Research of the ancient cultures, their customs, and their history	Product of historical forces	Mid	Firmer grasp of historical issues of the text	Too far removed from the history	Higher
Translation Studies	Provide a clear, readable translation based on the best manuscripts	Understanding of the receiving culture's language along with the meanings of the text for the best translation	Product of dynamic interpretation	Mid	Pursuing a version of the Bible in one's own tongue and thought world	Reflects our own opinions about the text's meaning	Lower

Figures of Speech

Bob Smith. *Basics of Bible Interpretation*. Waco: Word Publishers, 1978. pp. 113-120.

One of the most enlightening aspects of language is the study of figurative expressions. Milton Terry introduces us to this subject with keen insight:

The natural operations of the human mind prompt men to trace analogies and make comparisons. Pleasing emotions are excited and the imagination is gratified by the use of metaphors and similes. Were we to suppose a language sufficiently copious in words to express all possible conceptions, the human mind would still require us to compare and contrast our concepts, and such a procedure would soon necessitate a variety of figures of speech. So much of our knowledge is acquired through the senses, that all our abstract ideas and our spiritual language have a material base. "It is not too much to say," observes Max Muller, "that the whole dictionary of ancient religion is made up of metaphors. With us these metaphors are all forgotten. We speak of spirit without thinking of breath, of heaven without thinking of sky, of pardon without thinking of a release, of revelation without thinking of a veil. But in ancient language every one of these words, nay, every word that does not refer to sensuous objects, is still in a chrysalis stage, half material and half spiritual, and rising and falling in its character according to the capacities of its speakers and hearers."[1]

What potent possibilities, then, lie in concepts conveyed by figurative language! So, moving to specifics, let's explore the various figures of speech. I'll list some of them, along with illustrations of their use on the following pages.

[1] Milton S. Terry. *Biblical Hermeneutics*. Grand Rapids: Zondervan Publishing House, n.d. p. 244.

Figures of Speech

SIMILE (similis = like)	A formal comparison using "as...so" or "like" to express resemblance. *"Even so, husbands should love their own wives as their own bodies..."* (Ephesians 5:28).
METAPHOR (Meta+phero = a carrying over)	An implied comparison, a word applied to something it is not, to suggest a resemblance. *"Benjamin is a ravenous wolf..."* (Genesis 49:27).

IRONY (Eiron = a dissembling speaker)	The speaker or writer says the very opposite of what he intends to convey. *"...you are the people and wisdom will die with you"* (Job 12:1).
METONYMY (Meta+onoma = a change of name)	One word is used in place of another to portray some actual relationship between the things signified. *"Kill the passover..."* (Exodus 12:21 KJV) where the paschal lamb is meant.
HYPERBOLE (Huper+bole) = a throwing beyond	Intentional exaggeration for the purpose of emphasis, or magnifying beyond reality. *"If your right eye causes you to sin, pluck it out and throw it away..."* (Matthew 5:29).
PERSONIFICATION (to make like a person)	Inanimate objects are spoken of as persons, as if they had life. *"The sea looked and fled..."* (Psalm 114:3).
APOSTROPHE (apo+strepho = to turn from)	Turning from the immediate hearers to address an absent or imaginary person or thing. *"Ah, sword of the Lord! How long till you are quiet?"* (Jeremiah 47:6).
SYNECDOCHE (sun+ekdechomai = to receive from and associate with)	Where the whole is put for a part, or a part for the whole, an individual for a class and vice-versa. *"And we were in all 276 souls..."* in Acts 27:37, where soul is used for the whole person.

Simile

First, let's compare simile and metaphor. Ephesians 5:22-27 is a simile, making a formal comparison between Christ and the church on the one hand, and husbands and wives on the other. The words "as . . . so" or "even so" make this very clear. And this figure heightens our interest and dignifies the marriage relationship, especially if we see it in outline form, like this:

AS with CHRIST AND THE CHURCH	SO with HUSBANDS AND WIVES
CHRIST LOVED THE CHURCH and gave himself up for her (Ephesians 5:25)	*HUSBANDS, LOVE your WIVES as CHRIST LOVED the CHURCH* (Ephesians 5:25)
"THAT he might sanctify her" (Ephesians 5:26) i.e. that we might be put to the intended use for which he created us: a) as an expression of his own *LIFE* and *CHARACTER* b) to fulfill our calling, enjoy our God-given ministries c) and much more (you add the rest)	THAT the husband might sanctify his wife. i.e. that she might SHARE HIS LIFE, be his helper, etc. a) expressing her own personality and life in Christ b) employing her gifts in a spiritual ministry. c) be the *ruler* of the home, in all that means to her husband and children
"THAT he might present the church to himself in splendor" (Ephesians 5:27) i.e. that he might enjoy the benefits stemming from his unselfish love – in enjoying his Bride. And lead us on to the fulfillment of our manhood and womanhood by his love.	THAT the husband might seek his wife's fulfillment, and enjoy her, i.e. that he may enjoy the beauty and glory of her fulfilled womanhood, as he undertakes the responsibility of his headship leading her with the leadership of love to ultimate fulfillment
"THAT she might be holy and without blemish" (Ephesians 5:27). i.e. that his work in us may go on to completion, that we may be wholly his.	THAT the husband be faithful, hanging in there, i.e. that his commitment may be steadfast and permanent, in spite of problems.
"Having cleansed her by the washing of water with the word" (Ephesians 5:26) Based on *COMMUNICATION* which his loving heart initiates – to keep us close, mutually enjoying our love relationship.	Husbands are to keep communication channels open, remembering that *LOVE finds a way to COMMUNICATE, and it's his initiative* if he is going to love as CHRIST LOVED.

Metaphor

By contrast, a metaphor is not so straightforward. It communicates an impression more by implication. In the expressions, *"You are the salt of the earth . . ."* (Matthew 5:13) and *"You are the light of the world"* (Matthew 5:14), our Lord Jesus is multiplying metaphors to communicate graphic truth about the determinative role Christians are to play in affecting the world. In those early days, salt was the major means of arresting corruption in meat or fish, so the figure is not lost on those who listened to Jesus. Light, in any age, enables us to function with any degree of confidence. It dispels darkness. When we can't see, we're in trouble! The words "salt" and "light" are used as implied comparison. These metaphors speak with penetrating force, even though they are implicit in nature.

Irony

The use of irony as a figure of speech, though it has a bite to it, often has its humorous side. Our Lord was using both effects when he said, ". . . how can you say to your brother, 'Brother, let me take out the speck that is in your eye,' when you yourself do not see the log that is in your own eye?" (Luke 6:42).

In 1 Corinthians 4:8 the apostle Paul uses irony with great force, "Already you are filled! Already you have become rich! Without us you have become kings! And would that you did reign, so that we might share the rule with you." As we read on, Paul proceeds to contrast the state of the apostles as being the last—not the first, as spectacles to the world, as fools. Then he uses irony again, "We are fools for Christ's sake, but you are wise in Christ. We are weak, but you are strong. You are held in honor, but we in disrepute" (1 Corinthians 4:10). Can you imagine how the Corinthian Christians must have felt the shame of their misplaced value systems, how this pointed word of sarcasm must have punctured their swollen pride in men? Would that we should review our value systems, today, and discover the only ground of boasting—the Lord Jesus and his life in us.

Metonymy

Then there's metonymy (a change of name). Speaking to the Pharisees concerning Herod, Christ says "Go and tell that fox . . ." (*Luke* 13:32) and with one word he characterized that politically crafty king. And, "The way of the fool is right in his own eyes . . ." (Proverbs 12:15) where *eyes* represents the way he sees things, or his mental perspective. And, ". . . *the tongue* of the wise brings healing" (Proverbs 12:18) in which tongue stands for what the wise one says, his words of wisdom.

In the New Testament, "Then went out to him Jerusalem and all Judea and all the region about the Jordan . . ." (Matthew 3:5) in which it is obvious that *people*, not places, are meant in the mention of these various regions. Then, we look at "You cannot drink the cup of the Lord and the cup of demons. You cannot partake of the table of the Lord and the table of demons" (1 Corinthians 10:21). Here *cup* and *table* are used for what they contain and what they offer. Again, in Romans 3:30 *the circumcision* is used to represent the Jewish people, while *uncircumcision* refers to the Gentiles.

I'm sure from these examples you can see how commonly metonymy is used in the Bible. We use the same figure today when we call a person "a tiger" or "a kitten."

Hyperbole

Painting a picture larger than life by intentional exaggeration beyond reality is a common feature of our own speech, so hyperbole (*a throwing beyond*) should be thoroughly familiar to us.

In the anguish of his torment Job indulges in this kind of language. More graphically than any other form of speech it expresses the awfulness of his feeling of affliction.

> And now my soul is poured out within me; days of affliction have taken hold of me.
>
> The night racks my bones, and the pain that gnaws me takes no rest.
>
> With violence it seizes my garment; it binds me about like the collar of my tunic.
>
> God has cast me into the mire, and I have become like dust and ashes.
>
> I cry to thee and thou dost not answer me; I stand, and thou dost not heed me.
>
> Thou hast turned cruel to me; with the might of thy hand thou dost persecute me.
>
> Thou liftest me up on the wind, thou makest me ride on it, and thou tossest me about in the roar of the storm.
>
> Yea, I know that thou wilt bring me to death, and to the house appointed for all living
>
> – Job 30:16-23

Certainly we get the keen sense of his utter despair from this highly expressive, but extravagant, language.

The apostle John in the New Testament uses hyperbolic language in this statement: "But there are also many other things which Jesus did; were every one of them to be written, I suppose that the world itself could not contain the books that would be written" (John 21:25). If we considered Christ's eternal existence, perhaps this statement could betaken literally, but if we limit it to the deeds of the Lord Jesus in his humanity (which I believe is what John has in mind) then it is clearly a use of hyperbole.

Personification

Referring to inanimate objects as if they possessed life and personality is especially evident in the language of imagination and feeling. In Numbers 16:32,". . . the earth opened its mouth and swallowed them up . . ." speaks of Korah and his men. Here the earth is personified as having a mouth to devour these men.

The Lord Jesus uses personification in, "O Jerusalem, Jerusalem, killing the prophets and stoning those who are sent to you! How often would I have gathered your children together as a hen gathers her brood under her wings, and you would not!" (Matthew 23:37). The city of Jerusalem is here personified. Our Lord's concern was for its people, yet he addresses the city as if it were they.

Again, our Lord personifies *tomorrow* in these words: "Therefore do not be anxious about tomorrow, for tomorrow will be anxious for itself " (Matthew 6:34). Here *tomorrow* is invested with characteristics of human personality, as being beset with anxious cares.

Apostrophe

This is a strange but graphic figure which sounds as if the speaker were talking to himself in a sort of externalized soliloquy. For instance, David says to his dead son, "O my son Absalom, my son, my son Absalom! Would I had died instead of you, O Absalom, my son, my son!" (2 Samuel 18:33). What a moving expression of David's grief this is; no other mode of expression could be quite so expressive in this instance.

Then there is the use of this figure in which the kings of earth address a fallen city, "Alas! alas! thou great city, thou mighty city, Babylon! In one hour has thy judgment come!" (Revelation 18:10).

This figure of speech seems best adapted to the expression of deep emotion. As such, it readily grabs our attention and draws out our interest.

Synechdoche

Here's one most of us never heard of, but which we frequently use in everyday speech. We say, "This is his hour" when we don't really mean an hour just sixty minutes long. We mean this is his time of glory, or suffering, or whatever we associate with his current experience. We have substituted a part for the whole. In Scripture it occurs in such passages as this: in Judges 12:7 we are told Jephthah was buried "in the cities of Gilead" (Hebrew) though actually only one of those cities is meant; in Luke 2:1 "all the world" is used to mean the world of the Roman Empire; in Deuteronomy 32:41 "if I whet the lightning of my sword" the word lightning is used for the flashing edge of the gleaming blade.

Perhaps now we have seen enough of the prevalence and expressive value of figures of speech to help us appreciate the color and realism they lend to the language of the Bible. Also, interpretively, our review should take some of the mystery out of our encounters with these forms, in studying the Bible.

Bible Study Tools Worksheet

Read through the following Scripture passage and then answer the questions that follow using a *Strong's Concordance*, *Vine's Expository Dictionary of Old and New Testament Words*, and the *New Bible Dictionary*.

Romans 4 (ESV)

What then shall we say was gained by Abraham, our forefather according to the flesh? [2] For if Abraham was justified by works, he has something to boast about, but not before God. [3] For what does the Scripture say? "Abraham believed God, and it was counted to him as righteousness." [4] Now to the one who works, his wages are not counted as a gift but as his due. [5] And to the one who does not work but trusts him who justifies the ungodly, his faith is counted as righteousness, [6] just as David also speaks of the blessing of the one to whom God counts righteousness apart from works: [7] "Blessed are those whose lawless deeds are forgiven, and whose sins are covered; [8] blessed is the man against whom the Lord will not count his sin." [9] Is this blessing then only for the circumcised, or also for the uncircumcised? We say that faith was counted to Abraham as righteousness. [10] How then was it counted to him? Was it before or after he had been circumcised? It was not after, but before he was circumcised. [11] He received the sign of circumcision as a seal of the righteousness that he had by faith while he was still uncircumcised. The purpose was to make him the father of all who believe without being circumcised, so that righteousness would be counted to them as well, [12] and to make him the father of the circumcised who are not merely circumcised but who also walk in the footsteps of the faith that our father Abraham had before he was circumcised. [13] For the promise to Abraham and his offspring that he would be heir of the world did not come through the law but through the righteousness of faith.

1. Use your concordance to identify the word that is translated "justified" in verse 2 and then write down the word and its Strong's number in the space below:

   Greek word _____ Strong's number _____

2. Look up this word in your *Vine's Expository Dictionary* and read the entry for this word. What does this information add to your understanding of the word and the passage?

   _____
   _____
   _____
   _____

3. Use your concordance to identify the word that is translated "walk" in verse 12 and then write down the word and its Strong's number in the space below.

   Greek word _____ Strong's number _____

4. Look up this word in *Vine's Expository Dictionary* and read the entry.

   Why do you think the Apostle Paul chose this word rather than one of the other Greek words for walking? What does knowing the definition of this word for "walk" add to your understanding of this passage?

   _____
   _____
   _____
   _____

5. Using the *New Bible Dictionary*, look up and read the article on "Abraham." In what way does this deepen your understanding of the Scripture passage?

   _____
   _____
   _____
   _____

Use of Reference Tools for Interpreting the Bible

Rev. Dr. Don L. Davis

	Cross-Reference Aids and Topical Concordances	**Theological Workbooks, Dictionaries, and Studies**	**Bible Dictionaries, Bible Atlases, and Customs References**
Purpose	To associate different texts together on a given subject, theme, or issue	To provide an understanding of the meanings of a word or phrase in light of its theological significance	To provide background on the history, culture, social customs, and/or life of the biblical periods
Stage Where Most Beneficial	Finding Biblical Principles	Understanding the Original Situation and Finding Biblical Principles	Understanding the Original Situation
Procedures	1. Find the reference you want to check. 2. Look up the other texts associated with passage in the reference. 3. Associate the verse with a particular theme. 4. Check the theme against those citations given.	1. Attribute the verse or passage you are studying with a particular theme. 2. Find the word or concept you would like to research. 3. Read on the background of the word in the reference or dictionary 4. Associate your text with the theme, gleaning what is helpful and discarding what is not relevant for the purpose of your study	1. Select an item, theme, issue, or custom you need help in understanding. 2. Check the item in the reference text provided. 3. Make note on the background of the issue, and factor the new information in your overall account of the passage.
Benefits	Find texts on same subject throughout the Bible Outlines provided to help digest all Scriptures on a different subject	Thorough scholarship on the various theological usages and meanings of a particular Bible word, wording, or phrase	Wealth of information given on the various sociology, anthropology, historical accounts, customs, society, geography and data on the original situation
Key Caution	Dig deeply into the text BEFORE you begin to look at other similar materials	Do not be confused by the VARIETY of usages and meanings of a theological idea	Stay focused on the meaning of the text and not merely its CONTEXT
Reliability	Good	Very Good	Excellent

	Bible Handbooks, Study Bible, and Commentaries	Topical Bibles, Textbooks, and Thematic Studies	Lexical Aids, Inter-linear Translations, and Word Studies
Purpose	To give a scholarly opinion as to the background, context, and meaning of the text	To give a sophisticated outline of passages on a given theme	To provide insight into the meaning, usage, and grammar of the biblical words and language
Stage Where Most Beneficial	Understanding the Original Situation and Finding Biblical Principles	Finding Biblical Principles	Understanding the Original Situation and Finding Biblical Principles
Procedures	1. After you have completed your own preliminary study, select a commentary or two you will check your findings against. 2. Check your findings against 2-3 other authors to see if yours harmonizes with the meanings they provide.	1. After you have done your study and made a preliminary judgment as to what you believe the passage teaches, assign your passage a biblical or theological theme. 2. Using that theme, look in the topical reference tools to check other texts on the same subject and incorporate their meanings into your study. 3. Do not be afraid to modify your findings if the new data illumines your study.	1. Select the words or phrases in the passage which serve as key words to define in order to understand the overall meaning of the passage. 2. Using a concordance, lexicon, or other linguistic tool, look at the various meanings of the word in the context of the book, the author, the author's contemporaries, the Bible, and finally, the period. 3. Allow the richness of the biblical meanings to nuance your study's claims on what the passage meant to its original hearers and what it means today.
Benefits	Excellent scholarly opinions on both the background and meaning of the various texts of Scripture	Rich, thorough presentations on various topics, themes, and theological concepts being dealt with in a passage	Abundant expert knowledge given on every phase of the design, use, and meaning of the biblical languages in their own historical and religious setting
Key Caution	Do your own study and reflection before you RELY on the opinion of your favorite interpreter	Do not make a topical listing of texts the SUBSTITUTE for deep digging into individual texts and passages for truth	Do not pretend that a knowledge of the original meanings of the key words DISQUALIFIES a sound knowledge of the text in your own language
Reliability	Good	Good	Excellent

How to Interpret a Narrative (Story)
Rev. Dr. Don L. Davis

All stories have a particular shape and possess a number of elements that make it possible to experience the truth of the story, whether historical or imaginative, in a way that is powerful, challenging, and entertaining.

The Elements of Narrative Study

I. **Note with special care the SETTING of the story.**

   A. Place: where geographically is the story taking place?

   B. Physical surroundings: what are the details physically?

   C. Temporal (time) setting: what are the time elements of the story?

   D. Cultural-historical surroundings: what details of culture or history are present?

II. **Identify the CHARACTERS of the story.**

   A. Who are the prime characters in the story? The "hero" and "villain"?

   B. Note the precise order and details of the actions, conversation, and events of the characters.

   C. How are the characters shown to us?

      1. Direct descriptions

      2. Indirect characterization

         a. Appearance

         b. Words and conversation

         c. Thoughts and attitudes

         d. Influence and effects

         e. Actions and character

   D. How are the characters tested, and what choices do they make?

   E. How do the characters grow or decline (rise or fall) in the story?

III. **Watch for the author's POINT-OF-VIEW and VOICE.**

   A. Note the author's comments about the characters and events.

      1. Attitude (positive, negative, or neutral)

2. Judgment (negative or affirmative)

3. Conclusion (summarizing, absent, closure?)

B. Consider what voice the story is being written in:

1. The Omniscient narrator (the Holy Spirit)

2. The First-person testimonial

3. The Third-person narrator

IV. Detect the PLOT DEVELOPMENT within the story.

A. Note the exact order and details of the events and actions.

B. Note also how the story begins, develops, and ends.

C. Ask and answer questions about the actual plot.

1. Why did the events happen as they did?

2. Why did the characters respond as they did?

3. Could they have done things in a different manner?

D. Use John Legget's elements of story.

1. Doormat — the intro of the story

2. Complications — Conflicts, problems, issues, threats

3. Climax — Peak and turning point of the action

4. Denouement — How the story resolves itself

5. End — Finis!

V. Note the THEME of the story

A. What key principles and truths can be drawn out of this story?

B. What is the "commentary on living" portrayed in this story?

1. What is the story's view of "reality" (what is the world like, and what is our role in it?)

2. What is the story's view of "morality (i.e., what constitutes good and bad in the story?)

3. What is the story's view of "value and meaning" (i.e., what is of ultimate concern and importance in the story?)

C. How do the truths of the story intersect with the challenges, opportunities, threats, and issues of our lives?

The Compass of Narrative Elements: Charting a Course toward a Story's Meaning

Rev. Dr. Don L. Davis

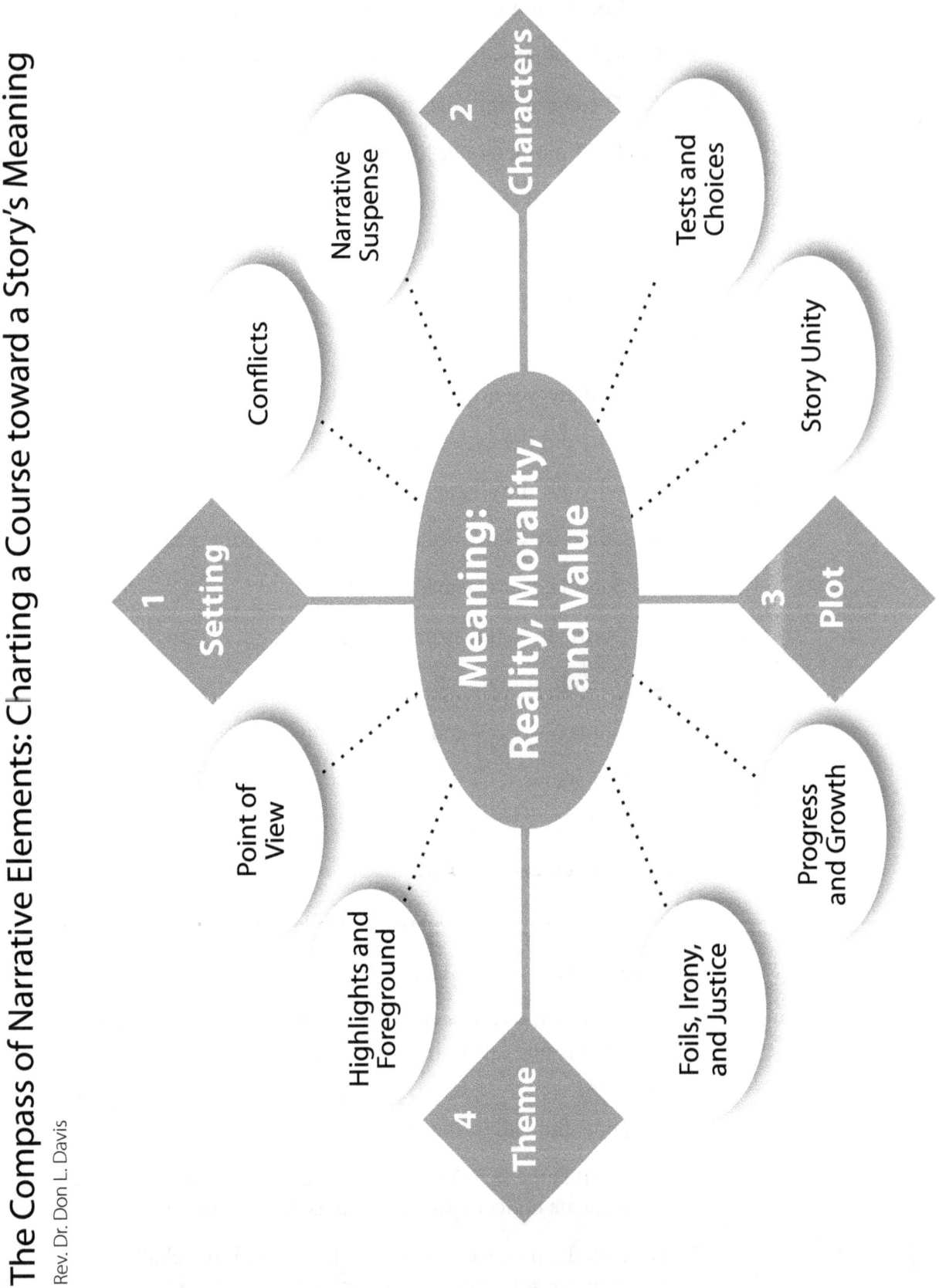

The Old Testament Witness to Christ and His Kingdom

Old Testament Witness to Christ and His Kingdom

Rev. Dr. Don L. Davis

Christ Is Seen in the Old Testament's:	Covenant Promise and Fulfillment	Moral Law	Christophanies	Typology	Tabernacle, Festival, and Levitical Priesthood	Messianic Prophecy	Salvation Promises
Passage	Genesis 12:1-3	Matthew 5:17-18	John 1:18	1 Corinthians 15:45	Hebrews 8:1-6	Micah 5:2	Isaiah 9:6-7
Example	The Promised Seed of the Abrahamic covenant	The Law given on Mount Sinai	Commander of the Lord's Army	Jonah and the great fish	Melchizedek, as both High Priest and King	The Lord's Suffering Servant	Righteous Branch of David
Christ As	Seed of the woman	The Prophet of God	God's present Revelation	Antitype of God's drama	Our eternal High Priest	The coming Son of Man	Israel's Redeemer and King
Where Illustrated	Galatians	Matthew	John	Matthew	Hebrews	Luke and Acts	John and Revelation
Exegetical Goal	To see Christ as heart of God's sacred drama	To see Christ as fulfillment of the Law	To see Christ as God's revealer	To see Christ as antitype of divine typos	To see Christ in the Temple cultus	To see Christ as true Messiah	To see Christ as coming King
How Seen in the New Testament	As fulfillment of God's sacred oath	As telos of the Law	As full, final, and superior revelation	As substance behind the historical shadows	As reality behind the rules and roles	As the Kingdom made present	As the One who will rule on David's throne
Our Response in Worship	God's veracity and faithfulness	God's perfect righteousness	God's presence among us	God's inspired Scripture	God's ontology: his realm as primary and determinative	God's anointed servant and mediator	God's resolve to restore his kingdom authority
How God Is Vindicated	God does not lie: he's true to his word	Jesus fulfills all righteousness	God's fullness is revealed to us in Jesus of Nazareth	The Spirit spoke by the prophets	The Lord has provided a mediator for humankind	Every jot and tittle written of him will occur	Evil will be put down, creation restored, under his reign

Summary of Messianic Interpretations in the Old Testament

Rev. Dr. Don L. Davis, adapted from James Smith, *The Promised Messiah*

Legend

EJ – Early Jewish Interpretation
NTA – New Testament Allusion
NTE – New Testament Exegesis
CF – Church Fathers

	Bible Reference	Summary of the Messianic Prophecy	EJ	NTA	NTE	CF
1	Genesis 3:15	One from the ranks of the seed of the woman will crush the head of the serpent	X	X		X
2	Genesis 9:25-27	God will come and dwell in the tents of Shem	X	X		X
3	Genesis 12:3; 18:18; 22:18; 26:4; 28:14	All nations of the earth will be blessed through the seed of Abraham, Isaac, and Jacob	X	X	X	X
4	Genesis 49:10-11	The scepter won't depart from Judah until Shiloh comes, and all the nations will be obedient to him	X	X		X
5	Numbers 24:16-24	A powerful ruler from Israel will come and crush the enemies of God's people	X	X		X
6	Deuteronomy 18:15-18	A prophet like Moses will come and all the righteous will listen to him		X	X	X
7	Deuteronomy 32:43	The angels of God commanded to rejoice as the Firstborn of God comes into the world		X		
8	1 Samuel 2:10	God will judge the ends of the earth but will give strength to his anointed	X			X
9	1 Samuel 2:35-36	A faithful Priest will come and dispense blessing upon the people				
10	2 Samuel 7:12-16	The Seed of David will sit upon an eternal throne and will build the house of God		X		X
11	Psalm 89	God's covenant to send Messiah through David cannot be revoked	X			
12	Psalm 132	God has chosen David and Zion		X		
13	Psalm 8	The Son of Man is made a little lower than the angels, and is exalted as ruler over all creation		X	X	X
14	Psalm 40	Messiah volunteers to enter the world, to suffer, and is delivered			X	X
15	Psalm 118	Messiah survives the power of death to become the chief Cornerstone, the Capstone of God's building			X	X
16	Psalm 78:1-2	Messiah will speak to the people in parables			X	
17	Psalm 69	Messiah's zeal for the house of God will bring hatred and abuse, but his enemies will receive their just dues			X	X

	Bible Reference	Summary of the Messianic Prophecy	EJ	NTA	NTE	CF
18	Psalm 109	The one who betrays Messiah will suffer a terrible fate			X	X
19	Psalm 22	After unparalleled suffering, Messiah conquers death and rejoices with his brethren			X	X
20	Psalm 2	Messiah is enthroned in Zion, defeats his opposition, and rules over creation	X		X	X
21	Psalm 16	Yahweh will not allow Messiah to see corruption in Sheol			X	X
22	Psalm 102	Messiah the Creator is eternal, though suffering severe persecution				X
23	Psalm 45	Messiah is God, and has been anointed by God to sit upon an eternal throne; his people are his lovely bride	X			X
24	Psalm 110	Messiah is a priest-king after the order of Melchizedek, and he sits at the right hand of God, ruling over all humankind	X		X	X
25	Psalm 72	Messiah reigns over a universal and righteous kingdom of blessing	X			X
26	Psalm 68	Messiah wins a great victory, then ascends back on high	X		X	X
27	Job 9:33; 16:19-21; 17:3; 33:23-28	A Mediator, Interpreter, Advocate, and Witness will walk in the latter days upon the earth				
28	Job 19:23-27	A Redeemer will stand upon the earth in the latter days and the righteous will see him				X
29	Joel 2:23	A Wonderful Teacher will arise and usher in an age of great abundance	X			X
30	Hosea 1:10-2:1	A Second Moses will lead God's people out of bondage into a glorious new era			X	
31	Hosea 3:5	After the exile, God's people will serve Yahweh their God, and David their king	X			
32	Hosea 11:1	God calls his Son, the Second Israel, out of Egypt			X	
33	Isaiah 4:2-6	The beautiful and glorious Shoot of Yahweh will be the pride of the remnant of Israel	X			
34	Isaiah 7:14-15	A virgin will conceive and bear a son whose name will be called Immanuel			X	X
35	Isaiah 8:17-18	Messiah waits for the time of his coming, and he and his children are signs and wonders in Israel		X	X	
36	Isaiah 9:1-7	Messiah will bring light to Galilee and one will sit on the throne of David to usher in the reign of God in righteousness and justice	X	X		X
37	Isaiah 11:1-16	A Shoot from the stem of Jesse will be filled with the Spirit of Yahweh, and will usher into the earth a Kingdom of righteousness and peace	X	X	X	X

	Bible Reference	Summary of the Messianic Prophecy	EJ	NTA	NTE	CF
38	Isaiah 16:5	Downtrodden peoples will look to the house of David for justice and lovingkindness				
39	Isaiah 28:16	God is going to lay in Zion a tried and tested Stone, a precious Cornerstone	X	X	X	X
40	Isaiah 30:19-26	The people of God will see their divine Teacher and will enjoy his abundant blessing as a result of listening to him	X			
41	Isaiah 32:1-2	A Leader of the future will be a shelter from the storm, like water in a dry place				
42	Isaiah 33:17	The eyes of the people of God will see the King in his beauty				
43	Isaiah 42:17	Yahweh's Servant will bring forth justice to the nations, and will be a Covenant to the people, a Light to the nations	X		X	X
44	Isaiah 49:1-13	Yahweh's Servant is divinely appointed to teach, to raise up the tribes of Jacob, and to be a Light to the Gentiles	X			X
45	Isaiah 50:4-11	Yahweh's Servant is an obedient disciple who endures suffering and indignity				X
46	Isaiah 52:13-53:12	God's Servant is rejected, suffers horribly for the sins of others, dies, but then sees his seed and is satisfied	X	X	X	X
47	Isaiah 55:3-5	A son of David will be made a Witness, Leader, and Commander for the peoples				X
48	Isaiah 59:20-21	A Redeemer will come to penitent Zion	X		X	
49	Isaiah 61:1-11	Messiah has been anointed by the Spirit of Yahweh to proclaim the Good News to the poor, and liberty and deliverance to the captives	X		X	X
50	Micah 2:12-13	The divine Breaker will lead the people of God out of bondage	X			
51	Micah 5:1-5	A glorious Ruler will arise from Bethlehem to shepherd the people of God and give them victory over their enemies	X	X	X	X
52	Habakkuk 3:12-15	Yahweh comes forth from the salvation of his Anointed, and will strike through the head of the house of evil				
53	Jeremiah 23:5-6	God will raise up a Righteous Branch who will act wisely and execute justice and righteousness in the land	X			
54	Jeremiah 30:9, 21	Upon return from exile, God's people will serve David their King who will serve as Mediator and draw near to God for them	X			
55	Jeremiah 31:21-22	God will create a new thing in the land	X			X
56	Jeremiah 33:14-26	Yahweh will raise up his righteous Servant in the land, and will not fail to fulfill his promise to David and to Levi	X			

	Bible Reference	Summary of the Messianic Prophecy	EJ	NTA	NTE	CF
57	Ezekiel 17:22-24	A tender Twig from the house of David will become a stately Cedar with birds of every kind nesting under it	X			X
58	Ezekiel 21:25-27	The crown is removed from the last king of Judah until he comes whose right it is				
59	Ezekiel 34:23-31	God will set over those who return from Babylon one Shepherd, his servant, David		X		
60	Ezekiel 37:21-28	God's people will be united and will have one King, "My Servant David"		X		
61	Ezekiel 44:48	A Prince in the future age will be accorded honor, and through him sacrifices will be offered to God	X			
62	Daniel 7:13-14	One like a Son of Man will come before the Ancient of Days to receive an everlasting Kingdom and Dominion	X	X	X	X
63	Daniel 9:24-27	After 69 "weeks" of years, Messiah will appear, he will be cut off, and will cause sacrifice and oblation to cease	X			X
64	Haggai 2:6-9	After the shaking of the nations, the Desire of all Nations will come and fill the Temple of God with glory	X		X	
65	Haggai 2:21-23	Zerubbabel will be made God's signet Ring in the day when the thrones of kingdoms and the Gentiles are overthrown by Yahweh				
66	Zechariah 3:8-10	The Servant of Yahweh, his Shoot, is symbolized by Joshua the High Priest and by an engraved stone	X			X
67	Zechariah 6:12-13	A man whose name is Shoot shall build the Temple of the Lord, and he will be a Priest and a King	X			X
68	Zechariah 9:9-11	The King of Zion comes riding upon the foal of a donkey	X		X	X
69	Zechariah 10:3-4	God will send one who is the Cornerstone, the Tent Peg, the Battle Bow, the one who possesses all sovereignty	X			
70	Zechariah 11:4-14	Thirty pieces of silver thrown to the potter in the house of God			X	X
71	Zechariah 13:7	The sword of divine justice smites the Shepherd and the sheep are scattered			X	X
72	Malachi 3:1	The Lord's messenger will clear the way before him, and the Lord will suddenly come to his Temple	X	X	X	X
73	Malachi 4:2	The Sun of Righteousness will arise with healing in his wings	X	X		

Messiah Yeshua in Every Book of the Bible

Adapted from Norman L. Geisler, *A Popular Survey of the Old Testament*

Christ in the Books of the Old Testament

1. The Seed of the Woman (Genesis 3:15)
2. The Passover Lamb (Exodus 12:3-4)
3. The Atoning Sacrifice (Leviticus 17:11)
4. The Smitten Rock (Numbers 20:8, 11)
5. The Faithful Prophet (Deuteronomy 18:18)
6. The Captain of the Lord's Host (Joshua 5:15)
7. The Divine Deliverer (Judges 2:18)
8. The Kinsman Redeemer (Ruth 3:12)
9. The Anointed One (1 Samuel 2:10)
10. The Son of David (2 Samuel 7:14)
11. The Coming King (1 Kings)
12. The Coming King (2 Kings)
13. The Builder of the Temple (1 Chronicles 28:20)
14. The Builder of the Temple (2 Chronicles)
15. The Restorer of the Temple (Ezra 6:14-15)
16. The Restorer of the Nation (Nehemiah 6:15)
17. The Preserver of the Nation (Esther 4:14)
18. The Living Redeemer (Job 19:25)
19. The Praise of Israel (Psalm 150:6)
20. The Wisdom of God (Proverbs 8:22-23)
21. The Great Teacher (Ecclesiastes 12:11)
22. The Fairest of Ten Thousand (Song of Solomon 5:10)
23. The Suffering Servant (Isaiah 53:11)
24. The Maker of the New Covenant (Jeremiah 31:31)
25. The Man of Sorrows (Lamentations 3:28-30)
26. The Glory of God (Ezekiel 43:2)
27. The Coming Messiah (Daniel 9:25)
28. The Lover of the Unfaithful (Hosea 3:1)
29. The Hope of Israel (Joel 3:16)
30. The Husbandman (Amos 9:13)
31. The Savior (Obadiah 21)
32. The Resurrected One (Jonah 2:10)
33. The Ruler in Israel (Micah 5:2)
34. The Avenger (Nahum 2:1)
35. The Holy God (Habakkuk 1:13)
36. The King of Israel (Zephaniah 3:15)
37. The Desire of Nations (Haggai 2:7)
38. The Righteous Branch (Zechariah 3:8)
39. The Sun of Righteousness (Malachi 4:2)

Christ in the Books of the New Testament

1. The King of the Jews (Matthew 2:2)
2. The Servant of the Lord (Mark 10:45)
3. The Son of Man (Luke 19:10)
4. The Son of God (John 1:1)
5. The Ascended Lord (Acts 1:10)
6. The Believer's Righteousness (Romans 1:17)
7. Our Sanctification (1 Corinthians 1:30)
8. Our Sufficiency (2 Corinthians 12:9)
9. Our Liberty (Galatians 2:4)
10. The Exalted Head of the Church (Ephesians 1:22)
11. The Christian's Joy (Philippians 1:26)
12. The Fullness of Deity (Colossians 2:9)
13. The Believer's Comfort (1 Thessalonians 4:16-17)
14. The Believer's Glory (2 Thessalonians 1:12)
15. The Christian's Preserver (1 Timothy 4:10)
16. The Christian's Rewarder (2 Timothy 4:8)
17. The Blessed Hope (Titus 2:13)
18. Our Substitute (Philemon 17)
19. The Great High Priest (Hebrews 4:15)
20. The Giver of Wisdom (James 1:5)
21. The Rock (1 Peter 2:6)
22. The Precious Promise (2 Peter 1:4)
23. The Life (1 John)
24. The Truth (2 John)
25. The Way (3 John)
26. The Advocate (Jude)
27. The King of kings and Lord of lords (Revelation 19:16)

Old Testament Names, Titles, and Epithets for the Messiah

Adapted from Norman L. Geisler, *A Popular Survey of the Old Testament*

1. Advocate, Job 16:19
2. Angel (messenger), Job 33:23
3. Anointed, 1 Samuel 2:19; Psalm 2:2
4. Battle-bow, Zechariah 10:4
5. Bethlehem's Ruler, Micah 5:2
6. Breaker, Micah 2:13
7. Commander, Isaiah 55:4
8. Cornerstone (Capstone), Psalm 118:22; Isaiah 28:16
9. Covenant of the People, Isaiah 42:6
10. Crusher, Genesis 3:15
11. David, Hosea 3:5; Jeremiah 30:9
12. Desire of all Nations, Haggai 2:7
13. Eternal One, Psalm 102:25-27
14. Eternal Priest, Psalm 110:4
15. Everlasting Father, Isaiah 9:6
16. Faithful Priest, 1 Samuel 2:35
17. Firstborn, Psalm 89:27
18. Forsaken Sufferer, Psalm 22
19. Foundation, Isaiah 28:16; Zechariah 10:4
20. God, Psalm 45:6-7
21. Head, Hosea 1:11; Micah 2:13
22. Healer, Isaiah 42:7
23. He who Comes, Psalm 118:26
24. Horn of David, Psalm 132:17
25. Immanuel, Isaiah 7:14
26. Interpreter, Job 33:23
27. Israel, Hosea 11:1; Isaiah 49:3
28. King, Psalm 2:5; Hosea 3:5
29. Lamp for David, Psalm 132:17
30. Last, Job 19:25
31. Launderer, Malachi 3:2
32. Leader, Isaiah 55:4
33. Liberator, Isaiah 42:7
34. Light, Isaiah 9:2
35. Light of the Gentiles, Isaiah 42:6; 49:6
36. Lord, Malachi 3:1
37. Man, Zechariah 6:12; 13:7
38. Man of Sorrows, Isaiah 53:3
39. Mediator, Job 33:23
40. Messenger of the Covenant, Malachi 3:1
41. Messiah-Prince, Daniel 9:25
42. Mighty God, Isaiah 9:6
43. Mighty Hero, Psalm 45:3
44. My Equal, Zechariah 13:7
45. Nail (peg), Zechariah 10:4
46. Our Peace, Micah 5:5
47. Parable Teller, Psalm 78:1-2
48. Pierced One, Zechariah 12:10
49. Poor and Afflicted, Psalm 69:29
50. Priestly Ruler, Jeremiah 30:21; Zechariah 6:13

51. Prince, Ezekiel 37:25; 44-48
52. Prince of Peace, Isaiah 9:6
53. Proclaimer of Good Tidings to the Poor, Isaiah 61:2
54. Prophet like Moses, Deuteronomy 18:15,18
55. Redeemer, Job 19:25; Isaiah 59:20
56. Refiner, Malachi 3:2
57. Refuge, Isaiah 32:1
58. Rejected Shepherd, Zechariah 11
59. Rejected Stone, Psalm 118:22
60. Righteous Shoot, Jeremiah 23:5; 33:15
61. Root out of Dry Ground, Isaiah 53:2
62. Ruler of all Nature, Psalm 8:5-8
63. Ruler of the Earth, Isaiah 16:5
64. Scepter, Numbers 24:17
65. Second Moses, Hosea 11:1
66. Seed of Abraham, Genesis 12:3; 18:18
67. Seed of David, 2 Samuel 2:12
68. Seed of the Woman, Genesis 3:15
69. Servant, Isaiah 42:1; 49:3, 6
70. Shade, Isaiah 32:2
71. Shelter, Isaiah 32:1
72. Shepherd, Ezekiel 34:23; 37:24
73. Shiloh, Genesis 49:10
74. Shoot, Zechariah 3:8; 6:12
75. Shoot from the Stump of Jesse, Isaiah 11:1
76. Shoot of Yahweh, Isaiah 4:2
77. Sign and Wonder, Isaiah 8:18
78. Signet Ring, Haggai 2:23
79. Son of God, 2 Samuel 7:14; Psalm 2:7
80. Son of Man, Psalm 8:4; Daniel 7:13
81. Star, Numbers 24:17
82. Stone, Zechariah 3:9
83. Substitutionary Sufferer, Isaiah 53
84. Sun of Righteousness, Malachi 4:5
85. Teacher, Isaiah 30:20
86. Teacher for Righteousness, Joel 2:23
87. Tender Shoot, Isaiah 53:2
88. Tender Twig, Ezekiel 17:22
89. Temple Builder, Zechariah 6:12
90. Tent Dweller, Genesis 9:26-27
91. Tested Stone, Isaiah 28:16
92. Trailblazer, Psalm 16:11
93. Victor, Psalm 68:18
94. Volunteer, Psalm 40:7
95. Water of Life, Isaiah 32:2
96. Witness, Job 16:19
97. Witness to the Peoples, Isaiah 55:4
98. Wonderful Counselor, Isaiah 9:6
99. Yahweh, Our Righteousness, Jeremiah 23:6
100. Zerubbabel, Haggai 2:23

Promise vs. Prediction:
The Apostolic Hermeneutic of the Old Testament
Adapted from Christopher J. H. Wright

And So It Was Fulfilled: Five Scenes of Jesus's Early Life				
Incident in Jesus's Life	**Matthew Citation**	**The Old Testament Reference**	**Commentary on the Actual Historical Context of the Old Testament Text**	**Hermeneutic Significance**
Assurance to Joseph concerning the child conceived in Mary	Matthew 1:18-25	Isaiah 7:14, the Immanuel sign given to King Ahaz by Isaiah	Immanuel prophecy was given as a sign to King Ahaz in his own historical context, and does not immediately provide any sense of a long range prediction of Messianic relevance	The Holy Spirit provided the Apostles with divine wisdom in making connections with not only the plain Messianic predictions, but also those aspects of the history of Israel which represent in a direct way some aspect of the life and ministry of Jesus. The ability to correlate particular events of Israel to the life and ministry of Messiah Jesus is precisely the nature of the apostolic Spirit-illumined hermeneutic which coincides with divine and Spirit-inspired Scripture. We are invited to exegete the Scriptures and make correlations in the same way as the Lord and the Apostles, although our connections should never be considered normative in the same way as theirs.
Jesus's birth in Bethlehem, the city of David	Matthew 2:1-12	Micah 5:2, prophecy of the Governor and Ruler of Israel to come from Bethlehem	A direct Messianic prediction about the birthplace of the future Governor of Israel and the nations	
The escape to Egypt, and the return from there	Matthew 2:13-15	Hosea 11:1, God's deliverance of his people Israel, his "son," out of Egypt at the Exodus	No prediction present; Hosea reference is a prophetic allusion to the Exodus of the people of God from Egypt.	
Herod's murder of the boys in Bethlehem	Matthew 2:16-18	Jeremiah 31:15, Jeremiah's lament for the Israelite nation who were going into exile, into Babylonian captivity	The Old Testament text is a figurative picture of the mourning of Rachel (Israel) at the time of the Exile in 587 BC after the fall of Jerusalem to the Babylonians. No explicit Messianic prediction is contained in the text.	
Jesus's family settlement in Nazareth of Galilee	Matthew 2:19-23	Several possible allusions in the Old Testament, Judges 13:5; 1 Samuel 1:11; Amos 2:10-11	Texts have relevance within their setting, but not in an explicit way to fulfill Messianic predictions.	

Messiah Jesus: Fulfillment of the Old Testament Types

Adapted from Norman Geisler, *To Understand the Bible, Look for Jesus*, pp. 38-41.

Messiah Jesus Fulfills the Tabernacle Types

Tabernacle Types	Jesus of Nazareth as the Antitype
The One Door	I am the Door John 10:9
The Brazen Altar	Gives his life as a ransom for many Mark 10:45
The Laver	If I do not wash you, you have no part with me John 13:8, 10; 1 John 1:7
The Lampstand	I am the Light of the Word John 8:12
The Shewbread	I am the Bread of Life John 6:48
The Altar of Incense	I am praying for them John 17:9
The Veil	This is my body Matthew 26:26
The Mercy Seat	I lay down my life for the sheep John 10:15

Contrast between Aaron's and Melchizedek's Priesthood

Nature of the Order	The Order of Aaron's Levitical Priesthood	The Order of Messiah Jesus's Priesthood (Melchizedek's Priesthood)
Consecration	Temporal and fading	Eternal priesthood Hebrews 7:21-23
Priest	Fallible, vulnerable to sin	Sinless and perfect Hebrews 7:26
Priesthood	Changeable	Unchangeable priesthood Hebrews 7:24
Ministry	Continual offering of sacrifice	Secured an eternal redemption once for all Hebrews 9:12, 26
Mediation	Imperfect representation	Perfect representation between God and humankind Hebrews 2:14-18
Sacrifice	Unable and insufficient to take the sin of the offenders away	Offered a single sacrifice for sin for all time Hebrews 10:11-12
Intercession	Was interrupted by weakness and death	Always lives to make intercession for us Hebrews 7:25

Messiah Jesus Fulfills the Levitical Sacrifices and Offerings

The Levitical Offering	How Offering Is Fulfilled in Jesus of Nazareth
The Burnt Offering	The perfection of his life Hebrews 9:14
The Meal Offering	The dedication and presentation of his life Hebrews 5:7; John 4:34
The Peace Offering	He is the peace of our relationships and souls Hebrews 4:1-2; Ephesians 2:14
The Sin Offering	He bore the penalty for our offense Hebrews 10:12; 1 John 2:2
The Trespass Offering	Provision for the offender Hebrews 10:20-21; 1 John 1:7

Messiah Jesus Fulfills the Levitical Feasts and Festivals

Levitical Feast (Leviticus 23)	The Fulfillment in Jesus of Nazareth
The Passover (April)	The death of Jesus Christ 2 Corinthians 5:17
Unleavened Bread (April)	Holy and humble walk for Jesus 1 Corinthians 5:8
First Fruits (April)	The resurrection of Messiah Jesus 1 Corinthians 15:23
The Feast of Pentecost (June)	Outpouring of the Spirit by the Father and the Son Acts 1:5; 2:4
Trumpets (September)	Messiah Jesus's regathering of the Nation Israel Matthew 24:31
The Day of Atonement (September)	Propitiation and cleansing through Jesus Romans 11:26
Tabernacles (September)	Rest and reunion with Messiah Jesus Zechariah 14:16-18

Principles Behind Prophecy

Rev. Dr. Don L. Davis

1. Prophecy provides divinely inspired truth about God, his universe, and his will.
   - Who is God and what is the nature of the "real"?
   - What is the truth, and how can we know it?
   - Where did we come from, why are we here, and how shall we act?

2. Prophecy originates and has its source in the Holy Spirit.
   - It is his gift (Romans 12:6; 1 Corinthians 12:10; Ephesians 4:8).
   - Prophet = "person of the Spirit," *pneumatikos* (1 Corinthians 14:37 and Hosea 9:7)
   - The hope of Moses (Numbers 11:16, 29; cf. Luke 10:1)

3. Diverse and various forms of revelation (Jeremiah 18:18, Law from the priest, counsel from the wise, and word from the prophet).
   - Lived in communities and guilds, some were attached to the temple, while others were priests (cf. 2 Kings 2:3ff.; Ezekiel 1:3; Jeremiah 1:1).
   - Sages and wisdom teachers were "recipients and mediators" of the divine gift (cf. Genesis 41:38; 2 Samuel 14:20; 16:23; 1 Kings 3:9, etc.).
   - Wisdom teacher and prophet both: Daniel.

4. Prophecy not self-authenticating: it must be judged valid.
   - Conflict existed between prophets within both the Old Testament and New Testament (cf. 1 Kings 22; Jeremiah 23; 28 and 2 Corinthians 11:4, 13; 1 John 4:1-3).
   - Prophetic claims must agree with Moses (Deuteronomy 13:1-5) and Jesus (Matthew 7:15; 24:11; 2 Peter 2:1).
   - If the word comes to pass, it is from the Lord (Deuteronomy 18:15-22).
   - All prophecy is to be examined for its truth value (1 Thessalonians 5:19-21).

5. The testimony of Jesus is the spirit of prophecy (Revelation 19:10).
   - Prophecy speaks to Messiah's suffering and glory (Luke 24:25-27; 44).
   - The prophetic Scriptures focus on his person and work (John 5:39-40).
   - Apostolic preaching connected him to their message (Acts 3:12-18; 10:43; 13:27; Romans 3:21-22; 1 Peter 1:10-12; 2 Peter 1:19-21).

Analytical vs. Christocentric Approach to Old Testament Study

Rev. Dr. Don L. Davis

An Analytical Approach	A Christocentric Approach
Focuses on individual verses, chapters, books, and sections in and of themselves	Focuses on how the content of book points to and gives witness to Messiah Jesus
Breaks Old Testament into many pieces for analysis and exegesis	Looks at Old Testament as single whole which gives single witness to Jesus
Concentrates on studying each book as its own self-contained unit	Concentrates on studying each book as it provides contribution to Christ's coming
Demands linguistic and socio-cultural expertise	Demands spiritual wisdom and discernment
Can only be legitimately done by experts	Can be done by all the saints of God
Difficult to give overview of Old Testament	Uses Christ as key to the interpretation of the Old Testament overview
Focuses on knowledge of content	Focuses on developing relationship to Christ
Hard to disciple others in knowledge of Old Testament and its contents	Designed to help teachers ground believers in the knowledge of Christ through the Old Testament
Can be remarkably boring and dry	Stirs the heart in longing and love for Jesus

The Prophetic Vision as Source of Biblical Faith Commitment

Rev. Dr. Don L. Davis

Faith is an essential part of human life. Humans are confessing, believing and trusting creatures. *And where we place our faith determines the world view which we will adopt. Put another way, our ultimate faith commitment sets the contours of our world view.* It shapes our vision for a way of life. People who doubt their world view are restless and feel they have no ground to stand on. They are often in the throes of a psychological crisis. *But the emotional crisis is fundamentally religious because our world view rests on a faith commitment.*

What is a faith commitment? It is the way we answer four basic questions facing everyone:

1) *Who am I?* Or, what is the nature, task, and purpose of human beings?

2) *Where am I?* Or, what is the nature of the world and universe I live in?

3) *What's wrong?* Or, what is the basic problem or obstacle that keeps me from attaining fulfillment? In other words, how do I understand evil?

4) *What is the remedy?* Or, how is it possible to overcome this hindrance to my fulfillment? In other words, how do I find salvation?

When we've answered these questions, that is, when our faith is settled, then we begin to see reality in some sensible pattern. *Out of our faith proceeds a world view, without which human life simply cannot go on.*

– Brian J. Walsh and J. Richard Middleton. *The Transforming Vision*. Downers Grove: InterVarsity Press, 1984. p. 35.

The Tabernacle of Moses

Vern Poythress, *The Shadow of Christ in the Law of Moses*, p. 17.

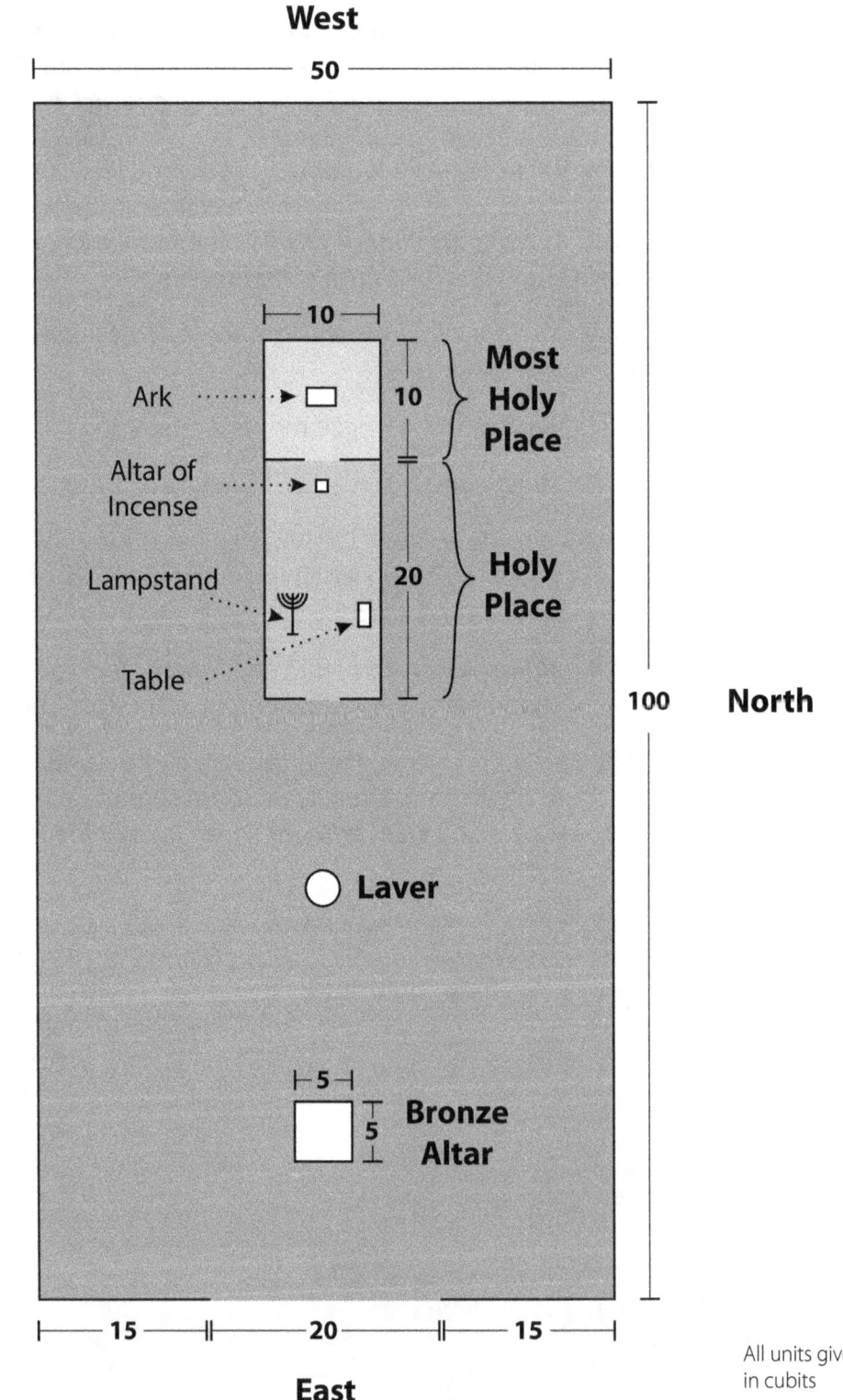

All units given in cubits

Arrangement of the Twelve Tribes around the Tabernacle

Vern S. Poythress, *The Shadow of Christ in the Law of Moses*

Tribes Encamped

Manasseh		Dan		Issachar
	Asher		Naphtali	
Ephraim		TABERNACLE		Judah
	Simeon		Gad	
Benjamin		Reuben		Zebulon

Tribes Marching

ARK

Zebulon　Issachar　Judah

TABERNACLE MATERIAL
(Gershon, Merari)

Gad　Simeon　Reuben

TABERNACLE FURNITURE
(Kohath)

Benjamin　Manasseh　Ephraim

Naphtali　Asher　Dan

Degrees of Authority Given to Fruit of Christocentric Use of the Old Testament

Rev. Dr. Don L. Davis

The Old Testament correlates with the New Testament, and through the aid of the Holy Spirit and the test of Scripture we may explore these connections between the people, events, and happenings of the Old Testament so as to understand how they testify of and foreshadow the Messiah, Jesus of Nazareth.

Unbiblical — **Plausible** — **Persuasive** — **Binding**

Denial of Scripture

Heresy

Denial of historic orthodoxy

Errors to avoid:

1. Assuming that no correlations are present

2. Assuming that something is there, but we can't see it

3. Assuming that something is there, I can see it, but I need not prove my associations

What is biblically provable

What is held by Christians

Everywhere

At all times

In all places

Hebrews 5:11-14;
1 Thessalonians 5:21;
John 7:24; Isaiah 8:19-29

The New Testament Witness to Christ and His Kingdom

Communicating Messiah: The Relationship of the Gospels

Adapted from N. R. Ericson and L. M. Perry. *John: A New Look at the Fourth Gospel*

	Matthew	Mark	Luke	John
Date	c. 65	c. 59	c. 61	c. 90
Chapters	28	16	24	21
Verses	1,071	666	1,151	879
Period	36 years	4 years	37 years	4 years
Audience	The Jews	The Romans	The Greeks	The World
Christ As	The King	The Servant	The Man	The Son of God
Emphasis	Sovereignty	Humility	Humanity	Deity
Sign	The Lion	The Ox	The Man	The Eagle
Ending	Resurrection	Empty Tomb	Promise of the Spirit	Promise of His Second Coming
Written In	Antioch?	Rome	Rome	Ephesus
Key Verse	27:37	10:45	19:10	20:30-31
Key Word	Kingdom	Service	Salvation	Believe
Purpose	Presentation of Jesus Christ		Interpretation of Jesus the Messiah	
Time to Read	2 hours	1 1/4 hours	2 1/4 hours	1 1/2 hours

Messianic Prophecies Cited in the New Testament

Rev. Dr. Don L. Davis

	NT Citation	OT Reference	Indication of the Fulfillment of the Messianic Prophecy
1	Matthew 1:23	Isaiah 7:14	The virgin birth of Jesus of Nazareth
2	Matthew 2:6	Micah 5:2	The birth of Messiah in Bethlehem
3	Matthew 2:15	Hosea 11:1	That Yahweh would call Messiah out of Egypt, the second Israel
4	Matthew 2:18	Jeremiah 31:15	Rachel weeping over infants slain by Herod seeking to destroy Messianic seed
5	Matthew 3:3	Isaiah 40:3	John the Baptist's preaching fulfills the Messianic forerunner of Isaiah
6	Matthew 4:15-16	Isaiah 9:1-2	Galilean ministry of Jesus fulfills Isaiah's prophecy of Messiah's light to the Gentiles
7	Matthew 8:17	Isaiah 53:4	Healing ministry of Jesus fulfills Isaiah prophecy regarding Messiah's power to exorcise and heal
8	Matthew 11:14-15	Isaiah 35:5-6; 61:1	Jesus's healing ministry confirms his identity as Yahweh's anointed Messiah
9	Matthew 11:10	Malachi 3:1	Jesus confirms John the Baptist's identity as the messenger of Yahweh in Malachi
10	Matthew 12:18-21	Isaiah 42:1-4	Jesus's healing ministry fulfills Isaiah's prophecy of Messiah's compassion for the weak
11	Matthew 12:40	Jonah 1:17	As Jonah was three days and nights in the belly of the sea monster, so Jesus would be in the earth
12	Matthew 13:14-15	Isaiah 6:9-10	The spiritual dullness of Jesus's audience
13	Matthew 13:35	Psalm 78:2	Messiah would teach in parables to the people
14	Matthew 15:8-9	Isaiah 29:13	Hypocritical nature of the audience of Jesus
15	Matthew 21:5	Zechariah 9:9	Triumphal entry of Messiah the King into Jerusalem upon the foal of a donkey
16	Matthew 21:9	Psalm 118:26-27	Hosannas to the King of Jerusalem
17	Matthew 21:16	Psalm 8:2	Out of the mouth of babes Yahweh declares salvation
18	Matthew 21:42	Psalm 118:22	The Stone which the builders rejected has become the Capstone
19	Matthew 23:39	Psalm 110:1	The enthronement of Yahweh's Lord
20	Matthew 24:30	Daniel 7:13	The Son of Man to come, of Daniel's prophecy, is none other than Jesus of Nazareth

	NT Citation	OT Reference	Indication of the Fulfillment of the Messianic Prophecy
21	Matthew 26:31	Zechariah 13:7	The Shepherd smitten by Yahweh and the sheep scattered
22	Matthew 26:64	Psalm 110:1	Jesus of Nazareth is the fulfillment of Daniel's Messianic Son of Man
23	Matthew 26:64	Daniel 7:3	Jesus will come in the clouds of heaven as Daniel's exalted ruler
24	Matthew 27:9-10	Zechariah 11:12-13	Messiah is betrayed for thirty pieces of silver
25	Matthew 27:34-35	Psalm 69:21	God's anointed is given wine mingled with gall
26	Matthew 27:35	Psalm 22:18	The soldiers cast lots for the garments of the Messiah
27	Matthew 27:43	Psalm 22:8	Messiah receives mockery and derision upon the cross
28	Matthew 27:46	Psalm 22:1	Messiah forsaken by God for the sake of others
29	Mark 1:2	Malachi 3:1	John the Baptist is the fulfillment of the prophecy regarding the Lord's messenger
30	Mark 1:3	Isaiah 40:3	John the Baptist is the voice calling in the wilderness to prepare the Lord's way
31	Mark 4:12	Isaiah 6:9	The spiritual dullness of the audience in regards to Messiah's message
32	Mark 7:6	Isaiah 29:13	Hypocrisy of the audience in their response to Messiah
33	Mark 11:9	Psalm 118:25	Hosanna's given to Messiah's entry as King into Jerusalem
34	Mark 12:10-11	Psalm 118:25	The stone which the builders rejected has become the chief cornerstone
35	Mark 12:36	Psalm 110:1	The Lord enthrones the Lord of David upon his throne in Zion
36	Mark 13:26	Daniel 7:13	Jesus is the prophesied Son of Man who will return in glory in the clouds
37	Mark 14:27	Zechariah 13:7	Jesus will be forsaken by his own, for the shepherd will be smitten and the sheep scattered
38	Mark 14:62	Daniel 7:13	Jesus is the Messiah, the Son of Man of Daniel's vision
39	Mark 14:62	Psalm 110:1	The Son of Man, who is Jesus, will come from the right hand of Yahweh
40	Mark 15:24	Psalm 22:18	Lots are cast for the garments of Messiah during his passion
41	Mark 15:34	Psalm 22:1	Messiah is forsaken by God for the redemption of the world
42	Luke 1:17	Malachi 4:6	John the Baptist will come in the power and the spirit of Elijah
43	Luke 1:76	Malachi 3:1	John goes before the Lord to prepare the way

	NT Citation	OT Reference	Indication of the Fulfillment of the Messianic Prophecy
44	Luke 1:79	Isaiah 9:1-2	Messiah will give light to those who dwell in darkness
45	Luke 2:32	Isaiah 42:6; 49:6	Messiah will be a light to the Gentiles
46	Luke 3:4-5	Isaiah 40:3	John is Isaiah's voice that cries in the wilderness to prepare the Lord's way
47	Luke 4:18-19	Isaiah 61:1-2	Jesus is Yahweh's servant, anointed by his Spirit to bring the good news of the Kingdom
48	Luke 7:27	Malachi 3:1	Jesus confirms John's identity as the preparer of the Lord's way
49	Luke 8:10	Isaiah 6:9	The dullness of the audience to Messiah Jesus
50	Luke 19:38	Psalm 118:26	Jesus fulfills in his entry into Jerusalem the Messianic prophecy of the King of Israel
51	Luke 20:17	Psalm 118:26	Jesus is Yahweh's stone which the builders rejected, which has become the Capstone
52	Luke 20:42-43	Psalm 110:1	David calls his lord the Messiah and Lord, who is enthroned in Zion by Yahweh
53	Luke 22:37	Isaiah 53:12	Messiah is classed among criminals
54	Luke 22:69	Psalm 110:1	Jesus will return from the right hand of God, from where he has been enthroned
55	Luke 23:34	Psalm 22:18	Lots are cast for the garments of Messiah
56	John 1:23	Isaiah 40:3	John's preaching is the fulfillment of Isaiah's prophecy about the forerunner of the Messiah
57	John 2:17	Psalm 69:17	Zeal for the house of the Lord will consume the Messiah
58	John 6:45	Isaiah 54:13	All those whom God teaches will come to Messiah
59	John 7:42	Psalm 89:4; Micah 5:2	Messiah, the seed of David, will be from Bethlehem
60	John 12:13	Psalm 118:25-26	Hosannas are given to Israel's triumphant Messiah King
61	John 12:15	Zechariah 9:9	The King of Israel enters Jerusalem upon the foal of a donkey
62	John 12:38	Isaiah 53:1	As Isaiah prophesied, few believed the report of Yahweh about his anointed one
63	John 12:40	Isaiah 6:10	Isaiah saw the glory of Messiah and spoke of the dullness of his audience to him
64	John 13:18; cf. 17:12	Psalm 41:9	Betrayal of Messiah by one of his intimate followers
65	John 15:25	Psalms 35:19; 69:4	Messiah will be hated without cause

	NT Citation	OT Reference	Indication of the Fulfillment of the Messianic Prophecy
66	John 19:24	Psalm 22:18	The garments of Messiah will be divided
67	John 19:28	Psalm 69:21	Messiah will be offered wine upon the cross
68	John 19:36	Exodus 12:46; Numbers 9:12; Psalm 34:20	Not one bone of the Messiah will be broken
69	John 19:37	Zechariah 12:10	The repentant nation of Israel will look upon him whom they have pierced
70	Acts 1:20	Psalms 69:25; 109:8	Judas is to be replaced with another
71	Acts 2:16-21	Joel 2:28-32	The Spirit is to be poured out in the last days upon all flesh
72	Acts 2:25-28	Psalm 16:8-11	Messiah could not undergo decay or corruption in Sheol
73	Acts 2:34-35	Psalm 110:1	Messiah is enthroned at Yahweh's right hand until his enemies are defeated
74	Acts 3:22-23	Deuteronomy 18:15, 19	God would raise up for the people a prophet like Moses
75	Acts 3:25	Genesis 22:18	All nations of the earth would be blessed in the seed of Abraham
76	Acts 4:11	Psalm 118:22	Messiah Jesus is the rejected stone whom God has made the cornerstone
77	Acts 4:25	Psalm 2:1	Yahweh will laugh at the opposition given by the nations to him and his anointed
78	Acts 7:37	Deuteronomy 18:15	Yahweh will give to Israel a prophet like Moses
79	Acts 8:32-33	Isaiah 53:7-9	Messiah Jesus is the Suffering Servant of Yahweh
80	Acts 13:33	Psalm 2:7	God has fulfilled the promise to Israel in Jesus by raising him from the dead
81	Acts 13:34	Isaiah 53:3	Messiah Jesus is the fulfillment of the sure mercies of David
82	Acts 13:35	Psalm 16:10	Messiah would not undergo corruption in the grave
83	Acts 13:47	Isaiah 49:6	Through Paul, the message of Messiah becomes a light to the nations
84	Acts 15:16-18	Amos 9:11-12	The dynasty of David is restored in Jesus, and Gentiles are welcomed into the Kingdom
85	Romans 9:25-26	Hosea 2:23; 1:10	Gentiles are to become the people of God
86	Romans 9:33; 10:11	Isaiah 28:16	Messiah becomes a stone of stumbling to those who reject God's salvation

	NT Citation	OT Reference	Indication of the Fulfillment of the Messianic Prophecy
87	Romans 10:13	Joel 2:32	Anyone calling on the name of the Lord will be saved
88	Romans 11:8	Isaiah 29:10	Israel through unbelief has been hardened to Messiah
89	Romans 11:9-10	Psalm 69:22-23	Judgment has hardened upon Israel
90	Romans 11:26	Isaiah 59:20-21	A deliverer will come from Zion
91	Romans 11:27	Isaiah 27:9	Forgiveness of sins will be given through a new covenant
92	Romans 14:11	Isaiah 45:23	All will be finally judged by Yahweh
93	Romans 15:9	Psalm 18:49	Gentiles praise God through faith in Messiah
94	Romans 15:10	Deuteronomy 32:43	God receives praise from the nations
95	Romans 15:11	Psalm 117:1	The peoples of the earth give God glory
96	Romans 15:12	Isaiah 11:10	Gentiles will hope in the root of Jesse
97	Romans 15:21	Isaiah 52:15	The Good News will be preached to those without understanding
98	1 Corinthians 15:27	Psalm 8:7	All things are under the feet of God's representative head
99	1 Corinthians 15:54	Isaiah 25:8	Death will be swallowed up in victory
100	1 Corinthians 15:55	Hosea 13:14	Death will one day lose its sting altogether
101	2 Corinthians 6:2	Isaiah 49:8	Now is the day of salvation through faith in Messiah Jesus
102	2 Corinthians 6:16	Ezekiel 37:27	God will dwell with his people
103	2 Corinthians 6:18	Hosea 1:10; Isaiah 43:6	Believers in Messiah Jesus are the sons and daughters of God
104	Galatians 3:8, 16	Genesis 12:3; 13:15; 17:8	The Scriptures, foreseeing Gentile justification by faith, preached the Gospel beforehand through the promise to Abraham, that all nations would be blessed in his seed
105	Galatians 4:27	Isaiah 54:1	Jerusalem is the mother of us all
106	Ephesians 2:17	Isaiah 57:19	Peace of Messiah Jesus is preached both to the Jew and the Gentile
107	Ephesians 4:8	Psalm 68:18	Messiah in his ascension has conquered and given gifts to us all by his grace
108	Ephesians 5:14	Isaiah 26:19; 51:17; 52:1; 60:1	The regeneration of the Lord has occurred; his light has shined on us

	NT Citation	OT Reference	Indication of the Fulfillment of the Messianic Prophecy
109	Hebrews 1:5	Psalm 2:7	Messiah is God's Son
110	Hebrews 1:5	2 Samuel 7:14	Messiah Jesus is the anointed Son of God
111	Hebrews 1:6	Deuteronomy 32:43	Angels worshiped Messiah when he entered the world
112	Hebrews 1:8-9	Psalm 45:6-7	Messiah Jesus is referred to as God by Yahweh in direct address
113	Hebrews 1:10-12	Psalm 102:25-27	The Son is the agent of God's creation and is eternal
114	Hebrews 1:13	Psalm 110:1	Messiah Jesus is enthroned at the Father's right hand
115	Hebrews 2:6-8	Psalm 8:4-6	All things have been made subject to the Son's authority
116	Hebrews 2:12	Psalm 22:22	Messiah Jesus is a brother to all of the redeemed
117	Hebrews 2:13	Isaiah 8:17-18	Messiah puts his trust in Yahweh God
118	Hebrews 5:5	Psalm 2:7	Messiah is God's Son
119	Hebrews 5:6	Psalm 110:4	Messiah is an eternal priest after the order of Melchizedek
120	Hebrews 7:17, 21	Psalm 110:4	Messiah Jesus is an eternal High Priest
121	Hebrews 8:8-12	Jeremiah 31:31-34	A new covenant has been made in the blood of Jesus
122	Hebrews 10:5-9	Psalm 40:6	The death of Messiah Jesus replaces the atoning system of Temple sacrifice
123	Hebrews 10:13	Psalm 110:1	Yahweh has enthroned Messiah Jesus as Lord
124	Hebrews 10:16-17	Jeremiah 31:33-34	The Holy Spirit bears witness to the sufficiency of the New Covenant
125	Hebrews 10:37-38	Habakkuk 2:3-4	He who will come will do so, in a little while
126	Hebrews 12:26	Haggai 2:6	All heaven and earth will be shaken
127	1 Peter 2:6	Isaiah 28:16	God lays a cornerstone in Zion
128	1 Peter 2:7	Psalm 118:22	The stone which the builders rejected, God has made the Capstone
129	1 Peter 2:8	Isaiah 8:14	Messiah is a stone of stumbling to those who do not believe
130	1 Peter 2:10	Hosea 1:10; 2:23	Gentiles through Messiah are now invited to become the people of God
131	1 Peter 2:22	Isaiah 53:9	The sinless Messiah Jesus was sacrificed for us

Preaching and Teaching Jesus of Nazareth as Messiah and Lord Is the Heart of All Biblical Ministry

Rev. Dr. Don L. Davis

Philippians 3:8 (ESV) – Indeed, I count everything as loss because of the surpassing worth of *knowing Christ [Messiah] Jesus my Lord*. For his sake I have suffered the loss of all things and count them as rubbish, in order *that I may gain Christ [Messiah]*.

Acts 5:42 (ESV) – And every day, in the temple and from house to house, they *did not cease teaching and preaching Jesus as the Christ [Messiah]*.

1 Corinthians 1:23 (ESV) – but we preach *Christ [Messiah] crucified*, a stumbling block to Jews and folly to Gentiles.

2 Corinthians 4:5 (ESV) – For what we proclaim is not ourselves, but *Jesus Christ [Messiah] as Lord*, with ourselves as your servants for Jesus' sake.

1 Corinthians 2:2 (ESV) – For I decided to know nothing among you except *Jesus Christ [Messiah] and him crucified*.

Ephesians 3:8 (ESV) – To me, though I am the very least of all the saints, this grace was given, *to preach to the Gentiles the unsearchable riches of Christ [Messiah]*.

Philippians 1:18 (ESV) – What then? Only that in every way, whether in pretense or in truth, *Christ [Messiah] is proclaimed*, and in that I rejoice. Yes, and I will rejoice.

Colossians 1:27-29 (ESV) – To them God chose to make known how great among the Gentiles are the riches of the glory of this mystery, which is *Christ [Messiah] in you, the hope of glory*. [28] Him we proclaim, warning everyone and teaching everyone with all wisdom, that we may *present everyone mature in Christ [Messiah]*. [29] *For this I toil, struggling with all his energy* that he powerfully works within me.

A Harmony of the Ministry of Jesus

Adapted from Walter M. Dunnett, *Exploring the New Testament*, p. 14.

Gospel	The Period of Preparation	The Period of Public Ministry		The Period of Suffering	The Period of Triumph
		Opening	Closing		
Matthew	1:1-4:16	4:17-16:20	16:21-26:2	26:3-27:66	28:1-20
Mark	1:1-1:13	1:14-8:30	8:31-13:37	14:1-15:47	16:1-20
Luke	1:1-4:13	4:14-9:21	9:22-21:38	22:1-23:56	24:1-53
John	1:1-34	1:35-6:71	7:1-12:50	13:1-19:42	20:1-21:25

Appearances of the Resurrected Messiah

Rev. Dr. Don L. Davis

	Appearance	Scripture
1	Appearance to Mary Magdalene	John 20:11-17; Mark 16:9-11
2	Appearance to the women	Matthew 28:9-10
3	Appearance to Peter	Luke 24:34; 1 Corinthians 15:5
4	Appearance to the disciples on the road to Emmaus	Mark 16:12-13; Luke 24:13-35
5	Appearance to the ten disciples, referred to as the "Eleven" (with Thomas absent)	Mark 16:14; Luke 24:36-43; John 20:19-24
6	Appearance to the Eleven with Thomas present one week later	John 20:26-29
7	Appearance to seven disciples by the Sea of Galilee	John 21:1-23
8	Appearance to five hundred	1 Corinthians 15:6
9	Appearance to James, the Lord's brother	1 Corinthians 15:7
10	Appearance to the eleven disciples on the mountain in Galilee*	Matthew 28:16-20
11	Appearance to his disciples at his ascension on the Mount of Olives*	Luke 24:44-53; Acts 1:3-9
12	Appearance to Stephen prior to his death as the Church's first martyr (witness)	Acts 7:55-56
13	Appearance to Paul on the road to Damascus	Acts 9:3-6; cf. 22:6-11; 26:13-18; 1 Corinthians 15:8
14	Appearance to Paul in Arabia	Acts 20:24; 26:17; Galatians 1:12, 17
15	Appearance to Paul in the Temple	Acts 22:17-21; cf. 9:26-30; Galatians 1:18
16	Appearance to Paul in prison in Caesarea	Acts 23:11
17	Appearance to John during his exile in Patmos	Revelation 1:12-20

* Items 10 and 11 describe the events commonly referred to as "The Great Commission" and "The Ascension," respectively.

Biblical Justification for the Resurrection of Messiah Jesus

Rev. Dr. Don L. Davis

	Reasons for His Resurrection	Scriptural Text
1	To fulfill the prophecy of Holy Scripture	Psalms 16:9-10; 22:22; 118:22-24
2	To demonstrate his true identity	Acts 2:24; Romans 1:1-4
3	To realize the promise of the Davidic covenant	2 Samuel 7:12-16; Psalm 89:20-37; Isaiah 9:6-7; Luke 1:31-33; Acts 2:25-31
4	To become the source of eternal life for all who believe in him	John 10:10-11; 11:25-26; Ephesians 2:6; Colossians 3:1-4; 1 John 5:11-12
5	To become the source of resurrection power to others	Matthew 28:18; Ephesians 1:19-21; Philippians 4:13
6	To be exalted as head over the Church	Ephesians 1:20-23
7	To demonstrate that God's imputation of our righteousness has been made complete	Romans 4:25
8	To reign until all enemies have been placed under his feet	1 Corinthians 15:20-28
9	To become the first fruits of the future resurrection	1 Corinthians 15:20-23
10	To assert the authority given to him by God to take his life back again	John 10:18

General Theology and Ethics

The Shadow and the Substance: Understanding the Old Testament as God's Witness to Jesus Christ

Rev. Dr. Don L. Davis

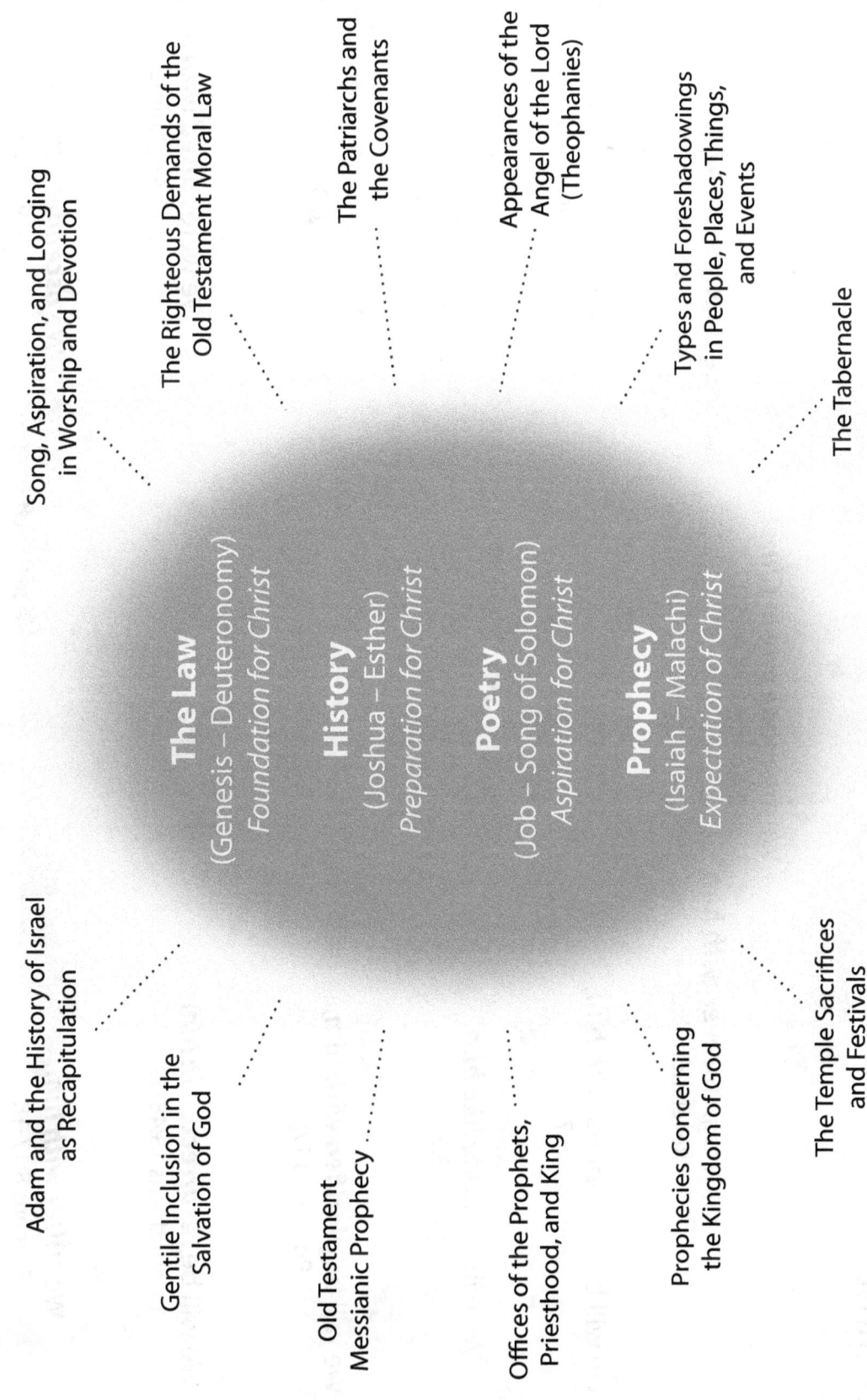

- Song, Aspiration, and Longing in Worship and Devotion
- The Righteous Demands of the Old Testament Moral Law
- The Patriarchs and the Covenants
- Appearances of the Angel of the Lord (Theophanies)
- Types and Foreshadowings in People, Places, Things, and Events
- The Tabernacle

The Law (Genesis – Deuteronomy) *Foundation for Christ*
History (Joshua – Esther) *Preparation for Christ*
Poetry (Job – Song of Solomon) *Aspiration for Christ*
Prophecy (Isaiah – Malachi) *Expectation of Christ*

- Adam and the History of Israel as Recapitulation
- Gentile Inclusion in the Salvation of God
- Old Testament Messianic Prophecy
- Offices of the Prophets, Priesthood, and King
- Prophecies Concerning the Kingdom of God
- The Temple Sacrifices and Festivals

In Christ

Rev. Dr. Don L. Davis

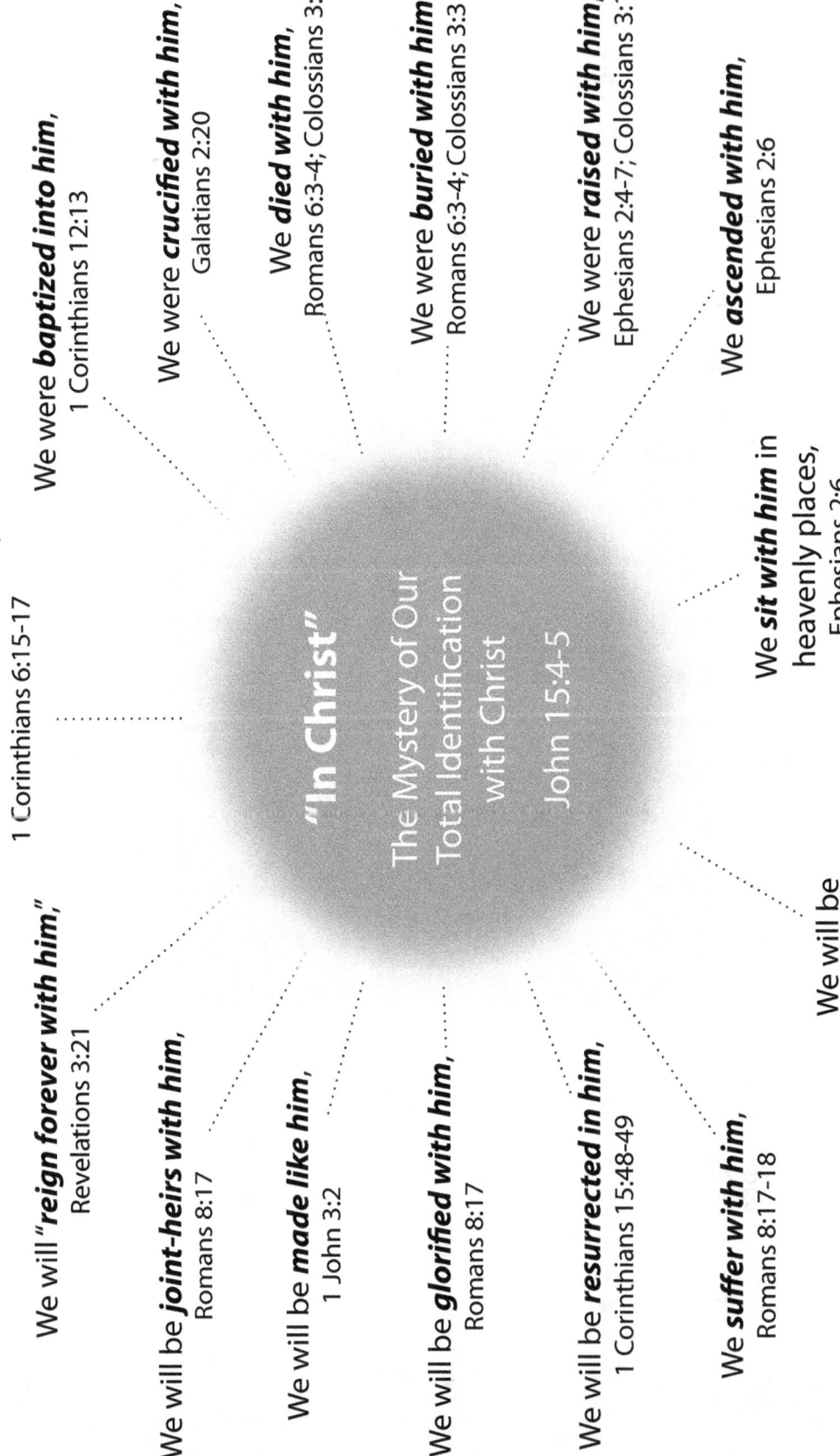

"In Christ"
The Mystery of Our Total Identification with Christ
John 15:4-5

- We are *made one in Christ*, 1 Corinthians 6:15-17
- We were *baptized into him*, 1 Corinthians 12:13
- We were *crucified with him*, Galatians 2:20
- We *died with him*, Romans 6:3-4; Colossians 3:3
- We were *buried with him*, Romans 6:3-4; Colossians 3:3
- We were *raised with him*, Ephesians 2:4-7; Colossians 3:1
- We *ascended with him*, Ephesians 2:6
- We *sit with him* in heavenly places, Ephesians 2:6
- We will be *caught up together with him*, 1 Thessalonians 4:13-18
- We *suffer with him*, Romans 8:17-18
- We will be *resurrected in him*, 1 Corinthians 15:48-49
- We will be *glorified with him*, Romans 8:17
- We will be *made like him*, 1 John 3:2
- We will be *joint-heirs with him*, Romans 8:17
- We will *"reign forever with him,"* Revelations 3:21

126 | Picturing Theology, Revised Edition

The Picture and the Drama: Image and Story in the Recovery of Biblical Myth

Rev. Dr. Don L. Davis

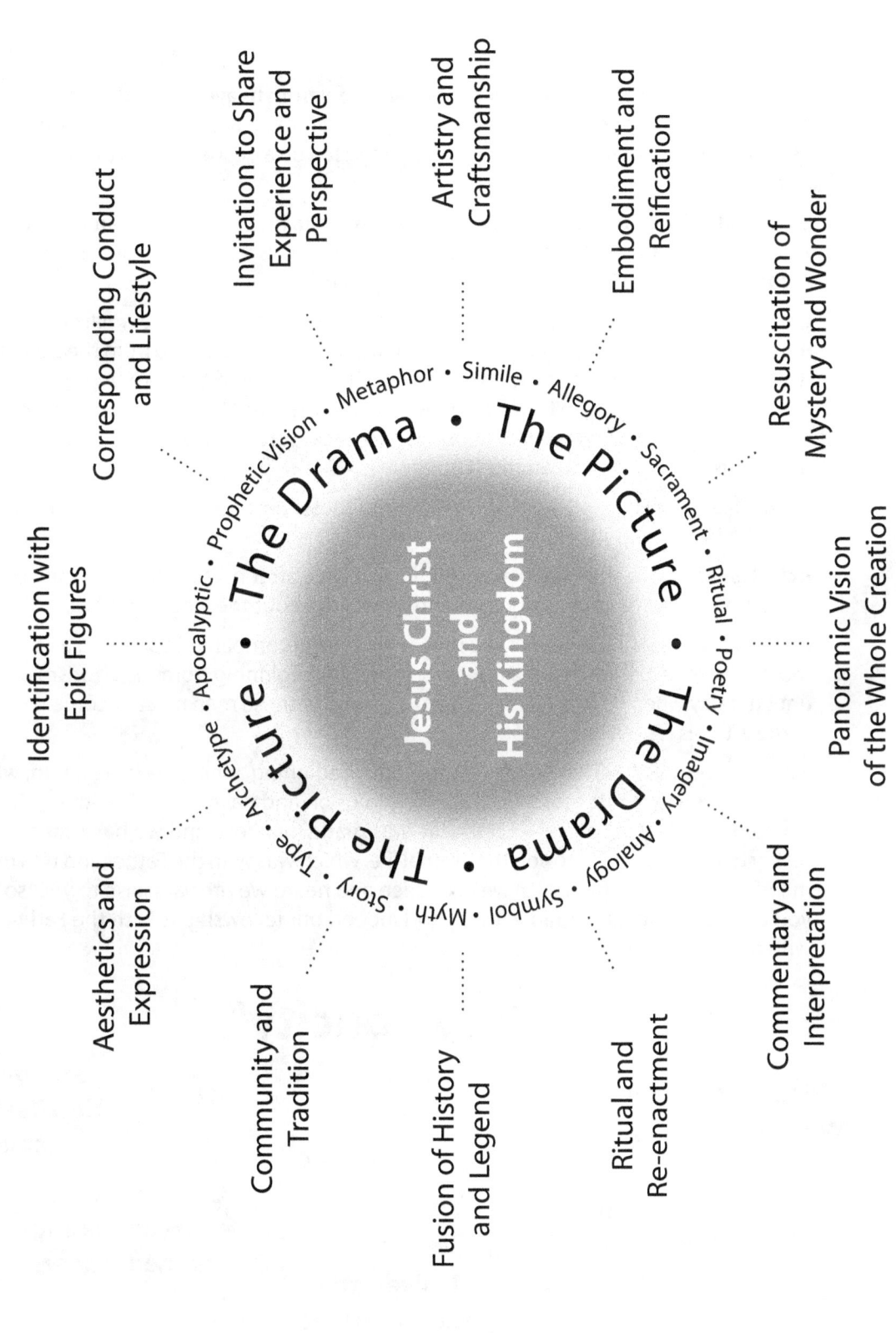

Apostolicity: The Unique Place of the Apostles in Christian Faith and Practice

Rev. Dr. Don L. Davis

Galatians 1:8-9 (ESV) – But even if we or an angel from heaven should preach to you a gospel contrary to the one we preached to you, let him be accursed. [9] As we have said before, so now I say again: If anyone is preaching to you a gospel contrary to the one you received, let him be accursed.

2 Thessalonians 3:6 (ESV) – Now we command you, brothers, in the name of our Lord Jesus Christ, that you keep away from any brother who is walking in idleness and not in accord with the tradition that you received from us.

Luke 1:1-4 (ESV) – Inasmuch as many have undertaken to compile a narrative of the things that have been accomplished among us, [2] just as those who from the beginning were eyewitnesses and ministers of the word have delivered them to us, [3] it seemed good to me also, having followed all things closely for some time past, to write an orderly account for you, most excellent Theophilus, [4] that you may have certainty concerning the things you have been taught.

John 15:27 (ESV) – And you also will bear witness, because you have been with me from the beginning.

Acts 1:3 (ESV) – To them he presented himself alive after his suffering by many proofs, appearing to them during forty days and speaking about the kingdom of God.

Acts 1:21-22 (ESV) – So one of the men who have accompanied us during all the time that the Lord Jesus went in and out among us, [22] beginning from the baptism of John until the day when he was taken up from us—one of these men must become with us a witness to his resurrection.

1 John 1:1-3 (ESV) – That which was from the beginning, which we have heard, which we have seen with our eyes, which we looked upon and have touched with our hands, concerning the word of life— [2] the life was made manifest, and we have seen it, and testify to it and proclaim to you the eternal life, which was with the Father and was made manifest to us— [3] that which we have seen and heard we proclaim also to you, so that you too may have fellowship with us; and indeed our fellowship is with the Father and with his Son Jesus Christ.

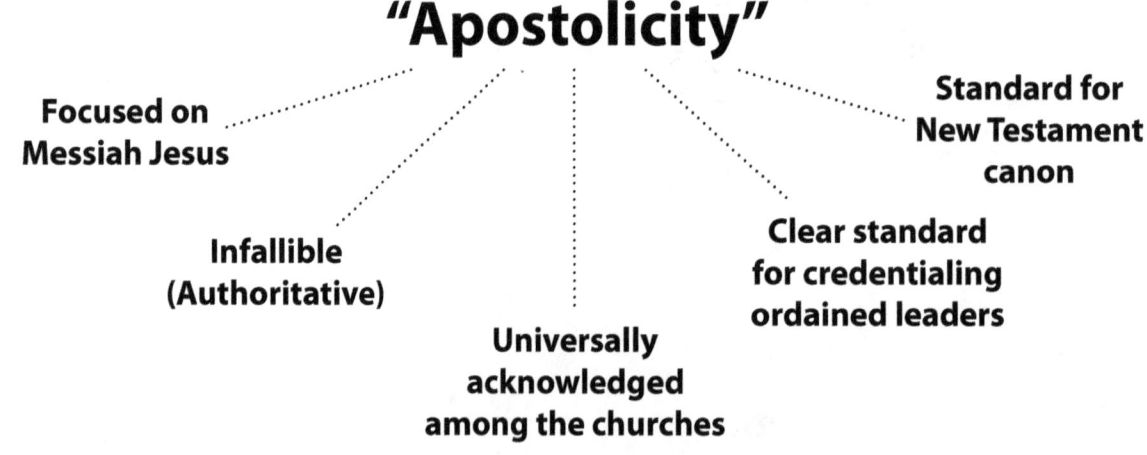

Giving Glory to God

Rev. Dr. Don L. Davis

John 17:3-4 (ESV) – And this is eternal life, that they know you the only true God, and Jesus Christ whom you have sent. [4] I glorified you on earth, having accomplished the work that you gave me to do.

It is amazing how we can misunderstand things. We think we know what something is all about, and we act on our wrong assumptions, and then we are amazed at how bad things are going, or are surprised when we learn that we were off in our thinking.

> One evening, a little girl was saying bedtime prayers with her mother. "Dear Harold, please bless Mother and Daddy and all my friends," she prayed. "Wait a minute", interrupted her mother, "who's Harold?" "That's God's name," was the answer. "Who told you that was God's name?" asked the mother. "I learned it in Sunday school, Mommy. 'Our Father, Who art in heaven, Harold be Thy name.'"
>
> – Bruce Larson

I believe that for many Christians today, the Christian life is primarily misconceived and misconstrued. While they believe they have a proper understanding of things, they are wrong, and like the little child, they continue to go on with their error, not knowing they have misconceived the purpose of the entire Christian vision.

This morning we are going to speak about the final purpose of all things, and the high aim of the Christian religion, all church life, and our *raison d'etre* (our reason for being). We exist for the glory of God!

I. What is the definition of glorifying God?

   A. *To glorify God* means that we give him what he is worthy of; worship is "worth-ship," giving to God what he is due by virtue of his person and work.

   B. *Glorifying God* means acknowledging him as our source, our significance, and our security in all that we are and do.

II. All Heaven and Earth were created in order to bring God glory.

All things that have life and exist, whether they are aware of it or not, were created by the hand of God in order to give him glory. He will get it from us, whether by life, or death, whether through honor or through tragedy.

A. Scriptures

1. Psalm 103:22

2. Psalm 145:10

3. Psalm 148:7-13

4. Proverbs 16:4

5. Romans 11:36

6. Philippians 2:9-11

7. Revelation 4:11

B. Illustrations and Principles

1. The key to effective living is living for the purpose that the Lord made you, understanding who you are, and why God put you here.

2. The Psalmist declares that everything that has breath ought to praise the Lord, Psalm 150:6.

3. In the not-too-distant future, God declares that all human beings everywhere will in fact acknowledge God as source, and give him the glory that he deserves, Revelation 5:12-14.

III. The redeemed of the Lord were selected by God in order to bring glory to him (1 Peter 4:11, 14).

While God intends for all things to praise him, he has especially brought his people to him in order that they might praise him in a higher mode. God saved you, cleansed you, brought you back from a life of sin and disgrace in order that you might now be a light, a trophy, a shining example of his grace and power. He saved you in order that you might glorify his name.

A. Scriptures

1. Isaiah 43:7, 21
2. 1 Peter 2:9-10
3. 1 Corinthians 10:31
4. Ephesians 1:5, 6, 12
5. Colossians 3:16-17
6. John 15:8
7. Ephesians 5:19-20

B. Illustrations

1. What is the glory of a thing? To do well what it was made for!
    a. A chainsaw
    b. A surgeon's scalpel
    c. A guitar
    d. We are his people, and the sheep of his hand, Psalm 95:6-7.
2. In letting our light shine, God receives more glory, Matthew 5:14-16.
3. We glorify God in proportion to our recognition of the good things that he has done for us.
    a. Isaiah 63:7
    b. Psalm 9:13-14

4. We are called to glorify God for his doings.

    a. We praise him for what he has done: Calvary.

    b. We praise him for what he is doing: Redemption.

    c. We praise him for what he is going to do: the Second Coming.

C. God's glory must be supreme in our minds.

    1. More than our safety, Acts 20:24

    2. More than our convenience, Hebrews 12:2-3

    3. More than our very lives, Philippians 1:20

God wants to be glorified in us no matter what, when we are poor or rich, when we are happy or miserable, whether we are healthy or sick. Yes, God can even be glorified in our illness! The following is a wonderful prayer by a beloved Christian from Norway, Ole Hallesby, which captures the Christian's attitude regarding illness: "Lord, if it will be to Your glory, heal suddenly. If it will glorify You more, heal gradually; if it will glorify You even more, may your servant remain sick awhile; and if it will glorify Your name still more, take him to Yourself in heaven."

IV. The essence of sin is to fail to give God his due; sin is robbing God of the glory that is rightfully due to him (Romans 3:23).

We can rob God of glory in at least four respects.

A. First, we can take for ourselves the glory that is reserved for God alone.

    1. Satan, Isaiah 14:13-20

    2. Herod, Acts 12:20-23

    3. Illustrations and Principles

        a. One of the hardest things in life is for us to know that God does things for his own sake, and not for our sake, Isaiah 48:11.

        b. The credit for all things belongs to God and not to us, Psalm 115:1.

    c. The tendency to take the credit usually occurs when we segment God off to a little part of our lives, rather than seeing everything we do as capable of honoring or dishonoring God—everything!

The well-known Christian author, Keith Miller, makes this point well: "It has never ceased to amaze me that we Christians have developed a kind of selective vision which allows us to be deeply and sincerely involved in worship and church activities and yet almost totally pagan [oblivious to God] in the day-in, day-out guts of our business lives and never realize it."

B. Second, we can rob God of the praise and adoration he deserves by ascribing the glory we owe to him alone to someone or something else, Isaiah 42:8.

   The threefold power grid of sin and substitute for God: money, sex, and power (greed, lust, and pride), 1 John 2:15-17; Exodus 20:2-3.

   It is possible to practice unconscious idolatry, even as a Christian, that is, to temporarily worship something else by giving it our love and allegiance.

   1. You may worship the god of pleasure.

   2. Many people today worship at the altar of greed and possession. (We live in a culture that glorifies acquisition, buying, selling, getting, as the most significant thing in our lives.)

Between 1983 and 1988, Americans bought 62 million microwave ovens, 88 million cars and light trucks, 105 million color television sets, 63 million VCR's, 31 million cordless phones, and 30 million telephone answering machines.

– Newsweek

   3. Do not worship the god of sport.

   4. Offer no sacrifices to the god of marriage and family.

   5. Do not seek to glorify the god of ethnicity and country.

6. You many not worship the god of work.

7. Do not bow down to the god of possessions

8. The god of Religion

9. Illustrations

    a. We as a society are more psyched over Michael Jordan and Michael Jackson than the Lord Jesus.

    b. The four C's: people are more committed to country, color, culture, and clan than Christ.

    c. What John Lennon said about the Beatles

C. Third, we can rob God of the glory that is due him by being indifferent to his praise—not really caring about it one way or another.

1. We can be unconcerned and even nonchalant about what we give to God, Malachi 1:7.

2. We can find giving glory to God contemptible (this is a fault and a problem of many young people who feel forced to believe in God because of their parent's faith), Malachi 1:7.

What do you suppose is the central task of one of the devil's tempters of human beings, what do they seek to do most?

C.S. Lewis, the author of *The Screwtape Letters*, suggests that it is to keep you indifferent to the things of God. In this book the devil counsels his nephew, Wormwood, on the subtleties and techniques of tempting people. The goal, he counsels, is not wickedness but indifference. Satan cautions his nephew to keep us, his prospect and patient, comfortable at all costs. If he should become concerned about anything of importance, encourage him to think about other little plans; not to worry, it could induce indigestion. Then the devil counsels his nephew to this eerie job description: "I, the devil, will always see to it that there are bad people. Your job, my dear Wormwood, is to provide me with the people who do not care."

See Philippians 2:21 in the New King James Version and The Living Bible.

D. Fourth, we can rob God of the glory that is due him by giving God less than he deserves, Malachi 1:6-8, 12-14.

   1. We can be stingy with our offerings to God, giving him the crumbs of our harvest and of our hearts, Malachi 3:8-10.

   2. We can give God sacrifices that are imperfect and filled with blemishes, Malachi 1:8, 13.

   3. We can give to God offerings that are polluted, stained by the unconfessed sin and wrong in our lives, (it is possible to come to church when things are a total mess in the rest of our lives), Malachi 1:7.

   4. Illustrations

      a. "Any old thing will do" syndrome

      b. God doesn't mind

      c. There are three kinds of people who live for the Lord.

There are three kinds of Christians who live for the Lord — the flint, the sponge and the honeycomb. To get anything out of a flint you must hammer it. Flint Christians give God a little, and only after a lot of hammering. And then you get only chips and sparks. To get water out of a sponge you must squeeze it, and the more you use pressure, the more you will get. Sponge Christians give God his due, but you have to constantly squeeze them in order to get them to participate. But the honeycomb just overflows with its own sweetness. A honeycomb Christian is full of God's heart and simply gives out of her abundant love and commitment to him. Which kind of Christian lifestyle do you lead right now?

V. The high calling of every Christian is to glorify God in all that we are, all we say, and all we do, 1 Corinthians 10:31.

   A. We are to glorify God in our bodies, 1 Corinthians 3:16-17; 6:19-20.

      1. Sexual Purity

      2. Physical health

B. We are to glorify God in our thoughts, Romans 8:5-8; 2 Corinthians 10:3-5.

   1. More than 19,000 thoughts per day, think four to five times as fast as a person can talk.

   2. The last battleground of your life is your thought life; be careful what you think about.

   3. Proverbs 23:7

C. We are to glorify God in the words of our conversation, 1 Corinthians 10:31; Ephesians 4:29, James 3:2.

   1. Attitude makes all the difference; more Christians dishonor God in their attitudes probably more than in any other single way.

   2. Attitudes are contagious and infectious, whether good or bad.

   3. Your tongue is connected to your heart.

   4. Not just profanity and cussing

   5. Negativism and sarcasm

   6. Complaining and murmuring

   7. Backbiting and gossip

D. We are to glorify God in our conduct and our character, Matthew 5:16; Ephesians 2:8-10.

   1. God can receive glory from the kind of things you do, just your everyday actions.

   2. Your character, your reputation is stitched to the reputation of Christ.

   3. No matter what you say, you can never go beyond the kind of conduct and life you are living.

E. We are to glorify God in all of our relationships, 1 Peter 2:11-12.

   1. In our marriages

   2. In our parenting

   3. In our extended family

4. With our brothers and sisters in the body of Christ
5. In our friendships
6. In our work relationships
7. In our neighborhood relationships

2 Thessalonians 1:11-12 (ESV) – To this end we always pray for you, that our God may make you worthy of his calling and may fulfill every resolve for good and every work of faith by his power, [12] so that the name of our Lord Jesus may be glorified in you, and you in him, according to the grace of our God and the Lord Jesus Christ.

God's Three-In-Oneness: The Trinity

Rev. Dr. Don L. Davis

The Church has not hesitated to teach the doctrine of the Trinity. Without pretending to understand, she has given her witness, she has repeated what the Holy Scriptures teach. Some deny that the Scriptures teach the Trinity of the Godhead on the ground that the whole idea of trinity in unity is a contradiction in terms; but since we cannot understand the fall of a leaf by the roadside or the hatching of a robin's egg in the nest yonder, why should the Trinity be a problem to us? "We think more loftily of God," says Michael de Molinos, "by knowing that He is incomprehensible, and above our understanding, than by conceiving Him under any image, and creature beauty, according to our rude understanding."

~ A. W. Tozer. *The Knowledge of the Holy*.
New York: Harper Collins, 1961. pp. 18-19.

"Glory be to the Father," sings the church, "and to the Son, and to the Holy Ghost." What is this? we ask—praise to three gods? No; praise to one God in three persons. As the hymn puts it, "Jehovah! Father, Spirit, Son! Mysterious Godhead! Three in One! This is the God whom Christians worship — the triune Jehovah. The heart of Christian faith in God is the revealed mystery of the Trinity. *Trinitas* is a Latin word meaning threeness. Christianity rests on the doctrine of the trinitas, the threeness, the tripersonality, of God.

~ J. I. Packer. *Knowing God*.
Downers Grove: InterVarsity Press, 1993. p. 65.

Questions to Ponder

- What is the relationship between understanding something and giving witness to something?

- Why do you suppose the Church's best testimony of the Trinity is captured in its hymns and worship as well as its doctrines and teachings?

- In what ways is a keen understanding of the nature of mystery so important in studying the doctrine of the Trinity?

- Why is understanding God as Trinity so important for both our own spiritual growth as well as our ministry to others?

Some Initial Difficulties in Pondering God as Trinity

- Beyond our ability to understand

- No earthly analogies exist

- Modernity, post-modernity, and the dominance of science: the character of our age

- Biblical illiteracy, theological novices, and no sermons

The Need for Wonder

- God is utterly incomprehensible as he is in himself.

- We must take off our sandals in the presence of such a being.

- Worship, not calculation, is the end of such reflection.

The Need for Submission

- The Scriptures are infallible as our rule of faith and practice.

- The Church's teaching must guide us true.

- Our wills, not our intellects must finally overcome our human inability to grasp that which cannot be fully grasped.

The doctrine of the Trinity is truth for the heart. The spirit of man alone can enter through the veil and penetrate into that Holy of Holies. "Let me seek Thee in longing," pleaded Anselm, "let me long for Thee in seeking; let me find Thee in love, and love Thee in finding." Love and faith are at home in the mystery of the Godhead. Let reason kneel in reverence outside.

A. W. Tozer. *The Knowledge of the Holy*. p. 20.

I. The biblical basis for the Trinity (Erickson, p. 97)[1]

  A. God is ONE.

   1. The unity of God is witnessed to in the Decalogue (i.e., the Ten Commandments), Exodus 20:2-4.

      a. The first commandment, Exodus 20:2-3.

      b. The second commandment, Exodus 20:4.

   2. The unity of God is testified in the Shema of Deuteronomy 6, (the Great Commandment of Jesus), Deuteronomy 6:4.

   3. The Old Testament witness

      a. Nehemiah 9:6

      b. Isaiah 42:8

      c. Isaiah 43:10

      d. Isaiah 44:6, 8

      e. Isaiah 45:6, 21-22

      f. Isaiah 46:9

      g. Zechariah 14:9

   4. The New Testament Witness

      a. James 2:19

      b. Mark 12:29-32

      c. John 5:44

      d. John 17:3

      e. 1 Corinthians 8:4, 6

      f. Ephesians 4:5-6

      g. 1 Timothy 2:5

---

[1] All references to Erickson in this outline refer to: Millard J. Erickson, Introducing Christian Doctrine. Grand Rapids: Baker Books, 1992.

B. The deity of Three is asserted (Erickson, p. 98).

Each person of the Godhead, (Father, Son, and Holy Spirit) is described as possessing the attributes which are affirmed of God alone.

1. The Father is God (universally asserted).

2. The Son is God (Philippians 2:5-11; John 1:1-18; Hebrews 1:1-12; John 8:58, etc.).

3. The Holy Spirit is God (Acts 5:3-4; John 16:8-11; 1 Corinthians 12:4-11; 3:16-17; Matthew 28:19; 2 Corinthians 13:14).

4. All three of these biblical personages share the same attributes together.

    a. Eternal, Romans 16:26 with Revelation 22:13; Hebrews 9:14

    b. Holy, Revelation 4:8, 15:4; Acts 3:14; 1 John 9:14

    c. True, John 7:28; 17:3; Revelation 3:7

    d. Omnipresent, Jeremiah 23:24; Ephesians 1:23; Psalm 139:7

    e. Omnipotent, Genesis 17:1 with Revelation 1:8; Romans15:19; Jeremiah 32:17

    f. Omniscient, Acts 15:18; John 21:17; 1 Corinthians 2:10-11

    g. Creator, Genesis 1:1 with Colossians 1:16; Job 33:4; Psalm 148:5 with John 1:3; and Job 26:13

    h. Source of eternal life, Romans 6:23; John 10:28; Galatians 6:8

    i. Raising Christ from the dead, 1 Corinthians 6:14 with John 2:19 and 1 Peter 3:18

C. God as THREE?: logical inference or biblical teaching (Erickson, p. 99)

1. Textual clues: the problem of 1 John 5:7

2. The plural form of the noun for God: Elohim, Genesis 1:26; Isaiah 6:8

3. The *Imago Dei* in humankind, Genesis 1:27 with 2:24

4. Equal naming: unity and plurality, Matthew 3:16-17; 28:19; 2 Corinthians 13:14

5. John the Apostle's threefold formula

    a. John 1:33-34

    b. John 14:16,26

    c. John 16:13-15

    d. John 20:21-22

6. The assertion of Jesus's oneness with the Father

    a. John 1:1-18

    b. John 10:30

    c. John 14:9

    d. John 17:21

II. Historical models and arguments for the Trinity (Erickson, p. 101)

A. The "Economic" View of the Trinity (Hippolytus and Tertullian)

1. No attempt to explore the eternal relations among the three members of the Trinity

2. Focus on creation and redemption: Son and Spirit are not the Father, but are inseparably with him in his eternal being

3. Analogy: the mental functions of a human being

B. Dynamic Monarchianism (Late 2nd and 3rd centuries)

Monarchianism = "sole sovereignty" (stress both the uniqueness and unity of God); both views of monarchianism are seeking to preserve the idea of God's oneness and unity

1. Originator: Theodotus

2. God was present in the life of the man, Jesus of Nazareth.

3. A working force upon, in, or through Jesus, but no real presence of God within Jesus

4. Before his baptism, Jesus was simply an ordinary (albeit virtuous) man, cf. Matthew 3:16-17.

5. At the baptism, the Spirit descended on Jesus and God's power flowed through him.

6. This view never became popular.

C. Modalistic Monarchianism

1. There is one Godhead which may be designated as Father, Son, or Spirit.

2. These terms do not stand for real distinctions of different personalities or members, but names appropriate for God's one working at different times.

3. Father, Son, and Spirit are the identical, ongoing revelations of the same, single person.

4. One person with three different names, activities, or roles

5. This view insufficient to take full biblical data seriously

D. The Orthodox Formulation (Erickson, pp.102-103)

1. The Council of Constantinople (381) and the view of Athanasius (293-373) and the "Cappadocian fathers" (Basil, Gregory of Nazianzus, and Gregory of Nyssa)

2. One *ousia* [substance] in three hypostases [persons] (a common substance but multiple, separate persons)

    a. The Godhead exists of only one essence

    b. The Godhead exists at one and the same time in three modes or beings or *hypostases* (persons)

3. The Cappadocian focus

    a. Individual *hypostases* is the *ousia* of Godhead.

    b. Each of the persons are distinguished by the characteristics or properties unique to him (like individual humans are to universal humanity).

4. Not tri-theism: belief in three gods. Why?

    a. "If we can find a single activity of the Father, Son, and Holy Spirit which is in no way different in any of the three persons, we must conclude that there is but one identical substance involved" (Erickson, p.102).

    b. The persons of the Trinity may be distinguished numerically as persons, but cannot be distinguished in their essence or substance (different in persons, one in being).

III. Essential elements, analogies, and implications of the Trinity (Erickson, 103)

A. Essential elements

1. God is one, not several.

2. The Father, Son, and Holy Spirit are each one divine. (Each possesses the attributes and qualities of the one true God.)

3. God's oneness and God's threeness are not, in reality, contradictory.

4. The Trinity is eternal.

5. Subordination among the persons does not suggest inferiority in their essence.

    a. The Son is subject to the Father.

    b. The Spirit is subject to the Father.

    c. The Spirit is subject to the Son as well as to the Father.

    d. This subordination is functional only; the subjection never speaks of inferiority.

6. The Trinity is incomprehensible.

B. The search for analogies of the Trinity

    1. Analogies from physical nature

        a. The egg: yolk, white, and shell

        b. Water: solid, liquid, and vaporous form

        c. Suggestive not persuasive

    2. Analogies from human personality: Augustine and De trinitate

        a. The analogy of the individual human self-conscious personality: self-referential thinking

        b. The analogy of interpersonal human relations: twins

C. Implications of the Doctrine of the Trinity

    1. Know God: Father, Son, and Holy Spirit

    2. Worship God: Father, Son, and Holy Spirit

    3. Pray to God: Father, Son, and Holy Spirit

    4. Obey God: Father, Son, and Holy Spirit

    5. Imitate God: Live in love, affection, and community

The Kingdom of God

Ethics of the New Testament:
Living in the Upside-Down Kingdom of God

Rev. Dr. Don L. Davis

True Myth and Biblical Fairy Tale: The Principle of Reversal

The Principle Expressed	Scripture
The poor shall become rich, and the rich shall become poor	Luke 6:20-26
The law breaker and the undeserving are saved	Matthew 21:31-32
Those who humble themselves shall be exalted	1 Peter 5:5-6
Those who exalt themselves shall be brought low	Luke 18:14
The blind shall be given sight	John 9:39
Those claiming to see shall be made blind	John 9:40-41
We become free by being Christ's slave	Romans 12:1-2
God has chosen what is foolish in the world to shame the wise	1 Corinthians 1:27
God has chosen what is weak in the world to shame the strong	1 Corinthians 1:27
God has chosen the low and despised to bring to nothing things that are	1 Corinthians 1:28
We gain the next world by losing this one	1 Timothy 6:7
Love this life and you'll lose it; hate this life, and you'll keep the next	John 12:25
You become the greatest by being the servant of all	Matthew 10:42-45
Store up treasures here, you forfeit heaven's reward	Matthew 6:19
Store up treasures above, you gain heaven's wealth	Matthew 6:20
Accept your own death to yourself in order to live fully	John 12:24
Release all earthly reputation to gain heaven's favor	Philippians 3:3-7
The first shall be last, and the last shall become first	Mark 9:35
The grace of Jesus is perfected in your weakness, not your strength	2 Corinthians 12:9
God's highest sacrifice is contrition and brokenness	Psalm 51:17
It is better to give to others than to receive from them	Acts 20:35
Give away all you have in order to receive God's best	Luke 6:38

A Theology of the Church in Kingdom Perspective

Rev. Dr. Don L. Davis and Rev. Terry G. Cornett

Representin': Jesus as God's Chosen Representative

Rev. Dr. Don L. Davis

To represent another

Is to be selected to stand in the place of another, and thereby fulfill the assigned duties, exercise the rights and serve as deputy for, as well as to speak and act with another's authority on behalf of their interests and reputation.

Jesus Fulfills the Duties of Being an Emissary

1. Receiving an *Assignment*, **John 10:17-18**
2. Resourced with an *Entrustment*, **John 3:34; Luke 4:18**
3. Launched into *Engagement*, **John 5:30**
4. Answered with an *Assessment*, **Matthew 3:16-17**
5. New assignment after *Assessment*, **Philippians 2:9-11**

The Temptation of Jesus Christ
Challenge to and Contention with God's Rep

Mark 1:12-13 (ESV)

The Spirit immediately drove him out into the wilderness. [13] *And he was in the wilderness forty days, being tempted by Satan*. And he was with the wild animals, and the angels were ministering to him.

The Baptism of Jesus Christ
Commissioning and Confirmation of God's Rep

Mark 1:9-11 (ESV)

In those days Jesus came from Nazareth of Galilee and was baptized by John in the Jordan. [10] And when he came up out of the water, immediately he saw the heavens opening and the Spirit descending on him like a dove. [11] And a voice came from heaven, "You are my beloved Son; with you I am well pleased."

The Public Preaching Ministry of Jesus Christ
Communication and Conveyance by God's Rep

Mark 1:14-15 (ESV)

Now after John was arrested, Jesus came into Galilee, proclaiming the gospel of God, [15] and saying, "The time is fulfilled, and the kingdom of God is at hand; repent and believe in the gospel."

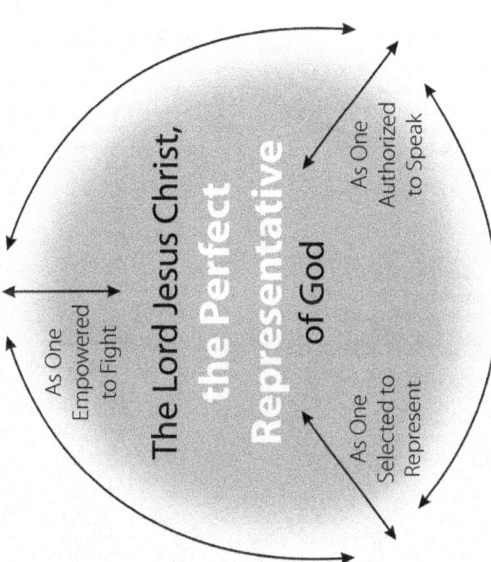

The Lord Jesus Christ, the Perfect Representative of God
- As One Authorized to Speak
- As One Selected to Represent
- As One Empowered to Fight

Faithfully Re-Presenting Jesus of Nazareth

Rev. Dr. Don L. Davis

Ephesians 4:17-19 (ESV) – Now this I say and testify in the Lord, that you must no longer walk as the Gentiles do, in the futility of their minds. [18] They are darkened in their understanding, alienated from the life of God because of the ignorance that is in them, due to their hardness of heart. [19] They have become callous and have given themselves up to sensuality, greedy to practice every kind of impurity.

Ephesians 4:20-23 (ESV) – But that is not the way you learned Christ! – [21] assuming that you have heard about him and were taught in him, as the truth is in Jesus, [22] to put off your old self, which belongs to your former manner of life and is corrupt through deceitful desires, [23] and to be renewed in the spirit of your minds.

Rediscover the Old Testament prophetic roots of the Messianic kingdom hope *(return)*

Faithfully Re-present Jesus of Nazareth

with ficelity to Holy Scripture in sync with apostolic tradition contextualizing biblical language without cultural distortion

Recognize the present cultural captivity of much evangelical Christian identity and practice (exile)

Re-experience and embrace the power of the New Testament apostolic vision and drama [myth] *(possession)*

Ephesians 4:24-25 (ESV) – and to put on the new self, created after the likeness of God in true righteousness and holiness. [25] Therefore, having put away falsehood, let each one of you speak the truth with his neighbor, for we are members one of another.

Models of the Kingdom

Howard A Snyder, March 2002.

1. **The Kingdom as Future Hope – the Future Kingdom**

    This has been a dominant model in the history of the Church. The emphasis is strongly on the future: a final culmination and reconciliation of all things which is more than merely the eternal existence of the soul. The model draws heavily on New Testament material. While some of the following models also represent future hope, here the note of futurity is determinative.

2. **The Kingdom as Inner Spiritual Experience – the Interior Kingdom**

    A "spiritual kingdom" to be experienced in the heart or soul; "beatific vision." Highly mystical, therefore individualistic; an experience that can't really be shared with others. Examples: Julian of Norwich, other mystics; also some contemporary Protestant examples.

3. **The Kingdom as Mystical Communion – the Heavenly Kingdom**

    The "communion of saints"; the Kingdom as essentially identified with heaven. Less individualistic. Often centers especially in worship and liturgy. Examples: John of Damascus, John Tauler; in somewhat different ways, Wesley and 19th and 20th-century revivalistic and Evangelical Protestantism. Kingdom is primarily other-worldly and future.

4. **The Kingdom as Institutional Church – the Ecclesiastical Kingdom**

    The dominant view of medieval Christianity; dominant in Roman Catholicism until Vatican II. Pope as Vicar of Christ rules on earth in Christ's stead. The tension between the Church and the Kingdom largely dissolves. Traces to Augustine's City of God, but was developed differently from what Augustine believed. Protestant variations appear whenever the Church and Kingdom are too closely identified. Modern "Church Growth" thinking has been criticized at this point.

5. **The Kingdom as Counter-System – the Subversive Kingdom**

    May be a protest to #4; sees the Kingdom as a reality which prophetically judges the sociopolitical order as well as the Church. One of the best examples: Francis of Assisi; also 16th century Radical Reformers; "Radical Christians" today; Sojourners magazine. Sees Church as counter-culture embodying the new order of the Kingdom.

6. **The Kingdom as Political State – the Theocratic Kingdom**

    Kingdom may be seen as a political theocracy; Church and society not necessarily to be organized democratically. Tends to work from Old Testament models, especially the Davidic Kingdom. Constantinian model; Byzantine Christianity a good example. Calvin's Geneva, perhaps, in a somewhat different sense. Problem of Luther's "two kingdoms" view.

7. The Kingdom as Christianized Society – the Transforming Kingdom

Here also the Kingdom provides a model for society, but more in terms of values and principles to be worked out in society. Kingdom in its fullness would be society completely leavened by Christian values. Post-millennialism; many mid-19th-century Evangelicals; early 20th-century Social Gospel. Kingdom manifested progressively in society, in contrast to premillennialism.

8. The Kingdom as Earthly Utopia – the Earthly Kingdom

May be seen as #7 taken to extreme. This view of the Kingdom is literally utopian. Tends to deny or downplay sin, or see evil as purely environmental. The view of many utopian communities (Cohn, Pursuit of the Millennium) including 19th-century U.S. and British examples. In a different way, the view of many of America's Founding Fathers. Most influential 20th-century example: Marxism. Liberation theology, to some degree. In a starkly different way: U.S. Fundamentalist premillennialism, combining this model with #1, #2 and/or #3 – Kingdom has no contemporary relevance, but will be literal utopia in the future. Thus similarities between Marxism and Fundamentalism.

God the Father

The Names of Almighty God

Rev. Dr. Don L. Davis

I. **The names of God**

   A. *Elohim*

   1. *Elohim* is a Hebrew plural form used more than two thousand times in the Old Testament, usually termed a "plural of majesty" of the general name for God.

   2. Derived from El, whose root meaning is "to be strong" (cf. Genesis 17:1; 28:3; 35:11; Joshua 3:10) or "to be preeminent." (Cf. Frank M. Cross, "El," in *Theological Dictionary of the Old Testament*, 6 vols., revised, edited by G. Johannes Botterweck and Helmer Ringgren [Grand Rapids: Eerdmans, 1977, 1:244].)

   3. Elohim is usually translated "God" in English translations.

   4. This name *emphasizes God's transcendence* (cf. that God is above all others who are called God). *Elohim* is the plural form of El; the terms seem to be interchangeable (cf. Exodus 34:14; Psalm 18:31; Deuteronomy 32:17, 21).

   5. *El* may signify in some texts (such as Isaiah 31:3) the "power and strength of God and the defenselessness of human enemies" (cf. Hosea 11:9). (Cf. 34. Helmer Ringgren, "*Elohim*," in *Theological Dictionary of the Old Testament*, 1:273–74.)

   B. *Adonai*

   1. The term *Adonai* (Heb. *Adhon* or *Adhonay*) in its root means "lord" or "master" and is usually translated "Lord" in English Bibles.

   2. It occurs 449 times in the Old Testament and 315 times with Yahweh. *Adhon* emphasizes the servant-master relationship (cf. Genesis 24:9) and suggests God's authority as Master, i.e., the One rules with absolute authority (cf. Psalm 8:1; Hosea 12:14).

   3. *Adonai* can be understood to mean "*Lord of all*" or "*Lord par excellence*" (cf. Deuteronomy 10:17; Joshua 3:11). (Cf. Merrill F. Unger and William White, Jr., eds., *Nelson's Expository Dictionary of the Old Testament* [Nashville: Nelson, 1980], pp. 228–29; and Otto Eissfeldt, "*Adhon*," in *Theological Dictionary of the Old Testament*, 1:59–72.)

C. *Yahweh* (Jehovah)

1. The name *Yahweh* translates the Hebrew *tetragrammaton* (four lettered expression) YHWH. Since the original name contained no vowels, it is uncertain how it should be pronounced. (For instance, the ASV translates it "Jehovah," whereas most modern translations simply render it "LORD" [to distinguish it from *Adonai*, "Lord"]).

2. Jewish scholars generally pronounce it as "*Adonai*" rather than voicing YHWH, out of respect for its sacredness.

3. It is used as a common designation (used 6,828 times in the Old Testament), and some suggest it may be related to the verb "to be." (Cf. Exodus 3:14–15 the Lord declares, "I AM WHO I AM...The Lord . . . has sent me to you. This is my name forever.)

4. *Yahweh* as the I AM connects to the "I AM" claims of Messiah Jesus (cf. John 6:35; 8:12; 10:9, 11; 11:25; 14:6; 15:1), who claimed equality with Yahweh.

5. *Yahweh*, the name of covenant relationship

    a. The name of the Abrahamic Covenant (Genesis 12:8)

    b. The name of the Exodus (Exodus 6:6; 20:2)

    c. A *unique relationship*: although the terms *Elohim* and *Adonai* were terms known to other peoples, Yahweh was unique to Israel.

II. Compound names: the name of God involving the names El (or Elohim) and Yahweh

A. *El Shaddai*

1. Translated "God Almighty"

2. Probably relates to the word *mountain*, suggesting the power or strength of God

3. The name of God as a covenant-keeping God (Genesis 17:1; cf. vv. 1–8)

B. *El Elyon*

   1. Translated "God Most High"

   2. This terms refers to *the supremacy of God.*

   3. *Yahweh* God is a god above all so-called gods (cf. Genesis 14:18–22). Melchizedek recognized him as "God Most High" inasmuch as he is possessor of heaven and earth (v. 19).

C. *El Olam*

   1. Translated the "Everlasting God"

   2. Emphasizes *the unchanging character of God* (Genesis 21:33; Isaiah 40:28)

D. Yahweh compound names

   1. Adonai-Yahweh, *"The Lord our Sovereign,"* Genesis 15:2, 8

   2. Yahweh-Jireh, *"The Lord will provide,"* Genesis 22:14

   3. Yahweh Elohim, *"The Lord God,"* Genesis 2:4-25

   4. Yahweh-Nissi , *"The Lord our banner,"* Exodus 17:15

   5. Yahweh-Rapha, *"The Lord our healer,"* Exodus 15:26

   6. Yahweh-Rohi, *"The Lord our shepherd,"* Psalm 23:1

   7. Yahweh-Shammah, *"The Lord is there,"* Ezekiel 48:35

   8. Yahweh-Hoseenu, *"The Lord our Maker,"* Psalm 95:6

   9. Yahweh-Shalom, *"The Lord our peace,"* Judges 6:24

   10. Yahweh-Sabbaoth, *"The Lord of armies,"* 1 Samuel 1:3

   11. Yahweh-Mekaddishkem, *"The Lord your sanctifier,"* Exodus 31:13

   12. Yahweh-Tsidkenu, *"The Lord our righteousness,"* Jeremiah 23:6

Theological Visions and Approaches
The Urban Ministry Institute

The following outline provides a bare bones overview of some of the philosophical approaches and understandings related to God and his relationship to the universe. Individuals pose different arguments for the existence of God and the relationship between God and his universe based on their 1) understanding of Scripture, 2) under-lying assumptions about the existence of God, 3) view of the material universe and world, and 4) the human capacity to know God (if he exists), and what that knowledge involves. Many modern approaches think of God's existence and all speech about God as the possibility of religion *within the bounds of knowledge*.

I. Principles of Natural Theology

  A. *Ontological argument* – Anselm *Proslogion*

   1. Logical necessity of God's existence by reason alone

   2. God = that than which no greater can be thought

   3. To exist in reality is greater than to exist merely in thought.

   4. "That than which no greater can be thought" must exist both in reality and in thought.

   5. Tautology – (argument in a circle) merely to define an entity as existing does not provide grounds for inferring its existence.

   6. Kant – a merchant cannot increase his wealth by adding zeroes to the figures in his accounts.

  B. *Cosmological argument* – existence of a first cause of the cosmos

   1. The things we observe in the world all have antecedent causes. Nothing is totally self-caused, and there must be a first cause.

   2. God is the Prime Mover and the First Cause.

  C. *Teleological argument* – (physico-teleological)

   1. Telos = end

   2. Things in our experience appear to serve ends beyond their devising or control. Purpose observed in nature, implying a cosmic mind.

   3. Key warrant: purpose does not occur without a Purposer.

D. *Moral argument* – People of different cultures and beliefs recognize certain basic moral values and obligations.

1. These universal values cannot be reduced to mere conventions.

2. These do not emerge from the material universe.

3. We can, therefore, posit a personal, moral being as the source of all moral values and as the One to whom all moral beings are ultimately responsible.

II. Facts about Natural Theology

A. Most prevalent in *Catholic theology*

B. *Calvinistic theology*: believes in a general revelation of God in nature and providence

1. Spoke of 'divinity' or 'sense of God' which was 'the seed of religion'

2. For sure and certain knowledge of God we must turn to the Word of God in Scripture

C. *Karl Barth*: rejected all natural theology on the grounds that God reveals himself in his Word, and is pointless to look elsewhere

D. *Emil Brunner*: argued for a natural theology based on such ideas as the image of God, general revelation, preserving grace, divine ordinances, point of contact, and the contention that race does not abolish nature but perfects it.

III. Dualism

A. A *dualism* exists when there are two substances, or powers, or modes, neither of which is reducible to the other.

1. Monism – there is only one substance, power, or mode.

2. Twins of all things

B. Four different contexts (God and creation)

1. Identifying God with his creation

    a. Metaphysical pantheism

    b. Mystical connection

2. God is distinct from his creation in the sense of its GROUND.

3. Unlike deism, God is its SUSTAINING CAUSE (both transcendently and imminently).

4. Difficulties: what is precisely the relationship between the divine and human action in creation

IV. Materialism

"The doctrine that whatever exists is either physical matter, or depends upon physical matter."

A. A philosophical position with definite ontological explanations (the denial of the existence of minds or spirits)

B. Research program and methodology with no such implications

C. Opposed by mind-body dualism

D. What of humanity as part of the creation, and life after death?

V. Deism

"Belief in a remote creator, uninvolved in the world whose mechanism he devised"

A. Stands for the abolition of dogma founded on alleged revelation

B. Promotes a natural religion with blessings bestowed on all by a beneficent God

C. Religion of moral law: "rationalists with a heart hunger for religion"

D. Non-christocentric worship of God

E. Ecclesiastical power as a hindrance of free thinking people

F. Fall and redemption is dismissed, its literary form regarded as crude, corrupt, and flawed

VI. Determinism

A. *Scientific determinism* – the form of every physical event is determined uniquely by the conjunction of events preceding it; discovering the interdependence and expressing it in laws.

B. *Theological determinism* – the form of all events is determined according to the "determinate counsel and foreknowledge of God" (Acts 2:23).

C. What of the *theodicy* questions? (Theodicy as the problem of evil happening to good or innocent persons)

D. Limited freedom or no freedom at all: what of the relationship between the material world, causative events, and the sovereignty of God?

The Father, Son, and Holy Ghost Share the Same Divine Attributes and Works: Supporting Scriptures

Adapted from Edward Henry Bickersteth, *The Trinity*. Grand Rapids: Kregel Publications, 1957. Rpt. 1980.

Attribute of God	God the Father	God the Son	God the Holy Spirit
God Is Eternal (Deuteronomy 33:27)	Isaiah 44:6; Romans 16:26	John 8:58; Revelation 1:17-18	Hebrews 9:14
God Created All Things (Revelation 4:11) and Is the Source of Life (Deuteronomy 30:20)	Psalms 36:9; 100:3; 1 Corinthians 8:6	John 1:3-4; Colossians 1:16	Genesis 1:2; Psalms 33:6; 104:30; Job 33:4; John 7:38-39; Romans 8:11
God Is Incomprehensible (1 Timothy 6:16) and Omniscient (Jeremiah 16:17)	Isaiah 46:9-10; Matthew 11:27; Hebrews 4:13	Matthew 11:27; John 21:17	Isaiah 40:13-14; 1 Corinthians 2:10; John 16:15
God Is Omnipresent (Jeremiah 23:24)	Acts 17:27-28	Matthew 18:20; 28:20	Psalm 139:7-10
God Is Omnipotent (2 Chronicles 20:6) and Sovereignly Acts as He Chooses (Job 42:2)	Luke 1:37; Ephesians 1:11	John 14:14; Matthew 11:27	Zechariah 4:6; Romans 15:19; 1 Corinthians 12:11
God Is True, Holy, Righteous, and Good (Psalm 119)	Psalm 34:8; John 7:28; 17:11, 25	John 10:11; 14:6; Acts 3:14	1 John 5:6; John 14:26; Psalm 143:10
God is the Source of Strength for His People (Exodus 15:2)	Psalm 18:32	Philippians 4:13	Ephesians 3:16
God Alone Forgives and Cleanses from Sin (Psalms 51:7; 130:3-4)	Exodus 34:6-7	Mark 2:7-11	1 Corinthians 6:11; Hebrews 9:14
God Gave Humanity the Divine Law Which Revealed His Character and Will (2 Timothy 3:16)	Ezekiel 2:4; Isaiah 40:8; Deuteronomy 9:10	Matthew 24:35; John 5:39; Hebrews 1:1-2	2 Samuel 23:2; 2 Peter 1:21; Romans 8:2
God Dwells in and among the People Who Believe in Him (Isaiah 57:15)	2 Corinthians 6:16; 1 Corinthians 14:25	Ephesians 3:17; Matthew 18:20	John 14:17; 1 Corinthians 6:19; Ephesians 2:22
God Is the Supreme, Highest Being Who Has No Equal, Who Reigns as Lord and King over All Creation, and Who Alone Is to Be Worshiped and Glorified	Isaiah 42:8; Psalm 47:2; 1 Timothy 6:15; Matthew 4:10; Revelation 22:8-9	John 20:28-29; Revelation 17:14; Hebrews 1:3, 6-8	Matthew 12:31; Luke 1:35; 2 Corinthians 3:18; 1 Peter 4:14; John 4:24

God the Son

The Self-Consciousness of Jesus Christ

Rev. Dr. Don L. Davis

Prophetic Orientation

John 17:25-26 (ESV) – O righteous Father, even though the world does not know you, I know you, and these know that you have sent me. [26] I made known to them your name, and I will continue to make it known, that the love with which you have loved me may be in them, and I in them.

John 5:34 (ESV) – Not that the testimony that I receive is from man, but I say these things so that you may be saved.

John 3:11 (ESV) – Truly, truly, I say to you, we speak of what we know, and bear witness to what we have seen, but you do not receive our testimony.

John 5:30 (ESV) – I can do nothing on my own. As I hear, I judge, and my judgment is just, because I seek not my own will but the will of him who sent me.

John 8:26 (ESV) – I have much to say about you and much to judge, but he who sent me is true, and I declare to the world what I have heard from him.

John 12:47-49 (ESV) – If anyone hears my words and does not keep them, I do not judge him; for I did not come to judge the world but to save the world. [48] The one who rejects me and does not receive my words has a judge; the word that I have spoken will judge him on the last day. [49] For I have not spoken on my own authority, but the Father who sent me has himself given me a commandment—what to say and what to speak.

God-Consciousness

John 5:17 (ESV) – But Jesus answered them, "My Father is working until now, and I am working."

John 5:19-20 (ESV) – So Jesus said to them, "Truly, truly, I say to you, the Son can do nothing of his own accord, but only what he sees the Father doing. For whatever the Father does, that the Son does likewise. [20] For the Father loves the Son and shows him all that he himself is doing. And greater works than these will he show him, so that you may marvel."

John 8:26 (ESV) – I have much to say about you and much to judge, but he who sent me is true, and I declare to the world what I have heard from him.

John 8:42 (ESV) – Jesus said to them, "If God were your Father, you would love me, for I came from God and I am here. I came not of my own accord, but he sent me."

John 14:10 (ESV) – Do you not believe that I am in the Father and the Father is in me? The words that I say to you I do not speak on my own authority, but the Father who dwells in me does his works.

The Self-Consciousness of Jesus Christ

Divine Representation

John 5:30 (ESV) – I can do nothing on my own. As I hear, I judge, and my judgment is just, because I seek not my own will but the will of him who sent me.

John 6:38 (ESV) – For I have come down from heaven, not to do my own will but the will of him who sent me.

John 14:10 (ESV) – Do you not believe that I am in the Father and the Father is in me? The words that I say to you I do not speak on my own authority, but the Father who dwells in me does his works.

John 17:8 (ESV) – For I have given them the words that you gave me, and they have received them and have come to know in truth that I came from you; and they have believed that you sent me.

Apocalyptic Imagination

John 5:21-22 (ESV) – For as the Father raises the dead and gives them life, so also the Son gives life to whom he will. [22] The Father judges no one, but has given all judgment to the Son.

John 11:23-26 (ESV) – Jesus said to her, "Your brother will rise again." [24] Martha said to him, "I know that he will rise again in the resurrection on the last day." [25] Jesus said to her, "I am the resurrection and the life. Whoever believes in me, though he die, yet shall he live, [26] and everyone who lives and believes in me shall never die. Do you believe this?"

John 4:25-26 (ESV) – The woman said to him, "I know that Messiah is coming (he who is called Christ). When he comes, he will tell us all things." [26] Jesus said to her, "I am, I who speak to you am he."

Mark 14:61-62 (ESV) – But he remained silent and made no answer. Again the high priest asked him, "Are you the Christ, the Son of the Blessed?" [62] And Jesus said, "I am, and you will see the Son of Man seated at the right hand of Power, and coming with the clouds of heaven."

The Principle of Substitution

Rev. Dr. Don L. Davis

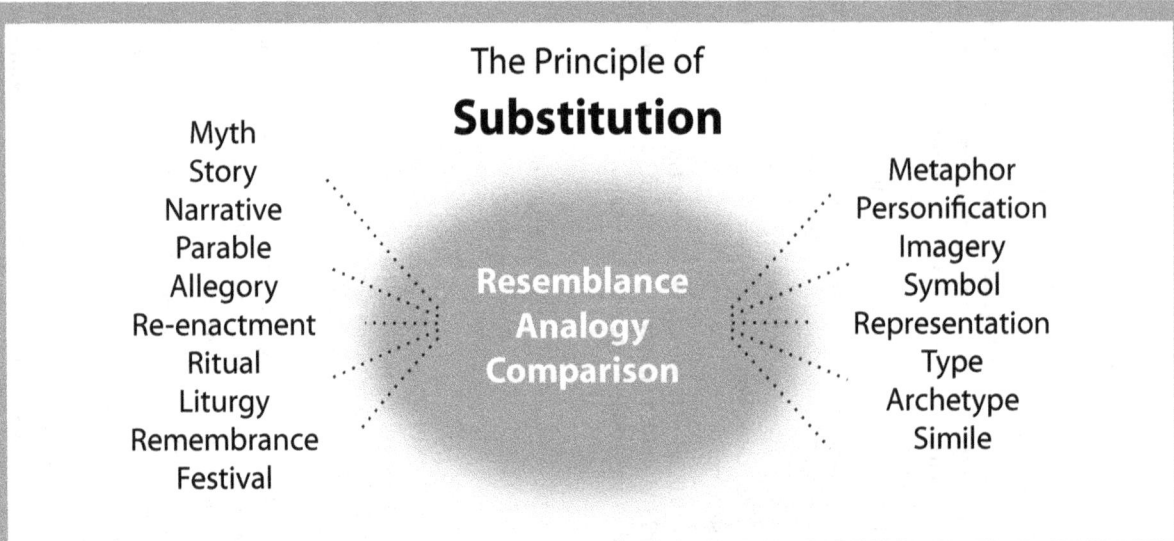

The Principle of **Substitution**

Myth
Story
Narrative
Parable
Allegory
Re-enactment
Ritual
Liturgy
Remembrance
Festival

Resemblance
Analogy
Comparison

Metaphor
Personification
Imagery
Symbol
Representation
Type
Archetype
Simile

$$\frac{A}{B} :: \frac{C}{D}$$

"As a *shepherd* is to *sheep*
so *the Lord* is to *his people*."

Analysis of Imagistic and Narratival Substitution

1. Main subject of discourse or religious idea

2. A concrete image or narrative derived from a cultural fund or reservoir of images and stories

3. Analogy-resemblance-comparison of selected elements or characteristics of (2) to illumine the nature of (1)

4. Implicit or explicit association, comparison, and identification of the two together

5. New understanding and experience of (1) through its association and identification with (2) representing new knowledge

*The Lord is my Shepherd,
I shall not want for anything.* – Psalm 23:1

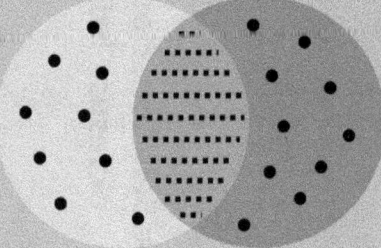

The Lord · A Shepherd

Levels of Association

1. The Holy Spirit's inspiration of associations

2. The cultural fund of associations for societal meaning

3. The missiological association to communicate truth

Rules of Association

1. No analogy is perfect

2. Selection of elements to compare is critical

3. Theology explores connections and possible connections

4. Creative connection demands mastery of core images and stories

Portrayals of Jesus in the New Testament Books

Adapted from John Stott, *The Incomparable Christ*

The Thirteen Letters of Paul				
Approximate Date of Writing	Period	Group	Letters	How Messiah Is Presented
48-49	End of 1st missionary journey	A polemical letter	Galatians	Christ the Liberator
50-52	During 2nd missionary journey	The early letters	1 and 2 Thessalonians	Christ the Coming Judge
53-57	During 3rd missionary journey	The major letters	Romans, 1 and 2 Corinthians	Christ the Savior
60-62	During 1st imprisonment in Rome	The prison letters	Colossians, Philemon, Ephesians, and Philippians	Christ the Supreme Lord
62-67	During release and 2nd imprisonment	The pastoral letters	1 and 2 Timothy and Titus	Christ the Head of the Church
General Epistles and Revelation				
Before 70	During the Pauline and Petrine ministry	Epistle to believing Jews	Hebrews	Christ our Great High Priest
40-50	First book of the New Testament to be written	General epistles	James	Christ our Teacher
64-67	Early period of persecution	General epistles	1 and 2 Peter	Christ our Exemplary Sufferer
90-100	Toward end of Apostle's ministry	General epistles	1, 2, and 3 John	Christ our Life
66-69	Threat and rise of early apostasy	General epistles	Jude	Christ our Advocate
95	Written while in exile	Prophecy	Revelation	King of Kings and Lord of lords

The Miracles of Jesus

Adapted from *The Bible Made Easy*. Peabody: Hendrickson Publishers, 1997.

#	Miracle	Reference
1	Water changed to wine	John 2:1-11
2	Nobleman's son healed	John 4:46-54
3	Lame man by the Bethesda pool	John 5:1-9
4	Man born blind	John 9:1-41
5	Lazarus raised from the dead	John 11:1-44
6	153 fish captured	John 21:1-11
7	Jesus walks on water	John 6:19-21
8	5,000 people fed	John 6:5-13
9	Demon-possessed man loosed	Luke 4:33-35
10	Peter's mother-in-law healed	Luke 4:38-39
11	Large catch of fish	Luke 5:1-11
12	Leper cleansed	Luke 5:12-13
13	Paralyzed man restored	Luke 5:18-25
14	Shriveled hand made whole	Luke 5:5-10
15	Centurion's steward healed	Luke 7:1-10
16	Widow's dead son raised	Luke 7:11-15
17	The storm calmed	Luke 8:22-25
18	The man with Legion exorcised	Luke 8:27-35
19	Jairus's daughter raised	Luke 8:41-56
20	Woman with hemorrhage healed	Luke 8:43-48
21	Demon-possessed boy delivered	Luke 8:43-48
22	Mute, demon-possessed man healed	Luke 9:38-43
23	Crippled woman straightened	Luke 13:11-13
24	Ten lepers cleansed	Luke 17:11-19
25	Blind Bartimeus made well	Luke 18:35-43
26	Malchus's ear restored	Luke 22:50-51
27	Two blind men healed	Matthew 9:27-31
28	Demon-possessed mute healed	Matthew 9:32-33
29	Coin in the fish's mouth	Matthew 17:24-27
30	Woman's daughter made whole	Matthew 15:21-28
31	4,000 people fed	Matthew 15:32-38
32	Fig tree cursed	Matthew 21:18-22
33	Deaf and mute man healed	Mark 7:31-37
34	Blind man restored	Mark 8:22-26
35	Man with dropsy healed	Luke 14:1-4

The Parables of Jesus

Adapted from *The Bible Made Easy*. Peabody: Hendrickson Publishers, 1997.

#	Parable	Reference
1	The Good Samaritan	Luke 10:30-37
2	The Lost Sheep	Luke 15:4-6
3	The Lost Coin	Luke 15:8-10
4	The Prodigal Son	Luke 15:11-32
5	The Dishonest Manager	Luke 16:1-8
6	The Rich Man and Lazarus	Luke 16:1-8
7	The Servants	Luke 17:7-10
8	The Persistent Widow	Luke 18:2-5
9	The Talents	Luke 19:12-27
10	The Wicked Tenants	Luke 20:9-16
11	New Cloth	Luke 5:36
12	New Wine	Luke 5:37-38
13	The House on the Rock	Luke 6:47-49
14	Two Debtors	Luke 7:41-43
15	The Sower	Luke 8:5-8
16	The Lamp	Luke 16:1-12
17	The Watching Servants	Luke 12:35-40
18	The Persistent Friend	Luke 11:5-8
19	The Rich Fool	Luke 12:16-21
20	The Faithful Steward	Luke 12:42-48
21	The Fruitless Fig Tree	Luke 13:6-9
22	The Leafless Fig Tree	Luke 21:29-31
23	The Mustard Seed	Luke 13:18-19
24	The Leaven	Luke 13:20-21
25	The Wedding Guests	Luke 14:7-14
26	The Great Banquet	Luke 14:16-24
27	Tower Building and Warfare	Luke 14:28-33
28	The Pharisee and the Publican	Luke 18:10-14
29	The Returning House Owner	Mark 12:1-9
30	The Growing Seed	Mark 4:26-29
31	The Weeds	Matthew 13:24-30
32	The Hidden Treasure	Matthew 13:44
33	The Pearl of Great Price	Matthew 13:45-46
34	The Net	Matthew 13:47-48
35	The Unforgiving Servant	Matthew 18:23-24
36	The Workers in the Vineyard	Matthew 20:1-16
37	The Two Sons	Matthew 21:28-31
38	The Ten Virgins	Matthew 25:1-13
39	The Sheep and the Goats	Matthew 25:31-36
40	The Wedding Banquet	Matthew 22:2-14

The Life of Christ according to Seasons and Years

Adapted from Ray E. Baughman, *The Life of Christ Visualized*

Key Events – Spring	M	M	L	J	Key Events – Summer	M	M	L	J	Key Events – Fall	M	M	L	J
Birth at Bethlehem, shepherds, angels			2:1-20							Baptism of Jesus (Jordan River)	3:1-17	1:9-11	3:1-18, 21-37	
Adoration of Simeon, Anna, wise men	2:1-12		2:21-38							Temptation (Wilderness of Judea)	4:1-11	1:12-13	4:1-13	
Bethlehem babies killed	2:16-18									Testimony of John the Baptist				1:15-34
Into Egypt (Flight of Joseph, Mary, and Jesus)	2:13-15									Jesus's first five disciples (Jordan)				1:35-51
Egyptian exile ended, settled in Nazareth	2:19-23		2:39-40											
Search for Jesus (12 years old, visit to Jerusalem)			2:41-52											
Cana, changing water into wine (first miracle)				2:1-11	First Passover during ministry (Jerusalem)				2:13	Woman at the well (Sychar)				4:5-42
Capernaum (first sojourn at future home)				2:12	First cleansing of the Temple (Jerusalem)				2:14-25	Nobleman's son made well (Jesus at Cana and son at Capernaum)				4:43-54
					Nicodemus's interview (Jerusalem)				3:1-21	Jesus preaches in synagogues of Galilee, is well received (first Galilean tour)		1:14-15	4:14-22	
					Judean ministry of John and Jesus				3:22-36					
					Jesus leaves Judea as John is imprisoned (Machaerus)	4:12-17	1:14	3:19-20	4:1-4					
Belligerent rejection (1st), at Nazareth	4:18-22		4:23-30		Impotent man at the pool (Jerusalem)				5:1-47	Kingdom of heaven parables by the sea (Capernaum)	13:1-53	4:1-34	8:4-18	
Large catch of fish, call of disciples (Galilee)		1:16-20	5:1-11		Disciples pluck grain (Galilee)	12:1-8	2:23-28	6:1-5		Stilling the sea and the wind	8:18-27	4:35-41	8:22-25	
Demoniac healed (Capernaum)	8:14-17	1:21-28	4:31-37		Man with withered hand (Capernaum)	12:9-21	3:1-12	6:6-11		Demoniac in graveyard, swine into the sea (Gadarenes)	8:28-34	5:1-20	8:26-39	
Peter's mother-in-law healed	4:23-25	1:29-34	4:38-41		Jesus chooses twelve apostles (Galilee)		3:13-19	6:12-16		Crossing back over the sea to Capernaum and four miracles; Jairus's daughter raised; woman touches Messiah's garment	9:18-26	5:21-43	8:40-56	
Galilean Tour (2nd) with four disciples		1:35-39	4:42-44		Sermon on the Mount (Horns of Hattin)	5:1-8:1		6:17-49		Two blind men; dumb demoniac healed	9:27-34			
Leper healed (sent to Jerusalem)	8:2-4	1:40-45	5:12-16		Centurion's servant healed (Capernaum)	8:5-13		7:1-10						
Roof opened for sick man (Capernaum)	9:1-8	2:1-12	5:17-26		Widow's son raised (Nain)			7:11-17						
Call of Matthew, his party (Capernaum)	9:9-17	2:13-22	5:27-39		John's disciples inquire of Jesus (Galilee)	11:2-30		7:18-35						
					First anointing of Jesus's feet (Capernaum)			7:36-50						
					Galilean tour (3rd) with disciples			8:1-3						
					Demon possessed, blind– dumb man healed (Capernaum?)	12:22-33	3:22-30							
					Beelzebub charged against Jesus	12:24-25	3:20-21, 31-35							
					Friends and family believe he is insane	12:46-50		8:19-21						

Key Events – Spring	M	M	L	J	Key Events – Summer	M	M	L	J	Key Events – Fall	M	M	L	J
Second rejection at Nazareth	13:54-58	6:1-6			Feeding of the 5,000 (Sea of Galilee)	14:13-21	6:30-44	9:10-17	6:1-15	Tabernacle Feast (Jerusalem)				7:1-8:1
Twelve sent forth (4th Galilean tour)	9:35-11:1	6:6-13	9:1-6		Walking on water, Bread of Life discourse	14:22-36	6:45-56		6:16-71	Adulterous woman				8:2-11
John the Baptist's death (Machaerus)	14:1-12	6:14-29	9:7-9		Eating with unwashed hands (Capernaum)	15:1-20	7:1-23			Light of the world				8:12-59
					Daughter of Syrophoenician healed (Phoenicia)	15:21-28	7:24-30			Man born blind healed			10:1-24	9:1-41
					Deaf and dumb man healed		7:31-37			Good Shepherd discourse			10:25-37	
					Feeding of the 4,000 (Decapolis)	15:29-31	8:1-9			Seventy sent out (Judea)			10:38-42	
					Pharisees and Sadducees seek a sign	15:32-38	8:10-12			Supper at Mary and Martha's (Bethany)				
					Warning against false teaching	15:39-16:4	8:13-21			Disciples taught to pray			11:1-13	
					Blind man healed at Bethsaida	16:5-12	8:22-26			Accused of tie with Beelzebub, demoniac healed			11:14-36	
					Peter's good confession (Caesarea Philippi)	16:13-20	8:27-30	9:18-21		Eating with Pharisee			11:37-54	
					Foretelling death, resurrection, second coming	16:21-28	8:31-32	9:22-27		Hypocrisy denounced (Judea)			12:1-21	
					Transfiguration (Mount Hermon	17:1-13	9:2-13	9:28-36		Parables on service			12:22-13:9	
					Demon-possessed boy healed	17:14-21	9:14-29	9:37-42		Healing of a crippled woman			13:10-21	
					Foretells death and resurrection (to Galilee)	17:22-23	9:30-32	9:43-44		Feast of Dedication (Jerusalem)				10:22-39
					Coin in fish's mouth (Capernaum)	17:24-27	9:33-50	9:46-62						
					Instructions to disciples	18:1-35								
Teaching in Perea, warned about Herod			13:22-35	10:40-42	Sunday – Triumphal Entry	21:1-11	11:1-11	19:28-44	12:12-19	Earthquake as angel rolls away the stone	28:1-4			
Healing of man on Sabbath			14:1-6		Monday – Second cleansing of the Temple	21:12-22	11:12-26	19:45-48	12:20-50	Women visit tomb	28:5-8	16:1-8	24:1-10	20:1-2
Parables on humility, rewards, excuses, discipleship			14:7-35		Tuesday – Jesus challenged, Olivet Discourse	21:23-26:5; 26:14-16	11:27-14:2, 10-11	20:1-22:6		Peter and John visit tomb			24:11-12	20:3-10
Lost sheep, coin, son			15:1-32		Thursday – Passover supper, Upper Room Discourse, Gethsemane, Arrest	26:17-56	14:12-52	22:7-53		Jesus appears to Mary Magdalene (Jerusalem)		16:9-11		20:11-18
Rich man and Lazarus			16:1-17:10		Friday – Trial, Crucifixion, burial	26:57-27:66	14:53-15:47	22:54-23:56	18:12-19:42	Jesus appears to other women	28:9-10			
Raising of Lazarus (Bethany)				11:1-44	Saturday – in the tomb					Guards report to rulers	28:11-15			
Conspiring to kill Jesus				11:45-57						Jesus appears to disciples on the road to Emmaus (& Simon)		16:12-13	24:13-35	
Ten lepers healed (Samaria)			17:11-37							Jesus appears to 10 disciples			24:36-43	20:19-25
Answered prayer, divorce, little children, rich young ruler	19:1-20:16	10:1-31	18:1-30							Jesus appears to all, w/ Thomas		16:14		20:26-31
Foretold death and resurrection	20:17-28	10:32-45	18:31-34							Jesus appears to 7 disciples by the sea of Galilee (second miracle of the fish)				21:1-25
Blind man of Jericho	20:29-34	10:46-52	18:35-43							Jesus appears to 500 disciples (cf. 1 Corinthians 15:5-7)				
Zacchaeus's transformation			19:1-27											
Last stop, 2nd anointing	26:6-13	14:3-9	12:1-11							The Ascension (Acts 1:9-12)	28:16-20	16:15-18	24:44-53	
												16:19-20		

God the Holy Spirit

Spiritual Gifts Specifically Mentioned in the New Testament

Rev. Terry G. Cornett

Administration	1 Corinthians 12:28	The ability to bring order to Church life
Apostleship	1 Corinthians 12:28; Ephesians 4:11	The ability to establish new churches among the unreached, nurture them to maturity, and exercise the authority and wisdom necessary to see them permanently established and able to reproduce; and/or A gift unique to the founding of the Church age which included the reception of special revelation and uniquely binding leadership authority
Discernment	1 Corinthians 12:10	The ability to serve the Church through a Spirit-given ability to distinguish between God's truth (his presence, working, and doctrine) and fleshly error or satanic counterfeits
Evangelism	Ephesians 4:11	The passion and the ability to effectively proclaim the Gospel so that people understand it
Exhortation	Romans 12:8	The ability to give encouragement or rebuke that helps others obey Christ
Faith	1 Corinthians 12:9	The ability to build up the Church through a unique ability to see the unrealized purposes of God and unwaveringly trust God to accomplish them
Giving	Romans 12:8	The ability to build up a church through taking delight in the consistent, generous sharing of spiritual and physical resources
Healing	1 Corinthians 12:9; 12:28	The ability to exercise faith that results in restoring people to physical, emotional, and spiritual health
Interpretation	1 Corinthians 12:10	The ability to explain the meaning of an ecstatic utterance so that the Church is edified

Knowledge	1 Corinthians 12:8	The ability to understand scriptural truth, through the illumination of the Holy Spirit, and speak it out to edify the body; and/or The supernatural revelation of the existence, or nature, of a person or thing which would not be known through natural means
Leadership	Romans 12:8	Spiritually inspired courage, wisdom, zeal, and hard work which motivate and guide others so that they can effectively participate in building the Church
Mercy	Romans 12:8	Sympathy of heart which enables a person to empathize with and cheerfully serve those who are sick, hurting, or discouraged
Ministering (or Service, or Helping, or Hospitality)	Romans 12:7; 1 Peter 4:9	The ability to joyfully perform any task which benefits others and meets their practical and material needs (especially on behalf of the poor or afflicted)
Miracles	1 Corinthians 12:10; 12:28	The ability to confront evil and do good in ways that make visible the awesome power and presence of God
Pastoring	Ephesians 4:11	The desire and ability to guide, protect, and equip the members of a congregation for ministry
Prophecy	1 Corinthians 12:28; Romans 12:6	The ability to receive and proclaim openly a revealed message from God which prepares the Church for obedience to him and to the Scriptures
Teaching	1 Corinthians 12:28; Romans 12:7; Ephesians 4:11	The ability to explain the meaning of the Word of God and its application through careful instruction
Tongues	1 Corinthians 12:10; 12:28	Ecstatic utterance by which a person speaks to God (or others) under the direction of the Holy Spirit
Wisdom	1 Corinthians 12:8	Spirit-revealed insight that allows a person to speak godly instruction for solving problems; and/or Spirit-revealed insight that allows a person to explain the central mysteries of the Christian faith

St. Basil, the Nicene Creed, and the Doctrine of the Holy Spirit

Rev. Terry G. Cornett

The original Nicene Creed came out of the first worldwide gathering of Christian leaders at Nicea in Bithynia (what is now Isnik, Türkiye) in the year 325. It was called to deal with a heresy called Arianism which denied that Jesus was God and taught that he was instead the greatest created being. The council at Nicaea condemned Arianism and hammered out language that the bishops could use to teach their churches who Jesus truly was.

A little over 50 years later, however, additional challenges were being faced by the Church. A modified form of the Arian heresy was making a comeback; Macedonius, an Arian theologian, had been elected as Bishop of Constantinople in 341. A new problem had also emerged: some Christian bishops had begun teaching that the Holy Spirit was not God. Macedonius eventually became the leader of the sect of Pneumatomachi, whose distinctive tenet was that the Holy Spirit is not God but rather a created being similar to the angels. They taught that the Holy Spirit is subordinate to the Father and the Son and functions as their servant.

Basil[1] is one of the key ancient theologians who communicated and defended the biblical doctrine of the Holy Spirit against these heresies. Basil was a bishop of Caesarea who lived in the 4th century A.D. He wrote *De Spiritu Sancto* ("On the Holy Spirit") in 374 just a few years before his death in 379. This book defended the belief that the Holy Spirit is God. Basil worked tirelessly to see that a new Church council would be called to affirm this doctrine and see that it was taught in the churches.

In 381, shortly after Basil's death, a council of 150 bishops of the Eastern Church were gathered in Constantinople (modern day Istanbul, Türkiye). This council reaffirmed the fact that Jesus was fully God and then turned their attention to the question of the Holy Spirit which the Nicene council had left untouched. (The original Nicene Creed read simply, "We believe in the Holy Spirit"). Building on Basil's writings, the council turned this simple statement into a paragraph which explained more fully the person and work of the Holy Spirit.

---

1   Basil was born in 329, in the region of Pontus (now modern day Türkiye), to a wealthy and rather remarkable family. His grandfather, his father, his mother, his sister and his two younger brothers were all eventually named as saints by the Church. He received an outstanding education at schools in Caesarea, Constantinople, and Athens. Following his education Basil became first a monk in Pontus, then a presbyter (a pastoral position) at Caesarea (where he eventually became a bishop) and developed into a vigorous theologian as well. In these roles, he developed a reputation for personal integrity and great compassion. Even as a bishop he owned only one undergarment and one outer garment and did not eat meat at his table. He lived simply, treated his body harshly, and was personally involved with the distribution to the poor. Because of his personal integrity his many theological opponents through the years had difficulty finding anything wrong to charge him with.

This amended version of the original Nicene Creed (technically the Nicene-Constantinopolitan Creed) is commonly referred to simply as the "Nicene Creed" since it is the final version of the statement started at Nicea. It is accepted by Catholics, Orthodox[2], and Protestant Christians alike as the summary of scriptural teaching which separates orthodoxy from heresy.

---

[2] Although the Orthodox do not include the phrase "and the Son" (which was added at a later date) in the statement about the Spirit proceeding from the Father.

Examples of Denominational Statements on "Baptism in the Holy Spirit" Which Illustrate the Differing Views

Rev. Terry G. Cornett

Single Stage View

Evangelical Presbyterian Church

Excerpted from *Position Paper on the Holy Spirit,* www.epc.org/about-epc/position-papers/holy-spirit.html

As a denomination in the Reformed tradition, we subscribe to the ancient affirmation of orthodox Christian faith and believe in "one Lord, one faith, one baptism" (Ephesians 4:5). This baptism, while visibly expressed in the covenant sacrament that bears its name is invisibly the work of the Spirit that takes place at the time of the new birth. Paul expresses this truth in I Corinthians 12:13, when he tells the Corinthians ". . . we were all baptized by one Spirit into one body . . ."

Thus, we hold to the concept of the baptism in or with the Holy Spirit as the act of the Spirit that takes an unregenerate individual and, through the new birth, adopts him into the family of God. All the works of the Spirit that follow, then, are because of this initial baptism rather than separate from it.

Since Christians are called to ". . . be filled with the Spirit . . ." (Ephesians 5:18) all believers in Christ having been baptized into His body by the Holy Spirit should seek to experience the fulfillment of this command. We believe that Christians are called upon to proclaim a grace that reaches out to forgive, to redeem and to give new spiritual power to life through Jesus Christ and the infilling of the Holy Spirit." (*Book of Worship*, 1-3).

Multiple Stage View: Holiness

Church of the Nazarene

Excerpted from *Articles of Faith,* www.nazarene.org/gensec/we_believe.html

We believe that entire sanctification is that act of God, subsequent to regeneration, by which believers are made free from original sin, or depravity, and brought into a state of entire devotement to God, and the holy obedience of love made perfect.

It is wrought by the baptism with the Holy Spirit, and comprehends in one experience the cleansing of the heart from sin and the abiding, indwelling presence of the Holy Spirit, empowering the believer for life and service.

Entire sanctification is provided by the blood of Jesus, is wrought instantaneously by faith, preceded by entire consecration; and to this work and state of grace the Holy Spirit bears witness.

This experience is also known by various terms representing its different phases, such as "Christian perfection," "perfect love," "heart purity," "the baptism with the Holy Spirit," "the fullness of the blessing," and "Christian holiness."

We believe that there is a marked distinction between a pure heart and a mature character. The former is obtained in an instant, the result of entire sanctification; the latter is the result of growth in grace.

We believe that the grace of entire sanctification includes the impulse to grow in grace. However, this impulse must be consciously nurtured, and careful attention given to the requisites and processes of spiritual development and improvement in Christlikeness of character and personality. Without such purposeful endeavor one's witness may be impaired and the grace itself frustrated and ultimately lost.

Multiple Stage View: Pentecostal

Assemblies of God

Excerpted from *The Initial Physical Evidence of the Baptism in the Holy Spirit*, http://ag.org/top/position_papers/0000_index.cfm

The term baptism in the Holy Spirit is taken from Scripture. John the Baptist was the first to use it shortly before Jesus began His public ministry. He said, "He [Jesus] shall baptize you with the Holy Ghost" (Matthew 3:11). At the conclusion of His earthly ministry, Jesus referred to John's statement (Acts 1:5); and Peter, in reporting on the events in the home of Cornelius, also repeated the statement (Acts 11:16).

The baptism in the Spirit (also referred to herein as the Baptism) is subsequent to and distinct from the new birth. Scripture makes it clear there is an experience in which the Holy Spirit baptizes believers into the body of Christ (1 Corinthians 12:13), and there is the experience in which Christ baptizes believers in the Holy Spirit (Matthew 3:11). These cannot refer to the same experience since the agent who does the baptizing and the element into which the candidate is baptized are different in each case.

The distinctiveness of the experiences is illustrated in several places. The case of the Ephesian disciples is an example. After they stated they had experienced only John's baptism (Acts 19:3), Paul explained they were to believe on Christ Jesus.

Then these disciples were baptized in water, after which Paul laid hands on them and the Holy Spirit came on them. The lapse of time was brief between these disciples' believing on Christ and the Holy Spirit's coming upon them, but it was long enough for them to be baptized in water. The baptism in the Spirit was distinct from and subsequent to salvation.

The baptism in the Spirit is not an end in itself, but a means to an end. The scriptural ideal for the believer is to be continually filled with the Spirit. The Baptism is the crisis experience which introduces the believer to the process experience of living a Spirit-filled life.

The expression *initial physical evidence of the Baptism* refers to the first outward sign that the Holy Spirit has come in filling power. A study of Scripture indicates there was a physical sign by which observers knew that believers had been baptized in the Holy Spirit. The evidence always occurred at the very time the believers were baptized in the Spirit and not on some future occasion.

In the home of Cornelius there was convincing evidence of the Holy Spirit being poured out on the Gentiles (Acts 10:44-48). Later, when Peter was called upon to explain to the leaders of the church in Jerusalem his ministry in the home of Cornelius, he referred to observable evidence of the believers being baptized in the Holy Spirit. He cited this as the reason why he arranged for the believers to be baptized in water (Acts 11:15-17).

While speaking in tongues has initial evidential value, it is designed by God to be much more than evidence of a past experience. It also continues to bring enrichment to the individual believer in personal devotions, and to the congregation when accompanied by the interpretation of tongues.

Combination View: Pentecostal-Holiness

Church of God in Christ

Excerpted from *The Doctrines of the Church of God in Christ*, http://www.cogic.org/about-us/what-we-believe

We believe that the Baptism of the Holy Ghost is an experience subsequent to conversion and sanctification and that tongue-speaking is the consequence of the baptism in the Holy Ghost with the manifestations of the fruit of the spirit (Galatians 5:22-23; Acts 10:46, 19:1-6). We believe that we are not baptized with the Holy Ghost in order to be saved (Acts 19:1-6; John 3:5). When one receives a baptismal Holy Ghost experience, we believe one will speak with a tongue unknown to oneself according to the sovereign will of Christ. To be filled with the Spirit means to be Spirit controlled as expressed by Paul in Ephesians 5:18-19. Since the charismatic demonstrations were necessary to help the early church to be successful in implementing the command of Christ, we therefore, believe that a Holy Ghost experience is mandatory for all men today.

Combination View: Charismatic

Association of Vineyard Churches

Excerpted from *Vineyard Statement of Faith*, www.vineyardusa.org/about/beliefs/beliefs_index/faith/paragraph_07.htm

WE BELIEVE that the Holy Spirit was poured out on the Church at Pentecost in power, baptizing believers into the Body of Christ and releasing the gifts of the Spirit to them. The Spirit brings the permanent indwelling presence of God to us for spiritual worship, personal sanctification, building up the Church, gifting us for ministry, and driving back the kingdom of Satan by the evangelization of the world through proclaiming the word of Jesus and doing the works of Jesus.

WE BELIEVE that the Holy Spirit indwells every believer in Jesus Christ and that He is our abiding Helper, Teacher, and Guide. We believe in the filling or empowering of the Holy Spirit, often a conscious experience, for ministry today. We believe in the present ministry of the Spirit and in the exercise of all of the biblical gifts of the Spirit. We practice the laying on of hands for the empowering of the Spirit, for healing, and for recognition and empowering of those whom God has ordained to lead and serve the Church.

Areas of Disagreement among Christians Concerning Spiritual Gifts

Rev. Terry G. Cornett

I. What is the relationship between "natural talents or capacities" and "spiritual gifts"?

A. View #1 – Spiritual gifts are what the natural talents and abilities latent in every human being look like when they are energized, empowered, broadened, and redirected by the Spirit of God regenerating a person. This view is concerned to safeguard the fact that:

1. There is no discontinuity between the activity of the Spirit who creates and who recreates. (Salvation is restorative in nature making us the full human beings we were originally created to be.)

2. That God has chosen to work his gifts through human beings which includes using their minds, bodies, and personalities. He includes us in his work so that even though his power will enable us to do far more than mere human accomplishments, it is still at work in, with, and through us as we actually are.

3. God foreknew us and was at work prior to our salvation (cf. Jeremiah 1:5)

    a. Jeremiah 1:5 (ESV) – Before I formed you in the womb I knew you, and before you were born I consecrated you; I appointed you a prophet to the nations.

    b. Ephesians 2:10 (ESV) – For we are his workmanship, created in Christ Jesus for good works, which God prepared beforehand, that we should walk in them.

4. That even those who are unsaved and in rebellion against God rely on his creation and gifts of grace (suppressed, corrupted, or misdirected as they may be) for their very being and productivity.

    a. 1 Corinthians 4:7 (ESV) – For who sees anything different in you? What do you have that you did not receive? If then you received it, why do you boast as if you did not receive it? (Cf. Psalm 104.)

b. Matthew 5:45 (ESV) – . . . so that you may be sons of your Father who is in heaven. For he makes his sun rise on the evil and on the good, and sends rain on the just and on the unjust.

c. "The same God is God of creation and of new creation, working out both through his perfect will. . . . God's gracious purpose for each of us is eternal. It was formed and even "given" to us in Christ "before eternal time" (2 Timothy 1:9, literally); God chose us to be holy and destined us to be his sons through Jesus Christ "before the foundation of the world" (Ephesians 1:4-5); and the good works for which were re-created in Christ are precisely those "which God prepared beforehand." This fundamental truth that God planned the end from the beginning should warn us against . . . [too easily separating] . . . between nature and grace, between our pre-conversion and our post-conversion life" (John R. W. Stott, *Baptism and Fullness: The Work of the Holy Spirit Today*).

B. View #2 – Spiritual gifts are new supernatural abilities given to Christians which are only available to us through God's power and are able to accomplish things far beyond the reach of human ability.

This view is concerned to safeguard the fact that:

1. Salvation is transformative as well as restorative.

2. God is able to supply whatever is needed in a situation regardless of the resources we seem to have available. We are dependent upon God's Spirit, not our own resources.

3. Supernatural powers exceeding anything possible in the natural order are available to the body of Christ.

4. We all are commanded to seek certain spiritual gifts that are of benefit to the body (1 Corinthians 12:31 and 14:12). The gifts are always spoken of in relation to how they build up Christ's body. There is no scriptural reference to spiritual gifts apart from their use in and by the Church.

a. 1 Corinthians 1:26-29 (ESV) – For consider your calling, brothers: not many of you were wise according to worldly standards, not many were powerful, not many were of noble birth. [27] But God chose what is foolish in the world to shame the wise; God chose what is weak in the world to shame the strong; [28] God chose what is low and despised in the world, even things that are not, to bring to nothing things that are, [29] so that no human being might boast in the presence of God.

    b. Non-Christians have talents through common grace... but these are talents, not gifts. No unbeliever has a spiritual gift. Only believers are gifted spiritually....Talents depend on natural power, gifts on spiritual endowment (Leslie B. Flynn, 19 *Gifts of the Spirit*).

C. View #3 – A Middle Way which suggests that spiritual gifts can be either the energizing of God-given natural talents or the creation of entirely new talents.

1. Note that logically, at least, it is not necessary for these two views to be mutually exclusive. It is at least possible that both types of spiritual gifts exist, some that are latent and some that are new.

2. Perhaps a more useful way to think about this would be to remember that gifts are the "manifestation" of the Spirit for the common good.

3. The Spirit being manifested is the emphasis not the means by which it happens. It is always a "gracious gift" when this happens. It always happens solely because of the Spirit's decision and because of the Spirit's power. Thus, whether the Spirit chooses to empower a natural capacity or create an entirely new one, each is a "charisma" — a gift of grace. A God given ability to teach exercised by a non-believer is a gracious gift (given by the Spirit in creation) but it is not a "manifestation of the Spirit" until that person submits themselves to the Holy Spirit and uses that gift under his direction and for his purposes.

II. Are all the gifts listed in the New Testament available today?

A. Some traditions answer "No."

1. Some traditions argue for the ceasing of certain gifts: usually apostleship, prophecy, tongues and interpretation (sometimes miracles).

2. There are at least two theological reasons why this is believed.

    a. First, there is a concern for safeguarding God's revelation in Scripture.

If apostles, prophets, and tongues continue to function as a means of ongoing revelation, the integrity of Scripture is potentially put at risk. Again and again in the history of the Church, people have come along that claimed a new, prophetic revelation which contradicted or went beyond the claims of Scripture. The scriptural testimony to Jesus as God's final Word cannot be compromised and these theological traditions do not see a way to reconcile the possibility of new revelations with that fact.

b. Second, the role of the apostles as the "foundation" of the Church seems to imply a unique place in Church history.

The Gospels and the Book of Acts are seen as a pivot point of history during which God works uniquely and unrepeatably to change his revelation from the Old Covenant to the New Covenant. This is accomplished by the granting of new revelations (which form the New Testament Scriptures) and signs and wonders which confirm and establish this testimony as authentic. The Church now is to exist by the testimony of that Word, guarding the deposit of faith but not adding to it or subtracting from it.

(1) Jude 1:3 (ESV) – Beloved, although I was very eager to write to you about our common salvation, I found it necessary to write appealing to you to contend for the faith that was once for all delivered to the saints.

(2) Hebrews 1:1-3 (ESV) – Long ago, at many times and in many ways, God spoke to our fathers by the prophets, [2] but in these last days he has spoken to us by his Son, whom he appointed the heir of all things, through whom also he created the world. [3] He is the radiance of the glory of God and the exact imprint of his nature, and he upholds the universe by the word of his power. After making purification for sins, he sat down at the right hand of the Majesty on high.

(3) Galatians 1:8-9 (ESV) – But even if we or an angel from heaven should preach to you a gospel contrary to the one we preached to you, let him be accursed. [9] As we have said before, so now I say again: If anyone is preaching to you a gospel contrary to the one you received, let him be accursed.

B. Some traditions answer "Yes."

"All may agree that there appears no new revelation to be expected concerning God in Christ. But there appears to be no good reason why the living God, who both speaks and acts (in contrast to dead idols), cannot use the gift of prophecy to give particular local guidance to a church, nation or individual, or to warn or encourage by way of prediction as well as by reminders, in full accord with the written word of Scripture, by which all such utterances must be tested. Certainly the New Testament does not see it as the job of the prophet to be a doctrinal innovator, but to deliver the word the Spirit gives him in line with the truth once for all delivered to the saints (Jude 3), to challenge and encourage our faith" (J. P. Baker, "Prophecy," *New Bible Dictionary,* 2nd Edition, J. D. Douglas and others, eds.).

1. The ministry of Jesus and the example of the Apostles and the New Testament Church is our inspired model for ministry and all of them used miraculous gifts in ministry.

2. The only time that Scripture speaks to the question of when gifts will cease it refers to the return of Christ (1 Corinthians 13:8-12).

3. The Holy Spirit is free and sovereign. He can give (or withhold) any gift at any time for whatever purpose he chooses (1 Corinthians 12:11 – gives as he determines).

4. The Craig S. Keener reading (*Gift and Giver*—pp. 89-112) makes the basic arguments for the view that all are available.

The Role of the Holy Spirit in Spiritual Guidance

Rev. Terry G. Cornett

Through the Holy Spirit, God has made himself available to believers so that they can be in constant, friendship relationship with him, receiving ongoing guidance and direction as to what he wants from them.

I. Key Texts

A. Romans 8:14 (ESV) – For all who are led by the Spirit of God are sons of God.

B. Isaiah 63:10-14 (ESV) – But they rebelled and grieved his Holy Spirit; therefore he turned to be their enemy, and himself fought against them. [11] Then he remembered the days of old, of Moses and his people. Where is he who brought them up out of the sea with the shepherds of his flock? Where is he who put in the midst of them his Holy Spirit, [12] who caused his glorious arm to go at the right hand of Moses, who divided the waters before them to make for himself an everlasting name, [13] who led them through the depths? Like a horse in the desert, they did not stumble. [14] Like livestock that go down into the valley, the Spirit of the Lord gave them rest. So you led your people, to make for yourself a glorious name.

C. John 10:1-5 (ESV) – Truly, truly, I say to you, he who does not enter the sheepfold by the door but climbs in by another way, that man is a thief and a robber. [2] But he who enters by the door is the shepherd of the sheep. [3] To him the gatekeeper opens. The sheep hear his voice, and he calls his own sheep by name and leads them out. [4] When he has brought out all his own, he goes before them, and the sheep follow him, for they know his voice. [5] A stranger they will not follow, but they will flee from him, for they do not know the voice of strangers.

D. John 14:25-26 (ESV) – These things I have spoken to you while I am still with you. [26] But the Helper, the Holy Spirit, whom the Father will send in my name, he will teach you all things and bring to your remembrance all that I have said to you.

E. John 16:13 (ESV) – When the Spirit of truth comes, he will guide you into all the truth, for he will not speak on his own authority, but whatever he hears he will speak, and he will declare to you the things that are to come.

F. Acts 16:7-8 (ESV) – And when they had come up to Mysia, they attempted to go into Bithynia, but the Spirit of Jesus did not allow them. [8] So, passing by Mysia, they went down to Troas (cf. Acts 20:22-23).

II. Why is the guidance of the Holy Spirit so important?

Christian, then, recognizes that when faced with the alternatives of good and evil, there is no choice; one must do good. But the greater challenge comes when we are faced with multiple alternatives that are all morally good. The question then becomes, which is the good to which God is calling me? And the good then becomes the enemy of the best, since it is quite possible for us to fill our days doing good things but neglecting the one thing that we must do and to which we are called. . . . Every choice is then both a yes and a no. . . . If I take on this assignment or this job, it means saying no to other opportunities. If I choose to spend my day in this way, it means I am saying no to other activities that might have filled my day. And surely this is what makes decisions making a challenge: we cannot be everywhere and we cannot do everything. There are many good things that we might do, and we cannot do them all. Again, this would be a terrifying and impossible burden were it not for the providential care of God. He is a God who is present and alive in all that is–the land, the sea, and the sky–but also a God who is personally present in each one of us. We are not alone! This is exceedingly good news. . . . When we make a choice, the Spirit is with us. Indeed we speak of God as Shepherd, that is, as one who guides (Psalm 23). And we experience this guidance most keenly in our times of choosing. Still, our decision making is our responsibility; it is our act of choosing in response to the options, problems, and opportunities that are placed before us. God does not choose for us, and we cannot expect others to make our choices for us, not if we want to accept adult responsibility for our lives. Indeed the capacity to discern well and make wise decisions is a critical sign of spiritual maturity. And further, it is something that we learn as we mature in faith and grow in wisdom.

– Gordon T. Smith. *The Voice of Jesus: Discernment, Prayer, and the Witness of the Spirit.* pp 130-132.

III. How do we hear God's voice?

A. Know what God the Spirit has already spoken: God's Written Word

1. The Scriptures are the record of the Spirit's guidance. The Scriptures are not only the infallible judge of guidance or prophecy, they are also our training in the recognition of God's voice.

2. John 5:46-47 (ESV) – If you believed Moses, you would believe me; for he wrote of me. [47] But if you do not believe his writings, how will you believe my words?

B. Set your heart to obey

1. Usually, the problem is NOT with our hearing!

    a. Psalm 119:10 (ESV) – With my whole heart I seek you; let me not wander from your commandments!

    b. The fundamental question relating to guidance is not whether I will be able to hear God speak but whether I intend to obey what he says.

2. God is a competent, clear-speaking guide.

    a. John 10:2-5, 27 (ESV) – But he who enters by the door is the shepherd of the sheep. [3] To him the gatekeeper opens. The sheep hear his voice, and he calls his own sheep by name and leads them out. [4] When he has brought out all his own, he goes before them, and the sheep follow him, for they know his voice. [5] A stranger they will not follow, but they will flee from him, for they do not know the voice of strangers. . . . [27] My sheep hear my voice, and I know them, and they follow me.

    b. The metaphors of Scripture describe a God who will be heard!

        (1) The images given by God to describe his leadership are very helpful. God is a king, a parent, a shepherd. The biblical question is seldom, "How do we hear?" Jesus says quite confidently that his sheep know his voice. Like all kings or parents or shepherds, God has no difficulty communicating to us in ways that we will understand.

        (2) How many of us, for example, find that the IRS has difficulty communicating with us that we need to pay taxes? How many of us just forget about April 15th and never think about it again once it is passed?

        (3) How many of you as kids sat around and agonized whether you were going to be able to recognize your parent's voice. What initiative did you take as a child to make sure you could hear and understand your parents?

(4) In the same manner, God takes the initiative to communicate his will to his people.

c. If God is silent it usually means that we are either free to choose among the good choices he has placed at our disposal, or alternatively, that we are operating under a preexisting command.

   (1) If God wants us to do something, he will make it clear to the listening heart.

   (2) When God has a already communicated his will through the Scriptures, the question will not be hearing but obeying.

d. The importance of a listening heart

   The foundational ground rule: We cannot be ignoring God or running away from obedience and then claim that God is not saying anything.

   (1) God's Church as the natural environment for listening

   (a) The family analogy holds true. My children came home after school everyday, ate at my table, lived in my house, and participated in our family life. Because that was true, they could be confident that they were hearing what I wanted from them. We must do the same in our spiritual walk.

   (b) If we ignore our relationship with the family of God and do not spend time in his presence, and hearing his Word, he will speak, but we will likely not attend to his voice. On the other hand, active participation in family life is an important part of listening

   (c) In my own experience God often speaks to me at church. Sometimes through the sermon and sometimes along a line completely different from the sermon or worship emphasis. The point is that I am at his family table. He can speak through the preacher or he can simply capture my attention and speak directly to my heart but I must participate in the family to have a reasonable expectation of receiving direction. If we run away from time with God's family (like the prodigal son) we cannot, then, claim the excuse that we do not hear him saying anything.

(d) Hearing the voice of God is not a private function. It takes place in community. We hear the voice of God best when we listen along with others.

(e) Our pastors and spiritual leaders have a unique role to play in this process.

(f) Hebrews 13:17 (ESV) – Obey your leaders and submit to them, for they are keeping watch over your souls, as those who will have to give an account. Let them do this with joy and not with groaning, for that would be of no advantage to you.

(g) Consulting our pastoral leadership for their insights and counsel is a natural starting point for decisions where God's will is not clear.

(h) Our brothers and sisters in Christ are also a rich resource for speaking the mind of Christ to us.

(i) 1 Corinthians 12:7 (ESV) – To each is given the manifestation of the Spirit for the common good.

(j) 1 Corinthians 14:26 (ESV) – What then, brothers? When you come together, each one has a hymn, a lesson, a revelation, a tongue, or an interpretation. Let all things be done for building up.

(k) Proverbs 27:17 (ESV) – Iron sharpens iron, and one man sharpens another.

(l) Proverbs 11:14 (ESV) – Where there is no guidance, a people falls, but in an abundance of counselors there is safety.

(m) Listening to the voice of the Spirit necessarily means that we must listen to the counsel of the church community and its leaders.

(2) The role of attention

I make it my business to persevere in his Holy presence, wherein I keep myself by a simple attention and a general fond regard to God, which I may call an ACTUAL PRESENCE of God; or, to speak better, an habitual, silent, and secret conversation of the soul with God, which often causes me joys and raptures inwardly, and sometimes

also outwardly, so great that I am forced to use means to moderate them and prevent their appearance to others.
– Brother Lawrence quoted in Dallas Willard. *Hearing God.*

(3) A Prayer from Saint Anselm of Canterbury (1033-1109).

Teach me to seek you
And as I seek you, show yourself to me,
For I cannot seek you unless you show me how,
And I will never find you unless you show yourself to me.
Let me seek you by desiring you,
And desire you by seeking you;
Let me find you by loving you,
And love you in finding you.
Amen.

IV. For further reading:

Richard J. Foster. Chapter 12. "Guidance." *Celebration of Discipline: The Path to Spiritual Growth.* San Francisco: HarperSanFrancisco, 1998.

Gordon T. Smith. *The Voice of Jesus: Discernment, Prayer and the Witness of the Spirit.* Downers Grove, IL: InterVarsity Press, 2003.

Charles Stanley. *How to Listen to God.* Nashville: Thomas Nelson, 1985.

Mark Water. *Knowing God's Will Made Easier.* Peabody, MA: Hendrickson, 1998.

Denominational Statements on "Sanctification"
Rev. Terry G. Cornett

Statements from Lutheran, Reformed, and Baptist Denominations

Church of the Lutheran Brethren

https://clba.org/about#statementoffaith

Sanctification

Sanctification is God's gracious, continual work of spiritual renewal and growth in the life of every justified person. Through the means of grace, the Holy Spirit works to reproduce the character of Christ within the lives of all believers, instructing and urging them to live out their new nature. The Holy Spirit enables believers more and more to resist the devil, to overcome the world, and to count themselves dead to sin but alive to God in Christ Jesus. The Holy Spirit produces spiritual fruit in and bestows spiritual gifts upon all believers. He calls, empowers and equips them to serve God in the home, in the community, and as part of the Church Universal. The process of sanctification will be complete only when the believer reaches glory.

Presbyterian Church in America

http://www.pcanet.org/general/cof_chapxi-xv.htm#chapxiii

The Westminster Confession of Faith

CHAP. XIII. – Of Sanctification.

1. They, who are once effectually called, and regenerated, having a new heart, and a new spirit created in them, are further sanctified, really and personally, through the virtue of Christ's death and resurrection, by His Word and Spirit dwelling in them, the dominion of the whole body of sin is destroyed, and the several lusts thereof are more and more weakened and mortified; and they more and more quickened and strengthened in all saving graces, to the practice of true holiness, without which no man shall see the Lord.

2. This sanctification is throughout, in the whole man; yet imperfect in this life, there abiding still some remnants of corruption in every part; whence ariseth a continual and irreconcilable war, the flesh lusting against the Spirit, and the Spirit against the flesh.

3. In which war, although the remaining corruption, for a time, may much prevail; yet, through the continual supply of strength from the sanctifying Spirit of Christ, the regenerate part doth overcome; and so, the saints grow in grace, perfecting holiness in the fear of God.

Southern Baptist Convention

http://www.sbc.net/bfm/bfm2000.asp#iv

Salvation involves the redemption of the whole man, and is offered freely to all who accept Jesus Christ as Lord and Saviour, who by His own blood obtained eternal redemption for the believer. In its broadest sense salvation includes regeneration, justification, sanctification, and glorification. There is no salvation apart from personal faith in Jesus Christ as Lord.

1. Regeneration, or the new birth, is a work of God's grace whereby believers become new creatures in Christ Jesus. It is a change of heart wrought by the Holy Spirit through conviction of sin, to which the sinner responds in repentance toward God and faith in the Lord Jesus Christ. Repentance and faith are inseparable experiences of grace.

    Repentance is a genuine turning from sin toward God. Faith is the acceptance of Jesus Christ and commitment of the entire personality to Him as Lord and Saviour.

2. Justification is God's gracious and full acquittal upon principles of His righteousness of all sinners who repent and believe in Christ. Justification brings the believer unto a relationship of peace and favor with God.

3. Sanctification is the experience, beginning in regeneration, by which the believer is set apart to God's purposes, and is enabled to progress toward moral and spiritual maturity through the presence and power of the Holy Spirit dwelling in him. Growth in grace should continue throughout the regenerate person's life.

4. Glorification is the culmination of salvation and is the final blessed and abiding state of the redeemed.

    Genesis 3:15; Exodus 3:14-17; 6:2-8; Matthew 1:21; 4:17; 16:21-26; 27:22-28:6; Luke 1:68-69; 2:28-32; John 1:11-14, 29; 3:3-21, 36; 5:24; 10:9, 28-29; 15:1-16; 17:17; Acts 2:21; 4:12; 15:11; 16:30-31; 17:30-31; 20:32; Romans 1:16-18; 2:4; 3:23-25; 4:3ff.; 5:8-10; 6:1-23; 8:1-18, 29-39; 10:9-10, 13; 13:11-14; 1 Corinthians 1:18, 30; 6:19-20; 15:10; 2 Corinthians 5:17-20; Galatians 2:20; 3:13; 5:22-25; 6:15; Ephesians 1:7; 2:8-22; 4:11-16; Philippians 2:12-13; Colossians 1:9-22; 3:1ff.; 1 Thessalonians 5:23-24; 2 Timothy 1:12; Titus 2:11-14; Hebrews 2:1-3; 5:8-9; 9:24-28; 11:1-12:8,14; James 2:14-26; 1 Peter 1:2-23; 1 John 1:6-2:11; Revelation 3:20; 21:1-22:5.

Statements from Holiness Denominations

Church of the Nazarene

https://nazarene.org/what-we-believe/#AOF

Articles of Faith

We believe that entire sanctification is that act of God, subsequent to regeneration, by which believers are made free from original sin, or depravity, and brought into a state of entire devotion to God, and the holy obedience of love made perfect. It is wrought by the baptism with the Holy Spirit, and comprehends in one experience the cleansing of the heart from sin and the abiding, indwelling presence of the Holy Spirit, empowering the believer for life and service. Entire sanctification is provided by the blood of Jesus, is wrought instantaneously by faith, preceded by entire consecration; and to this work and state of grace the Holy Spirit bears witness. This experience is also known by various terms representing its different phases, such as "Christian perfection," "perfect love," "heart purity," "the baptism with the Holy Spirit," "the fullness of the blessing," and "Christian holiness."

We believe that there is a marked distinction between a pure heart and a mature character. The former is obtained in an instant, the result of entire sanctification; the latter is the result of growth in grace. We believe that the grace of entire sanctification includes the impulse to grow in grace. However, this impulse must be consciously nurtured, and careful attention given to the requisites and processes of spiritual development and improvement in Christlikeness of character and personality. Without such purposeful endeavor one's witness may be impaired and the grace itself frustrated and ultimately lost.

(Jeremiah 31:31-34; Ezekiel 36:25-27; Malachi 3:2-3; Matthew 3:11-12; Luke 3:16-17; John 7:37-39; 14:15-23; 17:6-20; Acts 1:5; 2:1-4; 15:8-9; Romans 6:11-13, 19; 8:1-4, 8-14; 12:1-2; 2 Corinthians 6:14-7:1; Galatians 2:20; 5:16-25; Ephesians 3:14-21; 5:17-18, 25-27; Philippians 3:10-15; Colossians 3:1-17; 1 Thessalonians 5:23-24; Hebrews 4:9-11; 10:10-17; 12:1-2; 13:12; 1 John 1:7, 9) ("Christian perfection," "perfect love": Deuteronomy 30:6; Matthew 5:43-48; 22:37-40; Romans 12:9-21; 13:8-10; 1 Corinthians 13; Philippians 3:10-15; Hebrews 6:1; 1 John 4:17-18 "Heart purity": Matthew 5:8; Acts 15:8-9; 1 Peter 1:22; 1 John 3:3 "Baptism with the Holy Spirit": Jeremiah 31:31-34; Ezekiel 36:25-27; Malachi 3:2-3; Matthew 3:11-12; Luke 3:16-17; Acts 1:5; 2:1-4; 15:8-9 "Fullness of the blessing": Romans 15:29 "Christian holiness": Matthew 5:1-7.29; John 15:1-11; Romans 12:1-15:3; 2 Corinthians 7:1; Ephesians 4:17-5:20; Philippians 1:9-11; 3:12-15; Colossians 2:20-3:17; 1 Thessalonians 3:13; 4:7-8; 5:23; 2 Timothy 2:19-22; Hebrews 10:19-25; 12:14; 13:20-21; 1 Peter 1:15-16; 2 Peter 1:1-11; 3:18; Jude 20-21)

Free Methodist Church

www.fmc-canada.org/articles.htm

Articles of Religion

Entire sanctification is that work of the Holy Spirit, subsequent to regeneration, by which the fully consecrated believer, upon exercise of faith in the atoning blood of Christ, is cleansed in that moment from all inward sin and empowered for service. The resulting relationship is attested by the witness of the Holy Spirit and is maintained by faith and obedience. Entire sanctification enables the believer to love God with all his heart, soul, strength, and mind, and his neighbor as himself, and it prepares him for greater growth in grace. (Leviticus 20:7-8; John 14:16-17; 17:19; Acts 1:8; 2:4; 15:8-9; Romans 5:3-5; 8:12-17; 12:1-2; 1 Corinthians 6:11; 12:4-11; Galatians 5:22-25; Ephesians 4:22-24; 1 Thessalonians 4:7; 5:23-24; 2 Thessalonians 2:13; Hebrews 10:14)

Wesleyan Church

www.wesleyan.org/doctrine.htm

The Articles of Religion

We believe that sanctification is that work of the Holy Spirit by which the child of God is separated from sin unto God and is enabled to love God with all the heart and to walk in all His holy commandments blameless. Sanctification is initiated at the moment of justification and regeneration. From that moment there is a gradual or progressive sanctification as the believer walks with God and daily grows in grace and in a more perfect obedience to God. This prepares for the crisis of entire sanctification which is wrought instantaneously when believers present themselves as living sacrifices, holy and acceptable to God, through faith in Jesus Christ, being effected by the baptism with the Holy Spirit who cleanses the heart from all inbred sin. The crisis of entire sanctification perfects the believer in love and empowers that person for effective service. It is followed by lifelong growth in grace and the knowledge of our Lord and Savior Jesus Christ. The life of holiness continues through faith in the sanctifying blood of Christ and evidences itself by loving obedience to God's revealed will.

Genesis 17:1; Deuteronomy 30:6; Psalm 130:8; Isaiah 6:1-6; Ezekiel 36:25-29; Matthew 5:8, 48; Luke 1:74-75; 3:16-17; 24:49; John 17:1-26; Acts 1:4-5, 8; 2:1-4; 15:8-9; 26:18; Romans 8:3-4; 1 Corinthians 1:2; 6:11; 2 Corinthians 7:1; Ephesians 4:13, 24; 5:25-27; 1 Thessalonians 3:10, 12-13; 4:3, 7-8; 5:23-24; 2 Thessalonians 2:13; Titus 2:11-14; Hebrews 10:14; 12:14; 13:12; James 3:17-18; 4:8; 1 Peter 1:2; 2 Peter 1:4; 1 John 1:7, 9; 3:8-9; 4:17-18; Jude 24.

Some of the Ways in Which Christians Disagree about Sanctification

Rev. Terry G. Cornett

I. Two key questions

A. The First Question: Can a person be entirely sanctified (completely free from sin), in this present life?

1. Reformed/Baptistic and some Pentecostal theologies say NO.

2. Holiness and some Pentecostal theologies say YES.

B. The Second Question: Does the experience of sanctification include a second distinct experience with God, received by grace through faith?

What you believe about the first question tends to influence what you believe about the second.

1. If you believe that complete holiness must wait for the transforming event of death or Christ's return, you hope to grow in holiness but there is no distinct point in this life where it can be achieved.

2. If you believe that complete holiness is attainable, you know it must come through a transforming event (you can't work your way into holiness). So holiness and Pentecostal-holiness groups say there is a distinct second experience.

II. Traditional Reformation teaching

A. Sanctification is begun at salvation and continues progressively until glorification. God completely sanctifies us positionally at the moment of salvation, but practical sanctification is worked out in our experience gradually and daily.

B. Sin is primarily defined as "falling short of God's glory."

C. Arguments in favor:

1. Jesus taught us to pray daily, "Forgive us our trespasses" (Matthew 6:12) and added "But if you do not forgive others their trespasses, neither will your Father forgive your trespasses" (Matthew 6:15).

2. The Corinthian church was identified by Paul as "sanctified by Christ Jesus and called to be holy" but in practice was anything but. Paul had to say in 1 Corinthians 3:3, "For you are still of the flesh. For while there is jealousy and strife among you, are you not of the flesh and behaving only in a human way?" Paul understood the difference between being sanctified in God's sight but not yet sanctified in practice.

   a. Experience teaches us that:

      (1) We sin.

      (2) People who claim perfection tend to become legalistic, condemning, boastful, and tend to deny sin when it occurs.

   b. Romans 7 – This passage is understood as describing Paul's experience following conversion.

   c. Complete sinless perfection is not attainable in this life. When the word "Perfect" occurs in Scripture it is understood as "complete" or "mature." Glorification is when sinlessness is achieved. Sanctification is the movement toward holiness that draws on the resources given at salvation.

   d. Most important historical proponent: Martin Luther

      Luther spoke about Christians as "*simul justus et peccator*"- at one and the same time a righteous man and a sinner. He believed that this paradox will not find resolution until faith become sight. Lutheranism in no way condones sin. Rather it recognizes "that where sin abounded, grace did much more abound."

III. Holiness movements

A. Sanctification is a second and distinct experience from salvation. Like salvation it is received by grace through faith and is frequently spoken of as "the Baptism in the Holy Spirit."

Entire Sanctification more commonly designated as "sanctification," "holiness," "Christian perfection," or "perfect love," represents that second definite stage in Christian experience wherein, by the baptism with the Holy Spirit, administered by Jesus Christ, and

received instantaneously by faith, the justified believer is delivered from inbred sin, and consequently is saved from all unholy tempers, cleansed from all moral defilement, made perfect in love and introduced into full and abiding fellowship with God.

– Doctrinal Statement of The First General Holiness Assembly held in Chicago, May, 1885
[Robert M. Anderson, *Vision of the Disinherited*]

B. Sin is primarily defined as "knowing, willful disobedience."

1. The concept of Christian Perfection [entire sanctification] is carefully defined.

    Perfection is not: perfect knowledge (ignorance remains), not freedom from mistakes, not free from weakness or character flaws, not free from temptation, not free from the need to grow, [See John Wesley, *On Christian Perfection*] It is not, a loss of the ability to sin. There is no point, short of glorification, where people could not fall.

    Perfection is: Walking in love by faith so that one does not sin willfully and habitually.

2. There is still a process of sanctification that follows the event of sanctification.

    I believe this perfection is always wrought in the soul by a simple act of faith; consequently in an instant. But I believe [in] a gradual work, both preceding and following that instant. As to the time, I believe this instant generally is the instant of death, the moment before the soul leaves the body. But I believe it may be ten, twenty, or forty years before. I believe it is usually many years after justification.

    – Brief Thoughts on Christian Perfection. *The Works of John Wesley*. Vol. 11, p. 466.

    Some holiness groups disagree with Wesley about timing. They believe entire sanctification can, and should, come more quickly.

C. Arguments for:

1. It is commanded by Jesus and the Apostles

    Matthew 5:48 – "Therefore you are to be perfect, as your heavenly Father is perfect." Compare with Apostle's injunction (1 John 5:3 – This is love for God: to obey his commands. And his commands are not burdensome).

2. It is the logical implication of what happens when an all-powerful God sets his Spirit to work against sin in our lives.

3. It seems to be frequently assumed by Scripture to be what happens in the life of the believer.

4. Romans 7 – This passage is understood as describing Paul's experience before conversion.

D. Most important historical proponent: John Wesley (who learned from the Puritan writer William Law)

E. Key Document: "A Plain Account of Christian Perfection."

Wesley's key concern was to avoid conceding the possibility of perfection because he felt it impugned God's nature and power. (Don't say that God cannot or will not do what he clearly desires). It is an issue of faith for Wesley. Even if he had never seen this happen he would still believe in God's ability to accomplish his desire for our holiness.

IV. Putting it together: theological common ground and key implications

What Reformed and Holiness Christians agree on:

A. Sanctification is becoming like Christ and is the aim of the Christian life. [Scripture teaches us that this [holiness] is the goal of our calling- John Calvin, "Institutes of the Christian Religion].

B. Sanctification begins at the moment of salvation and faith is its sole condition (Doctrinal Minutes of the Methodist Conferences 1744-47).

C. Sanctification is both imputed and imparted and comes only by the grace of God.

D. Sanctification involves both a unique point of decision[1] and an on-going process of living out that decision.

---

1 For Reformed theology this point is conversion; for Holiness theologies it is conversion and a second experience of grace with the Holy Spirit.

General Christian Ministry

The Hump
Rev. Dr. Don L. Davis • 1 Timothy 4:9-16; Hebrews 5:11-14

The Baby Christian
The New Believer and the Spiritual Disciplines

Awkwardness

Unskillfulness

Mistakes

Roughness

Sporadic Behavior

Uncomfortableness

Inefficiency

Novice-Level Performance

Heart Desire
A Clear Goal
Feasible Plan
Solid Support
Correct Knowledge
Faithful Effort
Good Examples
Extended Period of Time
Longsuffering

Regular, correct application of the spiritual disciplines

The Mature Christian
The Mature Believer and the Spiritual Disciplines

Faithful Application

Gracefulness

Automatic Response

Comfortableness

Personal Satisfaction

Excellence

Expertise

Training Others

Fit to Represent: Multiplying Disciples of the Kingdom of God

Rev. Dr. Don L. Davis • Luke 10:16 (ESV) – *The one who hears you hears me, and the one who rejects you rejects me, and the one who rejects me rejects him who sent me.*

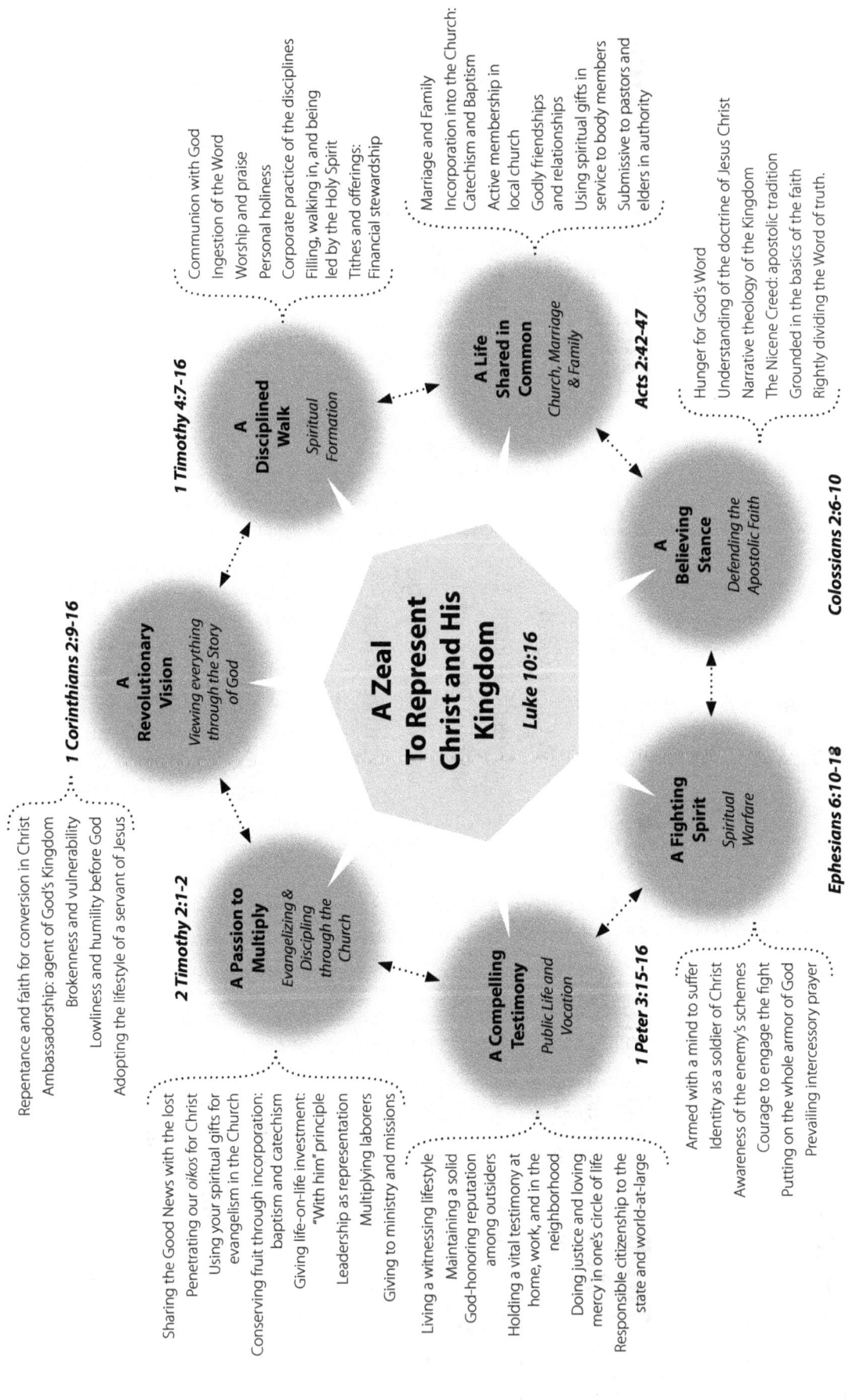

Our Declaration of Dependence: Freedom in Christ

Rev. Dr. Don L. Davis, January 11, 2003

It is important to teach morality within the realm of freedom (i.e., Galatians 5:1, "It is for freedom Christ has set you free"), and always in the context of using your freedom in the framework of bringing God glory and advancing Christ's Kingdom. I emphasize the "6-8-10" principles of 1 Corinthians, and apply them to all moral issues.

1. 1 Corinthians 6:9-11, Christianity is about transformation in Christ; no amount of excuses will get a person into the Kingdom.

2. 1 Corinthians 6:12a, We are free in Christ, but not everything one does is edifying or helpful.

3. 1 Corinthians 6:12b, We are free in Christ, but anything that is addictive and exercising control over you is counter to Christ and his Kingdom.

4. 1 Corinthians 8:7-13, We are free in Christ, but we ought never to flaunt our freedom, especially in the face of Christians whose conscience would be marred and who would stumble if they saw us doing something they found offensive.

5. 1 Corinthians 10:23, We are free in Christ; all things are lawful for us, but neither is everything helpful, nor does doing everything build oneself up.

6. 1 Corinthians 10:24, We are free in Christ, and ought to use our freedom to love our brothers and sisters in Christ, and nurture them for other's well being (cf. Gal. 5.13).

7. 1 Corinthians 10:31, We are free in Christ, and are given that freedom in order that we might glorify God in all that we do, whether we eat or drink, or anything else.

8. 1 Corinthians 10:32-33, We are free in Christ, and ought to use our freedom in order to do what we can to give no offense to people in the world or the Church, but do what we do in order to influence them to know and love Christ, i.e., that they might be saved.

This focus on freedom, in my mind, places all things that we say to adults or teens in context. Often, the way in which many new Christians are discipled is through a rigorous taxonomy (listing) of different vices and moral ills, and this can at times give them the sense that Christianity is an anti-act religion (a religion of simply not doing things), and/or a faith overly concerned with not sinning. Actually, the moral focus in Christianity is on freedom, a freedom won at a high price, a freedom to love God and advance the Kingdom, a freedom to live a surrendered life before the Lord. The moral responsibility of urban Christians is to live free in Jesus Christ, to live free unto God's glory, and to not use their freedom from the law as a license for sin.

The core of the teaching, then, is to focus on the freedom won for us through Christ's death and resurrection, and our union with him. We are now set free from the law, the principle of sin and death, the condemnation and guilt of our own sin, and the conviction of the law on us. We serve God now out of gratitude and thankfulness, and the moral impulse is living free in Christ. Yet, we do not use our freedom to be wiseguys or knuckle-heads, but to glorify God and love others. This is the context in which we address the thorny issues of homosexuality, abortion, and other social ills. Those who engage in such acts feign freedom, but, lacking a knowledge of God in Christ, they are merely following their own internal predispositions, which are not informed either by God's moral will or his love.

Freedom in Christ is a banner call to live holy and joyously as urban disciples. This freedom will enable them to see how creative they can be as Christians in the midst of so-called "free" living which only leads to bondage, shame, and remorse.

Thirty-Three Blessings in Christ
Rev. Dr. Don L. Davis

Did you know that 33 things happened to you at the moment you became a believer in Jesus Christ? Lewis Sperry Chafer, the first president of Dallas Theological Seminary, listed these benefits of salvation in his *Systematic Theology, Volume III* (pp. 234-266). These points, along with brief explanations, give the born-again Christian a better understanding of the work of grace accomplished in his/her life as well as a greater appreciation of his/her new life.

1. In the eternal plan of God, the believer is:

    a. *Foreknown* – Acts 2:23; 1 Peter 1:2, 20. God knew from all eternity every step in the entire program of the universe.

    b. *Predestined* – Romans 8:29-30. A believer's destiny has been appointed through foreknowledge to the unending realization of all God's riches of grace.

    c. *Elected* – Romans 8:38; Colossians 3:12. He/she is chosen of God in the present age and will manifest the grace of God in future ages.

    d. *Chosen* – Ephesians 1:4. God has separated unto himself his elect who are both foreknown and predestined.

    e. *Called* – 1 Thessalonians 6:24. God invites man to enjoy the benefits of his redemptive purposes. This term may include those whom God has selected for salvation, but who are still in their unregenerate state.

2. A believer has been *redeemed* – Romans 3:24. The price required to set him/her free from sin has been paid.

3. A believer has been *reconciled* – 2 Corinthians 6:18, 19; Romans 5:10. He/she is both restored to fellowship by God and restored to fellowship with God.

4. A believer is related to God through *propitiation* – Romans 3:24-26. He/she has been set free from judgment by God's satisfaction with his Son's death for sinners.

5. A believer has been *forgiven* all trespasses – Ephesians 1:7. All his/her sins are taken care of – past, present, and future.

6. A believer is vitally *conjoined to Christ* for the judgment of the old man "unto a new walk" – Romans 6:1-10. He/she is brought into a union with Christ.

7. A believer is *"free from the law"* – Romans 7:2-6. He/she is both dead to its condemnation, and delivered from its jurisdiction.

8. A believer has been made a *child of God* – Galatians 3:26. He/she is born anew by the regenerating power of the Holy Spirit into a relationship in which God the First Person becomes a legitimate Father and the saved one becomes a legitimate child with every right and title – an heir of God and a joint heir with Jesus Christ.

9. A believer has been *adopted as an adult child* into the Father's household – Romans 8:15, 23.

10. A believer has been *made acceptable to God* by Jesus Christ – Ephesians 1:6. He/she is made *righteous* (Romans 3:22), *sanctified* (set apart) positionally (1 Corinthians 1:30, 6:11); *perfected forever in his/her standing and position* (Hebrews 10:14), and *made acceptable in the Beloved* (Colossians 1:12).

11. A believer has been *justified* – Romans 5:1. He/she has been declared righteous by God's decree.

12. A believer is *"made right"* – Ephesians 2:13. A close relation is set up and exists between God and the believer.

13. A believer has been *delivered from the power of darkness* – Colossians 1:13; 2:13. A Christian has been delivered from Satan and his evil spirits. Yet the disciple must continue to wage warfare against these powers.

14. A believer has been *translated into the Kingdom of God* – Colossians 1:13. The Christian has been transferred from Satan's kingdom to Christ's Kingdom.

15. A believer is *planted* on the Rock, Jesus Christ – 1 Corinthians 3:9-15. Christ is the foundation on which the believer stands and on which he/she builds his/her Christian life.

16. A believer is a *gift from God to Jesus Christ* – John 17:6, 11, 12, 20. He/she is the Father's love gift to Jesus Christ.

17. A believer is *circumcised in Christ* – Colossians 2:11. He/she has been delivered from the power of the old sin nature.

18. A believer has been made a *partaker of the Holy and Royal Priesthood* – 1 Peter 2:5, 9. He/she is a priest because of his/her relation to Christ, the High Priest, and will reign on earth with Christ.

19. A believer is part of a *chosen generation, a holy nation and a peculiar people* – 1 Peter 2:9. This is the company of believers in this age.

20. A believer is a *heavenly citizen* – Philippians 3:20. Therefore he/she is called a stranger as far as his/her life on earth is concerned (1 Peter 2:13), and will enjoy his/her true home in heaven forever.

21. A believer is in *the family and household of God* – Ephesians 2:1, 9. He/she is part of God's "family" which is composed only of true believers.

22. A believer is in *the fellowship of the saints* – John 17:11, 21-23. He/she can be a part of the fellowship of believers with one another.

23. A believer is in *a heavenly association* – Colossians 1:27; 3:1; 2 Corinthians 6:1; Colossians 1:24; John 14:12-14; Ephesians 5:25-27; Titus 2:13. He/she is a partner with Christ now in life, position, service, suffering, prayer, betrothal as a bride to Christ, and expectation of the coming again of Christ.

24. A believer has *access to God* – Ephesians 2:18. He/she has access to God's grace which enables him/her to grow spiritually, and he/she has unhindered approach to the Father (Hebrews 4:16).

25. A believer is within *the "much more" care of God* – Romans 5:8-10. He/she is an object of God's love (John 3:16), God's grace (Ephesians 2:7-9), God's power (Ephesians 1:19), God's faithfulness (Philippians 1:6), God's peace (Romans 5:1), God's consolation (2 Thessalonians 2:16-17), and God's intercession (Romans 8:26).

26. A believer is *God's inheritance* – Ephesians 1:18. He/she is given to Christ as a gift from the Father.

27. A believer *has the inheritance of God himself* and all that God bestows – 1 Peter 1:4.

28. A believer has *light in the Lord* – 2 Corinthians 4:6. He/she not only has this light, but is commanded to walk in the light.

29. A believer is *vitally united to the Father, the Son and the Holy Spirit* – 1 Thessalonians 1:1; Ephesians 4:6; Romans 8:1; John 14:20; Romans 8>9; 1 Corinthians 2:12.

30. A believer is blessed with *the earnest or firstfruits of the Spirit* – Ephesians 1:14; 8:23. He/she is born of the Spirit (John 3:6), and baptized by the Spirit (1 Corinthians 12:13), which is a work of the Holy Spirit by which the believer is joined to Christ's body and comes to be "in Christ," and therefore is a partaker of all that Christ is. The disciple is also indwelt by the Spirit (Romans 8:9), sealed by the Spirit (2 Corinthians 1:22), making him/her eternally secure, and filled with the Spirit (Ephesians 5:18) whose ministry releases his power and effectiveness in the heart in which he dwells.

31. A believer is *glorified* – Romans 8:18. He/she will be a partaker of the infinite story of the Godhead.

32. A believer is *complete in God* – Colossians 2:9, 10. He/she partakes of all that Christ is.

33. A believer *possesses every spiritual blessing* – Ephesians 1:3. All the riches tabulated in the other 32 points made before are to be included in this sweeping term, "all spiritual blessings."

Come Thou Fount of every blessing
Tune my heart to sing Thy grace;
Streams of mercy, never ceasing,
Call for songs of loudest praise
Teach me some melodious sonnet,
Sung be flaming tongues above.
Praise the mount! I'm fixed upon it,
Mount of God's unchanging love.

Here I raise my Ebenezer;
Hither by Thy help I'm come;
And I hope, by Thy good pleasure,
Safely to arrive at home.
Jesus sought me when a stranger,
Wandering from the field of God;
He, to rescue me from danger,
Interposed His precious blood.

O to grace how great a debtor
Daily I'm constrained to be!
Let that grace now like a fetter,
Bind my wandering heart to Thee.
Prone to wander, Lord, I feel it,
Prone to leave the God I love;
Here's my heart, O take and seal it,
Seal it for Thy courts above.

Come Thou Fount of Every Blessing
Robert Robinson, 1757

Substitute Centers to a Christ-Centered Vision: Goods and Effects Which Our Culture Substitutes as the Ultimate Concern

Rev. Dr. Don L. Davis

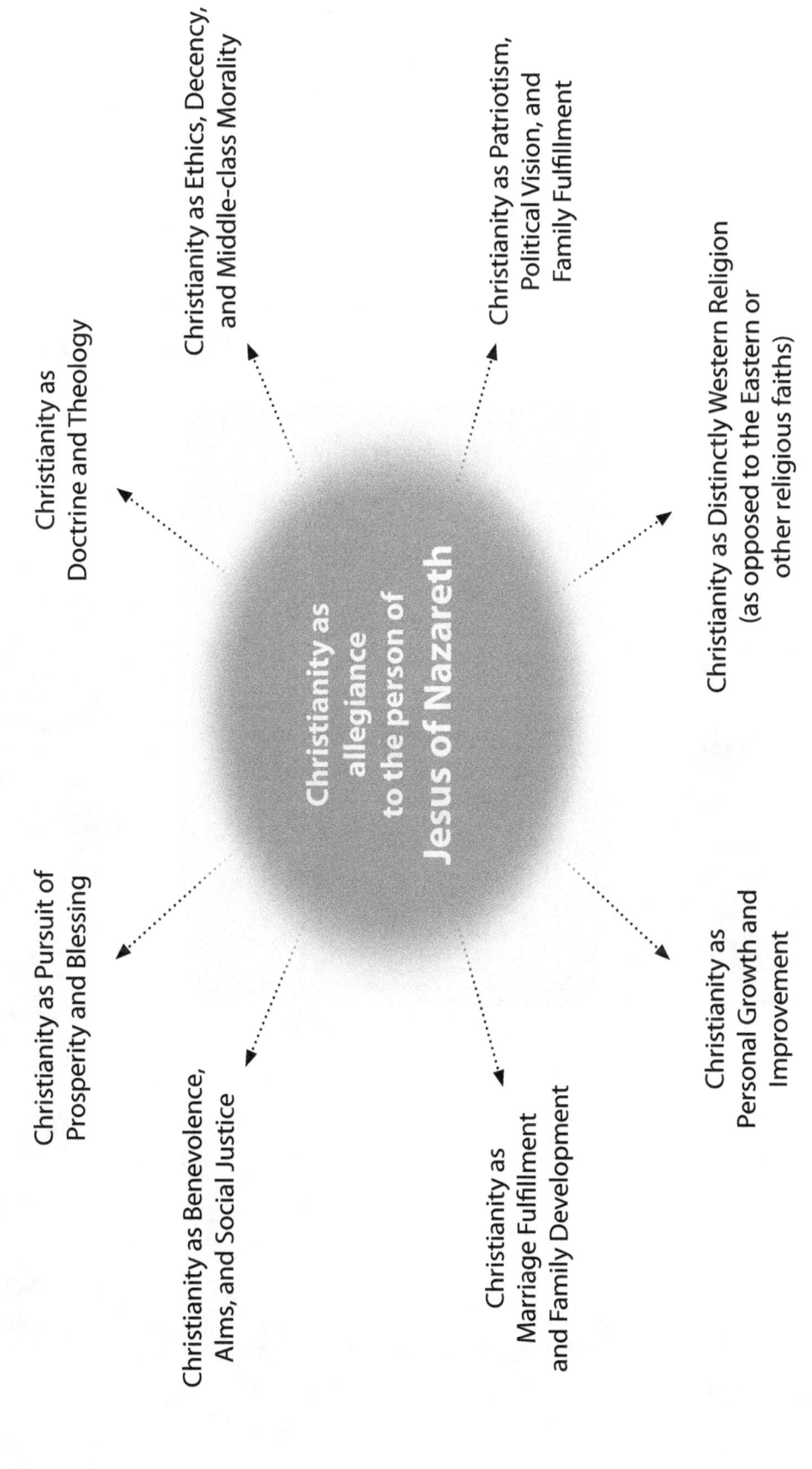

Theology of the Church

The Lord's Supper: Four Views

Rev. Terry G. Cornett

	Transubstantiation	Consubstantiation	Reformed	Memorialist
Groups	Roman Catholic	Lutheran	Presbyterian and other Reformed Churches, Episcopalians	Baptists, Mennonites, Pentecostals
Key Person	Thomas Aquinas	Martin Luther	John Calvin	Ulrich Zwingli
Presence of Christ	After being consecrated by the priest, the bread changes into Christ's body and the wine changes into Christ's blood so that Christ is present in the elements themselves	The elements do not change but Christ is actually present in, with, and under the elements of bread and wine	Christ is not literally present in the elements since Christ's body is in heaven. Christ is spiritually present and at work in the partaking of the elements through the Holy Spirit when received in faith.	Christ is not present in the elements either literally or spiritually.
What Takes Place	Spiritual food is given to the soul which strengthens the participant spiritually and cleanses them from venial sins, Christ's sacrifice on the cross is made present anew at each mass.	Sins are forgiven and the new covenant promises are reconfirmed. Unless the elements are received in faith, the sacrament has no benefit.	As the elements are received in faith, the partaker receives spiritual nourishment which strengthens the soul, is brought close to the presence of Christ and has a renewed experience of God's grace.	Christ's command is obeyed and Christ's death is commemorated so that the partaker is reminded of the benefits of salvation accomplished by his sacrificial death. Love for God is renewed through the remembering of his love for us.
Key Verses	John 6:53-58 Matthew 26:26 1 Corinthians 10:16	Matthew 26:26 1 Corinthians 10:16	John 6:63; 16:7 Colossians 3:1	Luke 22:19 1 Corinthians 11:24-25
Term Used	Sacrament	Sacrament	Sacrament	Ordinance
Who Presides	Priest	Ordained Minister	Church Leaders (Clergy or Laity)	Church Leaders (Clergy or Laity)

Perception and Truth

Rev. Dr. Don L. Davis

Levels of Perception

What is really happening
What is apparent
What you see
What others see
What the enemy sees
What the enemy wants you to think about what you see
What God sees
What God wants you to know about what you see

The Present Situation
What's going on here?
What does this mean?

① The So-Called "Facts" of the Matter
What is apparent to all of us
What we're going through
Our initial reactions and categories

② The Common Prognosis
What usually happens
What we can expect
What is feels like

③ Opinions of Key People
- Leaders
- Experts
- Friends and Family
- Significant Others

④ Your Current Spiritual, Experiential, and Psychological Predisposition ("Habits of the Heart")
State of unawareness
Distraction and preoccupation
Proneness to doubt

Keen spiritual awareness
Spiritually alert
Sober and ready to fight

⑤ The Lying Persuasion of the Enemy ("Dirty Fighter")
Awareness of deep inadequacy
Fear of vulnerability
Impossibility of change
Certainty of chronic bondage
Prospect of failure

⑥ The Testimony of the Divine Promise
Certainty of God's supply
Assurance of safety
Possibility of radical transformation
Power of Divine deliverance
Affirmation of victory

Paul's Partnership Theology:
Our Union with Christ and Partnership in Kingdom Ministry

Adapted from Brian J. Dodd. *Empowered Church Leadership.* Downers Grove: InterVarsity Press, 2003.

The apostolic fondness for Greek terms compounded with the prefix syn (with or co-)

English Translation of the Greek Term	Scripture References
Co-worker (*Synergos*)	Romans 16:3, 7, 9, 21; 2 Corinthians 8:23; Philippians 2:25; 4:3; Colossians 4:7, 10, 11, 14; Philemon 1, 24
Co-prisoner (*Synaichmalotos*)	Colossians 4:10; Philemon 23
Co-slave (*Syndoulous*)	Colossians 1:7; 4:7
Co-soldier (*Systratiotes*)	Philippians 2:25; Philemon 2
Co-laborer (*Synathleo*)	Philippians 4:2-3

Six Kinds of New Testament Ministry for Community

Rev. Dr. Don L. Davis

Type	Greek	Text	Task
Proclamation	*evanggelion*	Romans 1:15-17	Preaching the Good News
Teaching	*didasko*	Matthew 28:19	To make disciples of Jesus
Worship	*latreuo*	John 4:20-24	Ushering into God's presence
Fellowship	*agape*	Romans 13:8-10	The communion of saints
Witness	*martyria*	Acts 1:8	Compelling testimony to the lost
Service	*diakonia*	Matthew 10:43-45	Caring for the needs of others

The Role of Women in Ministry

Rev. Dr. Don L. Davis

While it is plain that God has established a clearly designed order of responsibility within the home, it is equally clear that women are called and gifted by God, led by his own Spirit to bear fruit worthy of their calling in Christ. Throughout the New Testament, commands are directed specifically to women to submit, with the particular Greek verb *hupotasso*, occurring frequently which means "to place under" or "to submit" (cf. 1 Timothy 2:11). The word also translated into our English word "subjection" is from the same root. In such contexts these Greek renderings ought not to be understood in any way except as positive admonitions towards God's designed framework for the home, where women are charged to learn quietly and submissively, trusting and working within the Lord's own plan.

This ordering of the woman's submission in the home, however, must not be misinterpreted to mean that women are disallowed from ministering their gifts under the Spirit's direction. Indeed, it is the Holy Spirit through Christ's gracious endowment who assigns the gifts as he wills, for the edification of the Church (1 Corinthians 12:1-27; Ephesians 4:1-16). The gifts are not given to believers on the criteria of gender; in other words, there is no indication from the Scriptures that some gifts are for men only, and the others reserved for women. On the contrary, Paul affirms that Christ provided gifts as a direct result of his own personal victory over the devil and his minions (cf. Ephesians 4:6ff.). This was his own personal choice, given by his Spirit to whomever he wills (cf. 1 Corinthians 12:1-11). In affirming the ministry of women we affirm the right of the Spirit to be creative in all saints for the well-being of all and the expansion of his Kingdom, as he sees fit, and not necessarily as we determine (Romans 12:4-8; 1 Peter 4:10-11).

Furthermore, a careful study of the Scriptures as a whole indicates that God's ordering of the home in no way undermines his intention for men and women to serve Christ as disciples and laborers together, under Christ's leading. The clear New Testament teaching of Christ as head of the man, and the man of the woman (see 1 Corinthians 11:4) shows God's esteem for godly spiritual representation within the home. The apparent forbidding of women to hold teaching/ruling positions appears to be an admonition to protect God's assigned lines of responsibility and authority within the home. For instance, the particular Greek term in the highly debated passage in 1 Timothy 2:12, *andros*, which has often times been translated "man," may also be translated "husband." With such a translation, then, the teaching would be that a wife ought not to rule over her husband.

This doctrine of a woman who, in choosing to marry, makes herself voluntarily submissive to "line up under" her husband is entirely consistent with the gist of the New Testament teaching on the role of authority in the Christian home. The Greek word *hupotasso*, which means to "line up under" refers to a wife's voluntary submission to her own husband (cf. Ephesians 5:22-23; Colossians 3:18; Titus 2:5; 1 Peter 3:1). This has nothing to do with any supposed superior status or capacity of the husband; rather, this refers to God's design of godly headship, authority which is given for comfort, protection, and care, not for destruction or domination (cf. Genesis 2:15-17; 3:16; 1 Corinthians 11:3). Indeed, that this headship is interpreted in light of Christ's headship over the Church signifies the kind of godly headship that must be given, that sense of tireless care, service, and protection required from godly leadership.

Of course, such an admonition for a wife to submit to a husband would not in any way rule out that women be involved in a teaching ministry (e.g., Titus 2:4), but, rather, that in the particular case of married women, that their own ministries would come under the protection and direction of their respective husbands (Acts 18:26). This would assert that a married woman's ministry in the Church would be given serving, protective oversight by her husband, not due to any notion of inferior capacity or defective spirituality, but for the sake of, as one commentator has put it, "avoiding confusion and maintaining orderliness" (cf. 1 Corinthians 14:40).

In both Corinth and Ephesus (which represent the contested Corinthian and Timothy epistolary comments), it appears that Paul's restriction upon women's participation was prompted by occasional happenings, issues which grew particularly out of these contexts, and therefore are meant to be understood in those lights. For instance, the hotly-contested test of a women's "silence" in the church (see both 1 Corinthians 14 and 1 Timothy 2) does not appear in any way to undermine the prominent role women played in the expansion of the Kingdom and development of the Church in the first century. Women were involved in the ministries of prophecy and prayer (1 Corinthians 11:5), personal instruction (Acts 18:26), teaching (Titus 2:4-5), giving testimony (John 4:28-29), offering hospitality (Acts 12:12), and serving as co-laborers with the apostles in the cause of the Gospel (Philippians 4:2-3). Paul did not relegate women to an inferior role or hidden status but served side-by-side with women for the sake of Christ "I urge Euodia and I urge Syntyche to live in harmony in the Lord. Indeed, true companion, I ask you also to help these women who have shared my struggle in the *cause* of the Gospel, together with Clement also and the rest of my fellow workers, whose names are in the book of life" (Philippians 4:2-3).

Furthermore, we must be careful in subordinating the personage of women *per se* (that is, their nature as women) versus their subordinated role in the marriage relationship. Notwithstanding the clear description of the role of women as heirs together of the grace of life in the marriage relationship (1 Peter 3:7), it is equally plain that the Kingdom of God has created a dramatic shift in how women are to be viewed, understood, and embraced in the kingdom community. It is plain that in Christ there is now no difference between rich and poor, Jew and Gentile, barbarian, Scythian, bondman and freemen, as well as man and woman (cf. Galatians 3:28; Colossians 3:11). Women were allowed to be disciples of a Rabbi (which was foreign and disallowed at the time of Jesus), and played prominent roles in the New Testament church, including being fellow laborers side by side with the apostles in ministry (e.g., see Euodia and Syntyche in Philippians 4:1ff.), as well as hosting a church in their houses (cf. Phoebe in Romans 16:1-2, and Apphia in Philemon 1).

In regards to the issue of pastoral authority, I am convinced that Paul's understanding of the role of equippers (of which the pastor-teacher is one such role, cf. Ephesians 4:9-15) is not gender specific. In other words, the decisive and seminal text for me on the operation of gifts and the status and function of offices are those New Testament texts which deal with the gifts (1 Corinthians 12:1-27; Romans 12:4-8; 1 Peter 4:10-11, and Ephesians 4:9-15). There is no indication in any of these formative texts that gifts are gender-specific. In other words, for the argument to hold decisively that women were never to be in roles that were pastoral or equipping in nature, the simplest and most effective argument would be to show that the Spirit simply would never even consider giving a woman a gift which was not suited to the range of callings which she felt a calling towards. Women would be forbidden from leadership because the Holy Spirit would never grant to a woman a calling and its requisite gifts because she was a woman. Some gifts would be reserved for men, and women would never receive those gifts.

A careful reading of these and other related texts show no such prohibition. It appears that it is up to the Holy Spirit to give any person, man or woman, any gift that suits him for any ministry he wishes them to do, as he wills (1 Corinthians 12:11 "But one and the same Spirit works all these things, distributing to each one individually as he wills"). Building upon this point, Terry Cornett has even written a fine theological essay showing how the New Testament Greek for the word "apostle" is unequivocally applied to women, most clearly shown in the rendering of the female noun, "Junia" applied to "apostle" in Romans 16:7, as well as allusions to co-laboring, for instance, with the twins, Tryphena and Tryphosa, who "labored" with Paul in the Lord (16:12).

Believing that every God-called, Christ-endowed, and Spirit-gifted and led Christian ought to fulfill their role in the body, we affirm the role of women to lead and instruct under godly authority that submits to the Holy Spirit, the Word of God, and is informed by the tradition of the Church and spiritual reasoning. We ought to expect God to give women supernatural endowments of grace to carry out his bidding on behalf of his Church, and his reign in the Kingdom of God. Since men and women both reflect the *Imago Dei* (i.e., image of God), and both stand as heirs together of God's grace (cf. Genesis 1:27; 5:2; Matthew 19:4; Galatians 3:28; 1 Peter 3:7), they are given the high privilege of representing Christ together as his ambassadors (2 Corinthians 5:20), and through their partnership to bring to completion our obedience to Christ's Great Commission of making disciples of all nations (Matthew 28:18-20).

A Theology of the Church

Rev. Dr. Don L. Davis and Rev. Terry G. Cornett ©1996 World Impact Press

The Church Is an Apostolic Community Where the Word Is Rightly Preached

I. **A community of calling**

   A. The essential meaning of Church is Ekklesia: those who have been *"called out"* in order to be *"called to"* a New Community.

   1. Like the Thessalonians, the Church is called out from idolatry to serve the living God and called to wait for his Son from heaven.

   2. The Church is called out in order that it may belong to Christ (Romans 1:6). Jesus speaks of the Church as "my *ekklesia*" that is the "called out ones" who are his unique possession (Matthew 16:18; Galatians 5:24; James 2:7).

   3. The components of God's call:

      a. The foundation is God's desire to save (John 3:16; 1 Timothy 2:4).

      b. The message is the good news of the Kingdom (Matthew 24:14).

      c. The recipients are "whosoever will" (John 3:15).

      d. The method is through faith in the shed blood of Christ and acknowledgment of his lordship (Romans 3:25; 10:9-10; Ephesians 2:8).

      e. The result is regeneration and placement into the body of Christ (2 Corinthians 5:17; Romans 12:4-5; Ephesians 3:6; 5:30).

   B. The Church is called out.

   1. Called out of the world:

      a. The world is under Satan's dominion and stands in opposition to God.

      b. Conversion and incorporation in Christ's Church involves repentance (*metanoia*) and a transfer of kingdom allegiances.

c. The Church exists as strangers and aliens who are "in" but not "of" this world system.

2. Called out from sin:

   a. Those in the Church are being sanctified, set apart for holy action, so that they may live out their calling as saints of God (1 Corinthians 1:2; 2 Timothy 1:9; 1 Peter 1:15).

   b. The Church must be available for God's purpose and use (Romans 8:28-29; Ephesians 1:11; Romans 6:13).

   c. The Church must bring glory to God alone (Isaiah 42:8; John 13:31-32; 17:1; Romans 15:6; 1 Peter 2:12).

   d. The Church must now be characterized by obedience to God (2 Thessalonians 1:8; Hebrews 5:8-9; 1 John 2:3).

C. The Church is called to:

1. Salvation and new life

   a. Forgiveness and cleansing from sin (Ephesians 1:7; 5:26; 1 John 1:9).

   b. Justification (Romans 3:24; 8:30; Titus 3:7) in which God pronounces us guiltless as to the penalty of his divine law.

   c. Regeneration (John 3:5-8; Colossians 3:9-10) by which a "new self" is birthed in us through the Spirit.

   d. Sanctification (John 17:19; 1 Corinthians 1:2) in which we are "set apart" by God for holiness of life.

   e. Glorification and Life Eternal (Romans 8:30; 1 Timothy 6:12; 2 Thessalonians 2:14) in which we are changed to be like Christ and prepared to live forever in the presence of God (Romans 8:23; 1 Corinthians 15:51-53; 1 John 3:2).

2. Participation in a new community of God's chosen people (1 Peter 2:9-10)

   a. Members of Christ's body (1 Corinthians 10:16-17; 12:27).

   b. Sheep of God's flock under one Shepherd (John 10; Hebrews 13:20; 1 Peter 5:2-4).

   c. Members of God's family and household (Galatians 6:10; 1 Timothy 3:15).

d. Children of Abraham and recipients of covenant promise (Romans 4:16; Galatians 3:29; Ephesians 2:12).

   e. Citizens of the New Jerusalem (Philippians 3:20; Revelation 3:12).

   f. The firstfruits of the Kingdom of God (Luke 12:32; James 1:18).

3. Freedom (Galatians 5:1, 13)

   a. Called out of the dominion of darkness which suppresses freedom (Colossians 1:13-14).

   b. Called away from sin which enslaves (John 8:34-36).

   c. Called to God the Father who is the Liberator of his people (Exodus 6:6).

   d. Called to God the Son who gives the truth which sets free (John 8:31-36).

   e. Called to God the Spirit whose presence creates liberty (2 Corinthians 3:17).

II. A community of faith

A. The Church is a community of faith, which has, by faith, confessed Jesus as Lord and Savior.

Faith refers both to the content of our belief and to the act of believing itself. Jesus is the object (content) of our faith and his life is received through faith (our belief) in him and his word. In both of these senses, the Church is a community of faith.

1. The Church places its faith:

   a. in the Living Word (Jesus the Messiah),

   b. who is revealed in the written Word (Sacred Scripture),

   c. and who is now present, teaching and applying his Word to the Church (through the ministry of the Holy Spirit).

2. The Church guards the deposit of faith, given by Christ and the apostles, through sound teaching and the help of the Holy Spirit who indwells its members (2 Timothy 1:13-14).

B. Because it is a community of faith, the Church is also a community of grace.

   1. The Church exists by grace-through faith rather than through human merit or works (Galatians 2:21; Ephesians 2:8).

   2. The Church announces, in faith, the grace of God to all humanity (Titus 2:11-15).

   3. The Church lives by grace in all actions and relationships (Ephesians 4:1-7).

C. The Church is a community where the Scriptures are preached, studied, meditated upon, memorized, believed, and obeyed (Ezekiel 7:10; Joshua 1:8; Psalm 119; Colossians 3:16; 1 Timothy 4:13; James 1:22-25).

   1. The Church preaches the Gospel of the Kingdom, as revealed in Scripture, and calls people to repentance and faith which leads to obedience (Matthew 4:17; 28:19-20; Acts 2:38-40).

   2. The Church studies and applies the Scriptures through teaching, rebuking, correcting, and training in righteousness so that all members of the community are equipped to live godly lives characterized by good works (2 Timothy 3:16-17; 4:2).

   3. The Church intentionally reflects on the Scriptures in light of reason, tradition, and experience, learning and doing theology as a means of more fully understanding and acting upon truth (Psalm 119:97-99; 1 Timothy 4:16; 2 Timothy 2:15).

   4. The Church functions as a listening community which is aware of the Spirit's presence and relies upon him to interpret and apply the Scriptures to the present moment (John 14:25-26).

D. The Church contends for the faith that was once for all entrusted to the saints (Jude 3).

III. A community of witness

A. The Church witnesses to the fact that in the incarnation, life, teaching, death and resurrection of Jesus the Christ, God's Kingdom has begun (Mark 1:15; Luke 4:43; 6:20; 11:20; Acts 1:3; 28:23; 1 Corinthians 4:20; Colossians 1:12-13).

   1. The Church proclaims Jesus as Christus Victor whose reign will:

a. Rescind the curse over creation and humankind (Revelation 22:3).

b. Defeat Satan and the powers and destroy their work (1 John 3:8).

c. Reverse the present order by defending and rewarding the meek, the humble, the despised, the lowly, the righteous, the hungry, and the rejected (Luke 1:46-55; 4:18-19; 6:20-22).

d. Propitiate God's righteous anger (Galatians 3:10-14; 1 John 2:1-2).

e. Create a new humanity (1 Corinthians 15:45-49; Ephesians 2:15; Revelation 5:9-10).

f. Destroy the last enemy: death (1 Corinthians 15:26).

2. Ultimately, the very Kingdom itself will be turned over to God the Father, and the freedom, wholeness, and justice of the Lord will abound throughout the universe (Isaiah 10:2-7; 11:1-9; 53:5; Micah 4:1-3; 6:8; Matthew 6:33; 23:23; Luke 4:18-19; John 8:34-36; 1 Corinthians 15:28; Revelation 21).

B. The Church witnesses by:

1. Functioning as a sign and foretaste of the Kingdom of God; the Church is a visible community where people see that:

a. Jesus is acknowledged as Lord (Romans 10:9-10).

b. The truth and power of the Gospel is growing and producing fruit among every kindred, tribe, and nation (Acts 2:47; Romans 1:16; Colossians 1:6; Revelation 7:9-10).

c. The values of God's Kingdom are accepted and acted upon (Matthew 6:33).

d. God's commands are obeyed on earth as they are in heaven (Matthew 6:10; John 14:23-24).

e. The presence of God is experienced (Matthew 18:20; John 14:16-21).

f. The power of God is demonstrated (1 Corinthians 4:20).

g. The love of God is freely received and given (Ephesians 5:1-2; 1 John 3:18; 4:7-8).

h. The compassion of God is expressed in bearing each other's burdens, first within the Church, and then, in sacrificial service to the whole world (Matthew 5:44-45; Galatians 6:2, 10; Hebrews 13:16).

i. The redemptiveness of God transcends human frailty and sin so that the treasure of the Kingdom is evident in spite of being contained in earthen vessels (2 Corinthians 4:7).

2. Performing signs and wonders which confirm the Gospel (Mark 16:20; Acts 4:30; 8:6, 13; 14:3; 15:12; Romans 15:18-19; Hebrews 2:4)

3. Accepting the call to mission

   a. Going into all the world to preach the Gospel (Matthew 24:14; 28:18-20; Acts 1:8; Colossians 1:6).

   b. Evangelizing and making disciples of Christ and his Kingdom (Matthew 28:18-20; 2 Timothy 2:2).

   c. Establishing churches among those unreached by the Gospel (Matthew 16:18; 28:19; Acts 2:41-42; 16:5; 2 Corinthians 11:28; Hebrews 12:22-23).

   d. Displaying the excellencies of Christ's Kingdom by engendering freedom, wholeness, and justice in his Name (Isaiah 53:5; Micah 6:8; Matthew 5:16; 12:18-20; Luke 4:18-19; John 8:34-36; 1 Peter 3:11).

4. Acting as a prophetic community

   a. Speaking the Word of God into situations of error, confusion, and sin (2 Corinthians 4:2; Hebrews 4:12; James 5:20; Titus 2:15).

   b. Speaking up for those who cannot speak up for themselves so that justice is defended (Proverbs 31:8-9).

   c. Announcing judgment against sin in all its forms (Romans 2:5; Galatians 6:7-8; 1 Peter 4:17).

   d. Announcing hope in situations where sin has produced despair (Jeremiah 32:17; 2 Thessalonians 2:16; Hebrews 10:22-23; 1 Peter 1:3-5).

      e. Proclaiming the return of Jesus, the urgency of the hour, and the reality that soon every knee will bow and every tongue confess that Jesus is Lord to the glory of God the Father (Matthew 25:1-13; Philippians 2:10-11; 2 Timothy 4:1; Titus 2:12-13).

The Church Is One Community
Where the Sacraments Are Rightly Administered

IV. A community of worship

  A. The Church recognizes that worship is the primary end of all creation.

    1. The worshiper adores, praises, and gives thanks to God for his character and actions, ascribing to him the worth and glory due his Person. This worship is directed to:

      a. The Father Almighty who is the Maker of all things visible and invisible.

      b. The Son who by his incarnation, death, and resurrection accomplished salvation and who is now glorified at the Father's right hand.

      c. The Spirit who is the Lord and Giver of Life.

    2. Worship is the primary purpose of the material heavens and earth, and all life therein (Psalms 148-150; Luke 19:37-40; Romans 11:36; Revelation 4:11; 15:3-4).

    3. Worship is the central activity of the angelic hosts who honor God in his presence (Isaiah 6; Revelation 5).

    4. Worship is the chief vocation of the "community of saints," all true Christians, living and dead, who seek to glorify God in all things (Psalm 29:2; Romans 12:1-2; 1 Corinthians 10:31; Colossians 3:17).

  B. The Church offers acceptable worship to God. This means:

    1. The worshipers have renounced all false gods or belief systems that lay claim to their allegiance and have covenanted to serve and worship the one true God (Exodus 34:14; 1 Thessalonians 1:9-10).

2. The worshipers worship:

    a. In Spirit – as regenerated people who, through saving faith in Jesus Christ, are filled with the Holy Spirit and under his direction.

    b. In Truth – understanding God as he is revealed in Scripture and worshiping in accordance with the teaching of the Word.

    c. In Holiness – Living lives that demonstrate their genuine commitment to serve the Living God.

C. The Church worships as a royal priesthood, wholeheartedly offering up sacrifices of praise to God and employing all its creative resources to worship him with excellence.

   1. The Christian Church is a people who worship, not a place of worship.

   2. The entire congregation ministers to the Lord, each one contributing a song, a word, a testimony, a prayer, etc. according to their gifts and capacities (1 Corinthians 14:26).

   3. The Church worships with the full range of human emotion, intellect, and creativity:

       a. Physical expression- raising of hands, dancing, kneeling, bowing, etc.

       b. Intellectual engagement- striving to understand God's nature and works.

       c. Artistic expression- through music and the other creative arts.

       d. Celebratory expression- the Church plays in the presence of God (Proverbs 8:30-31) experiencing "Sabbath rest" through festivals, celebrations, and praise.

   4. The Church worships liturgically by together reenacting the story of God and his people.

       a. The Church proclaims and embodies the drama of God's redemptive action in its ritual, tradition, and order of worship.

       b. The Church, like the covenant people Israel, orders its life around the celebration of the Lord's Supper and Baptism which reenact the story of God's salvation (Deuteronomy 16:3; Matthew 28:19; Romans 6:4; 1 Corinthians 11:23-26).

    c. The Church remembers the worship and service of saints through the ages, learning from their experiences with the Spirit of God (Deuteronomy 32:7; Psalms 77:10-12; 143:5; Isaiah 46:9; Hebrews 11).

5. The Church worships in freedom:

    a. Constantly experiencing new forms and expressions of worship which honor God and allow his people to delight in him afresh (Psalms 33:3; 40:3; 96:1; 149:1; Isaiah 42:9-10; Luke 5:38; Revelation 5:9).

    b. Being led by the Spirit so that its worship is responsive to God himself (2 Corinthians 3:6; Galatians 5:25; Philippians 3:3).

    c. Expressing the unchanging nature of God in forms that are conducive to the particular cultures and personalities of the worshipers (Acts 15).

6. The Church worships in right order, making sure that each act of worship edifies the body, and stands in accordance with the Word of God (1 Corinthians 14:12, 33, 40; Galatians 5:13-15, 22-25; Ephesians 4:29; Philippians 4:8).

D. The Church's worship leads to wholeness:

1. Health and blessing attend the worshiping community (Exodus 23:25; Psalm 147:1-3).

2. The community takes on the character of the One who is worshiped (Exodus 29:37; Psalm 27:4; Jeremiah 2:5; 10:8; Matthew 6:21; Colossians 3:1-4; 1 John 3:2).

V. A community of covenant

A. The Church is the gathering of those who participate in the New Covenant. This New Covenant:

1. Is mediated by Jesus Christ, the Great High Priest, and is purchased and sealed by his blood (Matthew 26:28; 1 Timothy 2:5; Hebrews 8:6; 4:14-16).

2. Is initiated and participated in only through the electing grace of God (Romans 8:29-30; 2 Timothy 1:9; Titus 1:1; 1 Peter 1:1).

3. Is a covenant of peace (Shalom) which gives access to God (Ezekiel 34:23-31; Romans 5:1-2; Ephesians 2:17-18; Hebrews 7:2-3).

4. Is uniquely celebrated and experienced in the Lord's Supper and Baptism (Mark 14:22-25; 1 Corinthians 10:16; Colossians 2:12; 1 Peter 3:21).

5. By faith, both imputes and imparts righteousness to the participants so that God's laws are put in the hearts and written on their minds (Jeremiah 31:33; Romans 1:17; 2 Corinthians 5:21; Galatians 3:21-22; Philippians 1:11; 3:9; Hebrews 10:15-17; 12:10-11; 1 Peter 2.24).

B. The Covenant enables us to understand and experience Christian sanctification:

1. Righteousness: right relationships with God and others (Exodus 20:1-17; Micah 6:8; Mark 12:29-31; James 2:8).

2. Truth: right beliefs about God and others (Psalm 86:11; Isaiah 45:19; John 8:31-32; 17:17; 1 Peter 1:22).

3. Holiness: right actions toward God and others (Leviticus 11:45; 20:8; Ecclesiastes 12:13; Matthew 7:12; 2 Corinthians 7:1; Colossians 3:12; 2 Peter 3:11).

C. The purpose of the New Covenant is to enable the Church to be like Christ Jesus:

1. Jesus is the new pattern for humanity:

    a. The second Adam (Romans 5:12-17; 1 Corinthians 15:45-49).

    b. The likeness into which the Church is fashioned (Romans 8:29; 1 John 3:2).

    c. His life, character, and teaching are the standard for faith and practice (John 13:17; 20:21; 2 John 6, 9; 1 Corinthians 11:1).

2. This covenant is made possible by the sacrifice of Christ himself (Matthew 26:27-29; Hebrews 8-10).

3. The apostolic ministry of the new covenant is meant to conform believers to the image of Christ (2 Corinthians 3; Ephesians 4:12-13).

D. The Covenant binds us to those who have gone before.

1. It recognizes that the Church is one (Ephesians 4:4-5).

2. It reminds us that we are surrounded by a cloud of witnesses who have participated in the same covenant (Hebrews 12:1).

3. It reminds us that we are part of a sacred chain:

   God-Christ-Apostles-Church.

4. It reminds us that we share the same:

   a. Spiritual parentage (John 1:13; 3:5-6; 2 Corinthians 1:2; Galatians 4:6; 1 John 3:9).

   b. Family likeness (Ephesians 3:15; Hebrews 2:11).

   c. Lord, faith and baptism (Ephesians 4:5).

   d. Indwelling Spirit (John 14:17; Romans 8:9; 2 Corinthians 1:22).

   e. Calling and mission (Ephesians 4:1; Hebrews 3:1; 2 Peter 1:10).

   f. Hope and destiny (Galatians 5:5; Ephesians 1:18; Ephesians 4:4; Colossians 1:5).

5. Causes us to understand that since we share the same covenant, administered by the same Lord, under the leadership of the same Spirit with those Christians who have come before us, we must necessarily reflect upon the creeds, the councils, and the actions of the Church throughout history in order to understand the apostolic tradition and the ongoing work of the Holy Spirit (1 Corinthians 11:16).

VI. A community of presence

A. "Where Jesus Christ is, there is the Church" – Ignatius of Antioch (Matthew 18:20).

B. The Church is the dwelling place of God (Ephesians 2:19-21):

1. His nation

2. His household

3. His temple

C. The Church congregates in eager anticipation of God's presence (Ephesians 2:22).

1. The Church now comes into the presence of God at every gathering:

   a. Like the covenant people in the Old Testament, the Church gathers in the presence of God (Exodus 18:12; 34:34; Deuteronomy 14:23; 15:20; Psalm 132:7; Hebrews 12:18-24).

   b. The gathered Church makes manifest the reality of the Kingdom of God by being in the presence of the King (1 Corinthians 14:25).

2. The Church anticipates the future gathering of the people of God when the fullness of God's presence will be with them all (Ezekiel 48:35; 2 Corinthians 4:14; 1 Thessalonians 3:13; Revelation 21:13).

D. The Church is absolutely dependent on the presence of the Spirit of Christ.

1. Without the presence of the Holy Spirit there is no Church (Acts 2:38; Romans 8:9; 1 Corinthians 12:13; Galatians 3:3; Ephesians 2:22; 4:4; Philippians 3:3).

2. The Holy Spirit creates, directs, empowers, and teaches congregations of believers (John 14:16-17, 26; Acts 1:8; 2:17; 13:1; Romans 15:13, 19; 2 Corinthians 3:18).

3. The Holy Spirit gives gifts to the Church so that it can accomplish its mission, bringing honor and glory to God (Romans 12:4-8; 1 Corinthians 12:1-31; Hebrews 2:4).

4. The Holy Spirit binds the Church together as the family of God and the body of Christ (2 Corinthians 13:14; Ephesians 4:3).

E. The Church is a Kingdom of priests which stands in God's presence (1 Peter 2:5, 9):

1. Ministering before the Lord (Psalm 43:4; Psalm 134:1-2).

2. Placing God's blessing on his people (Numbers 6:22-27; 2 Corinthians 13:14).

3. Bringing people before the attention of God (1 Thessalonians 1:3; 2 Timothy 1:3).

4. Offering themselves and the fruit of their ministry to God (Isaiah 66:20; Romans 12:1; 15:16).

F. The Church lives in God's presence through prayer.

1. Prayer as access to the Holy of Holies (Revelation 5:8).

2. Prayer as communion with God (Psalm 5:3; Romans 8:26-27).

3. Prayer as intercession.

    a. For the world (1 Timothy 2:1-2).

    b. For the saints (Ephesians 6:18-20, 1 Thessalonians 5:25).

4. Prayer as thanksgiving (Philippians 4:6; Colossians 1:3).

5. Prayer as the warfare of the Kingdom.

    a. Binding and loosing (Matthew 16:19).

    b. Engaging the principalities and powers (Ephesians 6:12,18).

The Church Is a Holy Community Where Discipline Is Rightly Ordered

VII. A community of reconciliation

A. The Church is a community that is reconciled to God: all reconciliation is ultimately dependent on God's reconciling actions toward humanity.

1. God's desire to reconcile is evidenced by sending his prophets and in the last days by his Son (Hebrews 1:1-2).

2. The incarnation, the life, the death, and the resurrection of Jesus are the ultimate acts of reconciliation from God toward humanity (Romans 5:8).

3. The Gospel is now a message of reconciliation, made possible by Christ's death, that God offers to humanity (2 Corinthians 5:16-20).

B. The Church is a community of individuals and peoples that are reconciled to each other by their common identity as one body.

1. By his death Christ united his people who are born of the same seed (1 John 3:9), reconciled as fellow citizens and members of a new humanity (Ephesians 2:11-22).

2. The Church community treats all members of God's household with love and justice in spite of differences in race, class,

gender, and culture because they are organically united by their participation in the body of Christ (Galatians 3:26-29; Colossians 3:11).

C. The Church is a community that is concerned for reconciliation among all peoples.

1. The Church functions as an ambassador that invites all people to be reconciled to God (2 Corinthians 5:19-20). This task of mission lays the foundation for all the reconciling activities of the Church.

2. The Church promotes reconciliation with and between all people.

   a. Because the Church is commanded to love its enemies (Matthew 5:44-48).

   b. Because the Church is an incarnational community which seeks, like Christ, to identify with those alienated from itself.

   c. Because the Church embodies and works for the vision of the Kingdom of God in which peoples, nations, and nature itself will be completely reconciled and at peace (Isaiah 11:1-9; Micah 4:2-4; Matthew 4:17; Acts 28:31).

   d. Because the Church recognizes the eternal plan of God to reconcile all things in heaven and on earth under one head, the Lord Jesus Christ, in order that the Kingdom may be handed over to God the Father who will be all in all (Ephesians 1:10; Romans 11:36; 1 Corinthians 15:27-28; Revelation 11:15, 21:1-17).

D. The Church is a community of friendship: friendship is a key part of reconciliation and spiritual development.

1. Spiritual maturity results in friendship with God (Exodus 33:11; James 2:23).

2. Spiritual discipleship results in friendship with Christ (John 15:13-15).

3. Spiritual unity is expressed in friendship with the saints (Romans 16:5, 9, 12; 2 Corinthians 7:1; Philippians 2:12; Colossians 4:14; 1 Peter 2:11; 1 John 2:7; 3 John 1:14).

VIII. A community of suffering

A. The Church community suffers because it exists in the world as "sheep among wolves" (Luke 10:3).

1. Hated by those who reject Christ (John 15:18-20).

2. Persecuted by the world system (Matthew 5:10; 2 Corinthians 4:9; 2 Timothy 3:12).

3. It is uniquely the community of the poor, the hungry, the weeping, the hated, the excluded, the insulted, and the rejected (Matthew 5:20-22).

4. It is founded on the example and experience of Christ and the apostles (Isaiah 53:3; Luke 9:22; 24:46; Acts 5:41; 2 Timothy 1:8; 1 Thessalonians 2:2).

B. The Church community imitates Christ in his suffering.

1. Because it purifies from sin (1 Peter 4:1-2).

2. Because it teaches obedience (Hebrews 5:8).

3. Because it allows them to know Christ more fully (Philippians 3:10).

4. Because those who share in Christ's suffering will also share in his comfort and glory (Romans 8:17-18; 2 Corinthians 1:5; 1 Peter 5:1).

C. The Church community suffers because it identifies with those who suffer.

1. The body of Christ suffers whenever one of its members suffers (1 Corinthians 12:26).

2. The body of Christ suffers because it voluntarily identifies itself with the despised, the rejected, the oppressed, and the unlovely (Proverbs 29:7; Luke 7:34; Luke 15:1-2).

D. The cross of Christ is both the instrument of salvation and the pattern for Christian life. The cross embodies the values of the Church community.

1. The cross of Christ is the most fundamental Christian symbol. It serves as a constant reminder that the Church is a community of suffering.

2. The basic requirement of discipleship is a willingness to take up the cross daily and follow Jesus (Mark 8:34; Luke 9:23; Luke 14:27).

IX. A community of works

A. "Works of Service" are the hallmark of Christian congregations as they do justice, love mercy, and walk humbly with God.

1. The leadership of the Church is charged with preparing God's people for "works of service" (Ephesians 4:12).

2. These good works are central to the new purpose and identity which is given us during the new birth. "For we are his workmanship, created in Christ Jesus for good works, which God prepared beforehand, that we should walk in them." (Ephesians 2:10).

3. These works of service reveal God's character to the world and lead people to give him praise (Matthew 5:16; 2 Corinthians 9:13).

B. Servanthood characterizes the Christian's approach to relationships, resources, and ministry.

1. The Church community serves based on the example of Christ who came "not to be served but to serve" (Matthew 20:25-28; Luke 22:27; Philippians 2:7).

2. The Church community serves based on the command of Christ and the apostles (Mark 10:42-45; Galatians 5:13; 1 Peter 4:10).

3. The Church community serves, first of all, "the least of these" according to the mandates of Christ's teaching (Matthew 18:2-5; 25:34-46; Luke 4:18-19).

C. Generosity and hospitality are the twin signs of kingdom service.

1. Generosity results in the giving of one's self and one's good for the sake of announcing and obeying Christ and his kingdom reign.

2. Hospitality results in treating the stranger, the foreigner, the prisoner, and the enemy as one of your very own people (Hebrews 13:2).

3. These signs are the true fruit of repentance (Luke 3:7-14; Luke 19:8-10; James 1:27)

D. Stewardship is the foundational truth which governs the way the Church uses resources in order to do "Works of Service."

1. Our resources (time, money, authority, health, position, etc.) belong not to ourselves but to God.

   a. We answer to God for our management of the things entrusted to us personally and corporately (Matthew 25:14-30).

   b. Money should be managed in such as way that treasures are laid up in heaven (Matthew 6:19-21; Luke 12:32-34; 16:1-15; 1 Timothy 6:17-19).

   c. Seeking first the Kingdom of God is the standard by which our stewardship is measured and the basis upon which more will be entrusted (Matthew 6:33).

2. Proper stewardship should contribute to equality and mutual sharing (2 Corinthians 8:13-15).

3. Greed is indicative of dishonest stewardship and a repudiation of God as the owner and giver of all things (Luke 12:15; 16:13; Ephesians 5:5; Colossians 3:5; 1 Peter 5:2).

E. Justice is a key goal of the Church as it serves God and others.

1. Doing justice is an essential part of fulfilling our service to God (Deuteronomy 16:20; 27:19; Psalm 33:5; 106:3; Proverbs 28:5; Micah 6:8; Matthew 23:23).

2. Justice characterizes the righteous servant but is absent from the hypocrite and the unrighteous (Proverbs 29:7; Isaiah 1:17; 58:1-14; Matthew 12:18-20; Luke 11:42).

Foundations of Christian Leadership

Discerning the Call: The Profile of a Godly Christian Leader

Rev. Dr. Don L. Davis

	Commission	Character	Community	Competence
Definition	Recognizes the call of God and replies with prompt obedience to his lordship and leading	Reflects the character of Christ in their personal convictions, conduct, and lifestyle	Regards multiplying disciples in the body of Christ as the primary role of ministry	Responds in the power of the Spirit with excellence in carrying out their appointed tasks and ministry
Key Scripture	2 Timothy 1:6-14; 1 Timothy 4:14; Acts 1:8; Matthew 28:18-20	John 15:4-5; 2 Timothy 2:2; 1 Corinthians 4:2; Galatians 5:16-23	Ephesians 4:9-15; 1 Corinthians 12:1-27	2 Timothy 2:15; 3:16-17; Romans 15:14; 1 Corinthians 12
Critical Concept	The Authority of God: God's leader acts on God's recognized call and authority, acknowledged by the saints and God's leaders	The Humility of Christ: God's leader demonstrates the mind and lifestyle of Christ in his or her actions and relationships	The Growth of the Church: God's leader uses all of his or her resources to equip and empower the body of Christ for his/her goal and task	The Power of the Spirit: God's leader operates in the gifting and anointing of the Holy Spirit
Central Elements	A clear call from God Authentic testimony before God and others Deep sense of personal conviction based on Scripture Personal burden for a particular task or people Confirmation by leaders and the body	Passion for Christlikeness Radical lifestyle for the Kingdom Serious pursuit of holiness Discipline in the personal life Fulfills role-relationships as bondslave of Jesus Christ Provides an attractive model for others in their conduct, speech, and lifestyle (the fruit of the Spirit)	Genuine love for and desire to serve God's people Disciples faithful individuals Facilitates growth in small groups Pastors and equips believers in the congregation Nurtures associations and networks among Christians and churches Advances new movements among God's people locally	Endowments and gifts from the Spirit Sound discipling from an able mentor Skill in the spiritual disciplines Ability in the Word Able to evangelize, follow up, and disciple new converts Strategic in the use of resources and people to accomplish God's task
Satanic Strategy to Abort	Operates on the basis of personality or position rather than on God's appointed call and ongoing authority	Substitutes ministry activity and/or hard work and industry for godliness and Christlikeness	Exalts tasks and activities above equipping the saints and developing Christian community	Functions on natural gifting and personal ingenuity rather than on the Spirit's leading and gifting
Key Steps	Identify God's call Discover your burden Be confirmed by leaders	Abide in Christ Discipline for godliness Pursue holiness in all	Embrace God's Church Learn leadership's contexts Equip concentrically	Discover the Spirit's gifts Receive excellent training Hone your performance
Results	Deep confidence in God arising from God's call	Powerful Christlike example provided for others to follow	Multiplying disciples in the Church	Dynamic working of the Holy Spirit

Investment, Empowerment, and Assessment:
How Leadership as Representation Provides Freedom to Innovate

Rev. Dr. Don L. Davis

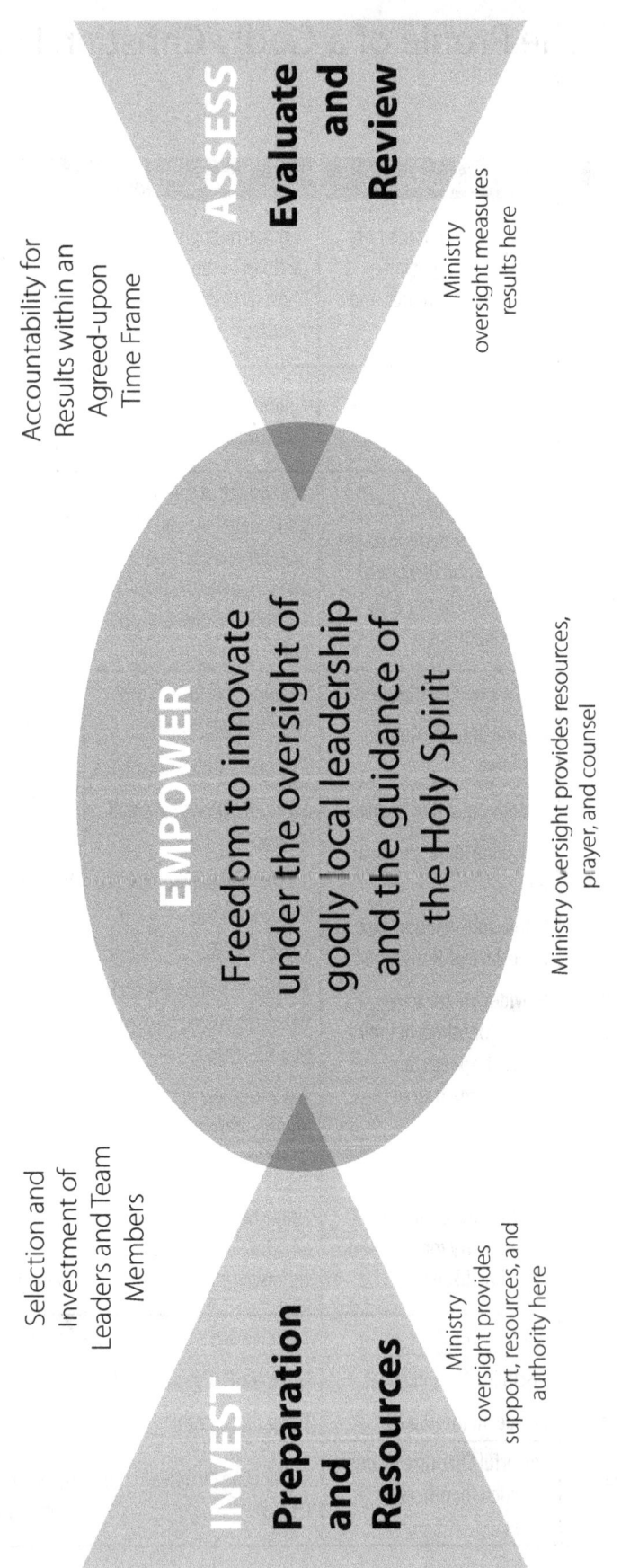

ASSESS — Evaluate and Review

Accountability for Results within an Agreed-upon Time Frame

Ministry oversight measures results here

- Evaluation by sending authority
- Review of results in light of task
- Faithfulness and loyalty assessed
- Overall evaluation of plan and strategy
- Critical evaluation of leadership performance
- Formal determination of operation's "success"
- Reassignment in light of evaluation

EMPOWER

Freedom to innovate under the oversight of godly local leadership and the guidance of the Holy Spirit

Ministry oversight provides resources, prayer, and counsel

INVEST — Preparation and Resources

Selection and Investment of Leaders and Team Members

Ministry oversight provides support, resources, and authority here

- Formal leadership selection
- Acknowledgment of personal call
- Determination of task and assignment
- Training in spiritual warfare
- Authorization to act defined and given
- Necessary resources given and logistics planned
- Commissioning: deputization formally recognized

Understanding Leadership as Representation: The Six Stages of Formal Proxy

Rev. Dr. Don L. Davis

> Luke 10:1 (ESV) After this the Lord appointed seventy-two others and sent them on ahead of him, two by two, into every town and place where he himself was about to go. . .
>
> Luke 10:16 (ESV) "The one who hears you hears me, and the one who rejects you rejects me, and the one who rejects me rejects him who sent me."
>
> John 20:21 (ESV) Jesus said to them again, "Peace be with you. As the Father has sent me, even so I am sending you."

Commissioning (1)
Formal Selection and Call to Represent

- Chosen to be an emissary, envoy, or proxy
- Confirmed by appropriate other who recognize the call
- Is recognized to be a member of a faithful community
- Calling out of a group to a particular role of representation
- Calling to a particular task or mission
- Delegation of position or responsibility

Equipping (2)
Appropriate Resourcing and Training to Fulfill the Call

- Assignment to a supervisor, superior, mentor, or instructor
- Disciplined instruction of principles underlying the call
- Constant drill, practice, and exposure to appropriate skills
- Recognition of gifts and strengths
- Expert coaching and ongoing feedback

Entrustment (3)
Corresponding Authorization and Empowerment to Act

- Delegation of authority to act and speak on commissioner's behalf
- Scope and limits of representative power provided
- Formal deputization (right to enforce and represent)
- Permission given to be an emissary (to stand in stead of)
- Release to fulfill the commission and task received

Mission (4)
Faithful and Disciplined Engagement of the Task

- Subordination of one's will to accomplish the assignment
- Obedience: carrying out the orders of those who sent you
- Fulfilling the task that was given to you
- Freely acting within one's delegated authority to fulfill the task
- Maintaining loyalty to those who sent you
- Using all means available to do one's duty, whatever the cost
- Full recognition of one's answerability to the one(s) who commissioned

Reckoning (5)
Official Evaluation and Review of One's Execution

- Reporting back to sending authority for critical review
- Formal comprehensive assessment of one's execution and results
- Judgment of one's loyalties and faithfulness
- Sensitive analysis of what we accomplished
- Readiness to ensure that our activities and efforts produce results

Reward (6)
Public Recognition and Continuing Response

- Formal publishing of assessment's results
- Acknowledgment and recognition of behavior and conduct
- Corresponding reward or rebuke for execution
- Review made basis for possible reassignment or recommissioning
- Assigning new projects with greater authority

Leadership As Representation

- The Revealed Will of God
- The Fulfillment of the Task and Mission
- Consent of Your Leaders

CONVICTION · CHARACTER · CONSCIENCE

Re-Presenting Messiah

Rev. Dr. Don L. Davis

"Gentilization" of modern Christian faith expressions

- Contextualization: freedom in Christ to enculturate the gospel
- Common modern portrayal of Messianic hope as Gentile faith
- Tendency of tradition/culture to usurp biblical authority
- Present day eclipse of biblical framework by "captivities"

Strange fires on the altar: examples of socio-cultural captivities

- Nationalism
- Capitalism
- Scientific rationalism
- Denominationalism
- Personal existentialism
- Asceticism/moralism
- Ethnocentrism
- Nuclear family life

Jesus's critique of socio-cultural captivity

- Bondage to religious tradition, Matthew 15:3-9
- Ignorance of Scripture and God's power, Matthew 22:29
- Zealous effort without knowledge, Romans 10:1-3

Hermeneutic habits that lead toward a syncretistic faith

- Selective choice of texts
- Tradition viewed as canon
- Cultural readings of texts
- Preaching and teaching based on eisegesis and audience
- Uncritical approaches to one's own doctrine and practice
- Apologetics for socio-cultural identity

"Paradigm paralysis" & biblical faith

- Blind to one's own historical conditionedness
- Limited vantage point and perspective
- Privilege and power: political manipulation
- Inability to receive criticism
- Persecution of opposite viewpoints and new interpretations of faith

---

Re-present Messiah Yeshua with passion and clarity

with fidelity to Scripture in sync with historic orthodoxy without cultural distortion without theological bias

Rediscover the Hebraic roots of the biblical Messianic hope (return)

Recognize the socio-cultural captivity of Christian profession (exile)

Rediscovery of the Jewish origins of biblical faith, John 4:22

YHWH as God of lovingkindness in covenant faithfulness

Messianic fulfillment in Old Testament: prophecy, type, story, ceremony, and symbol

Hebraic roots of the Promise: YHWH as a Warrior God

People of Israel as community of Messianic hope

Psalms and Prophets emphasize divine rulership of Messiah

Tracing the Seed

Seed of the Woman, Genesis 3:15
Seed of Shem, Genesis 9:26-27
Seed of Abraham, Genesis 12:3
Seed of Isaac and Jacob, Genesis 26:2-5; 28:10-15
Seed of Judah, Genesis 49:10
Seed of David, 2 Samuel 7

Suffering Servant of YHWH: humiliation and lowliness of God's Davidic king

Glimmers of Gentile salvation and global transformation

Live the adventure of New Testament apocalyptic myth (possession)

Apocalyptic as the "mother tongue and native language" of the apostles and early Church as eschatological community

Yeshua Messiah as the Cosmic Warrior: YHWH as God who wins ultimate victory over his enemies

Messiah Yeshua as Anointed One and Binder of the Strong Man: the Messianic Age to come inaugurated in Jesus of Nazareth

"Already/Not Yet" Kingdom orientation: The Reign of God as both manifest but not consummated

The Evidence and Guarantee of the Age to Come: The Spirit as down payment, first fruits, and seal of God

Paul's Team Members

Rev. Dr. Don L. Davis

Achaicus, A Corinthian who visited Paul at Philippi, 1 Corinthians 16:17.

Archippus, Colossian disciple whom Paul exhorted to fulfill his ministry, Colossians 4:17; Philemon 2.

Aquila, Jewish disciple Paul found at Corinth, Acts 18:2, 18, 26; Romans 16:3; 1 Corinthians 16:19; 2 Timothy 4:19.

Aristarchus, With Paul on 3rd journey, Acts 19:29; 20:4; 27:2; Colossians 4:10; Philemon 24.

Artemas, Companion of Paul at Nicopolis, Titus 3:12.

Barnabas, A Levite, cousin of John Mark, and companion with Paul in several of his journeys, cf. Acts 4:36, 9:27; 11:22, 25, 30; 12:25; chs. 13, 14, and 15; 1 Corinthians 9:6; Galatians 2:1, 9, 13; Colossians 4:13.

Carpus, Disciple of Troas, 2 Timothy 4:13.

Claudia, Female disciple of Rome, 2 Timothy 4.21.

Clement, Fellow-laborer at Philippi, Philippians 4:3.

Crescens, A disciple at Rome, 2 Timothy 4:10.

Demas, A laborer of Paul at Rome, Colossians 4:14; Philemon 24; 2 Timothy 4:10.

Epaphras, Fellow laborer and prisoner, Colossians 1:7; 4:12; Philemon 23.

Epaphroditus, Messenger between Paul and the churches, Philippians 2:25; 4:18.

Eubulus, Disciple of Rome, 2 Timothy 4:21.

Euodia, Christian woman of Philippi, Philippians 4:2

Fortunatus, Part of the Corinthian team, 1 Corinthians 16:17.

Gaius, 1) A Macedonian companion, Acts 19:29; 2) A disciple/companion in Derbe, Acts 20:4.

Jesus (Justus), A Jewish disciple at Colossae, Colossians 4:11.

John Mark, Companion of Paul and cousin of Barnabas, Acts 12:12, 15; 15:37, 39; Colossians 4:10; 2 Timothy 4:11; Philemon 24.

Linus, A Roman Companion of Paul, 2 Timothy 4:21.

Luke, Physician and fellow-traveler with Paul, Colossians 4:14; 2 Timothy 4:11; Philemon 24.

Onesimus, Native of Colossae and slave of Philemon who served Paul, Colossians 4:9; Philemon 10.

Hermogenes, A team member who abandoned Paul in prison, 2 Timothy 1:15.

Phygellus, One with Hermogenes turned from Paul in Asia, 2 Timothy 1:15.

Priscilla (Prisca), Wife of Aquila of Pontus and fellow-worker in the Gospel, Acts 18:2, 18, 26; Romans 16:3; 1 Corinthians 16:19.

Pudens, A Roman companion of Paul, 2 Timothy 4:21.

Secundus, Companion of Paul on his way from Greece to Syria, Acts 20:4.

Silas, Disciple, fellow laborer, and prisoner with Paul, Acts 15:22, 27, 32, 34, 40; 16:19, 25, 29; 17:4, 10, etc.

Sopater, Accompanied Paul to Syria, Acts 20:4.

Sosipater, Kinsman of Paul, Romans 16:21.

Silvanus, Probably same as Silas, 2 Corinthians 1:19; 1 Thessalonians 1:1; 2 Thessalonians 1:1.

Sosthenes, Chief Ruler of the Synagogue of Corinth, laborer with Paul there, Acts 18:17.

Stephanus, One of the first believers of Achaia and visitor to Paul, 1 Corinthians 1:16; 16:15; 16:17.

Syntyche, One of Paul's female "fellow workers" in Philippi, Philippians 4:2.

Tertius, Slave and person who wrote the Epistle to the Romans, Romans 16:22.

Timothy, A young man of Lystra with a Jewish mother and Greek father who labored on with Paul in his ministry, Acts 16:1; 17:14, 15; 18:5; 19:22; 20:4; Romans 16:21; 1 Corinthians 4:17; 16:10; 2 Corinthians 1:1, 19; Philippians 1:1; 2:19; Colossians 1:1; 1 Thessalonians 1:1; 3:2, 6; 2 Thessalonians 1:1; 1 Timothy 1:2, 18; 6:20; 2 Timothy 1:2; Philemon 1; Hebrews 13:23.

Titus, Greek disciple and co-laborer of Paul, 2 Corinthians 2:13; 7:6, 13, 14; 8:6, 16, 23; 12:18; Galatians 2:1, 3; 2 Timothy 4:10; Titus 1:4.

Trophimus, A Ephesian disciple who accompanied Paul to Jerusalem from Greece, Acts 20:4; 21:29; 2 Timothy 4:20.

Tryphena and Tryphosa, Female disciples of Rome, probably twins, who Paul calls laborers in the Lord, Romans 16:12.

Tychicus, A disciple of Asia Minor who accompanied Paul in various trips, Acts 20:4; Ephesians 6:21; Colossians 4:7; 2 Timothy 4:12; Titus 3:12.

Urbanus, Roman disciple and aid to Paul, Romans 16:9.

Nurturing Authentic Christian Leadership

Rev. Dr. Don L. Davis

Cliff On-One-Side	Cliff On-the Other-Side
Laying on hands too quickly	Always postponing delegation to the indigenous
Ignoring culture in leadership training	Elevating culture above truth
Demoting doctrine and theology	Supposing doctrine and theology as only criteria
Highlighting skills and gifts above availability and character	Substituting availability and character for genuine giftedness
Emphasizing administrative abilities above spiritual dynamism	Ignoring administration's role in spiritual vitality and power
Equating readiness with Christian perfection	Ignoring the importance of biblical standards
Limiting candidacy for leadership based on gender and ethnicity	Setting quotas of leadership based on gender and ethnicity
Seeing everyone as a leader	Seeing virtually no one as worthy to lead

Lording Over vs. Serving Among: Differing Styles and Models of Leadership

Adapted from George Mallone, *Furnace of Renewal*

Secular Authority	Servant Authority
Functions on the basis of power	Functions on basis of love and obedience
Primarily rules by giving orders	Serves as one who is under orders of another
Unwilling to fail: blame-shifts for leverage	Unafraid to receive responsibility for failure
Sees itself as absolutely necessary	Willing to be used and expended for the body
Drives others (cow-punching mentality)	Leads others (shepherding mentality)
Subjects others to threat of loss and pain	Builds others by encouragement and challenge
Consolidates power for maximum impact	Stewards authority for greatest good
Has gold, makes rules	Follows the Golden Rule
Uses position for personal advancement	Exercises authority to please the Master
Expects benefits from service	Expects to expend oneself in service to others
Strength, not character, is decisive	Character, not strength, carries most weight

Dealing with Old Ways
Adapted from Paul Hiebert

Delegation and Authority in Christian Leadership
Rev. Dr. Don L. Davis

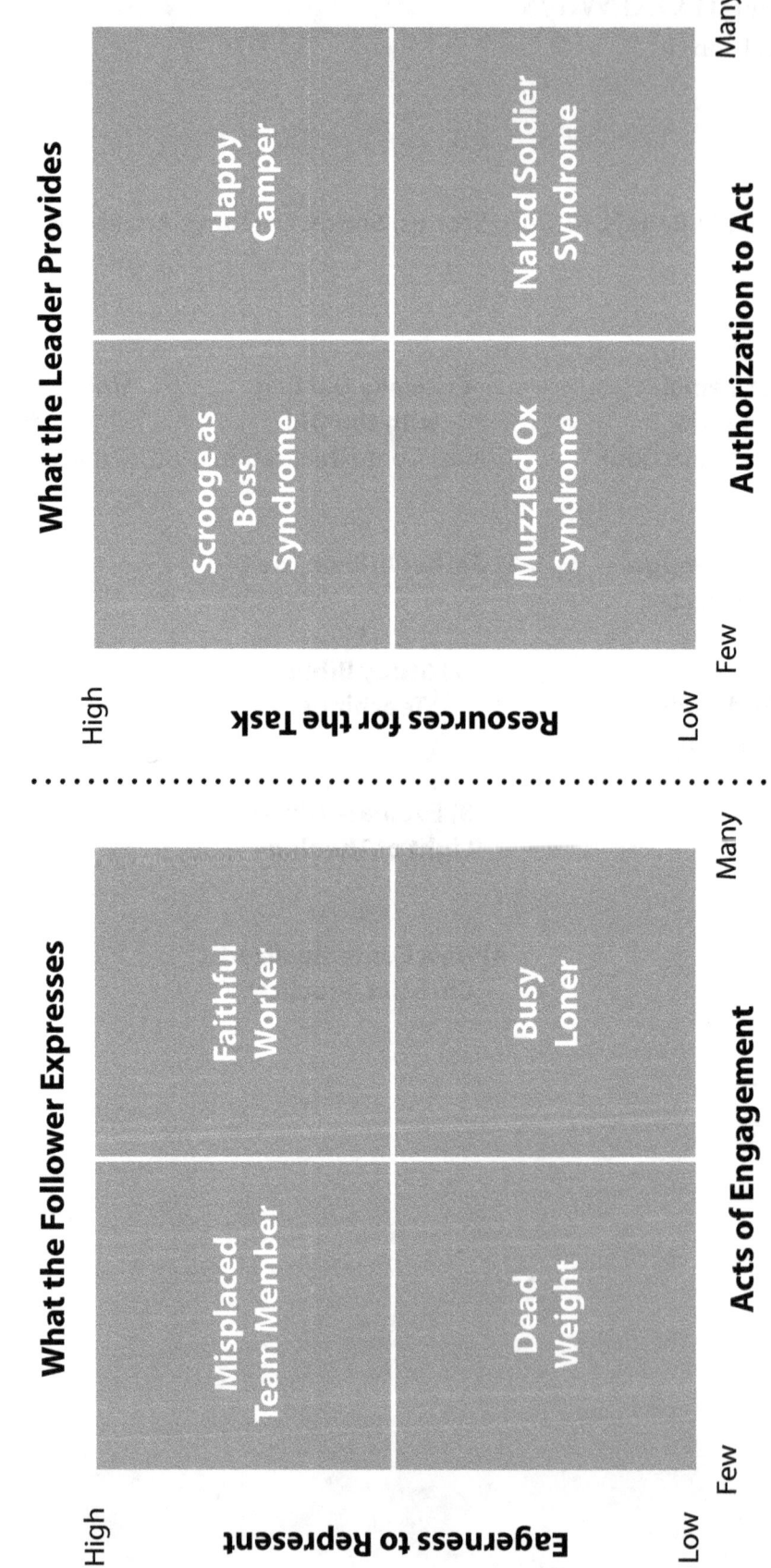

"You Can Pay Me Now, Or You Can Pay Me Later"

Rev. Dr. Don L. Davis

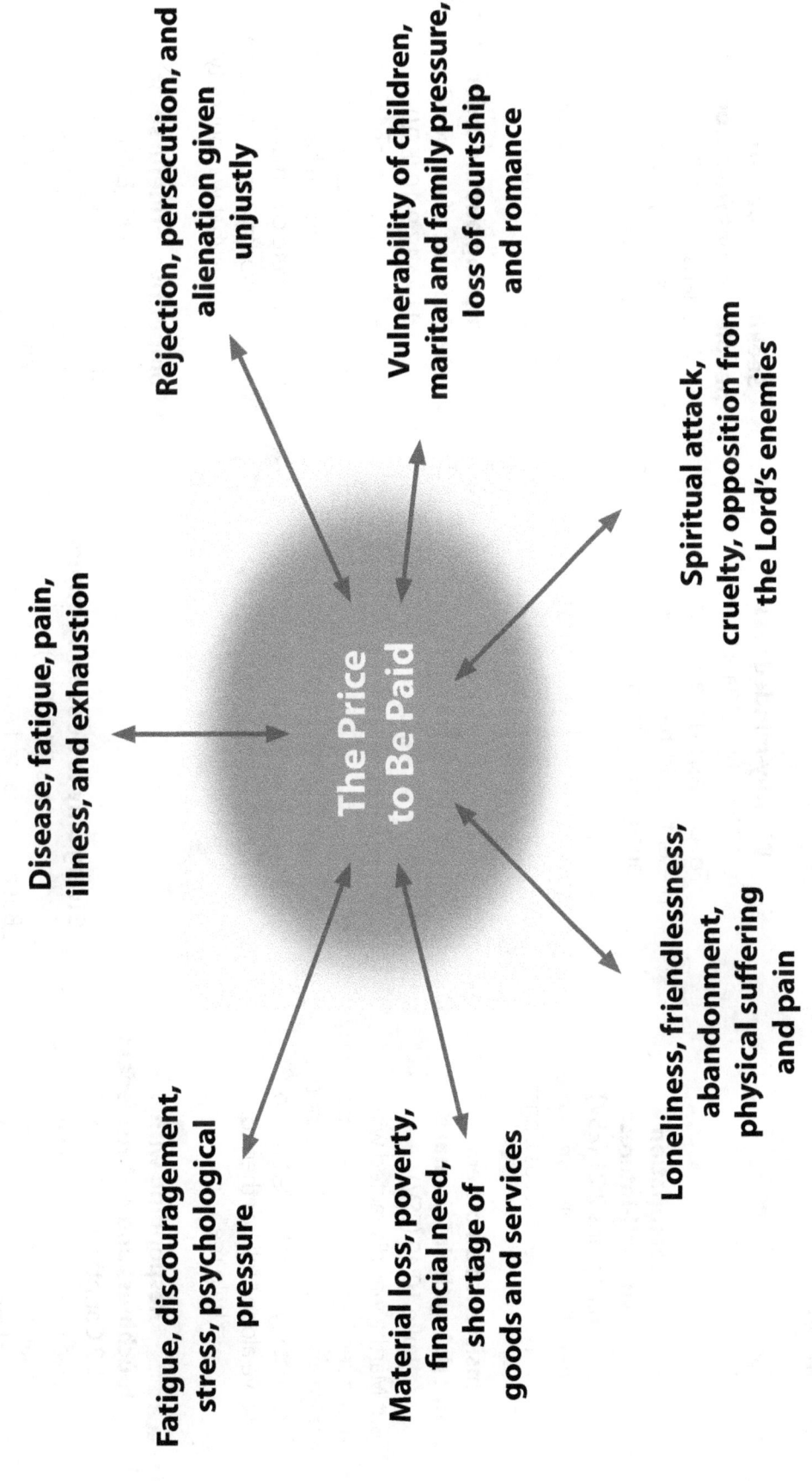

The Price to Be Paid

- Disease, fatigue, pain, illness, and exhaustion
- Rejection, persecution, and alienation given unjustly
- Vulnerability of children, marital and family pressure, loss of courtship and romance
- Spiritual attack, cruelty, opposition from the Lord's enemies
- Loneliness, friendlessness, abandonment, physical suffering and pain
- Material loss, poverty, financial need, shortage of goods and services
- Fatigue, discouragement, stress, psychological pressure

Hindrances to Christlike Servanthood

Rev. Dr. Don L. Davis

Hindrances to Christlike Servanthood

Seeking approval from people and not from God
Galatians 1:10 (ESV)

For am I now seeking the approval of man, or of God? Or am I trying to please man? If I were still trying to please man, I would not be a servant of Christ.

Scripting out the order and extent of our service
Luke 17:9-10 (ESV)

Does he thank the servant because he did what was commanded? So you also, when you have done all that you were commanded, say, "We are unworthy servants; we have only done what was our duty."

A Competitive, prideful spirit
Luke 18:11-12 (ESV)

The Pharisee, standing by himself, prayed thus: "God I thank you that I am not like other men, extortioners, unjust, adulterers, or even like this tax collector. [12] I fast twice a week; I give tithes of all that I get."

Giving only to be seen by others
Acts 5:1-2 (ESV)

But a man named Ananias, with his wife Sapphira, sold a piece of property, and with his wife's knowledge he kept back for himself some of the proceeds and brought only a part of it and laid it at the apostles' feet.

Responding with touchiness and defensiveness
2 Corinthians 12:19 (ESV)

Have you been thinking all along that we have been defending ourselves to you? It is in the sight of God that we have been speaking in Christ, and all for your upbuilding, beloved.

Insistence on others not doing their fair share
Luke 10:40 (ESV)

But Martha was distracted with much serving. And she went up to him and said, "Lord, do you not care that my sister has left me to serve alone? Tell her then to help me."

Preoccupation with self-interest
Philippians 2:21 (ESV)

They all seek their own interests, not those of Jesus Christ.

Worldly-mindedness
2 Timothy 4:10a (ESV)

For Demas, in love with this present world, has deserted me and gone to Thessalonica.

Practicing Christian Leadership

A Guide to Determining Your Worship Profile

Adapted from Robert Webber, *Planning Blended Worship*, Nashville: Abingdon Press, 1998

1. Which of the following categories best describes your church?

    ____ Affected by Catholic and mainline worship renewal

    ____ Affected by the Pentecostal, charismatic, or praise and worship renewal

    ____ Affected by the movement to blend traditional and contemporary worship

    ____ Not affected by any of the worship renewal movements

2. Identify the age make-up of the people in your church

    ____% over 65   ____% 18-34

    ____% 50-65   ____% under 18

    ____% 35-49

3. Of the eight common elements of worship renewal, which ones have made an impact on the worship of your church? Evaluate each of the areas on a scale of 1 (least impact) to 10 (most impact). Then take time to discuss those areas that are weakest.

    a. Our church draws from a biblical understanding of worship.
       1 2 3 4 5 6 7 8 9 10

    b. The worship of our church draws from the past, especially the early Church.
       1 2 3 4 5 6 7 8 9 10

    c. Our church has experienced a new focus on Sunday worship.
       1 2 3 4 5 6 7 8 9 10

    d. Our church draws from the music of the whole Church.
       1 2 3 4 5 6 7 8 9 10

    e. Our church has restored the use of the arts.
       1 2 3 4 5 6 7 8 9 10

    f. Our church follows the calendar of the Christian year effectively.
       1 2 3 4 5 6 7 8 9 10

    g. Our church has experienced the restoration of life in the sacred actions of worship.
       1 2 3 4 5 6 7 8 9 10

    h. The worship of our church empowers its outreach ministries.
       1 2 3 4 5 6 7 8 9 10

4. Evaluate the content, structure, and style of your worship. Again, use a scale of 1 ("That does not describe our church at all.") to 10 ("Yes, that is our church!"). Discuss areas of greatest weakness.

   a. The content of our worship is the full story of Scripture.
      1 2 3 4 5 6 7 8 9 10

   b. The structure of our worship is the universally accepted fourfold pattern.
      1 2 3 4 5 6 7 8 9 10

   c. The style of our worship is appropriate to our congregation and to the people we attract.
      1 2 3 4 5 6 7 8 9 10

5. Answer the following:

   a. The approach to worship in our church is based upon:
      Conceptual language / Symbolic language

   b. The communication style of our church will relate best to:
      Boosters / Boomers / Generation X
      All of the above

6. I would describe our church as: An old paradigm church/A new paradigm church

7. Draw from each of the previous questions to create a worship profile of the church. Do so by completing each of the following sentences:

   a. Our church has been affected by (which stream of worship renewal):

   b. Our age group is primarily:

   c. Of the eight aspects of worship renewal, we draw on:

   d. The content of our worship is:

   e. The structure of our worship is:

   f. The style of our worship is:

   g. Our approach to communication is:

8. To complete this study, comment on the kinds of changes you would like to see occur in the worship of your church.

Capturing God's Vision for His People: The "Enduring Solidarity" of Our Search for the Land of Promise

Hebrews 11:13-16 (ESV) – These all died in faith, not having received the things promised, but having seen them and greeted them from afar, and having acknowledged that they were strangers and exiles on the earth. [14] For people who speak thus make it clear that they are seeking a homeland. [15] If they had been thinking of that land from which they had gone out, they would have had opportunity to return. [16] But as it is, they desire a better country, that is, a heavenly one. Therefore God is not ashamed to be called their God, for he has prepared for them a city.

A whole galaxy of auxiliary images oscillate around the analogy of "the people of God" for Christians and the Christian church. These include in the Pauline letters the following: "God's elect" (Romans 8:33; Ephesians 1:4; Colossians 3:12), "Abraham's descendants" (Romans 4:16; Galatians 3:29; 4:26-28), "the true circumcision" (Philippians 3:3; Colossians 2:11), and even "Israel of God" (Galatians 6:16). All of these images assert, in some manner, an enduring solidarity of the people of the church with the people of Israel, whose history provides the church with an authoritative account of the principles and actions of God's past redemptive working. It is the task of exegesis and theology to spell out the nature of this relationship.

– Richard Longenecker, ed.
Community Formation in the Early Church and in the Church Today.
Peabody, MA: Hendrickson Publishers, 2002. p. 75.

Dynamics of Credible Spiritual Vision
Rev. Dr. Don L. Davis

Vision originates in calling

Vision presumes gifting

Vision assures confirmation

Vision inspires commitment

Vision identifies opportunity

Vision demands strategy

Vision requires resources

Calling
+
Gifting
+
Confirmation
+
Commitment
+
Opportunity
+
Strategy
+
Resources
=
Results for God

The Church Leadership Paradigm: The Case for Biblical Leadership

Rev. Dr. Don L. Davis

1. The *Kingdom of God* has come in the person of *Jesus of Nazareth*, and is now manifest through the Spirit in the Church.

2. The cities of the world, as strongholds of the devil, desperately need the *presence* and *witness* of the Church.

3. The Church cannot thrive and provide witness without *leadership*.

4. Authentic leadership in the Church must be *called by God, represent Jesus Christ, be gifted by the Spirit, and confirmed by others* in the body.

5. Called, endowed, and confirmed leaders must be given *authority, resources, and opportunity* in order to facilitate maturity and equip the saints for ministry.

Roles of Representational Leadership

Rev. Dr. Don L. Davis

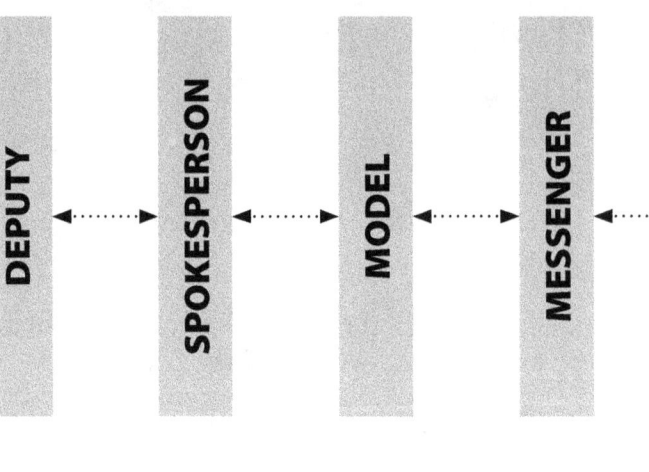

Roles of Representational Leadership

DEPUTY ↔ SPOKESPERSON ↔ MODEL ↔ MESSENGER ↔ AGENT

Things that may or may not have any bearing on the personal representation of another:

- **Background**
- **Experience**
- **Competence**
- **Confidence**
- **Opinion of Others**
- **Education**
- **Majority Acceptance**
- **Officials**
- **Traditional Ways of Promotion and Demotion**
- **Seniority**
- **Voting Habits**

Has someone granted to you the right and responsibility to stand for them in this situation?

What precisely have you been authorized to do and entrusted to steward or accomplish on behalf of the person who granted these rights to you?

What is at stake in my faithful accomplishment of my entrusted status – what will I gain or what will I forfeit with this charge?

A Sociology of Urban Leadership Development: A Tool for Assessment and Training

Rev. Dr. Don L. Davis

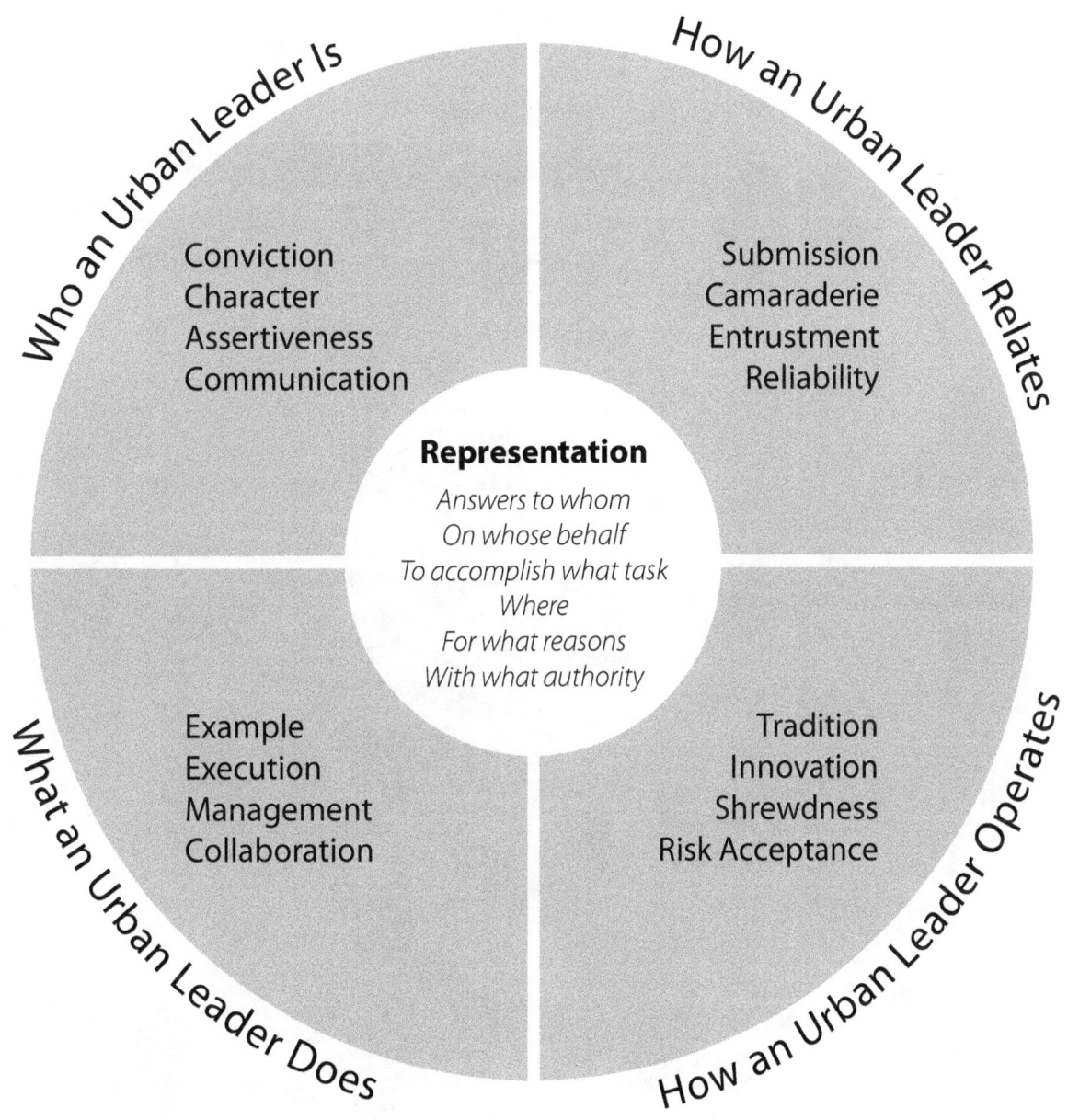

The Equipping Ministry

The Three-Step Model
Rev. Dr. Don L. Davis and Rev. Terry G. Cornett

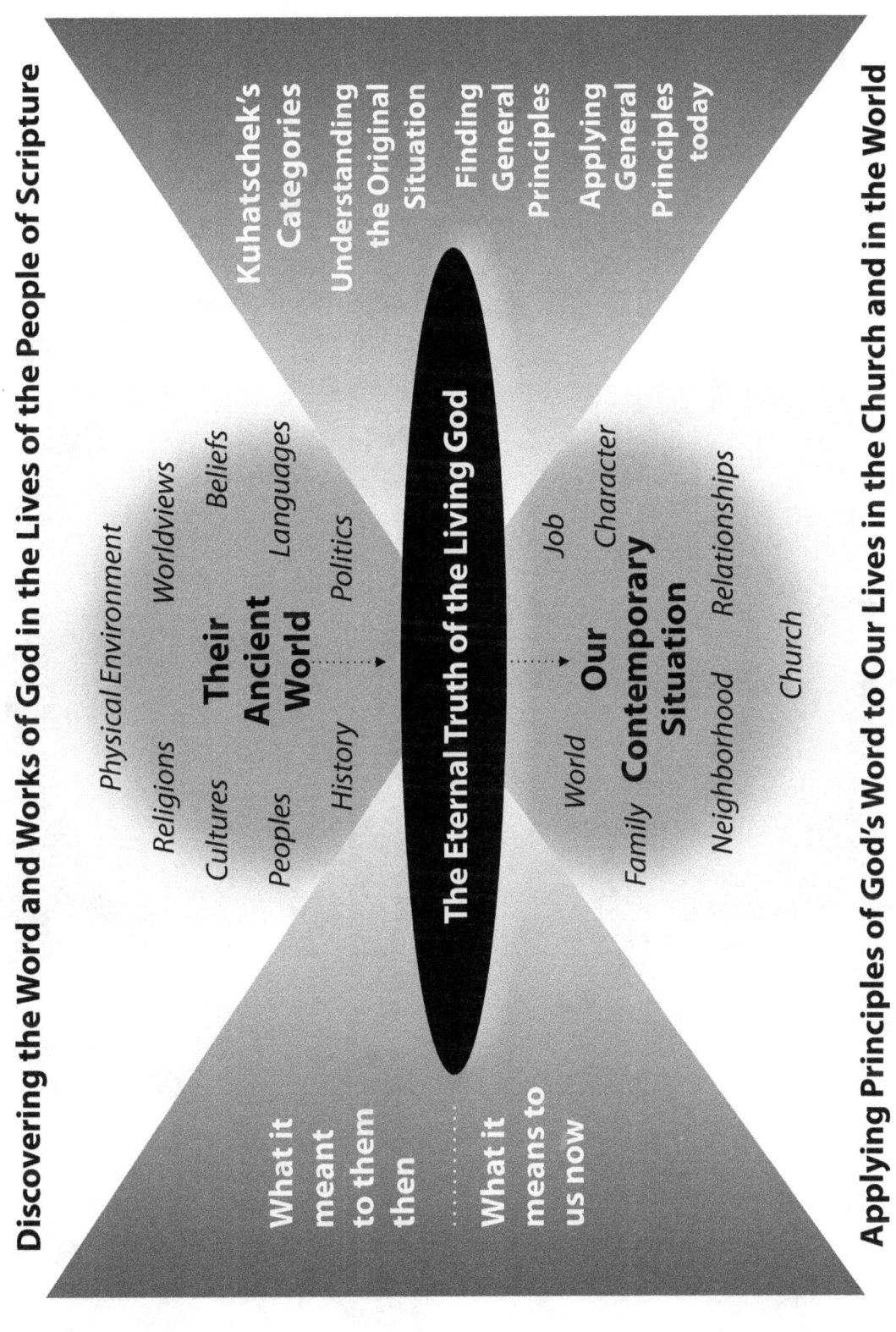

The Obedient Christian in Action
The Navigators

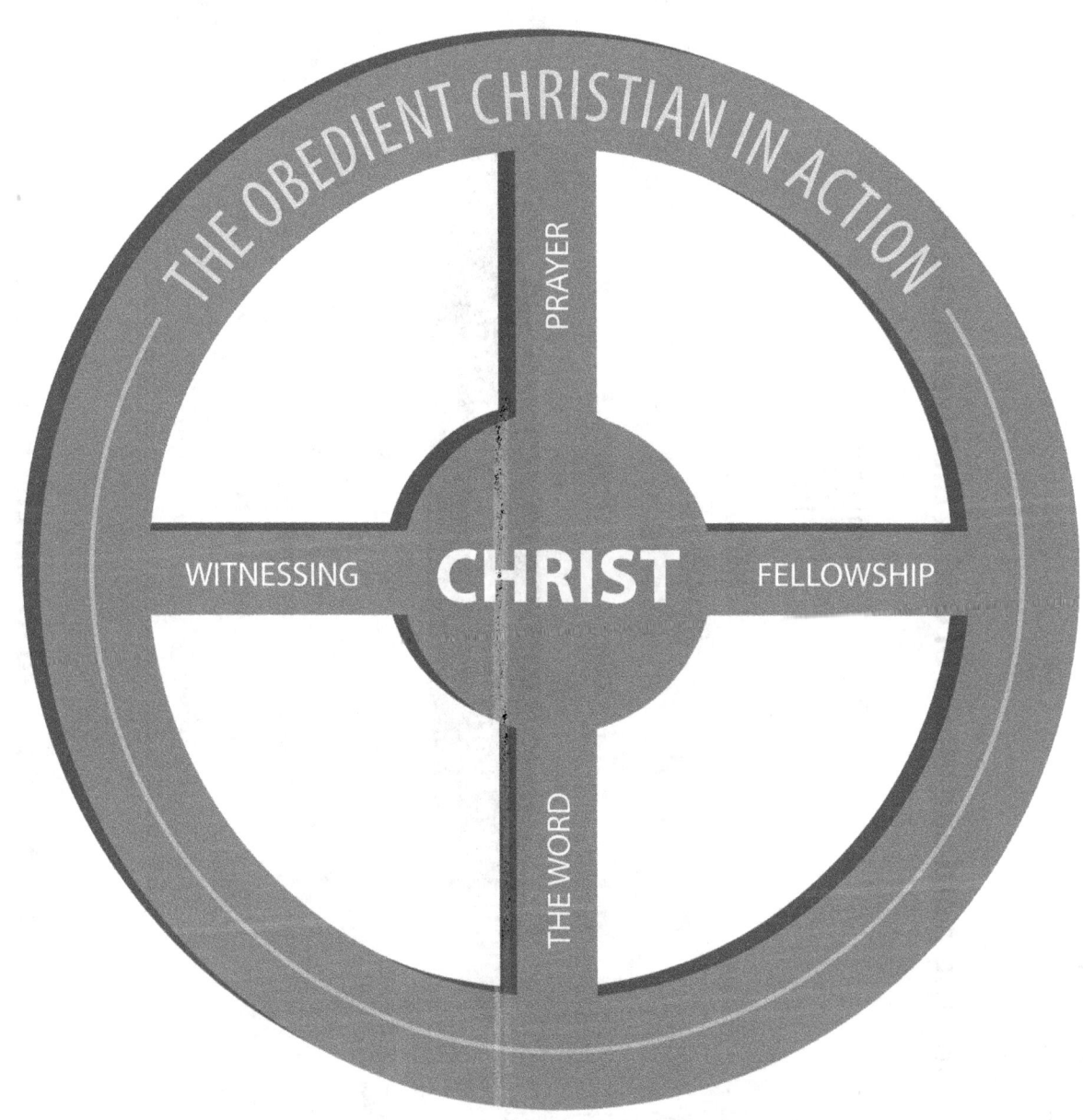

Spiritual Growth Diagrams

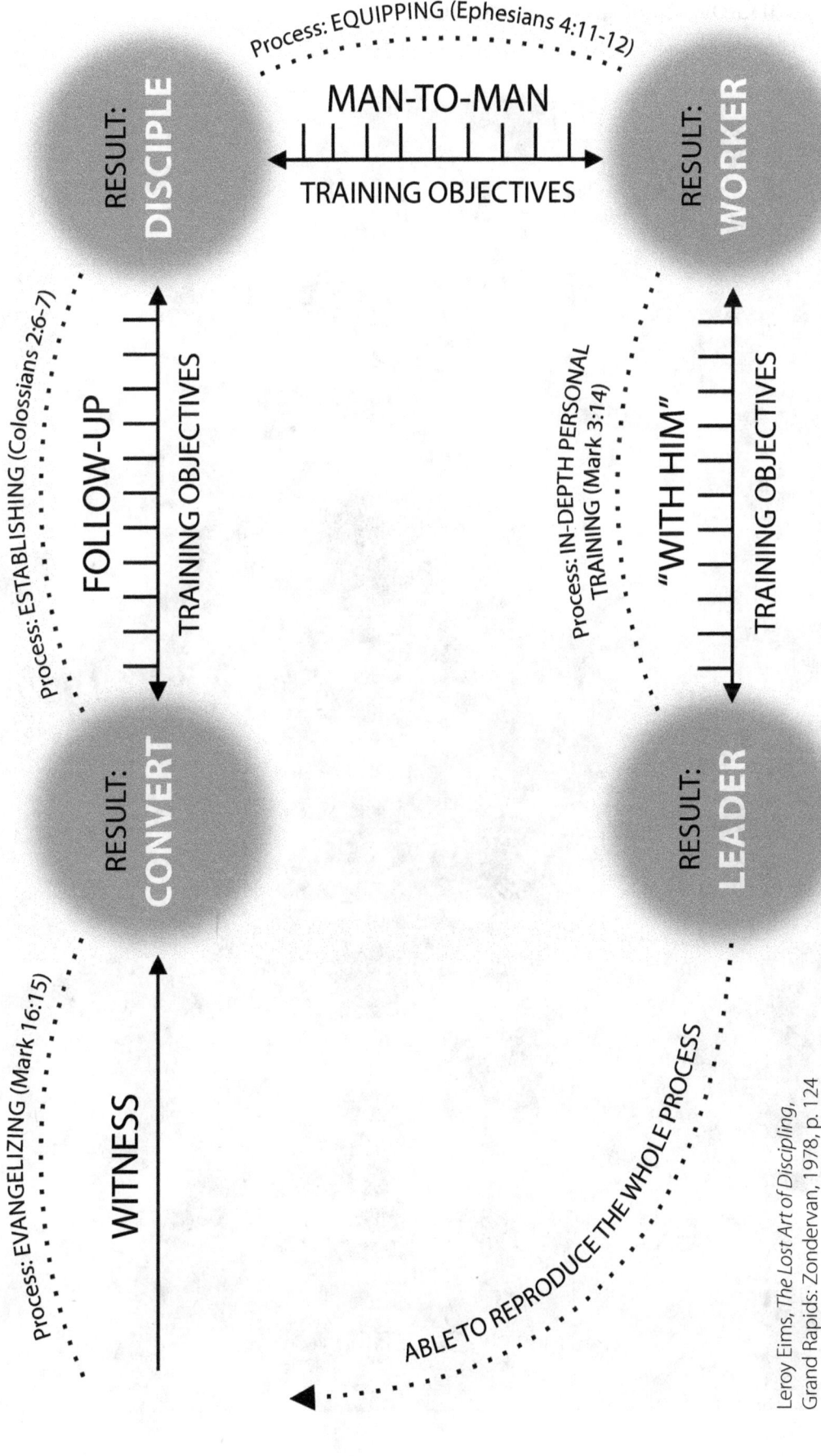

Leroy Eims, *The Lost Art of Discipling*, Grand Rapids: Zondervan, 1978, p. 124

Spiritual Growth Diagrams, continued
Adapted from Rick Warren, *The Purpose-Driven Church*, p. 144

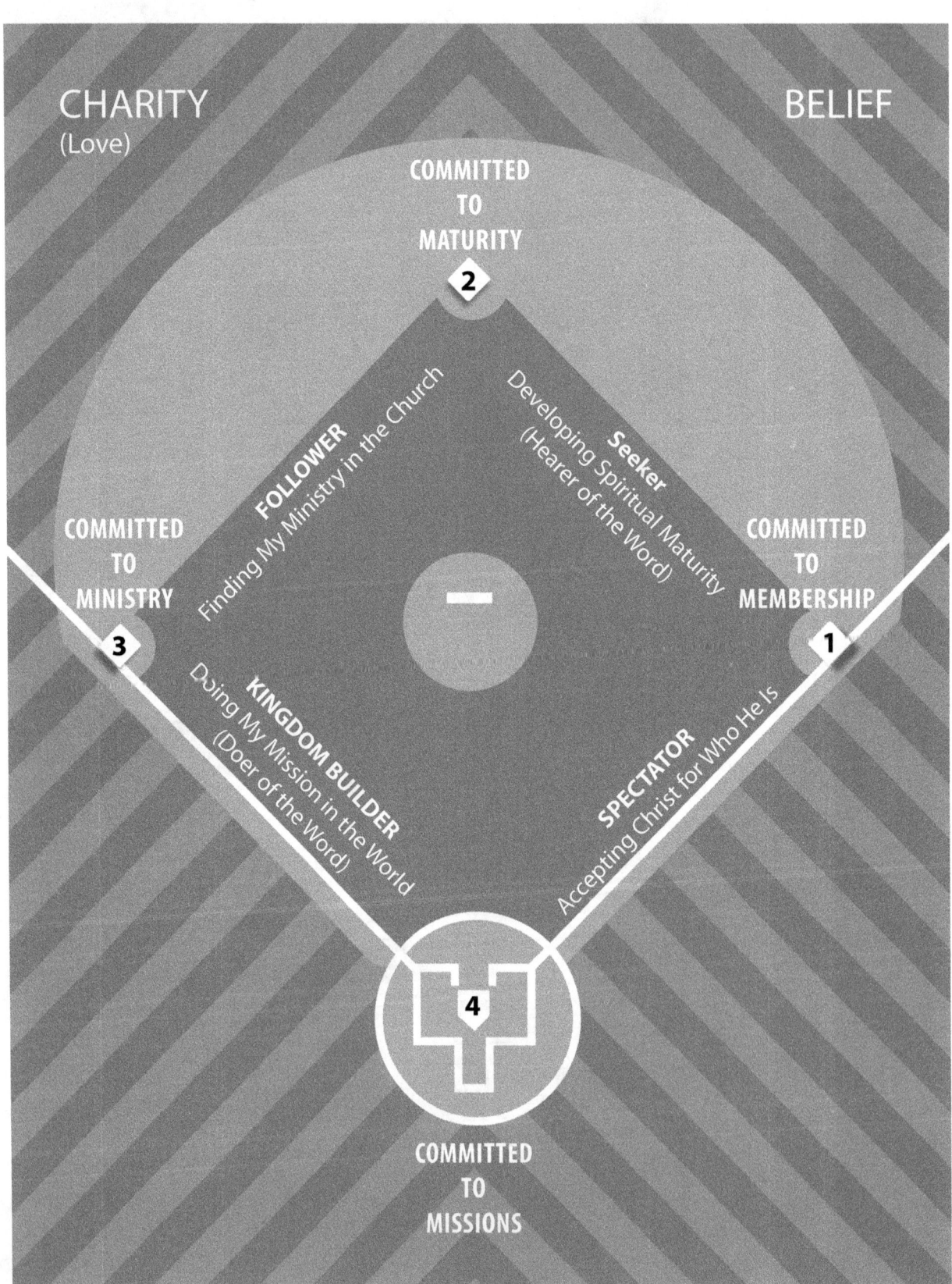

Living the Disciplines

Rev. Dr. Don L. Davis

1. Understand Why, Matthew 22:29

2. Study How, Ezra 7:10

3. Commit It to God, Psalm 5:1-3

4. Get Proper Guidance, Acts 8:30-31

5. Start Small, Luke 18:9-14

6. Begin Immediately, 2 Corinthians 6:1

7. Set Realistic Goals, Psalm 119:64

8. Recruit Partners, Psalm 34:1-4

9. Be Consistent, Daniel 6:5-10

10. Take Steps to Improve, 2 Peter 3:18

11. Help Others Grow, Hebrews 5:11-14

12. Keep It All in Focus, Philippians 1:20-21

Steps to Equipping Others

Rev. Dr. Don L. Davis

Step One

*You **become** a Master at it, striving toward mastery by practicing it with regularity, excellence, and enjoyment.* You must learn to do it, and do it excellently. While you need not be perfect, you should be able to do it, be doing it regularly, and growing in your practice of it. This is the most fundamental principle of all mentoring and discipling. You cannot teach what you do not know or cannot do, and when your Apprentice is fully trained, they will become like you (Luke 6:40).

Step Two

*You **select** an Apprentice who also desires to develop mastery of the thing, one who is teachable, faithful, and available.* Jesus called the Twelve to be with him, and to send them out to preach (Mark 3:14). His relationship was clear, neither vague nor coerced. The roles and responsibilities of the relationship must be carefully outlined, clearly discussed, and openly agreed upon.

Step Three

*You instruct and model the task **in the presence of and accompanied by** your Apprentice.* He/she comes alongside you to listen, observe, and watch. You do it with regularity and excellence, and your Apprentice comes along "for the ride," who is brought along to see how it is done. A picture is worth a thousand words. This sort of non-pressure participant observation is critical to in-depth training (2 Timothy 2:2; Philippians 4:9).

Step Four

*You do the task and **practice the thing together**.* Having modeled the act for your Apprentice in many ways and at many times, you now invite them to cooperate with you by becoming a partner-in-training, working together on the task. The goal is to do the task together, taking mutual responsibility. You coordinate your efforts, working together in harmony to accomplish the thing.

Step Five

*Your Apprentice does the task on their own, **in the presence of and accompanied by you**.* You provide opportunity to your Apprentice to practice the thing in your presence while you watch and listen. You make yourself available to help, but offer it in the background; you provide counsel, input, and guidance as they request it, but they do the task. Afterwards, you evaluate and clarify anything you may have observed as you accompanied your Apprentice (2 Corinthians 11:1).

Step Six

*Your Apprentice does the thing solo, practicing it regularly, automatically, and excellently **until mastery of the thing is gained**.* After your Apprentice has done the task under your supervision excellently, he/she is ready to be released to make the thing his/her own by habituating the act in his/her own life. You are a co-doer with your Apprentice; both of you are doing the task without coercion or aid from the other. The goal is familiarity and skillfulness in the task (Hebrews 5:11-15).

Step Seven

*Your Apprentice **becomes a Mentor of others**, selecting other faithful Apprentices to equip and train.* The training process bears fruit when the Apprentice, having mastered the thing you have equipped him/her to do, becomes a trainer of others. This is the heart of the discipling and training process (Hebrews 5:11-14; 2 Timothy 2:2)

Discipleship Diagram
Rev. Dr. Don L. Davis

2 Timothy 2:2 (ESV) – And what you have heard from me in the presence of many witnesses entrust to faithful men who will be able to teach others also.

Circle of Jewish Calendar

Robert Webber, The Biblical Foundations of Christian Worship. Peabody: Hendrickson, 1993. p. 191.

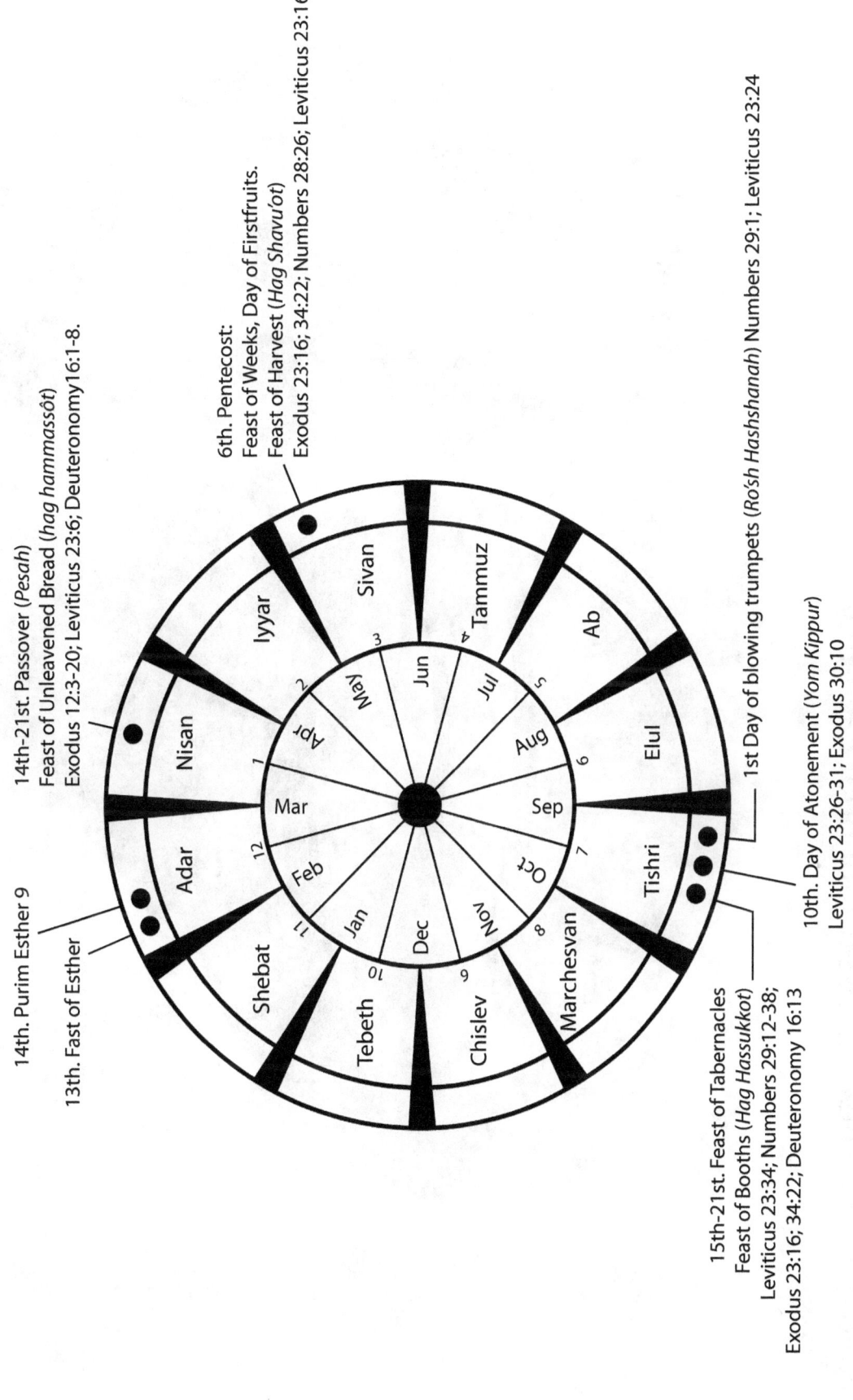

14th. Purim Esther 9

13th. Fast of Esther

14th–21st. Passover (*Pesah*)
Feast of Unleavened Bread (*hag hammassôt*)
Exodus 12:3–20; Leviticus 23:6; Deuteronomy 16:1–8.

6th. Pentecost:
Feast of Weeks, Day of Firstfruits.
Feast of Harvest (*Hag Shavu'ot*)
Exodus 23:16; 34:22; Numbers 28:26; Leviticus 23:16

1st Day of blowing trumpets (*Ro'sh Hashshanah*) Numbers 29:1; Leviticus 23:24

10th. Day of Atonement (*Yom Kippur*)
Leviticus 23:26–31; Exodus 30:10

15th–21st. Feast of Tabernacles
Feast of Booths (*Hag Hassukkot*)
Leviticus 23:34; Numbers 29:12–38;
Exodus 23:16; 34:22; Deuteronomy 16:13

Following the Life of Christ throughout Each Year

Rev. Dr. Don L. Davis

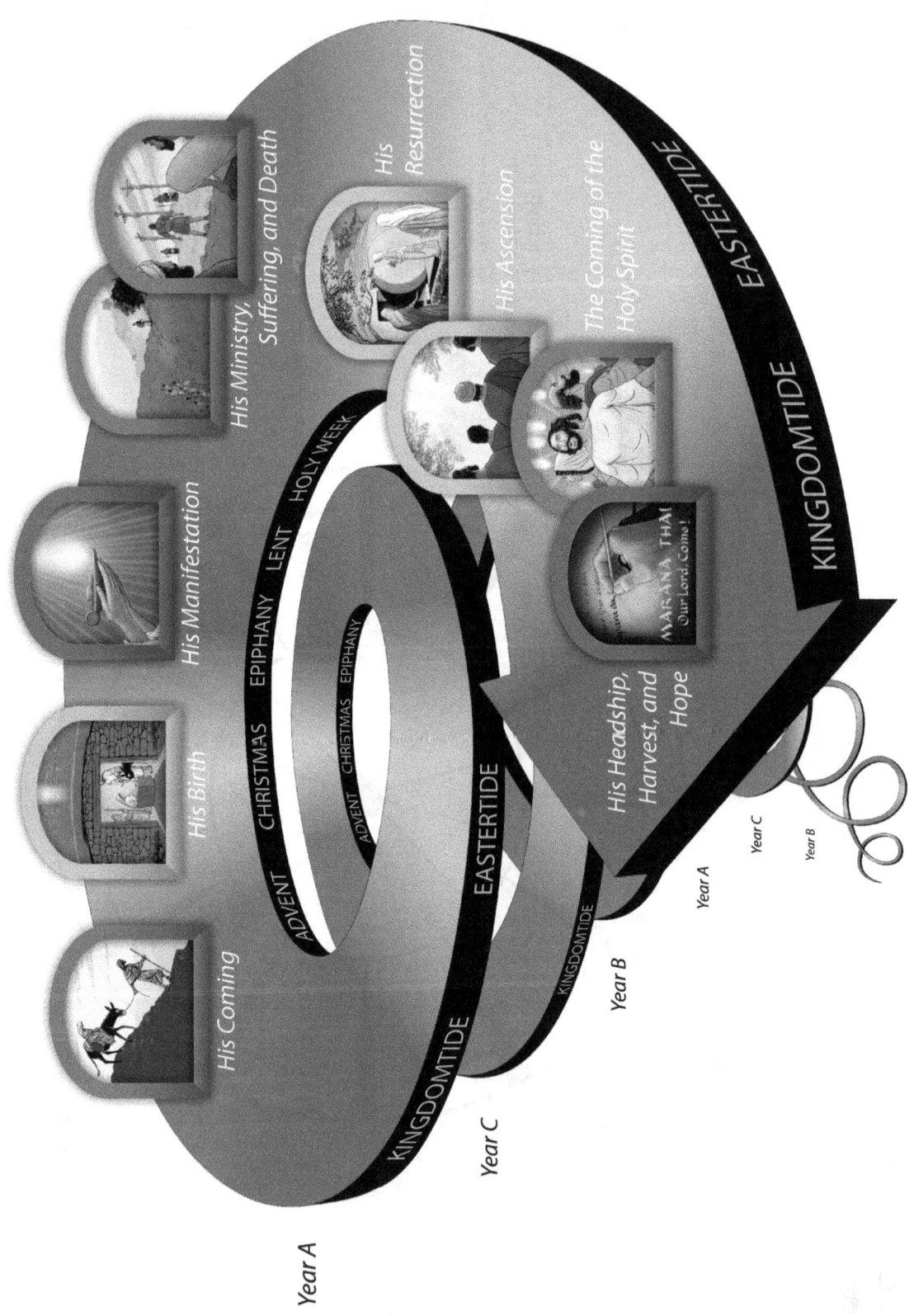

The Plot Line of the Church Year
Rev. Ryan Carter

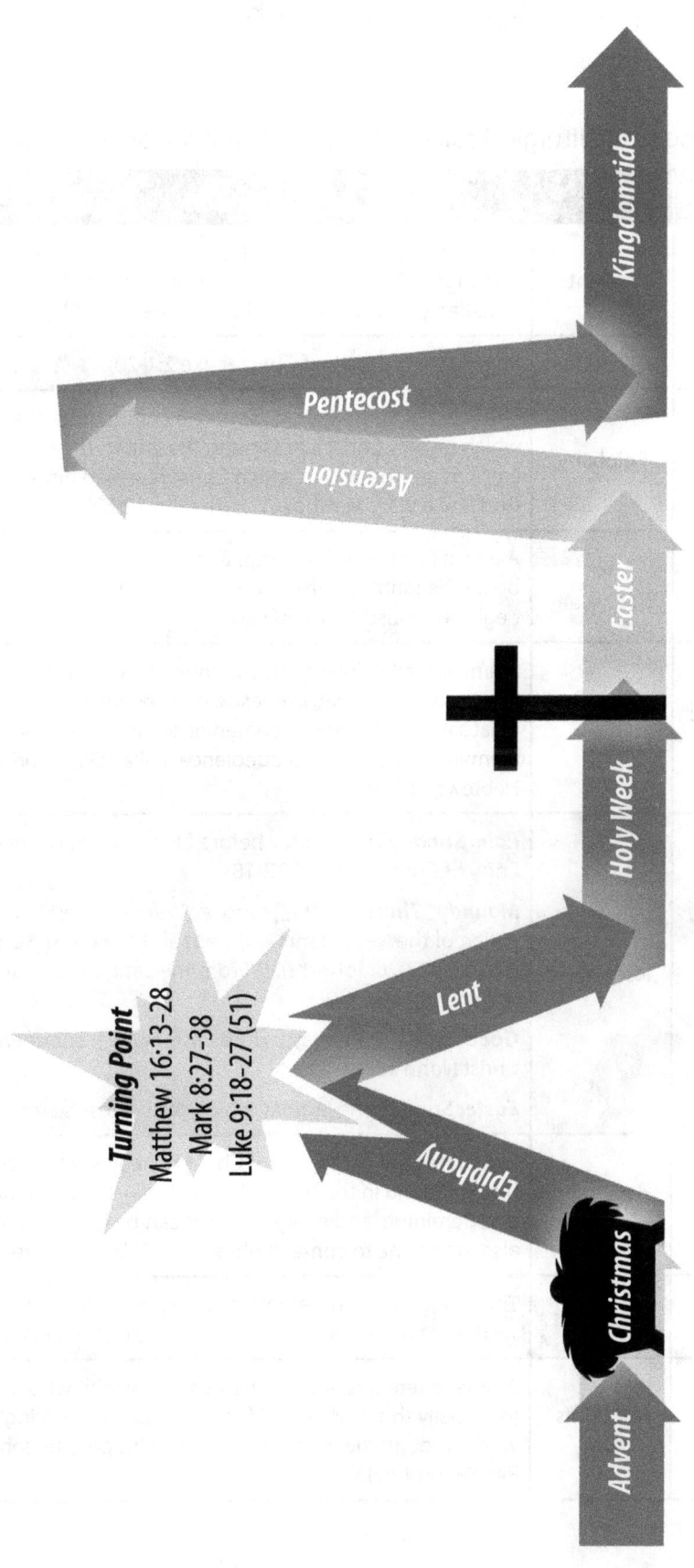

The Church Year (Western Church)

The Urban Ministry Institute

The purpose of the liturgical calendar is to relive the major events in Jesus's life in real time.

Date	Event	Purpose
Begins late Nov. or early Dec.	Advent	A season of anticipation and repentance which focuses on the First and Second Comings of Christ. The dual focus means that Advent both begins and ends the Christian year (Isaiah 9:1-7, 11:1-16; Mark 1:1-8).
Dec. 25	Christmas	Celebrates the Birth of Christ (Luke 2:1-20).
Jan. 6	Epiphany	The Feast of Epiphany on January 6 commemorates the coming of the Magi which reveals Christ's mission to the world. The entire season of Epiphany then emphasizes the way in which Christ revealed himself to the world as the Son of God (Luke 2:32; Matthew 17:1-6; John 12:32).
The seventh Wednesday before Easter	Ash Wednesday	A day of fasting and repentance that reminds us that we are disciples about to begin the journey with Jesus that ends in the cross (Luke 9:51). Ash Wednesday begins the observance of Lent.
40 days before Easter (excluding Sundays)	Lent	A time for reflection on the suffering and death of Jesus. Lent also emphasizes "death to self" so that, like Jesus, we prepare ourselves to obey God no matter what sacrifice it involves. Lenten observance calls for people to fast as a way of affirming this attitude of obedience (Luke 5:35; 1 Corinthians 9:27; 2 Timothy 2:4; Hebrews 11:1-3).
Movable depending on the date of Easter Sunday which occurs in March or April	Holy Week	*Palm Sunday* The Sunday before Easter which commemorates the Triumphal Entry of Christ (John 12:12-18). *Maundy* Thursday* The Thursday before Easter which commemorates the giving of the New Commandment and the Lord's Supper prior to Christ's Death (Mark 14:12-26; John 13). (* From the Latin mandatum novarum – "new commandment.") *Good Friday* The Friday before Easter which commemorates the crucifixion of Christ (John 18-19). *Easter Sunday* The Sunday which celebrates the resurrection of Christ (John 20).
40 days after Easter	Ascension Day	Celebrates the Ascension of Christ to heaven at which time God "seated him at his right hand in the heavenly realms, far above all rule and authority, power and dominion, and every title that can be given, not only in the present age but also in the one to come" (Ephesians 1:20b-21; 1 Peter 3:22; Luke 24:17-53).
7th Sunday after Easter	Pentecost	The day which commemorates the coming of the Holy Spirit to the Church. Jesus is now present with all his people (John 16; Acts 2).
Nov. 1	All Saints Day	A time to remember those heroes of the faith who have come before us (especially those who died for the Gospel). The living Christ is now seen in the world through the words and deeds of his people (John 14:12; Hebrews 11; Revelation 17:6).

The Church Year Follows the Ordering of the Gospels and Acts

Birth ↓ Ministry ↓ Passion ↓ Ascension ↓ Descent of the Spirit ↓ The Church through the Ages ↓ Second Coming	It begins with the birth of Christ (Advent to Epiphany).
	It then focuses on the revelation of his mission to the world (Epiphany).
	It reminds us that Jesus set his face toward Jerusalem and the cross (Ash Wednesday and Lent).
	It chronicles his final week, his crucifixion and his resurrection (Holy Week).
	It affirms his Ascension to the Father's right hand in glory (Ascension Day).
	It celebrates the birth of his Church through the ministry of his Spirit (Pentecost).
	It remembers the history of his Church throughout the ages (All Saints Day).
	Advent both ends the cycle and begins it again. It looks forward to his Second Coming as the conclusion of the Church year but also prepares to remember again his first coming and thus starts the Church year afresh.

Colors Associated with the Church Year

Christmas Season (Christmas Day through start of Epiphany): *White and Gold*

Epiphany Season: *Green*

Ash Wednesday and Lent: *Purple*

Holy Week

- Palm Sunday: *Purple*
- Maundy Thursday: *Purple*
- Good Friday: *Black*
- Easter Sunday: *White and Gold*

Ascension Day: *White and Gold*

Pentecost: *Red*

All Saints Day: *Red*

Advent Season (Fourth Sunday before Christmas through Christmas Eve): *Purple*

The Meaning of the Colors

Black	Mourning, Death
Gold	Majesty, Glory
Green	Hope, Life
Purple	Royalty, Repentance
Red	Holy Spirit (flame) Martyrdom (blood)
White	Innocence, Holiness, Joy

Spiritual Service Checklist

Rev. Dr. Don L. Davis

1. *Salvation*: Has this person believed the Gospel, confessed Jesus as Lord and Savior, been baptized, and formally joined our church as a member?

2. *Personal integrity*: Are they walking with God, growing in their personal life, and demonstrating love and faithfulness in their family, work, and in the community?

3. *Equipped in the Word*: How equipped is this person in the Word of God to share and teach with others?

4. *Support of our church*: Do they support the church through their presence, pray for the leaders and members, and give financially to its support?

5. *Submission to authority*: Does this person joyfully submit to spiritual authority?

6. *Identification of spiritual gifts*: What gifts, talents, abilities, or special resources does this person have for service, and what is their particular burden for ministry now?

7. *Present availability*: Are they open to be assigned to a task or project where we could use their service to build up the body?

8. *Reputation amongst leaders*: How do the other leaders feel about this person's readiness for a new role of leadership?

9. *Resources needed to accomplish*: If appointed to this role, what particular training, monies, resources, and/or input will they need to accomplish the task?

10. *Formal commissioning*: When and how will we make known to others that we have appointed this person to their task or project?

11. *Timing and reporting*: Also, if we dedicate this person to this role/task, when will they be able to start, and how long ought they serve before we evaluate them.

12. *Evaluate and re-commission*: When will we evaluate the performance of the person, and determine what next steps we ought to take in their leadership role at the church?

General Urban Mission

How to Start Reading the Bible

Rev. Don Allsman and Rev. Dr. Don L. Davis

1. Read individual passage, texts, and even books in light of the context of the whole Story of the Bible. How does it fit in God's redemptive plan to win all that was lost at the Fall?

2. Observe the situation. Put yourself in the setting, noticing the surroundings, the sights, the smells. Imagine what it must have been like.

3. Pay attention to commands, warnings, instructions, and inspiration that shape how you live and think so you can seek his Kingdom first.

Ways to Read through the Bible

Bible Reading Plan #1: From Genesis to Revelation

1. Start by reading through the book of John. This will give you an overview of Jesus's life and help you get some background as you read the rest of the Bible.

2. Go back to Genesis 1 and read straight through the Bible.

3. Do not get stuck on details, but read through the whole Bible to enjoy its richness and variety. Write down questions you have about words you don't understand or things that are confusing so you can ask someone or look them up later.

Bible Reading Plan #2: Chronological Reading Guide

You also can read through the Bible each year, reading the various books in the order that Christian scholars believe it was written.

Many believers read through the Scriptures together every year "chronologically" (through time), seeking to gain greater insight on the entire Story of God *as it occurred in historical order of events.*

A Schematic for a Theology of the Kingdom and the Church
The Urban Ministry Institute

The Reign of the One, True, Sovereign, and Triune God, the LORD God, Yahweh, God the Father, Son, and Holy Spirit

The Father	The Son
Love – 1 John 4:8 Maker of heaven and earth and of all things visible and invisible	Faith – Hebrews 12:2 Prophet, Priest, and King
Creation All that exists through the creative action of God	**Kingdom** The Reign of God expressed in the rule of his Son Jesus the Messiah
Revelation 8:18-31 > The eternal God, sovereign in power, infinite in wisdom, perfect in holiness, and steadfast in love, is the source and goal of all things.	**Freedom** (Slavery) Jesus replied, "I tell you the truth, everyone who sins is a slave to sin. Now a slave has no permanent place in the family but a son belongs to it forever. So if the Son sets you free, you will be free indeed." – John 8:34-36 (NIV)
Revelation 21:1-5 > O, the depth of the riches of the wisdom and knowledge of God! How unsearchable his judgments, and his paths beyond tracing out! Who has known the mind of the Lord? Or who has been his counselor? Who has ever given to God, that God should repay him? For from him and through him and to him are all things. To him be glory forever! Amen. – Romans 11:33-36 (NIV) (cf. 1 Corinthians 15:23-28; Revelation)	**Wholeness** (Sickness) But he was pierced for our transgressions, he was crushed for our iniquities; the punishment that brought us peace was upon him and by his wounds we are healed. – Isaiah 53:5 (NIV)
Isaiah 11:6-9 >	**Justice** (Selfishness) Here is my servant whom I have chosen, the one I love, in whom I delight; I will put my spirit on him and he will proclaim justice to the nations. He will not quarrel or cry out; no one will hear his voice in the streets. A bruised reed he will not break and a smoldering wick he will not put out till he leads justice to victory. – Matthew 12:18-20 (NIV)

The Spirit
Hope – Romans 15:13
Lord of the Church

Church
The one, holy, apostolic community which functions as a witness to (Acts 28:31) and a foretaste of (Colossians 1:12; James 1:18; 1 Peter 2:9; Revelation 1:6) the Kingdom of God

The Church is an apostolic community where the Word is rightly preached; therefore it is a community of:

Calling – It is for freedom that Christ has set us free. Stand firm, then, and do not let yourselves be burdened again by a yoke of slavery. – Galatians 5:1 (NIV) (cf. Romans 8:28-30; 1 Corinthians 1:26-31; Ephesians 1:18; 2 Thessalonians 2:13-14; Jude 1:1)

Faith – "If you do not believe that I am the one I claim to be, you will indeed die in your sins". . . . To the Jews who had believed him Jesus said, "If you hold to my teaching you are really my disciples. Then you will know the truth and the truth will set you free."- John 8:24b, 31-32 (NIV) (cf. Psalm 119:45; Romans 1:17; 5:1-2; Ephesians 2:8-9; 2 Timothy 1:13-14; Hebrews 2:14-15; James 1:25)

Witness – The Spirit of the Lord is upon me because he has anointed me to preach good news to the poor. He has sent me to proclaim freedom for the prisoners and recovery of sight for the blind, to release the oppressed, to proclaim the year of the Lord's favor. – Luke 4:18-19 (NIV) (cf. Leviticus 25:10; Proverbs 31:8; Matthew 4:17; 28:18-20; Mark 13:10; Acts 1:8; 8:4, 12; 13:1-3; 25:20; 28:30-31)

The Church is one community where the sacraments are rightly administered; therefore it is a community of:

Worship – Worship the Lord your God, and his blessing will be on your food and water. I will take away sickness from among you. – Exodus 23:25 (NIV) (cf. Psalm 147:1-3; Hebrews 12:28; Colossians 3:16; Revelation 15:3-4; 19:5)

Covenant – The Holy Spirit also testifies to us about this. First he says: "This is the covenant I will make with them after that time, says the Lord. I will put My laws in their hearts, and I will write them on their minds." Then he adds: "Their sins and lawless acts I will remember no more." – Hebrews 10:15-17 (NIV) (cf. Isaiah 54:10-17; Ezekiel 34:25-31; 37:26-27; Malachi 2:4-5; Luke 22:20; 2 Corinthians 3:6; Colossians 3:15; Hebrews 8:7-13; 12:22-24; 13:20-21)

Presence – And in him you too are being built together to become a dwelling in which God lives by his Spirit. – Ephesians 2:22 (NIV) (cf. Exodus 40:34-38; Ezekiel 48:35; Matthew 18:18-20)

The Church is a holy community where discipline is rightly ordered; therefore it is a community of:

Reconciliation – For he himself is our peace, who has made the two one and has destroyed the barrier, the dividing wall of hostility by abolishing in his flesh the law with its commandments and regulations. His purpose was to create one new man out of two, thus making peace and in this one body to reconcile both of them to God through the cross, by which he put to death their hostility. He came and preached peace to those who were far off and peace to those who were near. For through him we have access to the Father by one Spirit. - Ephesians 2:14-18 (NIV) (cf. Exodus 23:4-9; Leviticus 19:34; Deuteronomy 10:18-19; Ezekiel 22:29; Micah 6:8; 2 Corinthians 5:16-21)

Suffering – Therefore, since Christ suffered in his body, arm yourselves also with the same attitude, because he who has suffered in his body is done with sin. As a result, he does not live the rest of his earthly life for evil human desires, but rather for the will of God. – 1 Peter 4:1-2 (NIV) (cf. Luke 6:22; 10:3; Romans 8:17; 2 Timothy 2:3; 3:12; 1 Peter 2:20-24; Hebrews 5:8; 13:11-14)

Service – Jesus called them together and said, "You know that the rulers of the Gentiles lord it over them, and their high officials exercise authority over them. Not so with you. Instead, whoever wants to become great among you must be your servant, and whoever wants to be first must be your slave – just as the Son of Man did not come to be served, but to serve and to give his life as a ransom for many." – Matthew 20:25-27 (NIV) (cf. 1 John 4:16-18; Galatians 2:10)

From Deep Ignorance to Credible Witness
Rev. Dr. Don L. Davis

Level	Stage	Scripture References	Quote
8	**Witness – Ability to give witness and teach**	2 Timothy 2:2 / Matthew 28:18-20 / 1 John 1:1-4 / Proverbs 20:6 / 2 Corinthians 5:18-21	*And the things you have heard me say in the presence of many witnesses entrust to reliable men who will also be qualified to teach others. – 2 Timothy 2:2*
7	**Lifestyle – Consistent appropriation and habitual practice based on beliefs**	Hebrews 5:11-6:2 / Ephesians 4:11-16 / 2 Peter 3:18 / 1 Timothy 4:7-10	*And Jesus increased in wisdom and in stature, and in favor with God and man. – Luke 2:52*
6	**Demonstration – Expressing conviction in corresponding conduct, speech, and behavior**	James 2:14-26 / 2 Corinthians 4:13 / 2 Peter 1:5-9 / 1 Thessalonians 1:3-10	*Nevertheless, at your word I will let down the net. – Luke 5:5*
5	**Conviction – Committing oneself to think, speak, and act in light of information**	Hebrews 2:3-4 / Hebrews 11:1, 6 / Hebrews 3:15-19 / Hebrews 4:2-6	*Do you believe this? – John 11:26*
4	**Discernment – Understanding the meaning and implications of information**	John 16:13 / Ephesians 1:15-18 / Colossians 1:9-10 / Isaiah 6:10; 29:10	*Do you understand what you are reading? – Acts 8:30*
3	**Knowledge – Ability to recall and recite information**	2 Timothy 3:16-17 / 1 Corinthians 2:9-16 / 1 John 2:20-27 / John 14:26	*For what does the Scripture say? – Romans 4:3*
2	**Interest – Responding to ideas or information with both curiosity and openness**	Psalm 42:1-2 / Acts 9:4-5 / John 12:21 / 1 Samuel 3:4-10	*We will hear you again on this matter. – Acts 17:32*
1	**Awareness – General exposure to ideas and information**	Mark 7:6-8 / Acts 19:1-7 / John 5:39-40 / Matthew 7:21-23	*At that time, Herod the tetrarch heard about the fame of Jesus. – Matthew 14:1*
0	**Ignorance – Unfamiliarity with information due to naivete, indifference, or hardness**	Ephesians 4:17-19 / Psalm 2:1-3 / Romans 1:21; 2:19 / 1 John 2:11	*Who is the Lord that I should heed his voice? – Exodus 5:2*

Suffering:
The Cost of Discipleship and Servant-Leadership

Rev. Dr. Don L. Davis

To be a disciple is to bear the stigma and reproach of the One who called you into service (2 Timothy 3:12). Practically, this may mean the loss of comfort, convenience, and even life itself (John 12:24-25).

All of Christ's Apostles endured insults, rebukes, lashes, and rejections by the enemies of their Master. Each of them sealed their doctrines with their blood in exile, torture, and martyrdom. Listed below are the fates of the Apostles according to traditional accounts.

- Matthew suffered martyrdom by being slain with a sword at a distant city of Ethiopia.

- Mark expired at Alexandria, after being cruelly dragged through the streets of that city.

- Luke was hanged upon an olive tree in the classic land of Greece.

- John was put in a cauldron of boiling oil, but escaped death in a miraculous manner, and was afterward branded at Patmos.

- Peter was crucified at Rome with his head downward.

- James, the Greater, was beheaded at Jerusalem.

- James, the Less, was thrown from a lofty pinnacle of the temple, and then beaten to death with a fuller's club.

- Bartholomew was flayed alive.

- Andrew was bound to a cross, whence he preached to his persecutors until he died.

- Thomas was run through the body with a lance at Coromandel in the East Indies.

- Jude was shot to death with arrows.

- Matthias was first stoned and then beheaded.

- Barnabas of the Gentiles was stoned to death at Salonica.

- Paul, after various tortures and persecutions, was at length beheaded at Rome by the Emperor Nero.

The Way of Wisdom

Rev. Dr. Don L. Davis • Proverbs 2:1-9; 8:1-9; 1:7; 8:13

Sowing and Reaping (Galatians 6:7-8)

You will **sow**	What you **think about**
You will **reap** what you sow	How you **dress**
You will reap **more than** what you sow	How you **speak**
You will reap in **proportion** to what you sow	Who you **hang out with**
You will reap **in kind** as you sow	What you **listen to and look at**
You will reap in a **different season** than you sow	What you **read**
You determine what you sow	Where you **go**
You can **sow differently** than you did last year	How you **make decisions**
You reap more if you **cultivate and fertilize**	What your **goals** are
Your sowing can **affect what others reap** also	**What's important** to you

The Goal

Be like Jesus
1 Corinthians 11:2; Romans 8:29; Philippians 3:8-12

Loving God with all our heart
Deuteronomy 6:4-6; Matthew 22:34-40

Loving our neighbors as ourselves
Leviticus 19:18; Matthew 7:12

The Way of Life (Proverbs 1:7-8; 4:13; 8:10; 9:9; 10:17; 13:18; 15:32-33; 23:23)

The Narrow Way (Matthew 7:13-14)

Isaiah 26:1-9

Doctrine (The Way)

Rebuke (the way off)
2 Timothy 3:16-17; John 8:31-32; 1 John 4:6
Proverbs 9:9; 11:14; 12:15; 15:22; 19:20; 20:18; 24:6; 13:10; 15:10

Instruction in righteousness (On track)
Psalms 31:3; 48:14; Isaiah 42:16; Psalms 125; 4-5; 25:5; 27:11

Correction (the way back)
Proverbs 13:1; 19:20; Hebrews 5:8; Matthew 26:39; Psalms 31:3; 119:35; 143:10; Proverbs 6:20-23; Jeremiah 42:1-3

The Way That Leads to Death
Proverbs 14:12; 16:25; 1:24-33; 2:10-22; 15:9; 15:19, 24, 29; 13:15; Job 15:20; Psalm 107:17; Romans 2:9

Foundations for Christian Mission

Story: The Crux of Revelation

Rev. Ryan Carter

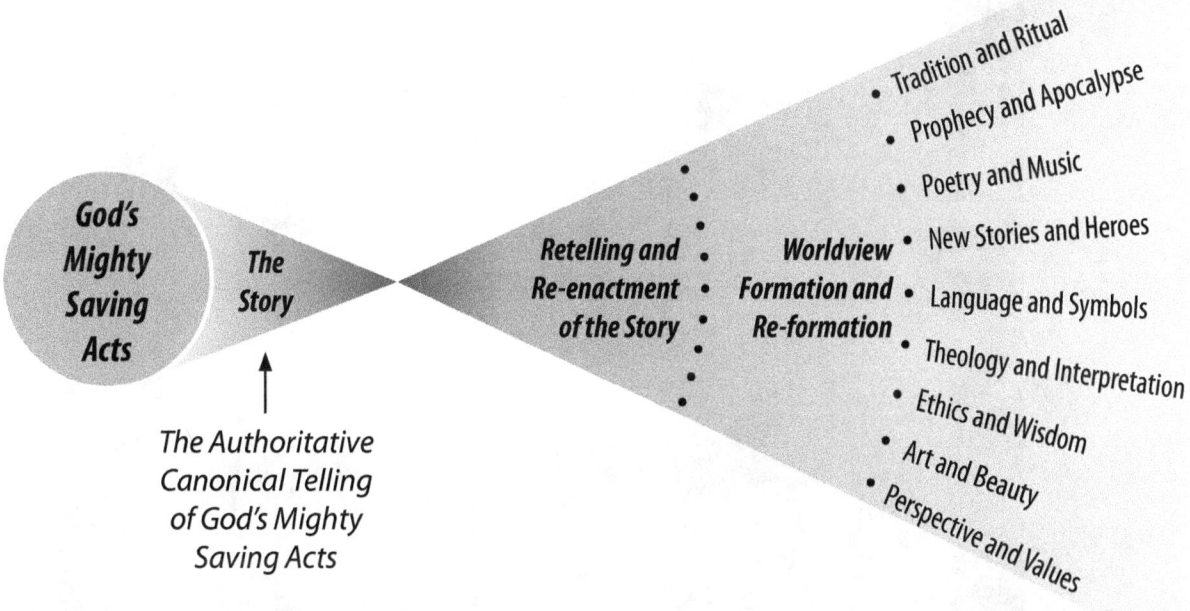

Developing Ears That Hear: Responding to the Spirit and the Word

Rev. Dr. Don L. Davis

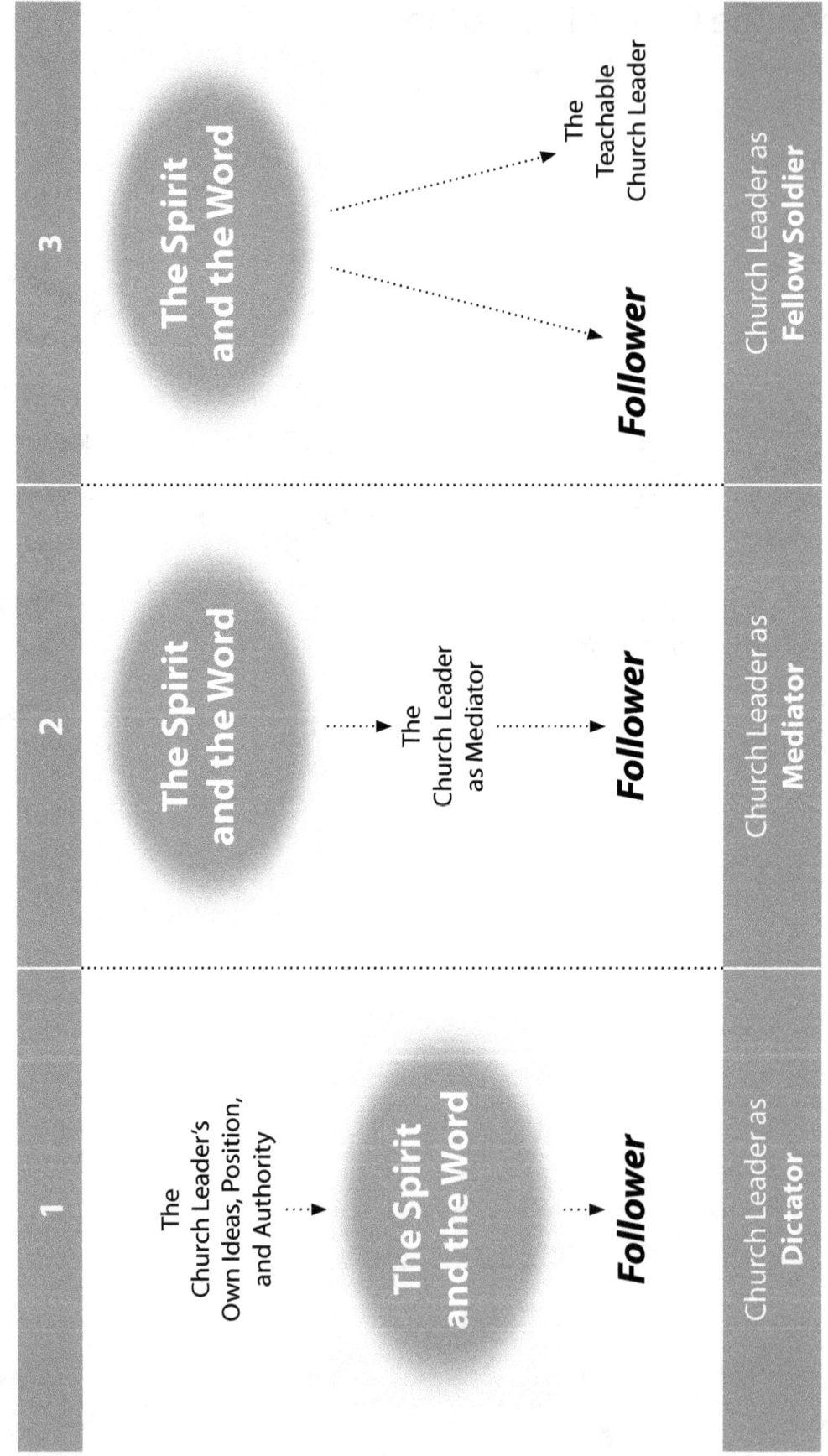

Toward a Hermeneutic of Critical Engagement

Rev. Dr. Don L. Davis

Replicare ~
to fold back; to fold again, to answer, to bend or twist together again

To respond in words, whether spoken or written, or in actions; to communicate in response back to the other; to twist together and connect one's own view with and/or against the view of the other as carefully as possible

(Caricature!)

Resonare ~
to sound again: to echo

To seek to find within the communication of the other some idea, belief, or statement with which one may empathize, sympathize, or find some commonality with

(Disconnection!)

Re + specere ~
to look, to look again

To consider worthy of reference, esteem, to treat with the highest sense of importance

(Disrespect!)

Respit ~
the act of looking back

To grant a period of open audience, to put off judgment and to suspend final conclusions on a matter until the argument of the other has been fully heard and understood

(Automatic judgment!)

Regarder ~
to look back, to guard

To pay attention, to take into careful consideration, to take into critical account the words, beliefs, and actions of another

(Disregard!)

Reflecter ~
to bend back, to mirror

To give back or exhibit as an image, likeness or outline; to reflect back; to reproduce accurately and clearly what the other has presented and communicated

(Generalization!)

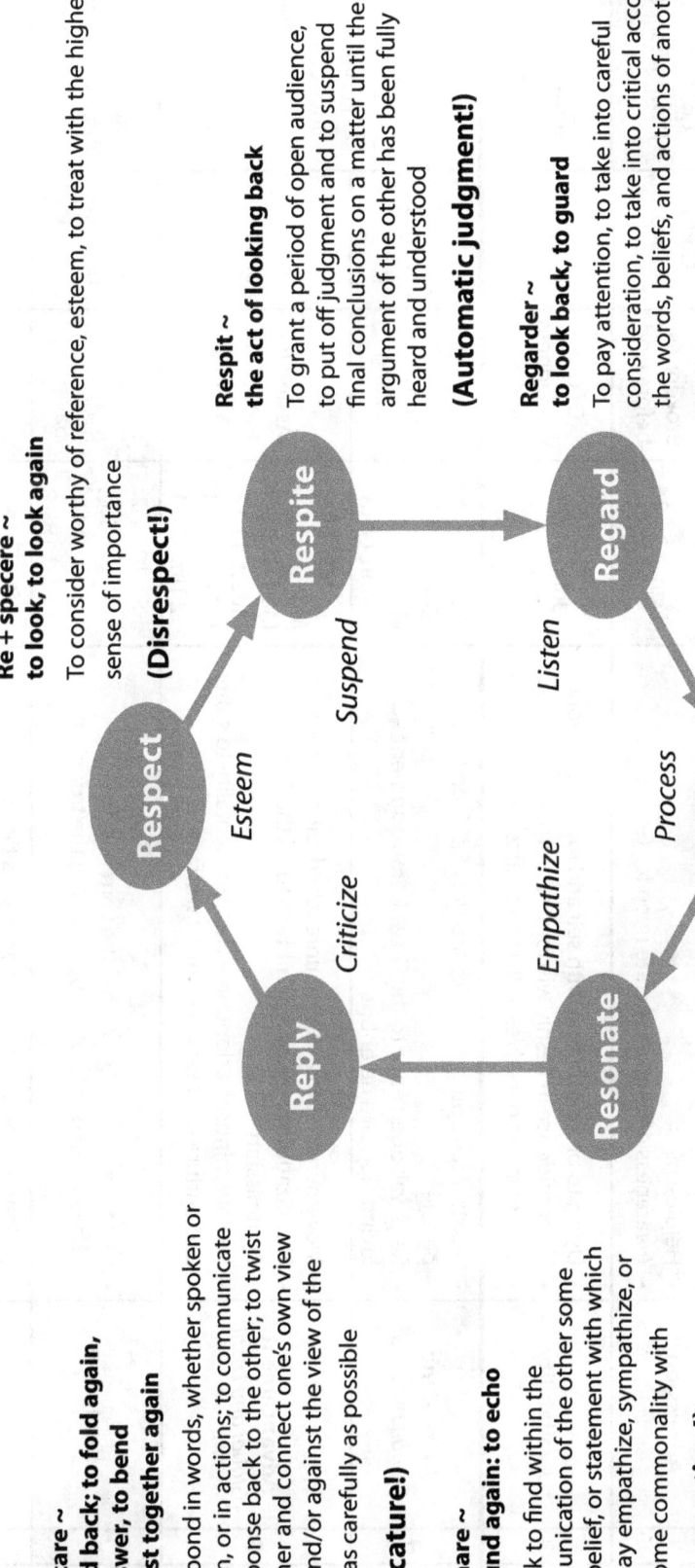

Assumptions about traditions:
1. Traditions deserve respect
2. Traditions ought not be prematurely judged
3. Traditions should be critically engaged
4. Traditions must be taken seriously
5. Traditions should be assessed
6. Traditions ought to be constructively utilized

Let God Arise! The Seven "A's" of Seeking the Lord and Entreating His Favor

Rev. Dr. Don L. Davis

		Theme	Scripture	Awareness		Concert of Prayer
1	**Adoration**	• Delight and enjoyment in God • Overwhelming gratefulness • Acknowledging God in his person and works	Ps. 29:1-2 Rev. 4-11 Rom. 11:33-36 Ps. 27:4-8	Of God's Majestic Glory		Gather to Worship and Pray
2	**Admission**	• Powerlessness • Helplessness • Awareness of one's desperate need for God	Ps. 34:18-19 Prov. 28:13 Dan. 4:34-35 Isa. 30:1-5	Of Our Brokenness before God	God's Face	Confess Your Powerlessness
3	**Availability**	• Dying to preoccupation with self and love of the world • No confidence in fleshly wisdom, resources, or method • Consecrating ourselves as living sacrifices to God	Rom. 12:1-5 John 12:24 Phil. 3:3-8 Gal. 6:14	Of Our Yieldedness to God		Surrender Your All to Christ
4	**Awakening** *Global and Local*	• Refreshment: outpouring of the Holy Spirit on God's people • Renewal: obedience to the Great Commandment – loving God and neighbor	Hos. 6:1-3 Eph. 3:15-21 Matt. 22:37-40 John 14:15	Asking for the Spirit's Filling	Fullness	
5	**Advancement** *Global and Local*	• Movements: outreaches to unreached, pioneer regions • Mobilization: of every assembly to fulfill the Great Commission • Military mindset: adopting a warfare mentality to suffer and endure hardness in spiritual warfare	Acts 1:8 Mark 16:15-16 Matt. 28:18-20 Matt. 11:12 Luke 19:41-42 2 Tim. 2:1-4	Asking for the Spirit's Moving	Fulfillment	Fervently Intercede on Behalf of Others
6	**Affirmation**	• Giving testimony over what the Lord has done • Challenging one another by speaking the truth in love	Ps. 107:1-2 Heb. 3:13 2 Cor. 4:13 Mal. 3:16-18	The Redeemed Saying So	The Faith	Encourage One Another in Truth and Testimony
7	**Acknowledgment**	• Waiting patiently on God to act by his timing and methods • Living confidently as though God is answering our petitions • Acting as if God will do precisely what he says he will do	Ps. 27:14 2 Chron. 20:12 Prov. 3:5-6 Isa. 55:8-11 Ps. 2:8	Keeping Our Eyes on the Lord	The Fight	Scatter to Work and Wait

"Seek the Lord" — Zechariah 8:18-23 • Isaiah 55:6 (rows 1-3)

"Entreat the Favor of the Lord" — Zechariah 8:18-23 • Jeremiah 33:3 (rows 4-7)

The Oikos Factor:
Spheres of Relationship and Influence
Rev. Dr. Don L. Davis

Survey: 42,000 asked: Who or what was responsible for your coming to Christ and your church:	
Special need	1-2%
Walk-in	2-3%
Pastor	5-6%
Visitation	1-2%
Sunday School	4-5%
Evangelistic crusade/TV	1/2%
Church program	2-3%
Friend or relative	75-90%!!

– Church Growth, Inc. Monrovia, CA

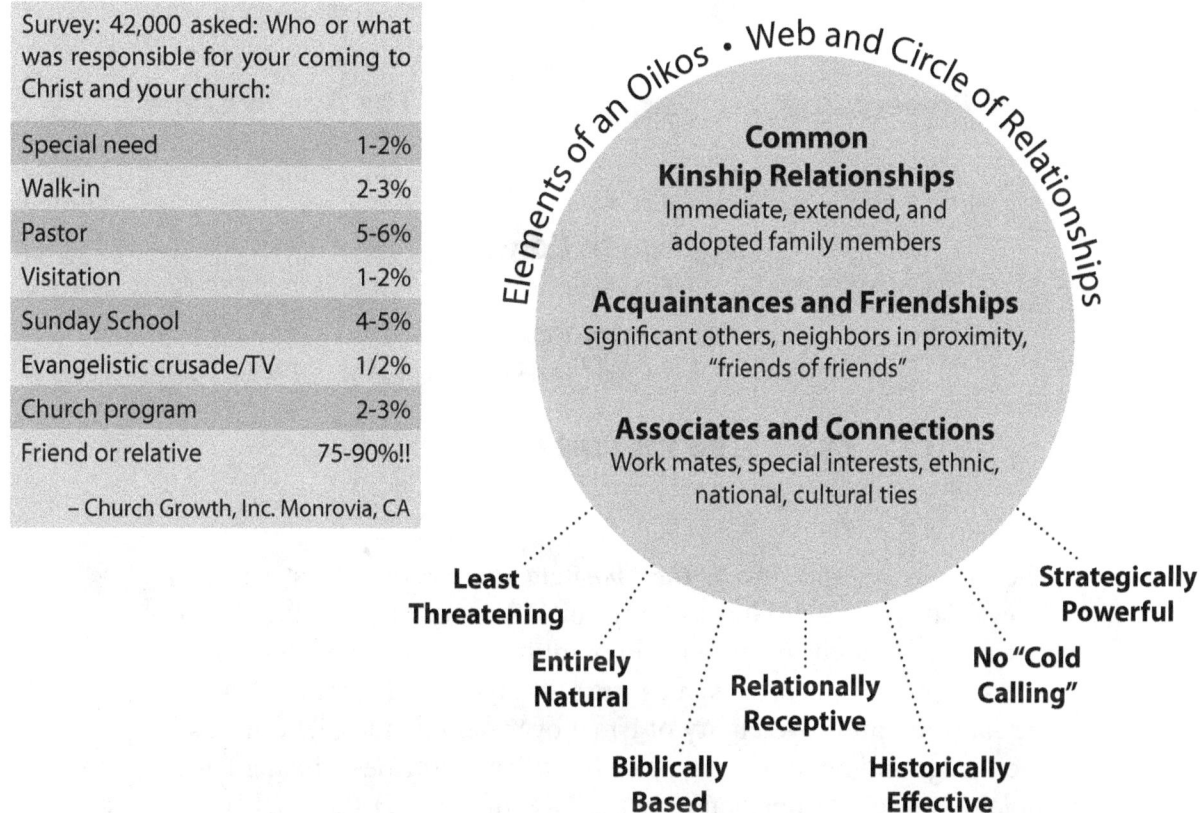

Elements of an Oikos • Web and Circle of Relationships

Common Kinship Relationships
Immediate, extended, and adopted family members

Acquaintances and Friendships
Significant others, neighbors in proximity, "friends of friends"

Associates and Connections
Work mates, special interests, ethnic, national, cultural ties

- Least Threatening
- Entirely Natural
- Biblically Based
- Relationally Receptive
- Historically Effective
- No "Cold Calling"
- Strategically Powerful

Oikos (household) in the Old Testament
"A household usually contained four generations, including men, married women, unmarried daughters, slaves of both sexes, persons without citizenship, and "sojourners," or resident foreign workers."
– Hans Walter Wolff, *Anthology of the Old Testament*.

Oikos (household) in the New Testament
Evangelism and disciple making in our New Testament narratives are often described as following the flow of the relational networks of various people within their *oikoi* (households), that is, those natural lines of connection in which they resided and lived (c.f., Mark 5:19; Luke 19:9; John 4:53; 1:41-45, etc.). Andrew to Simon (John 1:41-45), and both Cornelius (Acts 10-11) and the Philippian jailer (Acts 16) are notable cases of evangelism and discipling through *oikoi*.

Oikos (household) among the urban poor
While great differences exist between cultures, kinship relationships, special interest groups, and family structures among urban populations, it is clear that urbanites connect with others far more on the basis of connections through relationships, friendships, and family than through proximity and neighborhood alone. Oftentimes, the closest friends of urban poor dwellers are not immediately close by in terms of neighborhood; family and friends may dwell blocks, even miles away. Taking the time to study the precise linkages of relationships among the dwellers in a certain area can prove extremely helpful in determining the most effective strategies for evangelism and disciple making in inner city contexts.

Kingdom of God Timeline

Rev. Dr. Don L. Davis

The *"malkuth" of Yahweh, the "basileia tou Theou."* First century Palestinian Jews saw God as King, of his people Israel and all the earth. Yet, due to the rebellion of humankind and Satan and his angels, God's reign in the earth is yet future. It shall be: 1) nationalistic – the salvation and sovereignty of Israel over her enemies, 2) universal knowledge and reign of God, 3) *tsidkenu* (righteousness, justice) and *shalom* (peace), 4) obedience to the Law of God, 5) the final battle with the Gentile nations – Armageddon, 6) occur by a supernatural cataclysm realized at the end of time, 7) transformation of the heavens and earth to pre-Edenic splendor, 8) rule by the son of David-son of Man, 9) rescinding the effects of the curse, 10) the resurrection of the dead, 11) and judgment and destruction of all of God's enemies – sin, death, evil, the "world," the devil and his angels, and 12) eternal life.

Jesus's proclamation: **The Kingdom of God has now appeared in the life, person, and ministry of Messiah Jesus.** In Jesus's words (*kerygma*), his deeds of compassion (*diakonia*), his miracles, his exorcisms of demons, his passion, death, and resurrection, and the sending of the Spirit, **the promised-for Kingdom has come.** The Kingdom is both present and future; he announces **the presence of the future.** Present kingdom blessings include 1) the Church as sign and foretaste, 2) the pledge of the Holy Spirit, 3) the forgiveness of sin, 4) the proclamation of the Kingdom worldwide, 5) reconciliation and peace with God, 6) the binding of Satan, with authority given to Christ's disciples.

That We May Be One:
Elements of an Integrated Church Planting Movement among the Urban Poor

Rev. Dr. Don L. Davis

> It is a most invaluable part of that blessed "liberty wherewith Christ hath made us free," that in his worship different forms and usages may without offence be allowed, provided the substance of the Faith be kept entire; and that, in every Church, what cannot be clearly determined to belong to Doctrine must be referred to Discipline; and therefore, by common consent and authority, may be altered, abridged, enlarged, amended, or otherwise disposed of, as may seem most convenient for the edification of the people, "according to the various exigency of times and occasions."
>
> – 1789 Preface to the *Book of Common Prayer*. 1928 Episcopal edition.

Church Planting Movements among the Urban Poor = an integrated and aggressive advance of the Kingdom of God among the urban poor resulting in a significant increase of indigenous churches which fundamentally share in common a constellation of elements which provides them with a distinct and unique identity, purpose, and practice.

Ministry among the urban poor must be grounded in a vision and understanding of the liberty we have in Christ to conceive of coherent, integrated movements of followers of Jesus who because of shared experience, proximity, culture, and history determine to reflect their unique faith and practice in a way consistent with the historic faith but distinct to their life and times. This is not an arbitrary act; movements cannot ignore the nature of the one (unity), holy (sanctity), catholic (universality), and apostolic (apostolicity) Church, the one true people of God.

Nevertheless, as was affirmed by the emerging leaders of the then American Episcopal Church, the freedom that we have in Christ allows for different forms and usages of worship in the body of Christ without any offense whatsoever, as long as we are faithful to the historic orthodox beliefs of the Church as taught to us by the prophets and apostles of our Lord. Doctrine must remain anchored and complete; discipline, however, can be based on the contingencies and exigencies of the people who embrace them, as long as all that is shaped and conceived builds up the body of Christ, and glorifies God our Father through our Lord Jesus Christ.

"The congregations in an Integrated Church Planting Movement among the Urban Poor *will exhibit together:*"

1. *A shared history and identity* (i.e., *a common name and heritage*). CPMs among the urban poor will seek to link themselves to and identify themselves by a well defined and joyfully shared history and persona that all members and congregations share.

2. *A shared liturgy and celebration* (i.e., *a common worship*). CPMs among the urban poor should reflect a shared hymnody, practice of the sacraments, theological focus and imagery, aesthetic vision, vestments, liturgical order, symbology, and spiritual formation that enables us to worship and glorify God in a way that lifts up the Lord and attracts urbanites to vital worship.

3. *A shared membership, well-being, welfare, and support* (i.e., *a common order and discipline*). CPMs among the urban poor must be anchored in evangelical and historically orthodox presentations of the Gospel that result in conversions to Jesus Christ and incorporation into local churches.

4. *A shared catechism and doctrine* (i.e., *a common faith*). CPMs among the urban poor must embrace a common biblical theology and express it practically in a Christian education that reflects their commonly held faith.

5. *A shared church government and authority* (i.e., *a common polity*). CPMs among the urban poor must be organized around a common polity, ecclesial management, and submit to flexible governing policies that allow for effective and efficient management of their resources and congregations.

6. *A shared leadership development structure* (i.e., *a common pastoral strategy*). CPMs among the urban poor are committed with supplying each congregation with godly undershepherds, and seek to identify, equip, and support its pastors and missionaries in order that their members may grow to maturity in Christ.

7. *A shared financial philosophy and procedure* (i.e., *a common stewardship*). CPMs among the urban poor strive to handle all of their financial affairs and resources with wise, streamlined, and reproducible policies that allow for the good management of their monies and goods, locally, regionally, and nationally.

8. *A shared care and support ministry* (i.e., *a common service*). CPMs among the urban poor seek to practically demonstrate the love and justice of the Kingdom among its members and towards others in the city in ways that allow individuals and congregations to love their neighbors as they love themselves.

9. *A shared evangelism and outreach* (i.e., *a common mission*): CPMs among the urban poor network and collaborate among their members in order to clearly present Jesus and his Kingdom to the lost in the city in order to multiply new congregations in unreached urban areas as quickly as possible.

10. *A shared vision for connection and association* (i.e., *a common partnership*). CPMs among the urban poor must seek to make fresh connections, links, and relationships with other movements for the sake of regular communication, fellowship, and mission.

These principles of belonging, camaraderie, and identity lay the foundation for a new paradigm of authentic ecumenical unity, the kind that can lead to partnerships and collaboration of grand scope and deep substance. Below is a short overview of the TUMI biblical basis for the kind of partnerships which can fuel and sustain credible church planting movements among the urban poor.

God's Partners and Fellow Workers

1 Corinthians 3:1-9 (ESV) – But I, brothers, could not address you as spiritual people, but as people of the flesh, as infants in Christ. [2] I fed you with milk, not solid food, for you were not ready for it. And even now you are not yet ready, [3] for you are still of the flesh. For while there is jealousy and strife among you, are you not of the flesh and behaving only in a human way? [4] For when one says, "I follow Paul," and another, "I follow Apollos," are you not being merely human? [5] What then is Apollos? What is Paul? Servants through whom you believed, as the Lord assigned to each. [6] I planted, Apollos watered, but God gave the growth. [7] So neither he who plants nor he who waters is anything, but only God who gives the growth. [8] He who plants and he who waters are one, and each will receive his wages according to his labor. [9] For we are God's fellow workers. You are God's field, God's building.

To Facilitate Pioneer Church Planting Movements among America's Unreached C1 Communities

As a ministry of World Impact, TUMI is dedicated to generating and strategically facilitating dynamic, indigenous C1 church planting movements targeted to reach the 80% Window of America's inner cities. In order to attain this purpose, we will help form strategic alliances between and among urban missionaries and pastors, theologians and missiologists, churches and denominations, and other kingdom-minded individuals and organizations in order to trigger robust pioneer church planting movements that multiply thousands of culturally conducive evangelical C1 churches among America's urban poor. We will offer our expertise to assure that these churches in every way glorify God the Father in their Christ-centered identity, Spirit-formed worship and community life, historically orthodox doctrine, and kingdom-oriented practice and mission.

I. **Partnership₁ involves recognizing our fundamental unity in Christ: We share the same spiritual DNA.**

   A. *Our faith in Jesus has made us one together.*

   1. 1 John 1:3 (ESV) – that which we have seen and heard we proclaim also to you, so that you too may have fellowship with us; and indeed our fellowship is with the Father and with his Son Jesus Christ.

   2. John 17:11 (ESV) – And I am no longer in the world, but they are in the world, and I am coming to you. Holy Father, keep them in your name, which you have given me, that they may be one, even as we are one.

   B. *The organic unity between the Father and Son, and the people of God*, John 17:21- 22 (ESV) – that they may all be one, just as you, Father, are in me, and I in you, that they also may be in us, so that the world may believe that you have sent me. [22] The glory that you have given me I have given to them, that they may be one even as we are one.

   C. *Our unity leads to a common effort in glorifying God the Father of our Lord*, Romans 15:5-6 (ESV) – May the God of endurance and encouragement grant you to live in such harmony with one another, in accord with Christ Jesus, [6] that together you may with one voice glorify the God and Father of our Lord Jesus Christ.

   D. *God's will for the body is unity in mind and judgment*, 1 Corinthians 1:10 (ESV) – I appeal to you, brothers, by the name of our Lord Jesus Christ, that all of you agree and that there be no divisions among you, but that you be united in the same mind and the same judgment.

   E. *The Holy Spirit's baptism has made us of one spiritual body and spirit*, 1 Corinthians 12:12-13 (ESV) – For just as the body is one and has many members, and all the members of the body, though many, are one body, so it is with Christ. [13] For in one Spirit we were all baptized into one body— Jews or Greeks, slaves or free— and all were made to drink of one Spirit.

   F. *The very essence of biblical faith is unity*, Ephesians 4:4-6 (ESV) – There is one body and one Spirit—just as you were called to the one hope that belongs to your call [5] one Lord, one faith, one baptism, [6] one God and Father of all, who is over all and through all and in all.

G. *Our bond of partnership precludes unity with those not united to Christ*, 2 Corinthians 6:14-16 (ESV) – Do not be unequally yoked with unbelievers. For what partnership has righteousness with lawlessness? Or what fellowship has light with darkness? [15] What accord has Christ with Belial? Or what portion does a believer share with an unbeliever? [16] What agreement has the temple of God with idols? For we are the temple of the living God; as God said, "I will make my dwelling among them and walk among them, and I will be their God, and they shall be my people.

II. **Partnership$_2$ involves the sharing of monies, persons, and resources to fund a common cause: We share a common source, table, and pot.**

A. *The partnership between those who share the Word and receive it involves concrete blessing and giving.*

1. *The taught share with the teacher*, Galatians 6:6 (ESV) – One who is taught the word must share all good things with the one who teaches.

2. *Illustrated in the relationship of the Jew to the Gentile in the body*, Romans 15:27 (ESV) – They were pleased to do it, and indeed they owe it to them. For if the Gentiles have come to share in their spiritual blessings, they ought also to be of service to them in material blessings.

B. *The power of unity extends to those who are appointed by God to serve his people*, Deuteronomy 12:19 (ESV) – Take care that you do not neglect the Levite as long as you live in your land.

C. *Those who labor deserve the generous supply of those who benefit from that labor.*

1. *Christ's exhortation to the disciples*, Matthew 10:10 (ESV) – No bag for your journey, nor two tunics nor sandals nor a staff, for the laborer deserves his food.

2. *Illustrated from Old Testament Scripture and analogy*, 1 Corinthians 9:9-14 (ESV) – For it is written in the Law of Moses, "You shall not muzzle an ox when it treads out the grain." Is it for oxen that God is concerned? [10] Does he not speak entirely for our sake? It was written for our sake, because the plowman should plow in hope and the thresher thresh in hope of sharing in the crop. [11] If we have sown spiritual things among you, is it too much if we reap material things from you? [12] If others share this rightful claim on

you, do not we even more? Nevertheless, we have not made use of this right, but we endure anything rather than put an obstacle in the way of the gospel of Christ. [13] Do you not know that those who are employed in the temple service get their food from the temple, and those who serve at the altar share in the sacrificial offerings? [14] In the same way, the Lord commanded that those who proclaim the gospel should get their living by the gospel.

3. *Double honor: respect and sharing of resources*, 1 Timothy 5:17-18 (ESV) – Let the elders who rule well be considered worthy of double honor, especially those who labor in preaching and teaching. [18] For the Scripture says, "You shall not muzzle an ox when it treads out the grain," and, "The laborer deserves his wages."

D. *The Philippian relationship with Paul is a prototype of this kind of essential partnership.*

1. *From the beginning they shared tangibly with Paul*, Philippians 1:3-5 (ESV) – I thank my God in all my remembrance of you, [4] always in every prayer of mine for you all making my prayer with joy, [5] because of your partnership in the gospel from the first day until now.

2. *Epaphroditus was their messenger to transport their aid to Paul*, Philippians 2:25 (ESV) – I have thought it necessary to send to you Epaphroditus my brother and fellow worker and fellow soldier, and your messenger and minister to my need

3. *The Philippians were completely engaged in the support of Paul's ministry from the first*, Philippians 4:15-18 (ESV) – And you Philippians yourselves know that in the beginning of the gospel, when I left Macedonia, no church entered into partnership with me in giving and receiving, except you only. [16] Even in Thessalonica you sent me help for my needs once and again. [17] Not that I seek the gift, but I seek the fruit that increases to your credit. [18] I have received full payment, and more. I am well supplied, having received from Epaphroditus the gifts you sent, a fragrant offering, a sacrifice acceptable and pleasing to God.

III. Partnership₃ involves collaborating together as co-workers and co-laborers in the work of advancing the Kingdom: We share a common cause and task.

A. *Partnership assumes that each person and congregation brings their unique experience, perspective, and gifting to the table for use*, Galatians 2:6-8 (ESV) – And from those who seemed to be influential (what they were makes no difference to me; God shows no partiality)—those, I say, who seemed influential added nothing to me. [7] On the contrary, when they saw that I had been entrusted with the gospel to the uncircumcised, just as Peter had been entrusted with the gospel to the circumcised [8] (for he who worked through Peter for his apostolic ministry to the circumcised worked also through me for mine to the Gentiles).

B. *Authentic partnerships involve discerning the Lord's leading, opportunity, and blessing on those who are called to represent his interests in the places where he has led them*, Galatians 2:9-10 (ESV) – and when James and Cephas and John, who seemed to be pillars, perceived the grace that was given to me, they gave the right hand of fellowship to Barnabas and me, that we should go to the Gentiles and they to the circumcised. [10] Only, they asked us to remember the poor, the very thing I was eager to do.

C. *Partnership in terms of co-working and co-laboring involves a shared vision and commitment to a common cause*, e.g., Timothy, Philippians 2:19-24 (ESV) – I hope in the Lord Jesus to send Timothy to you soon, so that I too may be cheered by news of you. [20] For I have no one like him, who will be genuinely concerned for your welfare. [21] They all seek their own interests, not those of Jesus Christ. [22] But you know Timothy's proven worth, how as a son with a father he has served with me in the gospel. [23] I hope therefore to send him just as soon as I see how it will go with me, [24] and I trust in the Lord that shortly I myself will come also.

D. *Paul's unique words for his partners in the Gospel*

1. Co-worker (*synergos*), Romans 16:3, 7, 9, 21; 2 Corinthians 8:23; Philippians 2:25; 4:3; Colossians 4:7, 10, 11, 14; Philemon 1, 24.

2. Co-prisoner (*synaichmalotos*), Colossians 4:10; Philemon 23

3. Co-slave (*syndoulos*), Colossians 1:7, 4:7

4. Co-soldier (*systratiotes*) Philippians 2:25; Philemon 2

5. Co-laborer (*synatheleo*), Philippians 4:2-3

E. A brief listing of Paul's partners in ministry (these accompanied him at every phase and effort of the work, with diverse backgrounds, giftings, tasks, and responsibilities along the way of his ministry)

1. John Mark (Colossians 4:10; Philemon 24)
2. Artistarchus (Colossians 4:10; Philemon 24)
3. Andronicus and Junia (Romans 16:7)
4. Philemon (Philemon 1)
5. Epaphroditus (same as Epaphras) (Colossians 1:7; Philemon 23; Philippians 2:25)
6. Clement (Philippians 4:3)
7. Urbanus (Romans 16:9)
8. Jesus (Justus) (Colossians 4:11)
9. Demas (who later apostatized in the world), (Colossians 4:14; Philemon 24; 2 Timothy 4:20)
10. Tychicus (Colossians 4:7; Philippians 4:3)
11. Archippus (Philemon 2)
12. Euodia (Philippians 4:2-3)
13. Syntyche (Philippians 4:2-3)
14. Tertius (Romans 16:22)
15. Phoebe (Romans 16:1)
16. Erastus (Romans 16:23)
17. Quartus (Romans 16:23)
18. Tryphena (Romans 16:12)
19. Tryphosa (Romans 16:12)
20. Persis (Romans 16:12)
21. Mary (Romans 16:6)
22. Onesiphorus (2 Timothy 1:16-18)

IV. Implications of partnership principles in light of TUMI's vision

To Facilitate Pioneer Church Planting Movements among America's Unreached C_1 Communities

As a ministry of World Impact, TUMI is dedicated to generating and strategically facilitating dynamic, indigenous C_1 church planting movements targeted to reach the 80% Window of America's inner cities. In order to attain this purpose, we will help form strategic alliances between and among urban missionaries and pastors, theologians and missiologists, churches and denominations, and other kingdom-minded individuals and organizations in order to trigger robust pioneer church planting movements that multiply thousands of culturally conducive evangelical C1 churches among America's urban poor. We will offer our expertise to assure that these churches in every way glorify God the Father in their Christ-centered identity, Spirit-formed worship and community life, historically orthodox doctrine, and kingdom-oriented practice and mission.

A. *TUMI will help form strategic alliances to trigger urban church plant movements.*

B. *TUMI seeks to support dynamic movements which produce and sustain healthy C_1 churches.*

C. Clear implications of this for us

1. We don't recruit people to ourselves, but to participate in Christ's kingdom advance.

2. We don't own the vision, it is God's desire to impact the world, and we contribute alongside others.

3. Our contribution is no better or worse than others: we are co-laborers with others.

4. The work that others do will probably be more critical and fruitful than our own.

Bottom Line

There is virtually no limit to what we can accomplish if we as a team are willing to give our all for the sake of our common cause, if we do not care what role we have to play in order to win, nor care who gets the credit after the victory.

Selecting Credible Criteria for Independence: Navigating Toward a Healthy Transition

Rev. Dr. Don L. Davis

In order to establish a smooth transition from a missionary-led community to an indigenous, independent church community, we must identify and agree upon a clear criteria which would help us know when the transition is complete. In other words, everything depends on all of the key players' ability (i.e., missionaries, elders, and church community) to be crystal clear regarding our assumptions about what the transition involves and what we are seeking to accomplish. If, for any reason, we are unclear as to our expectations and directions together, we can easily misunderstand one another, and prolong the process, or even make the transition period unnecessarily painful.

The following categories are given as a guide, a criteria which may help you as leaders critically assess whether you have covered all necessary areas of transition. The list is suggestive, not exhaustive, and is not meant to be a final summary, but a tickler to help you think carefully through all of the issues necessary to make your period of transition an open and supportive one.

1. **A faithful group of converted, gathered, maturing disciples of Jesus**

    a. Solid conversions to Jesus Christ as Lord and Savior

    b. Self-identity as a separate Christian assembly with its own passionate spirituality, inspiring worship, and presence in the community

    c. Possess a clear sense of membership, ownership, belonging; able to bring new members in easily through strong orientation and loving relationships

    d. Clear sense of entering membership, disciplining members, restoring them

    e. Incorporating people smoothly into the life of the body (i.e., small group life, friendships, large group fellowship, etc.)

2. **Identified, commissioned, and released indigenous leaders**

    a. Selected by and for the body publicly and prayerfully

    b. Determiners of the church's direction and operation

    c. Accountable to the church's membership for their life and ministry

d. The body exercising wisdom as it determines which leaders to fund (i.e., how many it can afford to fund fully or partially), while at the same time relying on lay leaders and members to meet its needs as God leads

e. Acknowledged separately from missionary leadership as authority of the body

3. **Selection of its own pastor and pastoral staff**

    a. Creation of a charter/by-laws/constitution/covenant delineating role of pastor(s) and relationship to body

    b. Installation of a pastor duly ratified by membership and endorsed by leadership

    c. Formal recognition of pastor's authority and responsibility

    d. Affirmation of community's support and submission to pastoral leadership

4. **Limited and decreasing oversight, participation, and direction**

    a. Missionaries have surrendered all significant positions and authority

    b. Clear understanding of the role of the missionaries presently serving our body

    c. Distinct lines between missionaries and indigenous leaders in decision making and direction setting of the church

    d. Encouragement for missionaries to seek God's leading regarding new communities to target for new outreaches of the Gospel

5. **Distinctive and unique burden-driven, gift-oriented ministries of the Church**

    a. Clear mission and vision of the church's purpose and goals to mature and grow in number as God leads

    b. Reproducing new assemblies built into the DNA of our church (i.e., to fund and support other efforts of church planting around our city and beyond)

    c. Open doorways for members to explore ministry opportunities that coincide with the body's vision to mobilize its members to minister in their community.

d. Ongoing equipping of the body members by the pastoral staff to enable members to do the work of the ministry

e. Regular programming for worship, teaching, fellowship, and mission funded and directed by the church's personnel and members

6. **Generating non-missionary ministry resources and operating income**

    a. Deep conviction within the congregation that they will look to God alone as the source of supply to implement their vision

    b. Development of a plan to make the congregation financially free and independent of outside missionary support

    c. Clear guidelines under which support and aid can be given to the body

    d. Identifying independent sources for ongoing access to cash resources that would help support the effort

7. **Acquisition and stewardship of the church's equipment, resources, and facilities**

    a. Functional, user-friendly structures created to administer the church's business and stewardship

    b. Careful, ongoing inventory of the church's resources

    c. Clear record keeping of the church's funds and finances, purchases, and allocations

    d. Responsible purchase and upkeep of the church's equipment and facilities

8. **Development of its own new friends, siblings, volunteers, and partners**

    a. Recognition from other Christian communities, inside and outside community

    b. New relationships with outside churches or other organizations who would continue to support the effort with work groups and short term help

    c. New affiliation with church denominations or groups whose vision resonates with the church

    d. Associations to increase the effectiveness of the church's outreach and mission

Salvation as Joining the People of God
Rev. Terry G. Cornett

I. The most significant way to define salvation in the biblical context is to describe it as being joined to the people of God.

　A. Old Testament

　　1. The prototype Old Testament image of salvation is the Exodus where God "saved" his people from bondage and slavery in Egypt.

　　　a. To be saved meant to be joined to the people of God who were being delivered together out of bondage and placed directly under God's lordship, laws, protection, provision, and presence.

　　　b. Exodus 6:7 (ESV) – *I will take you as my own people*, and I will be your God. Then you will know that I am the LORD your God, who brought you out from under the yoke of the Egyptians (cf. Leviticus 26:12; Deuteronomy 4:20; Hosea 13:4).

　　2. God's selection of Israel as "his people" gave them a unique position among all the peoples of the earth.

　　　a. Deuteronomy 7:6 (ESV) – For you are a people holy to the LORD your God. *The LORD your God has chosen you out of all the peoples on the face of the earth to be his people, his treasured possession* (cf. Deuteronomy 14:2; 26:18; 33:29).

　　　b. Deuteronomy 27:9 (ESV) – Then Moses and the priests, who are Levites, said to all Israel, "Be silent, O Israel, and listen! *You have now become the people of the LORD your God.*"

　　3. The means of salvation for anyone outside of Israel was to join themselves to the people of God.

　　　a. Exodus 12:37-38, 48a (ESV) – The Israelites journeyed from Rameses to Succoth. There were about six hundred thousand men on foot, besides women and children. *Many other people went up with them*, as well as large droves of livestock, both flocks and herds. . . . *"An alien living among you who wants to celebrate the LORD'S Passover must have all the males in his household circumcised; then he may take part like one born in the land."*

b. Isaiah 56:3-8 (ESV) – *Let no foreigner who has bound himself to the LORD say,"The LORD will surely exclude me from his people." And let not any eunuch complain,"I am only a dry tree." For this is what the LORD says: "To the eunuchs who keep my Sabbaths, who choose what pleases me and hold fast to my covenant-to them I will give within my temple and its walls a memorial and a name better than sons and daughters; I will give them an everlasting name that will not be cut off. And foreigners who bind themselves to the LORD to serve him, to love the name of the LORD, and to worship him, all who keep the Sabbath without desecrating it and who hold fast to my covenant-these I will bring to my holy mountain and give them joy in my house of prayer. Their burnt offerings and sacrifices will be accepted on my altar; for my house will be called a house of prayer for all nations." The Sovereign LORD declares-he who gathers the exiles of Israel: "I will gather still others to them besides those already gathered."*

4. The New Testament suggests that even Moses (an ethnic Hebrew but raised culturally as an Egyptian and therefore a foreigner) had to make a conscious choice to join himself to the people of God in faith so that he could experience salvation.

   Hebrews 11:25 (ESV) – *He [Moses] chose to be mistreated along with the people of God* rather than to enjoy the pleasures of sin for a short time.

5. Summary: [In the Old Testament] salvation came, not by the man's mere merit, but because the man belonged to a nation peculiarly chosen by God ("Salvation," *International Standard Bible Encyclopedia* [Electronic ed.]. Cedar Rapids: Parsons Technology, 1998.).

B. New Testament

"... who gave himself for us to redeem us from all wickedness *and to purify for himself a people that are his very own, eager to do what is good*" (Titus 2:14).

1. Both Peter and Paul suggest that the New Testament view of salvation is equally concerned as the Old Testament with God calling out a people but that the people "called out" are bound to Christ and his Church rather than to a political or ethnic "nation."

a. 1 Peter 2:9-10 (ESV) – *But you are a chosen people, a royal priesthood, a holy nation, a people belonging to God*, that you may declare the praises of him who called you out of darkness into his wonderful light. *Once you were not a people, but now you are the people of God; once you had not received mercy, but now you have received mercy.*

b. Acts 15:14 (ESV) – Simon has described to us how God at first showed his concern *by taking from the Gentiles a people for himself.*

c. Ephesians 2:13, 19 (ESV) – But now in Christ Jesus you who once were far away have been brought near through the blood of Christ. . . . Consequently, you are no longer foreigners and aliens, *but fellow citizens with God's people and members of God's household.*

d. Romans 9:24-26 (ESV) – Even us, whom he also called, *not only from the Jews but also from the Gentiles?* As he says in Hosea: *"I will call them 'my people' who are not my people; and I will call her 'my loved one' who is not my loved one,"* and, *"It will happen that in the very place where it was said to them,'You are not my people,' they will be called 'sons of the living God.'"*

2. "On the other hand, while the [Gospel] message involved in every case is strict individual choice, yet the individual who accepted it entered into social relations with the others who had so chosen. *So salvation involved admission to a community of service* (Mark 9:35, etc.)" (International Standard Bible Encyclopedia [Electronic Edition]).

II. The metaphors of salvation: joined to a people

In human society, belonging to a "people" (family, clan, nation) happens through either:

- birth,

- adoption, or

- marrying into a family group

Thus, the New Testament language of salvation draws from these three primary metaphors to describe what happens at salvation.

A. Birth

1. John 1:12-13 (ESV) – Yet to all who received him, to those who believed in his name, he gave the right to become children of God – *children born not of natural descent*, nor of human decision or a husband's will, *but born of God.*

2. John 3:3 (ESV) – In reply Jesus declared, "I tell you the truth, *no one can see the Kingdom of God unless he is born again.*"

3. 1 Peter 1:23 (ESV) – *For you have been born again*, not of perishable seed, but of imperishable, through the living and enduring word of God.

4. 1 Peter 1:3 (ESV) – Praise be to the God and Father of our Lord Jesus Christ! *In his great mercy he has given us new birth into a living hope through the resurrection of Jesus Christ from the dead.*

B. Adoption

1. Romans 8:23 (ESV) – Not only so, but we ourselves, who have the firstfruits of the Spirit, groan inwardly *as we wait eagerly for our adoption as sons*, the redemption of our bodies.

2. Ephesians 1:4-6 (ESV) – For he chose us in him before the creation of the world to be holy and blameless in his sight. *In love he predestined us to be adopted as his sons through Jesus Christ*, in accordance with his pleasure and will - to the praise of his glorious grace, which he has freely given us in the One he loves.

3. Galatians 4:4-7 (ESV) – But when the time had fully come, God sent his Son, born of a woman, born under law, to redeem those under law, *that we might receive the full rights of sons.* Because you are sons, God sent the Spirit of his Son into our hearts, the Spirit who calls out, "Abba, Father." *So you are no longer a slave, but a son; and since you are a son, God has made you also an heir.*

C. Marriage

1. John 3:29 (ESV) – *The bride belongs to the bridegroom. The friend who attends the bridegroom waits and listens for him, and is full of joy when he hears the bridegroom's voice. That joy is mine, and it is now complete.* [Spoken by John the Baptist in reference to Christ.]

2. Ephesians 5:31-32 (ESV) – "For this reason *a man will leave his father and mother and be united to his wife, and the two will become one flesh.*" This is a profound mystery – *but I am talking about Christ and the Church.*

3. Revelation 19:7 (ESV) – Let us rejoice and be glad and give him glory! *For the wedding of the Lamb has come, and his bride has made herself ready.*

Evangelism and Spiritual Warfare

Translating the Story of God
Rev. Dr. Don L. Davis

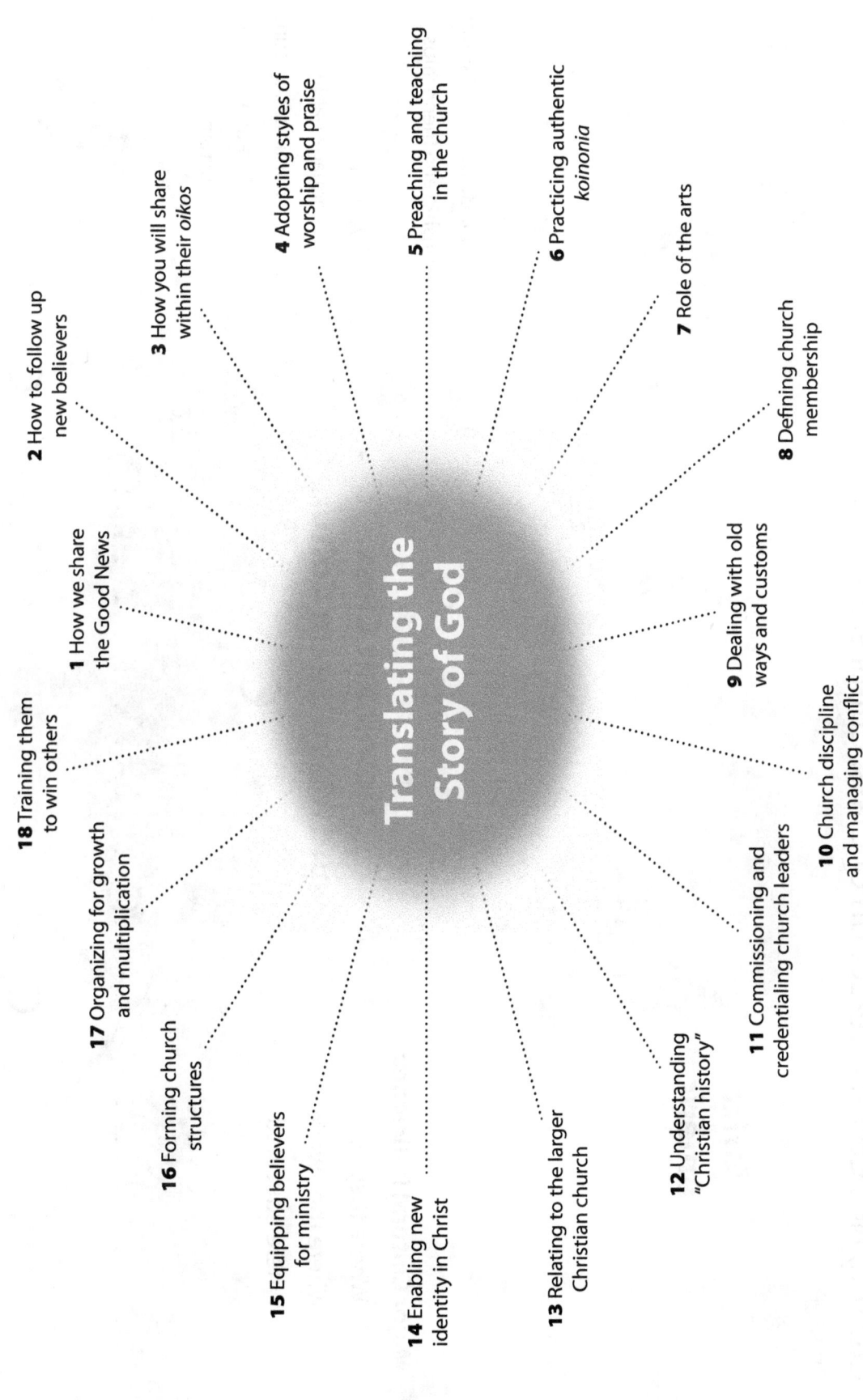

Translating the Story of God

1. How we share the Good News
2. How to follow up new believers
3. How you will share within their *oikos*
4. Adopting styles of worship and praise
5. Preaching and teaching in the church
6. Practicing authentic *koinonia*
7. Role of the arts
8. Defining church membership
9. Dealing with old ways and customs
10. Church discipline and managing conflict
11. Commissioning and credentialing church leaders
12. Understanding "Christian history"
13. Relating to the larger Christian church
14. Enabling new identity in Christ
15. Equipping believers for ministry
16. Forming church structures
17. Organizing for growth and multiplication
18. Training them to win others

Culture, Not Color: Interaction of Class, Culture, and Race

World Impact, Inc.

Asian

Hispanic

African-American

White

C_1, C_2, C_3 — **Dominant Class and Mainstream Culture**

Other Indicators of Culture:
Kinship and friendships
Upbringing
Values and norms
Language habits
Socio-economic background
Education
Customs

Major Cultural Indicators:
Where they live
Where they work
Where educated

Targeting Unreached Groups in Churched Neighborhoods
Mission Frontiers

Many different peoples!

Many homogeneous congregations

The extent of normal "outreach": Incorporating and gathering according to culture

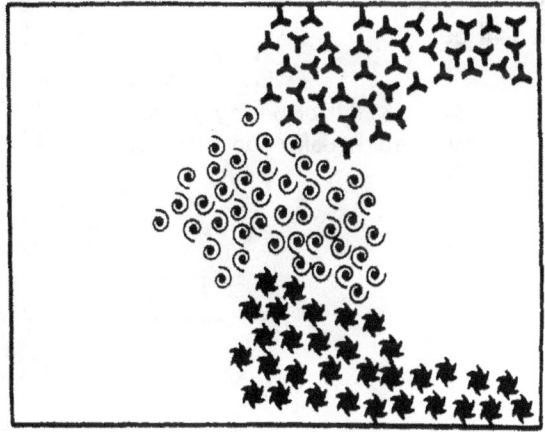

"So close and yet so far away": The unreached, unaffected neighbors

Receptivity Scale

The Holmes-Rahe Social Readjustment Scale indicates different events, in approximate order of their importance, that have an effect in producing periods of personal or family transition. The numbers on the right indicate the importance of the event relative to other transition-producing events. Various events may compound each other when an individual experiences more than one incident over a relatively short period of time. The higher the number, the more receptive the person is to the Gospel. For example, someone who was just married and is also having trouble with his or her boss will be more receptive than if either event had occurred separately. Also, the larger the number or accumulation of numbers, the longer the period of transition will last and the more intense it will be.

– Win Arn and Charles Arn. *The Master's Plan for Making Disciples*. 2nd ed. Grand Rapids: Baker Books, 1998. pp. 88-89.

The Holmes-Rahe Social Readjustment Scale

Event	Score
Death of Spouse	100
Divorce	73
Marital Separation	65
Jail Term	63
Death of Close Family Member	63
Personal Injury or Illness	53
Marriage	50
Fired from Work	47
Marital Reconciliation	45
Retirement	45
Change in Family Member's Health	44
Pregnancy	40
Sex Difficulties	39
Addition to Family	39
Business Readjustment	39
Change in Financial Status	38
Death of Close Friend	37
Change in Number of Marital Arguments	35
Mortgage or Loan over $75,000	31
Foreclosure of Mortgage or Loan	30
Change in Work Responsibilities	29
Son or Daughter Leaving Home	29
Trouble with In-Laws	29
Outstanding Personal Achievement	28
Spouse Starts Work	26
Starting or Finishing School	26
Change in Living Conditions	25
Revision of Personal Habits	24
Trouble with Boss	23
Change in Work Hours or Conditions	20
Change in Residence	20
Change in Schools	20
Change in Recreational Habits	19
Change in Social Activities	18
Mortgage or Loan under $75,000	18
Easter Season	17
Change in Sleeping Habits	16
Change in Number of Family Gatherings	15
Vacation	13
Christmas Season	12
Minor Violation of the Law	11

Relationship of Cost and Effectiveness in Disciple-Making Endeavors

Taken from Win Arn and Charles Arn, *The Master's Plan for Making Disciples*. 2nd ed. Grand Rapids: Baker Books, 1998. pp. 166

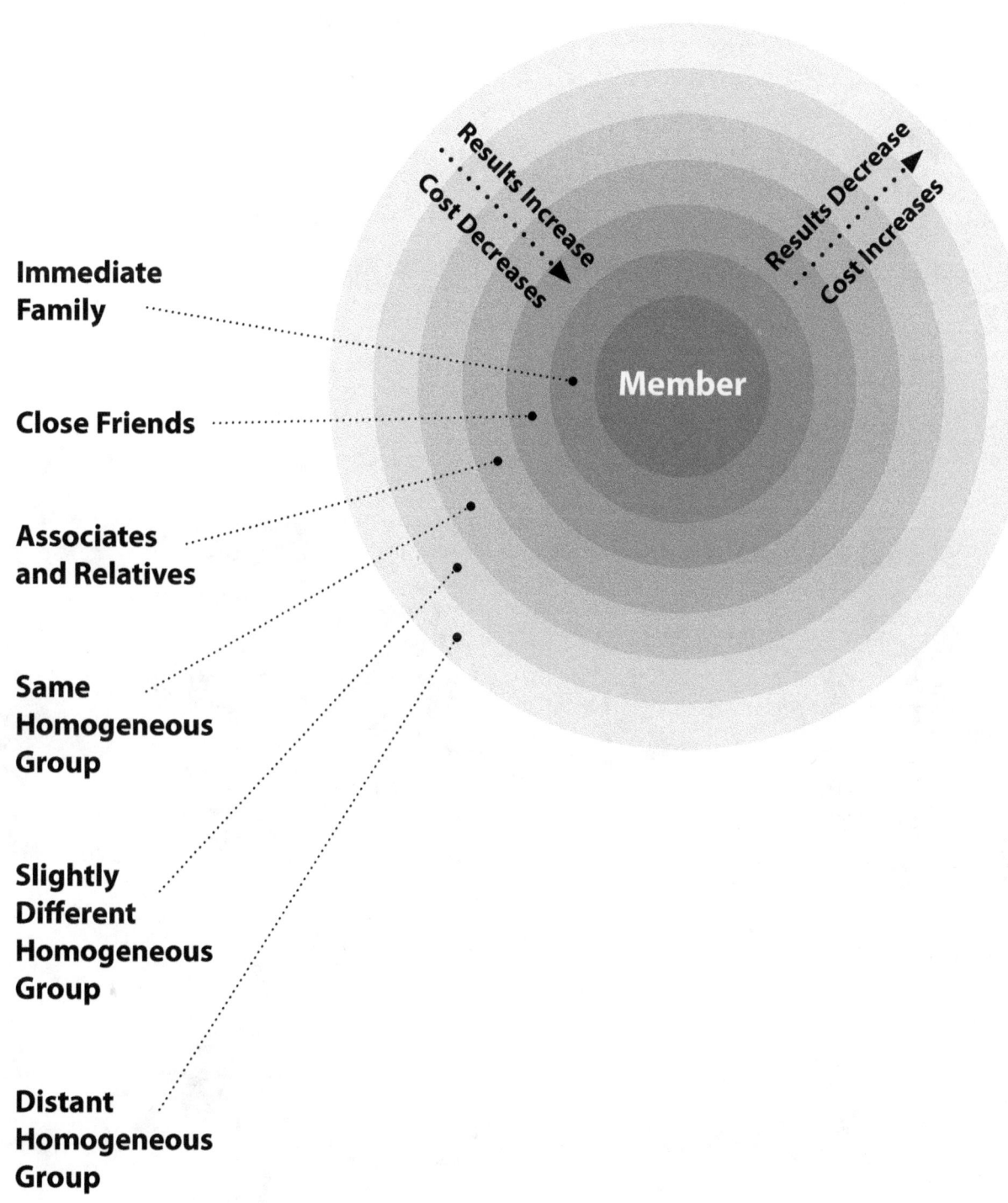

Focus on Reproduction

Equipping the Church Plant Team Member: Developing Workable Training Strategies

Rev. Dr. Don L. Davis

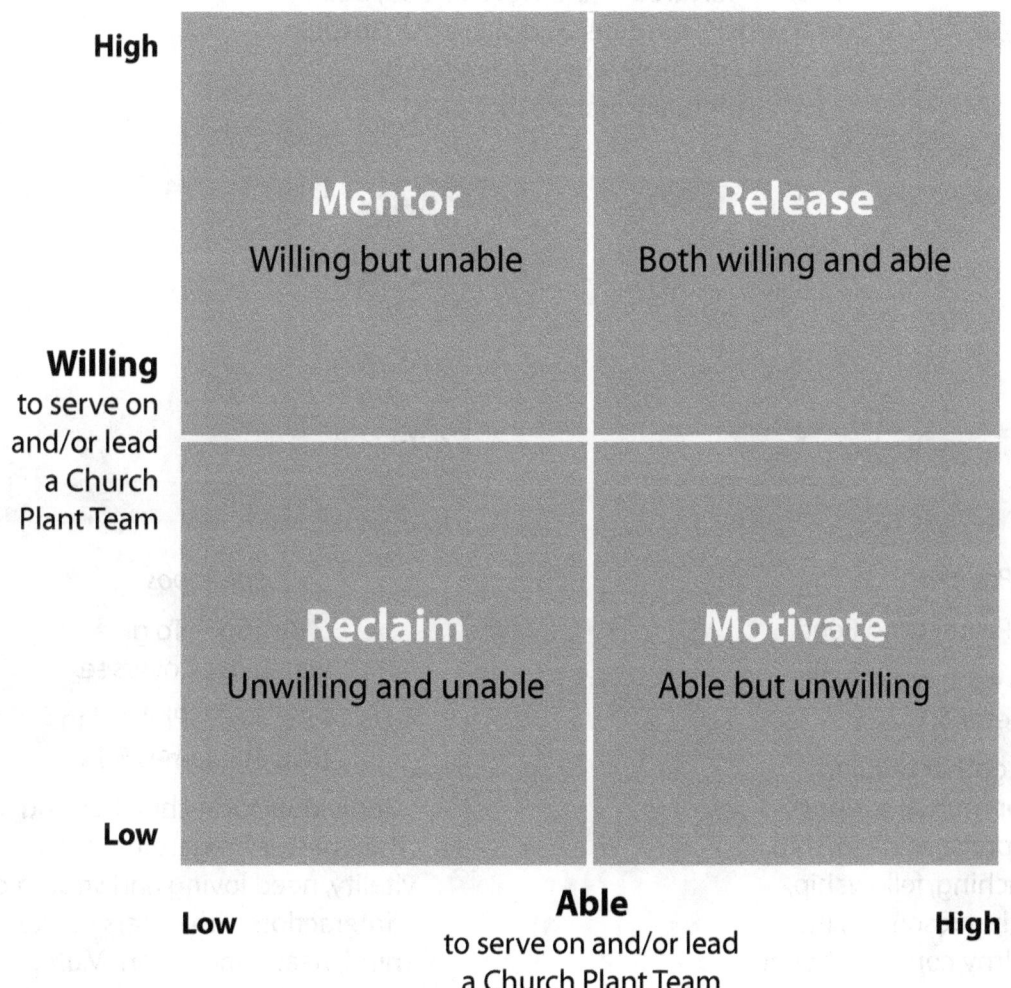

The Communal Context of Authentic Christian Leadership

Rev. Dr. Don L. Davis

Presbuteros

"Elder" – depth, maturity, and spiritual experience

Acts 20:28; Titus 1:5-7

Cells are the incubators of personal discipleship, where believers gather to worship, share their gifts, be nurtured in the Word of God, bear one another's burdens, and share the Gospel. Cells multiply when facilitated by spiritually mature disciples.

Poimen

"Pastor" – Protect and Feed

Ephesians 4:11; Acts 20:28; 1 Peter 5:1, 2

Vital cells gather regularly together for mutual support, large group praise and worship, biblical teaching, fellowship, and sharing resources in mission. Healthy congregational life demands godly pastoral care and oversight of the cells interacting together.

Episkopos

"Bishop" – To give watch over, oversee

Acts 14:23; 20:17; Philippians 1:1; Titus 1:5; James 5:14

Individual local churches and their pastors, regardless of their vitality, need loving and strategic interaction with others of like mind, heart, and vision. Multiple congregations in a given locale prosper greatly when supplied with solid bishop oversight.

Presbuteros, "an elder" is another term for the same person as bishop or overseer . . . . The term "elder" indicates the mature spiritual experience and understanding of those so described; the term "bishop" or "overseer," indicates the character of the work undertaken. According to the divine will and appointment, as in the New Testament, there were to be bishops in every local church, Acts 14:23; 20:17; Philippians 1:1; Titus 1:5; James 5:14."

– *Vine's Complete Expository Dictionary*. Nashville: Thomas Nelson Publishers, 1996. p. 195

Church Planting Models

Rev. Dr. Don L. Davis

The following questions are designed to help us explore the various options available to the cross-cultural urban church planter in establishing congregations among the poor. Our dialogue today hopefully will isolate some of the critical issues necessary for a church plant team to think through in order to make its selection as to what particular kind of church they ought to plant, given the culture, population, and other factors encountered in its particular mission field.

1. What is the definition of the phrase "church planting models"? Why might it be important to consider various options in planting a church among the poor in the city?

2. How would you characterize the various models (or other) which are available to an urban church plant team? What would you consider to be its strengths and/or weaknesses in regard to planting churches among the poor in the city?

    a. Founding pastor model – a leader moves into a community with a commitment to lead and shepherd the church that is planted.

    b. Church split model?! – a new church is formed due to fundamental disagreement over some issue of morality, Bible interpretation, or schism.

    c. Colonization model – a central assembly commissions an entire group (usually with leadership and members already organized) into an unreached community as a kind of ready-made nucleus of the church which is to be formed.

    d. Beachhead or Mother Church model – a strong, central congregation determines to become a kind of sending center and nurturing headquarters for new churches planted through its oversight and auspices, in the immediate area and/or beyond.

    e. Cell Church model – once centralized assembly which considers the heart of its life and ministry to occur in the cells which are connected structurally and pastorally to the central congregation; their participation together constitutes the church.

    f. Home Church model – a church, which although similar to a cell church model, is intentionally planted with greater attention given to the authority and autonomy of the gathering of Christians who meet regularly in their respective homes.

g. Missionary model – a church where a cross-cultural church planter seeks to plant a church among an unreached people with an intent from the beginning to help the church to be self-propagating, self-governing, and self-supporting.

3. What are the critical issues (e.g., culture, the tradition of the church planters, and contextualization) which ought to be factored most into selecting the appropriate model for planting a church cross-culturally in the city?

4. Of all the things which a church planter may be aware of, what do you believe is the central element he or she must understand in order to choose the "right" option for them?

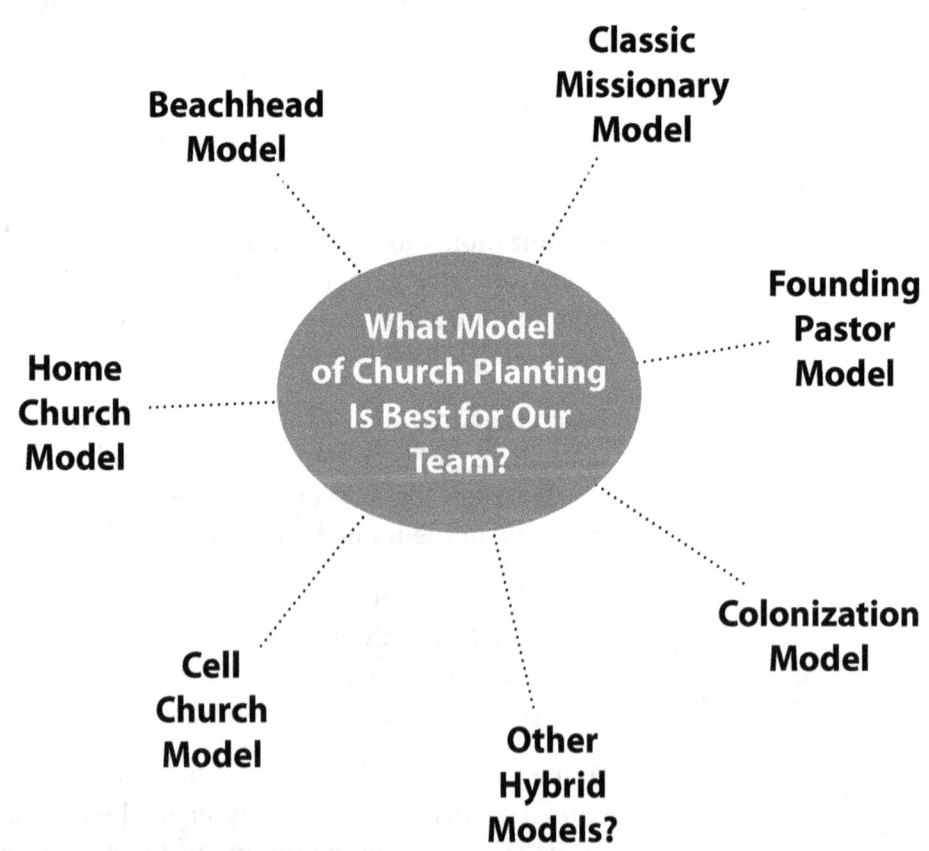

Overview of Church Plant Planning Phases

Rev. Dr. Don L. Davis

	Prepare	Launch	Assemble	Nurture	Transition
Definition	Forming a team of called members who ready themselves to plant a church under the Holy Spirit's direction	Penetrating the selected community by conducting evangelistic events among the target population	Gathering the cells of converts together to form a local assembly of believers, announcing the new church to the neighbors in the community	Nurturing member and leadership discipleship, enabling members to function in their spiritual gifts, and establishing solid infrastructure within the Christian assembly	Empowering the church for independence by equipping leaders for autonomy, transferring authority, and creating structures for financial independence
Purpose	Seek God regarding the target population and community, the formation of your church plant team, organizing strategic intercession for the community, and doing research on its needs and opportunities	Mobilize team and recruit volunteers to conduct ongoing evangelistic events and holistic outreach to win associates and neighbors to Christ	Form cell groups, Bible studies, or home fellowships for follow-up, continued evangelism, and ongoing growth toward public birth of the church	Develop individual and group discipleship by filling key roles in the body based on burden and gifting of members	Commission members and elders, install pastor, and foster church associations
Parent-Child Metaphor	Decision and Conception	Pre-natal Care	Childbirth	Growth and Parenting	Maturity to Adulthood
Question Focus During Dialogue	Questions about: • Preparing your team • The target community • Strategic prayer initiatives • Demographic studies	Questions about: • Character and number of evangelistic events • Communication and advertisement of events • Recruiting and coordinating volunteers • Identity and name of the outreach	Questions about: • Follow-up and incorporation of new believers • Make-up of small group life • The character of public worship • Initial church structures and procedures • Initial body life and growth • Cultural friendliness of church	Questions about: • Discipling individuals and leaders • Helping members identify gifts and burdens (teams) • Credentials for leadership • Church order, government and discipline	Questions about: • Incorporation • Affiliations and associations • Transferring leadership • Missionary transition • Ongoing reproduction
Cardinal Virtue	Openness to the Lord	Courage to engage the community	Wisdom to discern God's timing	Focus upon the faithful core	Dependence on the Spirit's ability
Critical Vice	Presumption and "paralysis of analysis"	Intimidation and haughtiness	Impatience and cowardice	Neglect and micromanagement	Paternalism and quick release
Bottom Line	Cultivate a period of listening and reflecting	Initiate your engagement with boldness and confidence	Celebrate the announcement of your body with joy	Concentrate on investing in the faithful	Pass the baton with confidence in the Spirit's continued working

Creating Coherent Urban Church Planting Movements: Discerning the Elements of Authentic Urban Christian Community

Rev. Dr. Don L. Davis

Core Evangelical Convictions

This circle represents its most fundamental convictions and commitments, its Affirmation of Faith, its commitment to the Gospel and those truths contained in the early Christian creeds (i.e., The Nicene Creed). These convictions are anchored in its confidence in the Word of God, and represent our unequivocal commitment to historic orthodoxy.

As members of the one, holy, apostolic, and catholic (universal) body of Christ, movements must be ready and willing to die for their core evangelical convictions. These convictions serve as the connection of the movements to the historic Christian faith, and as such, can never be compromised or altered.

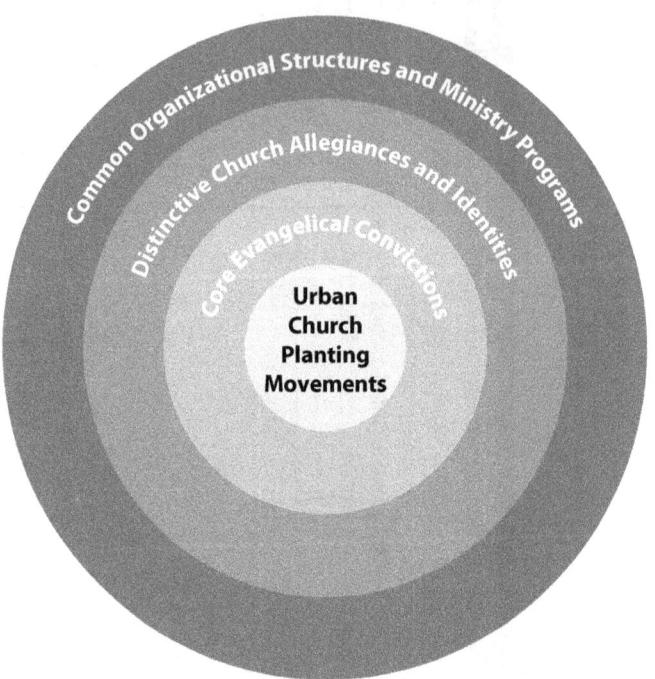

Distinctive Church Allegiances and Identities

This circle represents their distinctive church allegiances and identities. Urban church plant movements will coalesce around their own distinctive traditions, overseen by leaders who provide those movements with vision, instruction, and direction as they move forward together to represent Christ and his Kingdom in the inner city.

Specific traditions seek to express and live out this faithfulness to the Authoritative and Great Traditions through their worship, teaching, and service. They seek to make the Gospel clear within new cultures or sub-cultures, speaking and modeling the hope of Christ into new situations shaped by their own set of questions posed in light of their own unique circumstances. These movements, therefore, seek to contextualize the Authoritative Tradition in a way that faithfully and effectively leads new groups of people to faith in Jesus Christ, and incorporates those who believe into the community of faith that obeys his teachings and gives witness of him to others.

Urban church plant movements must be ready and willing to articulate and defend their unique distinctives as God's kingdom community in the city.

Common Organizational Structure and Ministry Programs

This circle represents the ways in which coherent urban church plant movements express their convictions and identity through their own distinct organizational structures and ministry programs. These structures and programs are designed and executed through their own specific strategies, policies, decisions, and procedures. The structures and programs represent their self-chosen methods of fleshing out their understanding of the faith as it pertains to their community purpose and mission. These are subject to change under their own legitimate processes as they apply accumulated wisdom in how best to accomplish their purposes in the city.

As communities of faith in Christ, urban church movements must be encouraged to dialogue about their structures and ministry programs in order to discover the best possible means to contextualize the Gospel and advance the Kingdom of God among their neighbors.

Apostolic Band: Cultivating Outreach for Dynamic Harvest

Rev. Dr. Don L. Davis

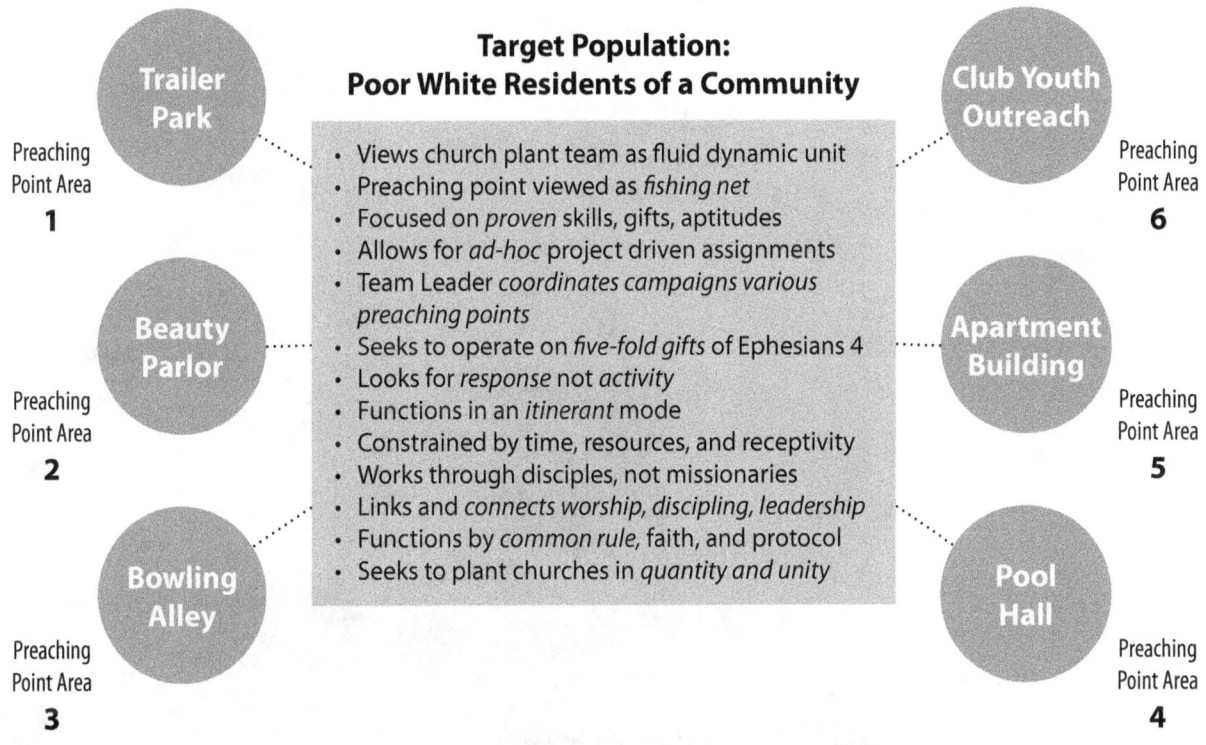

Target Population: Poor White Residents of a Community

- Views church plant team as fluid dynamic unit
- Preaching point viewed as *fishing net*
- Focused on *proven* skills, gifts, aptitudes
- Allows for *ad-hoc* project driven assignments
- Team Leader *coordinates campaigns various preaching points*
- Seeks to operate on *five-fold gifts* of Ephesians 4
- Looks for *response* not *activity*
- Functions in an *itinerant* mode
- Constrained by time, resources, and receptivity
- Works through disciples, not missionaries
- Links and *connects worship, discipling, leadership*
- Functions by *common rule*, faith, and protocol
- Seeks to plant churches in *quantity and unity*

Preaching Points (around diagram):
- Trailer Park — Preaching Point Area 1
- Beauty Parlor — Preaching Point Area 2
- Bowling Alley — Preaching Point Area 3
- Pool Hall — Preaching Point Area 4
- Apartment Building — Preaching Point Area 5
- Club Youth Outreach — Preaching Point Area 6

Principle Concepts

1. Itinerancy – an apostolic band functions <u>in multiple-contexts simultaneously</u> organized around a common target population
2. Commonality – an apostolic band uses <u>similar forms, methods, and protocols</u> to win and build converts
3. Authority – an apostolic band functions under a <u>common authority structure</u> and <u>leadership core</u>
4. Identity – an apostolic band plants <u>churches of a kind</u> with shared doctrine, practice, structures and traditions
5. Gifting – an apostolic band is organized around <u>the proven gifts</u> of the band, not availability and assignment alone
6. Fluidity – an apostolic band invests in <u>contacts who respond in</u> preaching points, giving the receptive their critical attention
7. Coordination – an apostolic band will <u>draft and employ select</u> individuals for contribution at critical times for particular projects
8. Consolidation – an apostolic band <u>consolidates the fruit in an area</u> with an eye toward movement and growth, not permanence
9. Discipline – an apostolic band functions according to an <u>order and structure</u>, equipping disciples in the disciplines of the faith
10. Germinal – an apostolic band seeks to <u>inaugurate and initiate spiritual birth and formation</u>, entrusting the lion's share of the congregation's growth and maturity to pastoral oversight

Definition of Terms

Apostolic Band – a fluid team of gifted, available, and committed workers assigned to play particular roles or accomplish specific tasks contributing to the outreach to a population

Preaching Point – a distinct area, venue, or place where people of the <u>target population live or gather</u>

Team Charter – a fluid agreement based on the prospective time and resources necessary to present the Gospel credibly to a target <u>population</u> in a given venue

Project Management – putting together a temporary group of people, strategies, and resources to <u>complete a particular task, outreach, or event</u>

The Church Plant Team: Forming an Apostolic Band
World Impact, Inc.

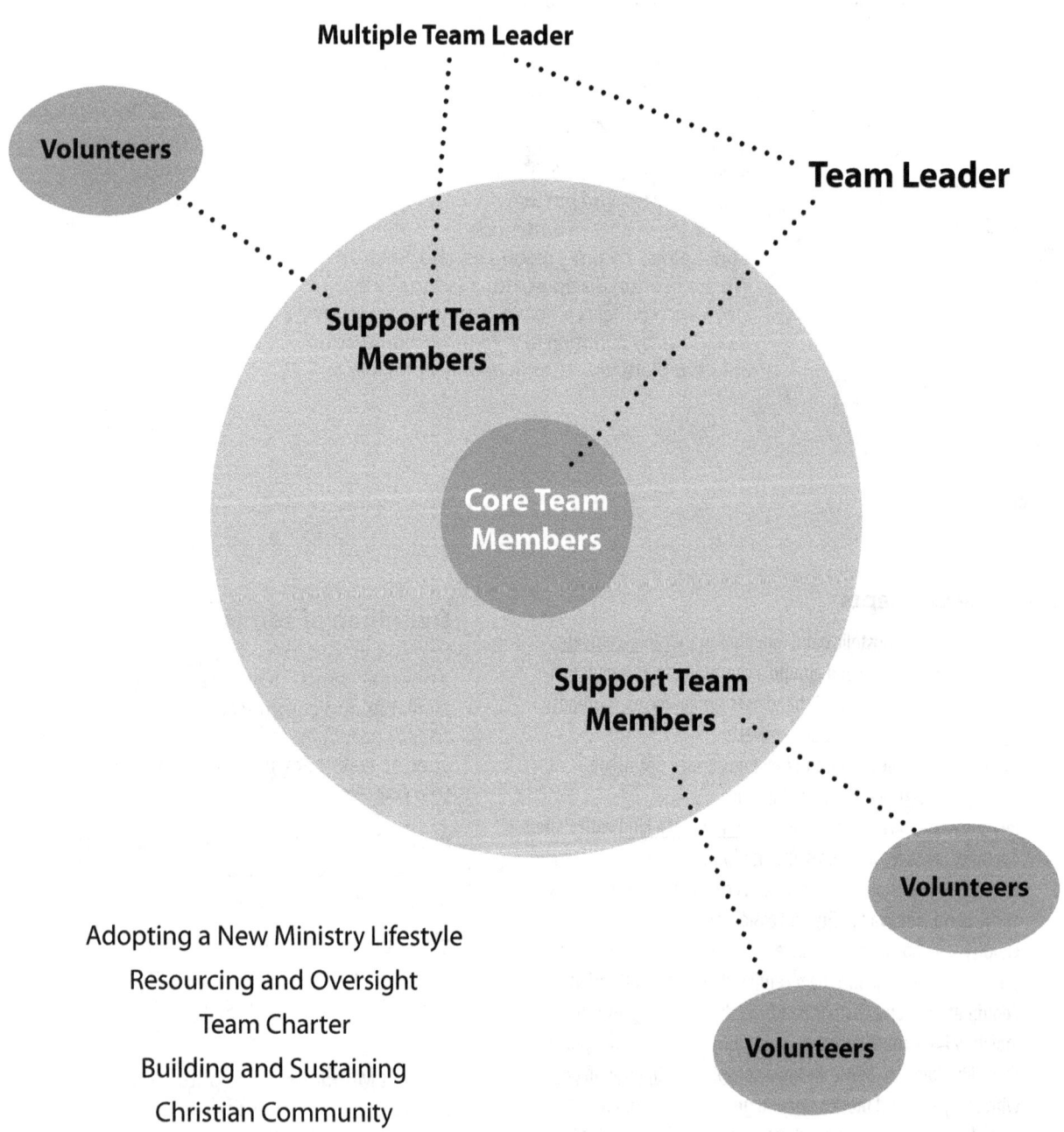

Adopting a New Ministry Lifestyle
Resourcing and Oversight
Team Charter
Building and Sustaining
Christian Community

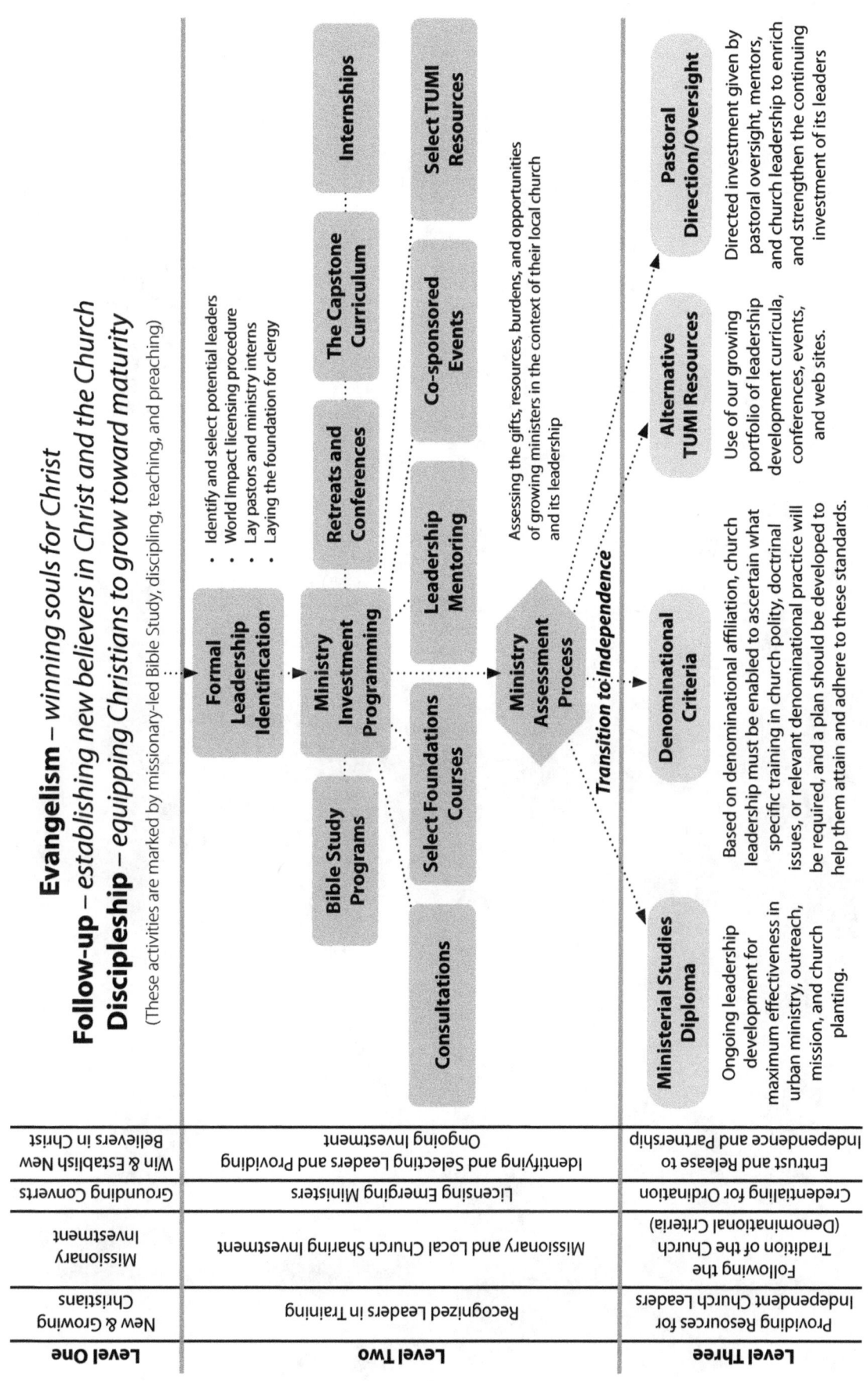

Doing Justice and Loving Mercy: Compassion Ministries

Five Views of the Relationship between Christ and Culture

Based on *Christ and Culture* by H. Richard Niebuhr, New York: Harper and Row, 1951

Christ against Culture	Christ and Culture in Paradox	Christ the Transformer of Culture	Christ above Culture	The Christ of Culture
Opposition	Tension	Conversion	Cooperation	Acceptance
Therefore come out from them and be separate, says the Lord. Touch no unclean thing, and I will receive you. - 2 Corinthians 6:17 (cf. 1 John 2:15)	Give to Caesar what is Caesar's, and to God what is God's. - Matthew 22:21 (cf. 1 Peter 2:13-17)	In putting everything under him, God left nothing that is not subject to him. Yet at present we do not see everything subject to him. - Hebrews 2:8 (cf. Colossians 1:16-18)	Indeed, when Gentiles, who do not have the law, do by nature things required by the law, they are a law for themselves. - Romans 2:14 (cf. Romans 13:1, 5-6)	Every good and perfect gift is from above, coming down from the Father of the heavenly lights, who does no change like shifting shadows. - James 1:17 (cf. Philippians 4:8)
Culture is radically affected by sin and constantly opposes the will of God. Separation and opposition are the natural responses of the Christian community which is itself an alternative culture.	Culture is radically affected by sin but does have a role to play. It is necessary to delineate between spheres: Culture as law (restrains wickedness), Christianity as grace (gives righteousness). Both are an important part of life but the two cannot be confused or merged.	Culture is radically affected by sin but can be redeemed to play a positive role in restoring righteousness. Christians should work to have their culture acknowledge Christ's lordship and be changed by it.	Culture is a product of human reason and is part of a God-given way to discover truth. Although culture can discern real truth, sin limits its capacities which must be aided by revelation. Seeks to use culture as a first step toward the understanding of God and his revelation.	Culture is God's gift to help man overcome his bondage to nature and fear and advance in knowledge and goodness. Human culture is what allows us to conserve the truth humanity has learned. Jesus's moral teaching moves human culture upward to a new level.
Tertullian, Menno Simons Anabaptists	Martin Luther Lutherans	St. Augustine, John Calvin Reformed	Thomas Aquinas Roman Catholic	Peter Abelard, Immanuel Kant Liberal Protestant

Advancing the Kingdom in the City: Multiplying Congregations with a Common Identity

Rev. Dr. Don L. Davis

Acts 2:41-47 (ESV) – So those who received his word were baptized, and there were added that day about three thousand souls. [42] And they devoted themselves to the apostles' teaching and fellowship, to the breaking of bread and the prayers. [43] And awe came upon every soul, and many wonders and signs were being done through the apostles. [44] And all who believed were together and had all things in common. [45] And they were selling their possessions and belongings and distributing the proceeds to all, as any had need. [46] And day by day, attending the temple together and breaking bread in their homes, they received their food with glad and generous hearts, [47] praising God and having favor with all the people. And the Lord added to their number day by day those who were being saved.

koinonia (pronunciation: [koy-nohn-ee'-ah])

Trinitarian Principle: Unity • Diversity • Equality

World Impact seeks to plant churches that are kingdom-oriented communities where Christ is exalted as Lord and the Kingdom of God is advanced in every facet of community life, and, we seek to do this in a way that respects and acknowledges the validity and significance of incarnating this community life in the receiving culture. In order to ensure the viability, protection, and flourishing of these congregations, we ought to explore forming close-knit associations between congregations where a common identity, confession, and faith are practiced, under a common oversight and governance, that connects in a fundamental way the resources and visions of each church without lording over them.

Following is a chart that sketches what might be the elements of such a common coalition of churches which would link their lives in a strategic way for the wellbeing and enrichment of the entire fellowship of churches.

Sharing a Common Identity, Purpose, and Mission	
A Common Name and Association	Understanding the churches as fundamentally linked in history, identity, legacy, and destiny
A Common Confession of Faith	Developing a common theological and doctrinal vision
A Common Celebration and Worship	Practicing a common liturgy with shared worship approaches
A Common Discipleship and Catechism	Sharing a common curriculum and process for welcoming, incorporating, and discipling new believers into our fellowship
A Common Governance and Oversight	Answering to a common accountability for leadership and care
A Common Service and Missionary Outreach	Developing integrated processes and programs of justice, good works, outreach, evangelism, and missions, both at home and throughout the world
A Common Stewardship and Partnership	Combining resources through consistent mutual contribution to maximize impact for the entire association

Benefits of a Common Movement

1. Sense of belonging through a shared faith and identity
2. Efficiency and economy of effort
3. Ability to plant multiple plants in many different venues and populations
4. Cultivating genuine unity and diversity, with a spirit of mutuality and equality among the congregations
5. Increased productivity and viability within our missions efforts and churches
6. Interchangeability and cross pollination
7. Ongoing support and encouragement of our leaders
8. Provide leverage for new projects and new initiatives
9. Standardized processes and procedures for incorporation and training
10. Greater opportunities for convocation and exposure to other like-minded believers

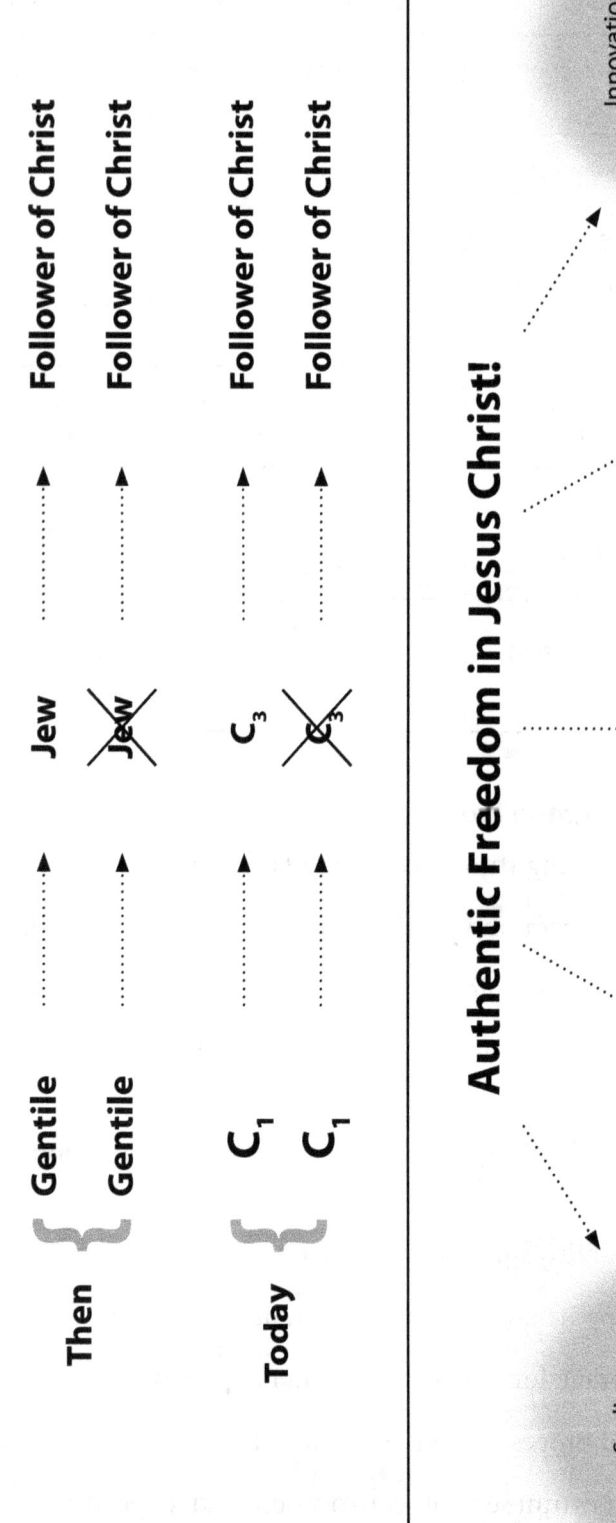

Empowering People for Freedom, Wholeness, and Justice
Theological and Ethical Foundations for World Impact's Development Ministries

Rev. Dr. Don Davis and Rev. Terry G. Cornett

Prologue: A Theology of Development

Love of God and love of neighbor have been pivotal themes of both Old and New Testament theology from their inception. From the time of the early Church forward, there has been a concern to demonstrate God's love and character to the world in word and deed, through faith and works, by both evangelistic proclamation and acts of justice and mercy.

Starting with its forerunners in Puritan, Pietistic, Moravian, and Wesleyan reform and revival movements, and extending into the modern Protestant missions movement, evangelical missionaries have combined a strong emphasis on evangelism and the establishment of churches with a serious attempt to engage in action that would foster justice and righteousness, especially on behalf of the poor and oppressed.

Evangelical reformers and missionaries have started schools and hospitals aimed at being accessible to the least advantaged segments of society, formed orphanages and worked for the reform of child labor laws, established businesses and cooperative ventures among the poor, supported legislation to abolish slavery and to ensure the protection of human rights, worked to upgrade the status of women in society, and mediated conflicts between warring groups and nations.[1]

Although Christians generally agree that evangelism and social action are important responsibilities of the Church, there is considerable variation in both the terms that are used to designate these responsibilities, and the way in which they are defined and placed in relation to one another. As a missions agency which is engaged in both of these activities, it is important to establish our definition of terms and a statement of the theological relationship which exists between these two tasks.

1. The Kingdom of God as the Basis of Evangelism, Church Planting, and Development

1.1 The Kingdom of God as the Basis for Mission

"Missiology is more and more coming to see the Kingdom of God as the hub around which all of mission work revolves" (Verkuyl 1978, 203). Evangelism, church-planting and development work are not based on a

---

1 See Paul E. Pierson' article, "Missions and Community Development: A Historical Perspective," (Elliston 1989, 1-22) for an introduction to the history of development work in evangelical missions and Donald W. Dayton's book "Discovering an Evangelical Heritage" (Dayton, 1988) for a helpful look at evangelical reform movements.

few isolated "proof-texts," but are an abiding response to the theme of the Kingdom which is woven throughout the scriptural record. The Kingdom of God embodies the essence of what God's mission (*Missio Dei*) in the world is and provides a basis for seeing how our own activities are intended to fit into God's overall plan.[2]

1.2 The Kingdom as Restoration

The Scriptures assert what human experience everywhere reveals; something has gone dramatically wrong with the world. The Bible teaches that the basis of this problem is humanity's rejection of God's rulership. The Genesis account of the Fall shows humanity repudiating God's right to give direction and boundaries to their decisions. From that time forward, evil filled the void left by the absence of God's loving rule. The world ceased to function correctly; death replaced life; disease replaced health; enmity replaced friendship; domination replaced cooperation; and scarcity replaced abundance. All human relationships with God and with each other were poisoned by the inner desire of each individual and social group to replace God's authority with their own rule.

In a response of grace to this situation, God decided not to reject and destroy the world, but to redeem it. He set in motion a plan to liberate the world from its bondage to evil powers, and to restore all things to perfection under his Kingly rule. Throughout the Scriptures this plan of reclamation is described as the "Kingdom of God," and insight into its nature and means of coming are progressively revealed.

Johannes Verkuyl summarizes the message of the Kingdom in this fashion:

> The heart of the message of the Old and New Testament is that God . . . is actively engaged in the reestablishment of His liberating dominion over the cosmos and all of humankind. In seeking out Israel, He sought all of us and our entire world, and in Jesus Christ He laid the foundation of the Kingdom. Jesus Christ the Messiah "promised to the fathers," is the auto basileia[3]: in Him the Kingdom has both come, and is coming in an absolutely unique way and with exceptional clarity. In His preaching Jesus divulges the riches, the thesaurus of that Kingdom: reconciliation, the forgiveness of sins, victory over demonic powers. Standing within the tradition of the Mosaic law, He expounds the core message of . . . the prophets; He accomplishes the reconciliation of the world to God; He opens the way to the present and future Kingdom which demands decisions of us in all aspects of life (Verkuyl 1993, 72).

---

2   See George Eldon Ladd (1974, 45-134), for an introduction to a biblical theology of the Kingdom.

3   That is, the One who in his own person fully embodies the rule of God.

1.3 Responsibilities for Those Who Seek God's Kingdom

The implications of the Kingdom of God for mission can be delineated in three central truths. A kingdom-centered theology and missiology will be concerned for:

- Evangelizing so that people are converted to Christ as Lord.

- Creating churches where people are discipled and bear fruit.

- Helping the Church live out its commitment to bring freedom, wholeness, and justice in the world.

Thus:

> *A truly Kingdom-centered theology . . . can never neglect the call for the conversion of persons among all peoples and religious communities. To everyone of whatever religious persuasion the message must be repeated: "The Kingdom of God is at hand; repent, and believe in the Gospel.". . . Kingdom-centered theology entails a call to recognition of the lordship of the King and new orientation to the constitution of His Kingdom. In the absence of this aspect, proclamation of the good news of the Gospel is impossible. A theology and missiology informed by the biblical notion of the rule of Christ will never fail to identify personal conversion as one of the inclusive goals of God's Kingdom . . .*
>
> *The Church . . . is raised up by God among all nations to share in the salvation and suffering service of the Kingdom . . . The Church constitutes the firstling, the early harvest of the Kingdom. Thus, although not limited to the Church, the Kingdom is unthinkable without the Church. Conversely, growth and expansion of the Church should not be viewed as ends but rather as means to be used in the service of the Kingdom. . . . The keys of the Kingdom have been given to the Church. It does not fulfill its mandate by relinquishing those keys but rather by using them to open up the avenues of approach to the Kingdom for all peoples and all population groups at every level of human society . . .*
>
> *Finally, the gospel of the Kingdom addresses itself to all immediate human need, both physical and mental. It aims to right what is wrong on earth. It enjoins engagement in the struggle for racial, social, cultural, economic, and political justice. . . . The good news of the Kingdom has to do with all of these things. For this reason missiology must bend its efforts to the erection of a multiplicity of visible signs of God's Kingdom throughout the length and breadth of this planet (Verkuyl 1993, 72-73).*

Evangelism, church planting and development spring from a common theological base: a desire to live out the implications of the Kingdom of God which has broken into this present age in the person of Jesus Christ, the King of kings. This Kingdom is both *already* and *not yet*. It is currently *forcefully advancing and spreading like yeast through dough*, but also awaiting the return of Christ when *every knee will bow* and there will be a *new heaven and a new earth*. Our evangelism and our development work acknowledge God's kingly rule, now, during a time when the world, as a whole, does not. We announce the good news of the in-breaking Kingdom of peace and justice, call people to repentance and salvation through faith in its King, hope in its inevitable complete triumph, and live out obedience to its commands and values in the present moment.

2. Kingdom Work

Since evangelism/church planting and development work are intimately related, those who engage in them often find that their roles and projects overlap. While this is both normal and good, a clear beginning definition of each role may help to minimize the confusion which can sometimes result from this process.

2.1 Missionaries

Missionaries are called to pioneer new outreaches that focus on the evangelization of peoples in unreached (or under-reached) areas, social classes, or cultural groups.

Therefore, we assert that:

> *Missionaries cross class and cultural barriers to evangelize and disciple unreached groups so that reproducing churches are formed among them and placed at the service of God's kingdom rule.*

2.2 Development Workers

Development workers are called to confront conditions and structures in the world that do not submit themselves to the rule of God.

Therefore, we assert that:

> *Development workers enable individuals, churches and communities to experience movement toward the freedom, wholeness, and justice of the Kingdom of God.*

2.3 The Common Link

Both missionaries and Christian development workers are united in their common commitment to further God's kingdom rule in all areas of life.

Missionary activity is centered around the proclamation of "good news" that calls people into the Kingdom of God through an experience of salvation and regeneration. It focuses on bringing unreached peoples, cultures, and subcultures into the community of the redeemed (i.e., "bringing the world into the Church"). All of this is done with an eye toward creating churches which can disciple their members to acknowledge God's rulership and live out the values of his Kingdom in their individual and corporate life.

Missionary activity also encompasses development that seeks to call every area of life into conformity with God's kingdom rule. It evaluates every concrete life-situation in light of the Lord's Prayer ("thy Kingdom come, thy will be done, on earth as it is in heaven") and engages in deeds of compassion, love, and justice that demonstrate the nature of God's divine plan for all peoples. It focuses on bringing God's rule to bear on every human relationship and structure (i.e., "bringing the Church into the world").

3. Theological Relationship between Evangelism and Development

3.1 A Partnership Relationship

Missionary evangelism and church-planting and Christian development work are partners in the process of proclaiming, demonstrating, and extending the rule of the King. Both are responses to the fact that God has announced his desire to reconcile the world to himself through the gift of his Son. Although each is a legitimate response to God's plan for the world, neither is a sufficient response in and of itself. Both word and deed are necessary components of the Church's announcement of, and faithfulness to, the Kingdom of God.

3.2 Interdependence and Interconnectedness

The relationship between Missions and Development is not a simple one. Their interconnectedness has many facets.

- *They are connected by a common goal.*

    Neither missionaries nor development workers are satisfied until God's reconciliation with man and man's reconciliation with man is completely realized. We believe that this makes both missions and development work Christocentric in orientation, since it is "in Christ" that God is reconciling the world to himself. Christ is the King. It is his sacrificial, reconciling death that provides the objective basis for reconciliation between humanity and God, and within human relationships and structures. It is his kingly authority and presence that allows the Kingdom to break into this present age destroying the works of darkness and creating authentic communities gathered under God's rule.

- *They retain a degree of independence from each other.*

   Evangelism and church-planting can sometimes be done without any immediate focus on development work. Conversely, development work can be sometimes be done without accompanying church-planting activity. Because both are authentic responses to God's activity in the world, they can, when appropriate, operate independently from each other. While each is a legitimate activity in its own right, it will obviously be healthier and more normal to find them occurring together.

- *They need each other for lasting effectiveness.*

   Without evangelism, there are no changed lives, no reconcilers who understand God's plan for man and society, and who undertake change in the power of the Spirit. Without development, the churches established by mission become withdrawn, and do not function as "salt and light" within their local and national communities. Missionary efforts are undermined when the existing church does not make visible in its life the effects of God's kingdom rule. The integration of the two is aptly expressed in Ephesians 2:8-10 which states, "For by grace you have been saved through faith. And this is not your own doing; it is the gift of God, [9] not a result of works, so that no one may boast. [10] For we are his workmanship, created in Christ Jesus for good works, which God prepared beforehand, that we should walk in them."

These facets may be summarized as "a threefold relationship between evangelism and social activity. First, Christian social activity [development] is a *consequence* of evangelism, since it is the evangelized who engage in it. Second, it is a *bridge* to evangelism, since it expresses God's love and so both overcomes prejudice and opens closed doors. Third, it is a *partner* of evangelism, so that they are 'like two blades of a pair of scissors or the two wings of a bird'" (Stott 1995, 52).

3.3   The Need for Specialization

Modern missions have seen the rise of both mission and development agencies. This occurs as organizations specialize in one component of the overall task God has given. This recognition of the need for specialization arose early on in the life of the Church.

J. Chongham Cho comments:

> *In Acts 6 . . . a distinction between evangelism and social action was made. This was not a division in essence but for the sake of practical efficacy of the church's mission and as the solution to a problem which arose in the church. This is a necessary deduction from the nature of the church as Christ's*

body. Although we should resist polarization between evangelism and social action, we should not resist specialization (Cho 1985, 229).

As a missions agency, our primary focus is evangelism and discipleship which results in the planting of indigenous churches. The fact that evangelism, church-planting and development are interconnected means that missions agencies, especially those who focus on the poor and oppressed, will engage in some form of development work. However, the mission agency must be careful to structure its development work so that it encourages the central task of evangelism and church-planting rather than detracts from it.[4] We should engage in development work which fosters the formation, health, growth, and reproducibility of indigenous churches among the poor.

Specialization allows organizations to maximize the training and resources that can be committed to a specific part of the overall task of mission. The development agency may engage in many good and necessary projects that have no immediate connection to evangelism and the planting and nurturing of emerging churches. The missions agency appreciates the many development agencies that engage in this type of work. Although the mission agency will want to network with them (and pray that God will vastly increase their number and effectiveness), the mission agency itself will focus on development projects that assist the task of evangelism, discipleship, and the establishment of indigenous churches. Without this commitment to specialization, the mission agency will lose its ability to accomplish its part of the larger task.

4. Development Work within Our Mission Agency

4.1 Statement of Purpose

While we recognize the legitimacy of engaging in development work for its own sake as a direct godly response to human need, we believe that we are called to specialize in development work that specifically supports and contributes to the task of evangelism, discipleship and church-planting. In light of this, we affirm the following statement.

The aim of World Impact's development ministries is to support the evangelism, discipleship, and church-planting goals of World Impact by:

- *Demonstrating the Love of Christ*

    Many oppressed people have little basis for understanding God's love for them and the essential justice and compassion of his character. Development work can provide a living witness to the love of Christ and his concern for justice and peace in urban neighborhoods. Holistic ministry can come alongside the verbal proclamation of the Gospel,

---

4   See Appendix A, following, for a variety of perspectives on how improperly implemented development work can adversely affect missionary work.

verifying its credibility and enriching the depth of understanding among its hearers. Development work can function pre-evangelistically to prepare people to genuinely listen to the claims of Christ and his message of salvation.

- *Empowering Emerging Churches*

    Emerging urban churches often have few physical resources with which to face the enormous needs of the city. Development work can partner with the pastors of planted-churches, giving access to resources and programs that can meet immediate needs within their congregation, encourage leadership development, and help their congregations engage in effective holistic outreach to their community.

- *Modeling the Implications of the Gospel*

    We cannot hope to reproduce churches committed to engage in a task they have never seen lived out in practice. We engage in development work because we expect newly planted churches to do likewise. We want to provide a living example that the Gospel will necessarily move from belief to action, from word to deed.

4.2 An Important Reminder

One cautionary note is in order. We cannot, through our own efforts, bring the Kingdom of God. As Paul Hiebert reminds us, "Our paradigms are flawed if we begin missions with human activity. Mission is not primarily what we do. It is what God does" (Hiebert 1993, 158). Evangelism, church-planting and development work all function, first and foremost, at the disposal of the Spirit of God. Knowing what should be done, and how we should do it, is never primarily determined through strategic diagrams or well-thought-out organizational approaches. Our first duty is to be faithful to the King, to listen to his instructions, and to respond to his initiatives.

An Ethic of Development

5. Introduction

We have stated that:

> Development workers enable individuals, churches and communities to experience movement toward the freedom, wholeness, and justice of the Kingdom of God.

The process by which we move toward this goal, and the decisions we make to achieve these ends must be guided by an ethic which is consistent with God's standard for human relationships.

Ethics has to do with human conduct and character. It is the systematic study of the principles and methods for distinguishing right from wrong and good from bad. A Christian ethic of development helps us make decisions about development issues in light of biblical revelation and theology. It enables us to think and act clearly so that we can discern what is right to do and how it should be done.

Ethics is concerned that our theology be applied to our behaviors and attitudes. It is not content to simply understand the truth. Instead, it continually seeks to help us discover how to apply the truth (and attempts to motivate us to do so). True ethical behavior means that ethical principles are understood, internalized, and applied to the situation through the development of specific strategies and practices. In an organization, true ethical behavior also requires that strategies and practices undergo regular testing, evaluation and refinement. This ensures that the organization is accomplishing in practice what it affirms in principle.

Finally, it should be noted that our experiences always confront us with paradoxes, anomalies and competing priorities. An ethic of development does not attempt to condense life into a neatly packaged system. Rather, it provides principles that will help us to clarify what is most important in the particular situation that are facing. Each ethical decision must involve discussion about how the various principles outlined below interrelate and about which are the most significant values for a given decision. Only in dialogue and in prayer can the correct decision be discerned.

The ethical principles of the Kingdom of God can be expressed in the values of freedom, wholeness, and justice. These values are the root and the fruit of doing development from a kingdom perspective.

6. World Impact's Development Work Is Committed to Freedom

Freedom is the ability to exercise our God-given capacity to make choices that express love. Therefore, development should engender freedom by helping individuals:

- Gain dignity and respect.

- Be empowered to make wise choices.

- Take responsibility for themselves and others.

This process involves helping individuals *understand* and *achieve* what they need to live freely in community as biblically responsible, self-directing, maturing servants of God's Kingdom. It implies the development of relationships characterized neither by dependence nor independence, but by loving *interdependence* that results in partnership, mutuality, and increased freedom.

6.1 Development affirms human beings as precious and unique in the sight of God, and believes that they have been granted unique capacities and potentials by God.

Explanation

As beings made in the image of God, every person regardless of station or place, is worthy of dignity and respect. People are to be cherished, nurtured, and provided for according to their intrinsic value and preciousness to God. Biblically based development will never exploit people for the sake of economic purposes or treat people as instruments, but instead will value them as ends-in-themselves, to be loved and respected for their worth before God.

Implications

- *People are to be given priority in every dimension of development.*

    Development should contribute to the potential for self-sufficiency, should enhance the quality of life, and should encourage good stewardship among those participating in the programs.

- *Mutual respect is foundational to authentic development.*

    For the poor, life in the urban community is full of inconvenience, difficulty, and shame. The needy daily experience the indignities of being poor in an affluent society. Oftentimes they are accused of moral laxity, subjected to stifling bureaucracies, and pre-judged as causing their own poverty through incompetence or lack of motivation. Development is sensitive to these messages which are given to the needy in our society. It recognizes that the poor are the objects of God's compassion and good news, chosen to be rich in faith and heirs to the Kingdom of God (James 2:5). Development seeks to demonstrate God's righteous cherishing of the poor through its specific actions and relationships.

    Aid not founded on genuine respect can easily humiliate the poor. Therefore, assistance offered to those in need must affirm their dignity and self-respect. Anything that diminishes the worth and significance of the poor in the development process is sinful and injurious to the well-being of all, both those offering the aid and those receiving it.

- *The workplace should operate as a caring community.*

    While an impersonal atmosphere characterizes many business environments, Christian development strives to create a relational framework for trainees and employees. Development workers and those participating in the development project must develop habit patterns of caring for each other beyond the constraints of the project at hand.

6.2 Development should empower people to take full responsibility for their own lives and to care for the needs of others.

Explanation

Development emerges from the conviction that all work is honorable. God has mandated that human beings earn their living with integrity and excellence. This mandate for individual work is grounded in God's initial command given to humankind at creation, and continues on and is reaffirmed in the teachings of the apostles. While God demands that his people be generous and hospitable to the needy and the stranger (2 Corinthians 9), God likewise commands all to work honestly with their own hands (1 Thessalonians 4), and further charges that those who refuse to work ought to correspondingly be denied benevolent aid, that is, "if anyone will not work, neither let him eat," (cf. 2 Thessalonians 3:10).

Development rejects the notion that the creation of wealth is intrinsically evil. Such a view is simplistic and fails to grapple with the biblical notion of Christian stewardship. Development aims to create abundance, but never for the sake of selfish gain or lustful greed. Rather, development takes seriously the biblical requirement that we work, not merely to meet our own needs, but so that from the abundance God has provided we may use our goods and resources to meet the needs of others, especially those who are our brothers and sisters in the body of Christ (cf. Ephesians 4; 2 Corinthians 8; Galatians 6). The biblical standard is that those who stole before they entered the Kingdom are to steal no more, but to work honorably in quietness and integrity, in order that they may have sufficient resources to meet their own needs, and have sufficient wealth to care for others. Development not only seeks to honor the needy by ensuring they can participate in the basic human right to work, it also challenges them to trust God to supply their needs through honorable labor that allows them to be providers for themselves and others.

Implications

- *Nothing can excuse a worker, leader, or professional from the perils and potentials of personal responsibility.*

    Christian workers are not exempt from the vices of laziness, slothfulness, mismanagement, and greed, and they will not be spared from the consequences of such habits and conduct.

- *It is a primary aim of development to increase the maturity of everyone involved in the process.*

    It is assumed that the maturing individual will be increasingly characterized by vision (establishing and owning life-long purposes, aspirations and priorities), responsibility (acting on those purposes, aspirations and priorities with motivation, perseverance and integrity), and wisdom (increasing in skill, understanding and the ability to discern and do what is right for themselves and others).

Maturing individuals should move from dependence toward autonomy, from passivity toward activity, from small abilities to large abilities, from narrow interests to broad interests, from egocentricity to altruism, from ignorance toward enlightenment, from self-rejection toward self-acceptance, from compartmentability toward integration, from imitation toward originality and from a need for rigidity toward a tolerance for ambiguity (Klopfenstein 1993, 95-96).

- *Decisions are best handled at the closest point to those affected.*

National policies and procedures exist to:

» Provide a framework for effective decision making.

» Express the values and purposes that are corporately shared.

» Ensure equity between peoples and projects at many different sites.

» Provide accountability which safeguards integrity.

Responsible decision making within a community assumes that there are mature individuals with a commitment to these common purposes and that open communication exists between the people involved. When these elements are present, most decision making should be done by the people who are responsible to implement the decisions. All decisions must take into consideration the local context and the unique people, relationships, and project conditions that are present.

- *Wages should be fair.*

When development work involves employment, the employee should be compensated equitably in relation to their contribution toward the success or profitability of the project.

- *Training programs should include teaching on the importance of stewardship and giving.*

The need for people to give to God, to others and to their community should be made explicit in the development process. Each person's self-identity as a contributor should be reinforced and the intrinsic connection between receiving and giving (Luke 6:38) should be established.

6.3 Development work must discourage the inclination toward dependency.

Explanation

Development emphasizes that each person should be trained and equipped to achieve their potential to be self-sustaining and self-directing. Creating or nurturing dependency undercuts the deep human need to be a co-creator with God in using our gifts to honor him, and finding our significance and place in the world. Dependency can occur from either end of the people-helping relationship; the developer can create a sense of his or her own indispensability which leads to dependency, or the trainee can easily refuse to progress and grow on to interdependence and depth. Dependency pollutes the process of authentic development by creating unhealthy relationships which damage the trainee's initiative and self-motivation.

Implications

- *Trainees must be required to demonstrated initiative.*

  The basic rule of thumb is "Don't do for people what they can do for themselves-even if it means that the project (or training) will go slowly" (Hoke and Voorhies 1989, 224). When too much is done for the people who are being assisted, the developer has taken from the trainees the opportunity to learn from their mistakes. Dependency, even when resulting from a spirit of benevolence and sympathy, inevitably stunts the growth of those who are so affected.

- *Development should avoid the extremes of authoritarian paternalism, on the one hand, and non-directive laissez-faire(ism) on the other.*

  Developers, by definition, are leaders, and cannot avoid their responsibility to mentor, train, teach, and provide direction to those they serve. Maintaining complete decision-making control, however, does not foster interdependent relationships. While close accountability is essential in the earliest stages of training, development workers must recognize the need to modify strategies and involvement based on the competency and ongoing progress of the learners.[5]

- *Projects should help trainees gain control of their own destiny.*

  Projects must be regularly evaluated to insure that they are not keeping people dependent on long-term employment by WIS. Projects which equip people to gain employment with existing businesses or start businesses of their own are the goal.

---

5 For a discussion of the Hersey-Blanchard training model that tailors leadership style to the competencies and attitudes of the trainee see Leadership Research (Klopfenstein, 1995).

7. Wholeness — Wholeness (*Shalom*) is the personal and communal experience of peace, abundance, goodness, soundness, well-being, and belonging. Wholeness is founded on *righteousness* (right relationships with God and man), *truth* (right beliefs about God and man), and *holiness* (right actions before God and man). Shalom is a gift of God and a sign of his Kingdom's presence.

7.1 Development should create an environment where cooperative relationships can flourish.

Explanation

Development that leads to wholeness acknowledges that human activity takes place in community. The web of relationships that occurs in the work environment (e.g. trainer to trainee, co-worker to co-worker, etc.), must reflect our values of Christian community.

Implications

- *People are not means to an end.*

  Development seeks, first of all, to develop people. This will necessarily involve equipping them (and holding them accountable to) accomplishing tasks. However, it is the maturing of the person, not the completion of the task that is always the primary end of development work.

- *All people in the development process should work for each other as if they are working for Christ himself.*

  Colossians 3:23-24 reminds us that our work is ultimately directed toward and rewarded by Christ. Development projects must operationalize this principle. This suggests that our work must be done with excellence, integrity, diligence, meekness, love and whatever other virtues are necessary for proper service to God.

- *Relational dynamics must be taken seriously.*

  A development project which produces an excellent product and equips people with marketable skills, but which is characterized by disharmony or disunity among its employees has not achieved its goal. The developer must seek to develop genuine community within the workplace.

7.2 Development activities should demonstrate the truth of the Gospel.

Explanation

1 John 3:18 exhorts us to love not merely with words or tongue, "but with actions and in truth." The love of Christ is given not to "souls" but to

whole persons. Development activities should minister unashamedly to the whole person and should serve as evangelism by example. Development work functions as a sign of the Kingdom by enabling people, families, and\ or communities to experience the love and care of Christ. This suggests that development workers must know Christ intimately and be able to communicate his love to others.

Implications

- *Development projects may emphasize mental, physical, social, or economic development.*

  All aspects of human need are of concern to the development worker. As the development worker's love for people takes shape in concrete actions, it should be their intent that people "may see your good deeds and praise your Father in heaven." (Matthew 5:16).

- *Development workers should be maturing disciples of Christ who are actively engaged in ongoing spiritual growth.*

  Who we are is more important than what we do. Only as development workers are actively seeking to live in Christ's love and listen to his Spirit, will they effectively communicate his love to those they work with.

- *Development workers must receive care for their own physical, mental, emotional, and spiritual health and development.*

  Development workers face unique pressures in dealing with human need. They often feel particular stress from standing in between, and identifying with, both the interests of the particular people they serve and the organization they represent (See Hiebert 1989, 83). Physical, emotional or spiritual burn-out is an ever present possibility. Therefore, it is important that development workers give adequate time and attention to maintaining their own health so that they can continue to effectively minister to the needs of others.

- *Development workers need to be specifically equipped in evangelism and an understanding of missions.*

  Christian development workers usually understand that development and evangelism should work in partnership, but are often undertrained in evangelism (See Hoke and Voorhies 1989). Development workers also need to receive general training in missions and management in addition to being trained for their specific task of development (See Pickett and Hawthorne 1992, D218-19) since many of their daily tasks require an understanding of these disciplines.

7.3 Development activities should be above reproach.

Explanation

Wholeness and holiness are inseparable concepts. The way in which development work is conducted will have a profound impact on its ability to effect transformation. For development work to contribute to the wholeness, soundness, and well-being of people it must take special care to sustain integrity in word and deed.

Implications

- *Development projects should maintain high ethical standards.*

    Lack of adequate funds or personnel and the pressures of immediate human need can tempt us to "cut corners" in the way we develop and administrate projects. This temptation must be resisted. Our product cannot be artificially separated from our process. Development projects must serve as a witness to the government, society at large, and the people they train through adherence to high ethical standards of business conduct.

- *Development projects must work within the framework of our 501(c)(3) non-profit status.*

    State and Federal laws limit the ability of non-profits to create situations where individuals directly receive wealth and resources from the corporation. (This prevents individuals inside and outside of the organization from abusing the non-profit status for personal gain). As programs are created to empower people and share resources, the development workers must make sure that they are structured in such a way that they fall within the legal guidelines.

- *Appeals to donors must not motivate by guilt, overstate the need, promise unrealistic results, or demean the dignity of aid recipients.*

    Compressing the complexity of human need and relationships into an appeal to donors is a difficult and complicated task. It is, however, necessary and important work. Development workers in the field should take personal responsibility for relaying needs and vision in an accurate manner to those involved in publishing printed materials about a project.

8. World Impact's Development Work Is Committed to Justice

Justice results from a recognition that all things belong to God and should be shared in accordance with his liberality and impartiality. Biblical justice is concerned both with equitable treatment and with the restoration of right relationship. It abhors oppression, prejudice and inequality because it understands that these separate people from each other and from God.

Development which is based on justice is an important step toward repairing damaged relationships between individuals, classes and cultures which may harbor suspicion and ill-will toward one another. Development work seeks to engender right actions which lead to right relationships.

8.1 Development is rooted in a biblical understanding of God as Creator and Ruler of the universe which demands that all things be reconciled in him.

Explanation

God has delegated to humanity the responsibility to be stewards of his world. This understanding manifests itself in concern for three broad categories of relationship: relations with God, relations with others, and relations with the environment (See Elliston 1989, *Transformation*, 176). Although these relationships were broken by the entrance of sin in the world, God's kingdom rule now demands their restoration.

Development recognizes that until the fullness of the Kingdom of Christ is manifested, there will inevitably be poverty, exploitation, and misery caused by sin's perversion of these three areas of relationship. This realization neither paralyzes nor discourages authentic Christian development. While understanding the nature of moral evil in the world, authentic development seeks to demonstrate models of justice and reconciliation which reflect the justice of Christ's Kingdom.

Implications

- *Development intends to move people toward right relationship with God.*

  Authentic reconciliation between people is based on their mutual reconciliation with God. Although "common grace" and the "image of God" provide a ground for some degree of reconciliation between all people, it is ultimately in right relationship with God through Christ that the most profound and lasting form of reconciliation can occur. Therefore, development work is eager to assist in preparing people for hearing the Gospel by witnessing to its truth and living out its implications.

- *Reconciliation between individuals, classes, and cultures is a key value.*

  Development will inevitably involve new ways of power-sharing, using resources, making decisions, enforcing policy, and relating to others. There is a need to innovate rather than simply imitate existing models. It is extremely important that the viewpoints of peoples from different classes and cultures be represented in the planning of any development project.

- *Development projects must not be wasteful of resources or harmful to the physical environment.*

    God's command to humankind is to recognize his ownership, and neither exploit nor destroy his earth, but to tend and care for it. Stewardship involves using the earth's resources to glorify him and meet the needs of our neighbors while keeping in mind our responsibility to future generations. Development must be sustainable, i.e., it must not simply consume resources but cultivate them as well.

8.2 Development recognizes the systemic and institutional foundations of producing wealth and experiencing poverty.

Explanation

The Bible delineates various moral vices that can lead to poverty in the lives of individuals (e.g., laziness, sloth, neglect of responsibility, cf. Proverbs 6; 24, etc.), However, it is also clear that poverty can be caused by large scale societal and economic factors that create conditions of need, oppression, and want (cf. Isaiah 1; 54; Amos 4, 5, etc.). Even a cursory reading of Scripture reveals that throughout biblical history the prophets condemned certain practices of business, politics, law, industry, and even religion that contributed to the imbalances among various groups within society, and led to the oppression of the poor. Development seeks to be prophetic by affirming that God is committed to the poor and the needy, and will not tolerate their oppression indefinitely. Development is not naive. It does not attribute all poverty in society to individual moral vice. On the contrary, struggling against injustice demands that people recognize the ever-present possibility of demonic influence in human structures (1 John 5:19).

Implications

- *Spiritual warfare is a key component of the development process.*

    Ephesians 6:12 reminds us that "we do not wrestle against flesh and blood, but against the rulers, against the authorities, against the cosmic powers over this present darkness, against the spiritual forces of evil in the heavenly places." Development work that does not intentionally and regularly set aside time for prayer and other spiritual disciplines is unlikely to effect lasting change. Development workers should have a plan for spiritual warfare that is as significant a focus as the plan for the development work itself.

    Development workers should also realize that their projects will experience spiritual attack. The accumulation of money or power within a project can be entry points for the perversion of that project despite its best intentions. Relationships between development project leaders, or between development workers and those they are training, can be twisted through the stress of conflict, jealousy, miscommunication, and cultural differences. Both personal relationships and institutional programs need to be protected from spiritual forces that would corrupt or destroy them. This requires an ongoing commitment to spiritual warfare, and to personal and corporate holiness.[6]

- *Development work should challenge unjust practices.*

  Development workers must prepare people to speak out against unjust practices in ways which demonstrate both the love and justice of God. While the non-profit organization is not itself a forum for political advocacy, it is responsible to train people to value justice and to make decisions in a moral context. In the marketplace, workers will be confronted by individual and systemic injustices and should be trained to respond to them in a manner which honors Christ and the values of his Kingdom.

- *The role of the Church in development must not be neglected.*

  Ephesians 2:14 records that it is "Christ himself" who is our peace and who has "destroyed the barrier, the dividing wall of hostility" between Jew and Gentiles. Reconciliation is rooted in the person and work of Christ and thus the importance of Christ's body, the Church, cannot be overlooked. Missionary development projects should both flow out of and result in dynamic churches.

8.3 Development does not seek to guarantee equality of outcome, but equality of opportunity.

Explanation

Development concentrates on providing an environment in which people can learn the importance and disciplines of work, gain skills which enhance the value of their work, and apply the disciplines and skills they acquire. However, no human endeavor is exempt from the moral force of our ability to choose, i.e., to decide whether or not to fully use the gifts, opportunities, and potentials we have been given. Because of variations of motivation, effort and preparation, differences in incomes are inevitable, and ought to be expected. Development programs should both teach and reward initiative.

---

[6] See Thomas McAlpine, *Facing the Powers* (McAlpine, 1991) for a helpful discussion of ways in which Reformed, Anabaptist, Charismatic, and Social Science perspectives share both differing perspectives and common ground in understanding and confronting spiritual powers.

Implications

- *Each trainee plays a critical role in their own success.*

    While the developers can offer a vast amount of expertise and aid in creating wealth for the trainees, many of the most important attributes necessary for prolonged success are controlled by the trainees. Without the requisite vision, energy, and commitment to do the work for long enough time so profits can be seen, success will not occur. These qualities arise from the drive and conviction of the trainees, not merely from the availability of the developers. Because of this, development cannot guarantee the success of all those involved in the project.

- *Faithful stewardship should lead to increased responsibility.*

    All development projects should have a plan for rewarding faithfulness, skill development, and diligence. Justice demands that increased effort lead to increased reward.

8.4 Development workers should respect cultural differences and strive to create a training style that is culturally conducive to those being empowered.

Explanation

Every human culture is "a blueprint that gives the individuals of a society a way of explaining and coping with life. It teaches people how to think, act and respond appropriately in any given situation. It allows people to work together based on a common understanding of reality. It organizes ways of thinking and acting into forms that can be passed on to others" (Cornett 1991, 2). Culture shapes every form of human activity from the observable behaviors (language, dress, food, etc.) to the internal thoughts and attitudes (thinking styles, definitions of beauty and worth, etc.). Understanding how a culture perceives reality, what it values, and how it functions is fundamental information for the development worker.

Although all human cultures are affected by sinful perspectives, attitudes and behaviors which must be confronted by the Gospel, human cultures themselves are celebrated by the Scriptures. The apostles confirmed that becoming a Christian did not entail having to change one's original culture (Acts 15). The vision of God's Kingdom from Old Testament (Micah 4) to New (Revelation 7:9) involves people from every nation, language and ethnicity. Missionaries from Paul onward have contextualized the Gospel, putting eternal truth in forms that could be understood and practiced by people of diverse cultures (See Cornett 1991, 6-9). Development workers, likewise, must respect cultural differences and seek to contextualize their instruction and resources (See Elliston, Hoke and Voorhies 1989).

Development workers have a unique interest in empowering groups that have been marginalized, oppressed or neglected by the larger society. This will frequently involve working with groups or individuals that are distinct from the dominant culture. Development work will effectively empower immigrants, unassimilated people groups, or people who have been victimized by race or class discrimination, only if it understands and respects the cultural distinctives of these groups.

Finally, development workers must prepare people to live and work in a pluralistic society. Learning how to successfully relate to customers and co-workers from other cultures has become a key component of job training. Although development work must start with the cultural context of those being assisted, it must also enable those workers to respect other cultures and to successfully work in the larger society.

Implications

- *Development workers should understand the culture(s) and sub-culture(s) of the people they work with.*

  Development workers should, first of all, gain a basic understanding of the nature of human culture and of strategies for developing effective cross-cultural training relationships.[7] They should gain the fundamental skills necessary for working in the cross-cultural environment (language acquisition, etc.). It is highly desirable for the development worker to have a mentor either from the culture or who is an experienced observer of the culture to assist in the training process.

- *The work environment should be functionally appropriate and aesthetically pleasing when viewed from the perspective of the culture(s) that work or do business there.*

  All human cultures desire environments that combine functionality with beauty. There is significant variation, however, in how beauty and functionality are defined, prioritized, and applied from one culture to another. The physical environment in which the development project occurs should take cultural concerns into account.

- *Development workers should be sensitive to how conflict is handled by the culture of the people they work among.*

  Conflict is an inevitable part of working together. It can be a healthy opportunity for growth if handled correctly. Cultural differences, however, can sabotage the process of conflict management. The development worker must take cultural attitudes toward directness/

---

7   Basic resources for gaining an understanding of culture include *The Missionary and Culture* (Cornett 1991), *Beyond Culture* (Hall 1976), *Christianity Confronts Culture* (Mayers 1974), *Ministering Cross-Culturally* (Lingenfelter and Mayers 1986) and *Cross-Cultural Conflicts: Building Relationships for Effective Ministry* (Elmer 1993).

indirectness, shame/guilt, individualism/collectivism, etc. seriously and adapt their conflict management style to reflect those concerns. They must also take seriously their responsibility to prepare people from sub-cultures to work within the dominant culture.

- *Development workers should be sensitive to roles or work that is considered degrading by the culture.*

  Although all honest work carries dignity before God, cultural perceptions of role and status have tremendous power to shape attitudes. Whenever possible, work should be chosen that is not repugnant to the culture. If this is not possible, careful preparation and training should be done to ensure that each person understands the necessity and dignity of the work involved. In some cases it may be necessary to challenge the cultural value system (see Miller, 1989) but this should be done sensitively and with adequate preparation and involvement of the trainees.

- *Developers should prepare trainees for situations that they are likely to encounter in the workplace.*

  People from event-oriented cultures, for example, need to understand the time-oriented culture that defines American business practices. Helping workers learn skills and disciplines for success in the larger society is an important part of the training process.

8.5 The goal of development is to glorify God through excellence and service, not merely to make a profit.

Explanation

In the ethics of the corporate world, the highest indicator of success is usually the profitability of the business. However, development work that is informed by kingdom values involves a broader vision. Development seeks to emphasize the importance of people-nurturing and training and the production of a quality product that meets human need.

Since producing quality Christian and professional leadership models is a high aim of our development efforts, we must unashamedly emphasize both external profits as well as internal gains. On the one hand, a business, if it is to survive, must be profitable and able to stand on its on. On the other hand, we must strive to produce men and women who are spiritually mature as well as professionally oriented and technically competent. The creation of wealth is not an end in itself; it is a by-product of engaging in business with an eye toward excellence, in the name of Christ.

Implications

- No skill will be taught or product produced simply because it is valued by society or likely to produce a profit.

    All skills and products must be consistent with the aims of justice, peace and wholeness that characterize the kingdom rule of Christ. Skills and modes of production that degrade human dignity and products that promote injustice, inequity, or human misery are not to be considered fitting for development regardless of their acceptance by the society at large.

- The aim of development work must not only be to help people obtain and generate resources but also to help them commit to using those resources on behalf of the Kingdom of God.

    Helping people to obtain education, skills or wealth is ultimately unproductive if these things are not placed at God's service and the service of others. Good development projects will offer people the opportunity to serve God not only with the profits from their labor but through the work itself. Developers must teach and model that work is an opportunity for service to God (Colossians 3:23-24).

9. The Need for Application

Each of the points listed above has a section titled "Explanation" and a section titled "Implications." However, for the paper to be complete one more step is necessary. Every implication must be accompanied by a series of applications. These applications should be created by development workers in the field, and structured for the unique needs of the local situation.

In creating these applications, the following guidelines should be followed:

- Each local ministry should thoroughly review the "Implications" sections and decide on specific steps which will enable them to apply these principles to their particular development project.

- These steps should be developed in a way that involves the people most affected by each development project.

- Once finalized, the application steps should be committed to writing.

- These applications should be regularly taught and reviewed.

- These applications should be included in each regularly scheduled evaluation done by the project.

- Following each scheduled evaluation, there should be a revising and updating of these applications based on what has been learned in experience.

Appendix A
Selected Quotes on the Role of Development Work within the Mission Agency

Christian social transformation differs from secular relief and development in that it serves in an integrated, symbiotic relationship with other ministries of the Church, including evangelism and church planting (Elliston 1989, 172).

My experience with scores of ministries among the poor has taught me that economic projects, when used as entrees into communities, do not facilitate church planting or growth. . . . the two goals—relief and church planting—are different. They are both Christian, and at times compatible. But many times they do not support each other well at all. . . . It appears that where workers enter a community with a priority to proclaim, many deeds of mercy, acts of justice and signs of power will occur. From these the church will be established. But when workers enter with a priority of dealing with economic need, they may assist the people economically very well, but they rarely establish as church. There is a time for both, and there are life callings to do both, but they must be distinguished (Grigg 1992, 163-64).

Avoid institutions if possible at the beachhead stage (community development programs unrelated to church planting, schools, clinics, etc.); they will come later. In Honduras we developed community development work but it grew out of the churches, not vice versa. We taught obedience to the great commandment of loving our neighbor in a practical way. A poverty program can aid church planting if the two are integrated by the Holy Spirit. But churches dependent on charitable institutions are almost always dominated by the foreign missionary and seldom reproduce (Patterson 1992, D-80).

All too often native pastors and churches have become preoccupied with ministries that attract Western dollars (such as orphan work) while neglecting more basic pastoral care and evangelism. Even development work, if not wisely administered, can hinder church growth (Ott 1993, 289).

There is a very real danger of recruiting missionary-evangelists primarily on the basis of their abilities and expertise. "Whatever your special interest is, we can use it in our mission"— this is an all-too-common approach to recruitment. As a result, many workers become frustrated when their special ability is not fully utilized; they react by simply "doing their thing" and contributing only indirectly to the task of planting growing churches. Consequently, the so-called secondary or supporting ministries have a way of becoming primary and actually eclipsing the central task! (Hesselgrave 1980, 112).

It is unfortunate that Christian service and witness often seem to be competing concerns in Christian outreach when, in fact, both are biblical and complementary.... One reason for this tension is that service enterprises such as hospitals and educational institutions have a way of preempting finances and energies so that evangelism and witness tend to get crowded out (Hesselgrave 1980 p. 328).

Since we believe in the unity of the Bible, we must say that 'The Great Commission is not an isolated command, (but) a natural outflow of the character of God... The missionary purpose and thrust of God...' Thus, we should not take the Great Commandment and the Great Commission as though they are mutually exclusive. We should take the Great Commandment—to love others—and the Great Commission—to preach—together, integrated in the mission of Jesus Christ, for it is the same Lord, who commanded and commissioned the same disciples and his followers. Therefore, as Di Gangi says, 'to communicate the gospel effectively we must obey the great commandment as well as the great commission' (Cho 1985, 229).

Works Cited

Cho, J. Chongham. "The Mission of the Church." See Nicholls, 1985.

Cornett, Terry G., ed. "The Missionary and Culture." *World Impact Ministry Resources*. Los Angeles: World Impact Mission Studies Training Paper, 1991.

Dayton, Donald W. *Discovering an Evangelical Heritage*. 1976. Peabody, MA: Hendrickson, 1988.

Elliston, Edgar J., ed. *Christian Relief and Development: Developing Workers for Effective Ministry*. Dallas: Word Publishing, 1989.

------. "Christian Social Transformation Distinctives." See Elliston, 1989.

Elliston, Edgar J., Stephen J. Hoke, and Samuel Voorhies. "Issues in Contextualizing Christian Leadership." See Elliston, 1989.

Grigg, Viv. "Church of the Poor." *Discipling the City*. 2nd ed. Ed. Roger S. Greenway. Grand Rapids: Baker Book House, 1992.

Hall, Edward T. *Beyond Culture*. Garden City, NY: Anchor Books, 1976.

Hesselgrave, David. *Planting Churches Cross-Culturally: A Guide for Home and Foreign Missions*. Grand Rapids: Baker Book House, 1980.

Hiebert, Paul G. "Evangelism, Church, and Kingdom." See Van Engen, et. al., 1993.

------. "Anthropological Insights for Whole Ministries." See Elliston, 1989.

Hoke, Stephen J. and Samuel J. Voorhies. "Training Relief and Development Workers in the Two-Thirds World." See Elliston, 1989.

Klopfenstein, David E. and Dorothy A. Klopfenstein. "Leadership Research." CityGates. 1 (1995): 21-26.

Klopfenstein, David, Dotty Klopfenstein and Bud Williams. *Come Yourselves Apart: Christian Leadership in the Temporary Community.* Azusa, CA: Holysm Publishing, 1993.

Ladd, George Eldon. *A Theology of the New Testament.* Grand Rapids: Wm. B. Eerdmans, 1974.

McAlpine, Thomas H. *Facing the Powers: What Are the Options?* Monrovia, CA: MARC-World Vision, 1991.

Miller, Darrow L. "The Development Ethic: Hope for a Culture of Poverty." See Elliston, 1989.

Nicholls, Bruce J., ed. *In Word and Deed: Evangelism and Social Responsibility.* Grand Rapids: Wm. B. Eerdmans, 1985.

Ott, Craig. "Let the Buyer Beware." *Evangelical Missions Quarterly*, 29 (1993): 286-291.

Patterson, George. "The Spontaneous Multiplication of Churches." See Winter and Hawthorne, 1992.

Pickett, Robert C. and Steven C. Hawthorne. "Helping Others Help Themselves: Christian Community Development." See Winter and Hawthorne, 1992.

Stott, John. "Twenty Years After Lausanne: Some Personal Reflections." *International Bulletin of Missionary Research.* 19 (1995): 50-55.

Van Engen, Charles, et. al., eds. *The Good News of the Kingdom: Mission Theology for the Third Millennium.* Maryknoll: Orbis Books, 1993.

Verkuyl, Johannes. *Contemporary Missiology: An Introduction.* Grand Rapids: Wm. B. Eerdmans, 1978.

------. "The Biblical Notion of Kingdom: Test of Validity for Theology of Religion." See Van Engen, et. al., 1993.

Winter, Ralph D. and Steven C. Hawthorne, eds. *Perspectives on the World Christian Movement: A Reader.* Rev. ed. Pasadena: William Carey Library, 1992.

Jesus and the Poor

Rev. Dr. Don L. Davis

Thesis: The heart of Jesus's ministry of the Kingdom was the transformation and renewal of the those on the underside of life, the poor. He demonstrated his personal heart vision in how he inaugurated his ministry, authenticated his ministry, defined the heart and soul of ministry, identifying himself directly with the poor.

I. Jesus inaugurated his ministry with an outreach to the poor.

  A. The inaugural sermon at Nazareth, Luke 4:16-21

  Luke 4:16-21 (ESV) – And he came to Nazareth, where he had been brought up. And as was his custom, he went to the synagogue on the Sabbath day, and he stood up to read. [17] And the scroll of the prophet Isaiah was given to him. He unrolled the scroll and found the place where it was written, [18] "The Spirit of the Lord is upon me, because he has anointed me to proclaim good news to the poor. He has sent me to proclaim liberty to the captives and recovering of sight to the blind, to set at liberty those who are oppressed, [19] to proclaim the year of the Lord's favor." [20] And he rolled up the scroll and gave it back to the attendant and sat down. And the eyes of all in the synagogue were fixed on him. [21] And he began to say to them, "Today this Scripture has been fulfilled in your hearing."

  B. The meaning of this inauguration

    1. The object of his attention: his choice of texts

    2. The object of his calling: his Spirit anointing

    3. The objects of his love:

        a. Good news to the poor

        b. Release to the captives

        c. Recovery of sight to the blind

        d. Letting the oppressed go free

    4. The object of his ministry: the Year of the Lord's favor

  C. *Ministry to the poor as the cornerstone of his inaugural ministry*

II. Jesus authenticated his ministry by his actions toward the poor.

    A. John's query regarding Jesus's authenticity, Luke 7:18-23

        Luke 7:18-23 (ESV) – The disciples of John reported all these things to him. And John, [19] calling two of his disciples to him, sent them to the Lord, saying, "Are you the one who is to come, or shall we look for another?" [20] And when the men had come to him, they said, "John the Baptist has sent us to you, saying, 'Are you the one who is to come, or shall we look for another?'" [21] In that hour he healed many people of diseases and plagues and evil spirits, and on many who were blind he bestowed sight. [22] And he answered them, "Go and tell John what you have seen and heard: the BLIND RECEIVE THEIR SIGHT, the lame walk, lepers are cleansed, and the deaf hear, the dead are raised up, the POOR HAVE GOOD NEWS PREACHED TO THEM. [23] And blessed is the one who is not offended by me."

    B. Will the real Messiah please stand up?

        1. The question of John, 19-20

        2. The actions of Jesus, 21 (the show-side of "show-and-tell")

        3. The explanation of his identity, 22-23

            a. Go and tell John what you have seen and heard.

            b. Blind seeing, lame walking, lepers cleansed, deaf hearing, dead being raised, the poor hearing the Gospel

    C. *Ministry to the poor is undeniable proof of the Messiah's identity.*

III. Jesus verified salvation in relation to one's treatment of the poor.

    A. The story of Zacchaeus, Luke 19:1-9

        Luke 19:1-9 (ESV) – He entered Jericho and was passing through. [2] And there was a man named Zacchaeus. He was a chief tax collector and was rich. [3] And he was seeking to see who Jesus was, but on account of the crowd he could not, because he was small of stature. [4] So he ran on ahead and climbed up into a sycamore tree to see him, for he was about to pass that way. [5] And when Jesus came to the place, he looked up and said to him, "Zacchaeus, hurry and come down, for I must stay at your house today." [6] So he hurried and came down and received him joyfully. [7] And when they saw it, they all grumbled, "He has gone in to be the guest of a man who is a sinner." [8] And Zacchaeus stood and said to the Lord, "Behold, Lord, the half of my goods I give to the poor. And if I have defrauded anyone of anything, I restore it fourfold." [9] And Jesus said to him, "Today salvation has come to this house, since he also is a son of Abraham."

1. The palpitations of Zacchaeus

2. The salutation of Zacchaeus (to Jesus)

3. The declaration of Zacchaeus

    a. Half of all I own I give to the poor.

    b. I restore those wrongly treated by me four-fold.

4. The salvation of Zacchaeus, vv. 9-10

B. Plucking Grain on the Sabbath, Matthew 12:1-8

Matthew 12:1-8 (ESV) – At that time Jesus went through the grainfields on the Sabbath. His disciples were hungry, and they began to pluck heads of grain and to eat. [2] But when the Pharisees saw it, they said to him, "Look, your disciples are doing what is not lawful to do on the Sabbath." [3] He said to them, "Have you not read what David did when he was hungry, and those who were with him: [4] how he entered the house of God and ate the bread of the Presence, which it was not lawful for him to eat nor for those who were with him, but only for the priests? [5] Or have you not read in the Law how on the Sabbath the priests in the temple profane the Sabbath and are guiltless? [6] I tell you, something greater than the temple is here. [7] And if you had known what this means, 'I DESIRE MERCY, AND NOT SACRIFICE,' you would not have condemned the guiltless. [8] For the Son of Man is lord of the Sabbath."

1. Disciples snacking on corn on the Sabbath

2. The Pharisees disputation: "Look, your disciples are doing what is not lawful to do on the sabbath."

3. Jesus's retort: "I desire mercy and not sacrifice."

    a. Mercy to the poor and broken, not ritual faithfulness

    b. Compassion for the broken, not religious discipline

C. *Ministry to the poor is the litmus test of authentic salvation.*

IV. Jesus identifies himself unreservedly with the poor.

A. Those who cannot repay you, Luke 14:11-15

Luke 14:11-14 (ESV) – "For everyone who exalts himself will be humbled, and he who humbles himself will be exalted." [12] He said also to the man who had invited him, "When you give a dinner or a banquet, do not invite your friends or your brothers or your relatives or rich neighbors, lest they also invite you in return and you be repaid. [13] But when you give a feast, invite the poor, the crippled, the lame, the blind, [14] and you will be blessed, because they cannot repay you. You will be repaid at the resurrection of the just."

B. The Judgment Seat of the King, Matthew 25:31-45

Matthew 25:34-40 (ESV) – Then the King will say to those on his right, "Come, you who are blessed by my Father, inherit the kingdom prepared for you from the foundation of the world. [35] For I was hungry and you gave me food, I was thirsty and you gave me drink, I was a stranger and you welcomed me, [36] I was naked and you clothed me, I was sick and you visited me, I was in prison and you came to me." [37] Then the righteous will answer him, saying, "Lord, when did we see you hungry and feed you, or thirsty and give you drink? [38] And when did we see you a stranger and welcome you, or naked and clothe you? [39] And when did we see you sick or in prison and visit you?" [40] And the King will answer them, "Truly, I say to you, as you did it to one of the least of these my brothers, you did it to me."

1. Two sets of people: sheep and goats

2. Two responses: one blessed and embraced, one judged and rejected

3. Two destinies: the sheep in the Kingdom inherited, prepared from the foundation of the world, the goats in the eternal fire prepared for the devil and his angels

4. Two reactions: one was hospitable, charitable, generous; the other apathetic, heartless, negligent

5. The same group of people: the hungry, the thirsty, the stranger, the naked, the sick, the prisoner

6. *The same standard: in the way you treated or mistreated these people, those on the underside of life, so you responded to me.*

C. Jesus made it appear as those who were least deserving but repentant would become heirs of the Kingdom.

Matthew 21:31 (ESV) – "Which of the two did the will of his father?" They said, "The first." Jesus said to them, "Truly, I say to you, the tax collectors and the prostitutes go into the kingdom of God before you."

Mark 2:15-17 (ESV) – And as he reclined at table in his house, many tax collectors and sinners were reclining with Jesus and his disciples, for there were many who followed him. [16] And the scribes of the Pharisees, when they saw that he was eating with sinners and tax collectors, said to his disciples, "Why does he eat with tax collectors and sinners?" [17] And when Jesus heard it, he said to them, "Those who are well have no need of a physician, but those who are sick. I came not to call the righteous, but sinners."

D. Ministry to the poor is ministry to the Lord Jesus – his identification with them is complete.

Conclusion: The heart and soul of Jesus's ministry was directed toward the transformation and liberation of those who were most vulnerable, most forgotten, most neglected. As disciples, may we demonstrate the same.